D0753704

Arthur Frommer's New World of Travel

Arthur Frommer's
New World of Travel

5th Edition

Arthur Frommer
Assisted by
Pauline Frommer

MACMILLAN • USA

Macmillan Travel
A Simon & Schuster Macmillan Company
1633 Broadway
New York, NY 10019

Copyright © 1988, 1989, 1990, 1991, 1996 by Arthur B. Frommer

All rights reserved. No part of this book may be reproduced or transmitted in any form or by any means, electronic or mechanical, including photocopying, recording, or by any information storage and retrieval system, without permission in writing from the publisher.

Macmillan is a registered trademark of Macmillan, Inc.

ISBN 0-02-860631-0
ISSN 0893-1895

Design by Amy Peppler-Adams, designLab, Seattle

Manufactured in the United States of America

To Pauline
from her proud father

About the Author

Arthur Frommer is America's foremost travel writer. Author of the famous *Europe on $5 a Day,* which launched the Frommer Travel Guide series, he has written scores of best-selling travel guides. He has been featured as a travel expert on the NBC Today Show, the Oprah Winfrey Show, and the Regis and Kathy Lee show. In addition to hosting his own popular nationwide radio call-in show, he also contributes to such leading publications as *Travel Holiday Magazine* and *Consumer's Digest.* A graduate of Yale University Law School, he served with U. S. Army Intelligence during the Korean War and later practiced law with the firm of the late Adlai Stevenson. He now devotes his full time to travel.

Contents

Preface

"Nel mezzo del cammin di nostra vita"—at a midpoint in the path of my life, to crib from Dante—I felt a sharp malaise about the state of American travel, and with my own role in it.

After 30 years of writing standard guide books, I began to see that most of the vacation journeys undertaken by Americans were trivial and bland, devoid of important content, cheaply commercial, and unworthy of our better instincts and ideals.

And overpriced, even in the budget realm.

Those travels, for most Americans, consist almost entirely of "sightseeing"—an activity as vapid as the word implies. We rove the world, in most cases, to look at lifeless physical structures of the sort already familiar from a thousand picture books and films. We gaze at the Eiffel Tower or the Golden Gate Bridge, enjoy a brief thrill of recognition, return home, and think we have traveled.

Only later do we ask: To what end did I travel? With what lasting rewards?

And these disappointments are not always reduced or affected by the decision to travel cheaply—as I once largely believed. Though the use of budget-priced facilities will *usually* result in a more meaningful trip—because they bring us closer to the realities of the countries through which we pass—they do not guarantee that condition. Even people staying in guesthouses and pensions can pass their days in senseless "sightseeing," trudging like robots to Trafalgar Square and various Changings of the Guard.

No. To me today, travel in all price ranges is scarcely worth the effort unless it is associated with people, with learning and ideas. To have meaning at all, travel must involve an encounter with new and different outlooks and beliefs. It must broaden our horizons, provide comparative lessons, show us how those in other communities are responding to their social and industrial problems. At its best, travel should challenge our preconceptions and most cherished views, cause us to rethink our assumptions, shake us a bit, make us broader-minded and more understanding.

It is toward achieving that kind of travel—that infinitely more memorable form of travel—that this yearly book hopes to contribute. Its method is to turn a spotlight on a host of little-known travel programs and organizations that surface each year, usually to benefit only the smallest portion of our population.

All over the world, and at home as well, a tiny segment of the travel industry is laboring to add valuable content to the travel experience:

• These are the people who operate ambitious study trips and scientific tours; they offer challenging, politically oriented journeys and excursions into the Emerging World.

• Their aim is to change your life. They experiment with new lifestyles and spiritual quests at yoga retreats and utopian communities, at tented Caribbean resorts and macrobiotic farms, at personal growth centers and adult summer camps.

• They sail the smallest of cruise ships into tiny ports and fishing villages unsullied by mass tourism.

• They practice "integrated tourism," using local facilities, and broadcast appeals for ethical tourism and tourism for the poor.

• They go on treks into the Himalayas or bicycle tours into the Dordogne.

• They enable Americans to study foreign languages at overseas schools, stay as guests in the homes of private families abroad, share the life and rhythm of Australian sheep farms, study 16th-century art with a connoisseur in the Belgian Ardennes.

• They promote homestays among people of accomplishment in Britain, or volunteer workcamps on the coasts of four continents.

But they are fledgling travel companies without funds to properly advertise their new approach; their trips, in consequence, are confined to the barest few.

In this book, hopefully, they will find their voice. Each new edition will attempt to introduce the best of them, and especially those with novel travel ideas: new themes of travel, new travel methods, new programs, new vacation possibilities, new and better ways of visiting old destinations, new destinations. Out of the welter of obscure new travel organizations emerging each year, surely one will lead to at least one new vacation activity for each of our readers.

One, did I say? Why not two or three? Travel should be no occasional fling, but a normal and frequent, integral part of one's life. Because alternative vacations are nearly always cheaper than the standard ones, they are the very best means for stretching your travel dollar; they are more effective in that regard than a whole host of heavily promoted rules for reducing travel costs. Though the traditional tourist will do well to continue obeying those rules, the unconventional traveler will reap the pleasures and rewards of far more frequent, far-ranging foreign travels.

Our ability to engage in that sort of travel is nothing short of a miracle. We are the first generation in human history to fly to other continents as easily as people once boarded a train to the next town. We are the first generation in human history for whom travel is not restricted to an affluent few, but is available to many.

We should not squander our opportunity. Travel, for too long, has been trivialized in the popular press and by the promoters of popular tours; it deserves better. It is an enduring subject of human concern, the essential requisite for a civilized life, perhaps the most effective tool for reducing foolish national pride and promoting a worldview.

It is too important a subject to be left to the commercial monoliths of the travel industry.

Hence, this book.

See you next year.

ARTHUR FROMMER
November 1995

The New World of Travel 1997

The lifeblood of the Arthur Frommer travel guides is the correspondence received from readers, commenting on the establishments recommended in the texts and recommending new establishments. Each such letter is carefully studied, and when a particular lead seems promising, it is followed up and personally checked.

It is hoped that *The New World of Travel* will receive similar assistance from its readers. A yearly publication, issued near the start of each year, *The New World of Travel* will constantly grow. And since much of its content relates to organizations that lack the means to market themselves properly, or come to the attention of a travel journalist, your help is invaluable in alerting me to the organizations—hospitality exchanges, alternative resorts, new travel clubs, and the like—that you have discovered.

If you become aware of a new travel organization, program, or development that deserves to be described in our next edition, *The New World of Travel 1997*, won't you please let me know about it? Send your letters to Arthur Frommer, *The New World of Travel*, 1841 Broadway, New York, NY 10023. All letters will be acknowledged, and all are warmly appreciated, in advance, by the author.

Introduction to a New Form of Vacation

To Americans of taste and intelligence, the standard holiday trip has frequently become, at best, a crushing bore, at worst a horror, a nightmare. All over the world, small-minded entrepreneurs, urged by profit, have nullified the charm, complexity, and distinctive qualities of numerous leading destinations.

And if this seems an exaggerated complaint, then let me cite several typical experiences familiar to every person who has recently traveled.

• You succumb to the ads for a winter charter program going to a once-quaint fishing village on Mexico's Pacific Coast. You arrive at a mini-metropolis thronged with crowds and lined with gaudy shops displaying mountains of earrings and mass-produced rugs. At the doors to restaurants, the wait for tables is three-quarters of an hour. In the lobbies of hotels, massed ranks of viewers watch U.S. football on satellite TV. Escaping to the beach, you are besieged by hawkers, assaulted by teenagers dropping from the skies in parasails, deafened by the motors of waterski boats.

• You join the strolling crowds in Spain's Toledo, heading for the church that displays El Greco's "Death and Burial of Count Orgaz." Arriving at the site, you jostle with 200 other clamoring visitors for a fleeting glimpse of the glass-protected painting, distanced by a crush of human bodies. You experience the same mob scenes at the Sistine Chapel, the Louvre, the Church of St. Bavo, the Nikko Shrine.

• You visit a medieval cathedral on the castle hill of Prague, and find yourself surrounded by a dozen clusters of tourists straining intently to hear the burst of commentary emerging from their suffering guides. As you seek to concentrate on the art and mood of the High Gothic era, you hear instead the distracting mini-lectures of a dozen touring companies, delivered in French and Russian, German and Japanese.

• You arrive, 10 minutes before curtain time, in the red-velvet-and-gilt setting of a Parisian music hall, where not a single other person is yet in sight. Suddenly the tour buses appear and the hall is instantly awash with foreigners carrying cameras and guidebooks. Tired dance numbers slouch onto the stage, their music canned, their theme without the slightest reference to even the popular culture of France. Broadly exaggerated imitations of French music hall variety ensue, done without finesse or talent—and hardly rehearsed. Totally contrived for the tourist, simple-minded, and infuriating.

Why are these scenes so frequently encountered?

• Because certain areas of the world are simply being visited by too many.

• Because tour buses, charter flights, and crowds of frantic, camera-toting visitors are spilling over from celebrated plazas, squares, beaches, and airports in the more popular, standard cities or islands.

• Because key attractions are besieged by throngs.

• Because, in response to the numbers, multi-national chains have thrown up massive, towering hotels that soon preempt the field, but only serve to separate their guests from the life and atmosphere surrounding them.

• Because large tour companies, intent on the bottom line, follow the course of least resistance, take you only to the famous and familiar, seek to simplify the travel experience, and make it as dumbly comforting, both mentally and physically, as possible.

The "New World" of Travel

How, under these circumstances, can a self-respecting, intellectually curious, spirited individual continue to travel?

The answer lies in a new approach, to new destinations, using new modes of travel and lodging, in search of learning. That "New World" of travel is broadly available to any reasonably energetic person, at lower costs than the standard form of vacation travel, and it is invigorating beyond compare, producing all the rewards (and more) that travel brought before the world became homogenized and mobbed. No matter what your age or resources, once you have taken a nonstandard trip, you will never again return willingly to the hackneyed variety.

The key objective is to experience events, lifestyles, attitudes, cultures, political outlooks, and theological views utterly different from what you ordinarily encounter at home. Unless that happens, why travel? Why endure the fatigue of transportation, and its associated burdens, just to reach a replica of your familiar surroundings? Unless vacation travel is a learning experience, unless it leaves you a bit different from what you were when you began, it is, in my view, a pointless physical exercise.

In seeking these rewards of nonstandard travel, you are now assisted by a growing multitude of small, alternative-travel companies or resorts—more than 1,200 described in this book—of which only a handful existed as recently as 10 years ago. The all-but-unnoticed emergence of this new segment of the travel industry—new tour operators, new facilities, new programs, new forms of lodging—is a major phenomenon. It reflects a massive dissatisfaction by large numbers of Americans with the simplistic travels offered by established travel firms and facilities. In effect, tens of thousands of our fellow citizens have opted for adventures of the mind when they travel, a New World of Travel.

Some, for want of assistance, have relied on do-it-yourself methods to enter the "New World," and those, too, are described in this book. Essentially, the effort is to stay ahead of the crowds, attempting always to select new destinations and unvisited areas for vacation travel. In each yearly edition of this book, I shall be searching for the as-yet-undiscovered: the places that deserve to be visited, but which for one reason or another— lack of government publicity, difficulty of access—have not to date become the subject of mass-volume commercial travel. And these, I suggest, are always the sites of memorable vacations.

But usually the process of alternative travel requires an organization; it often involves booking a program or facility that pursues themes or beliefs outside one's normal ken: New Age therapies or Eastern theologies, holistic healing or macrobiotics, utopian living or rebellious politics, Nicaragua or abstract art.

One engages in these novel travel pursuits not necessarily out of a sympathy for such credos, but to be fully alive, open to all thought, constantly questing. I happen to be, in my own beliefs, very much a rationalist, agnostic, suspicious of spiritual claims or sudden panaceas. And yet the most rewarding travels of my life have been those when I exposed myself to diametrically opposing beliefs, in a residential setting, among adherents to those other beliefs, and with an open mind.

Such is the classic travel experience, exhilarating and enlarging; the rest is mere tourism, and painfully dull. Not to have heard alternative viewpoints in the places where they prevail, not to have visited countries of the Emerging World or nations of eastern Europe, not to have met the people of other cultures in a nontouristic setting, is not to have lived in this century.

Which brings me to the final, key ingredient of productive, rewarding travel: *people*. We all know that the encounter with local people, on a human scale, away from hotels and buses, is the single most memorable event of any trip. Yet most of us pursue that goal of meeting people in an unplanned, helter-skelter fashion, simply hoping that lightning will strike.

The new approach to travel brings careful deliberation, even organization, to such meetings:

• First, by utilizing lodgings that are not standard hotels, but accommodations indigenous to their surroundings, operated by people representative of their respective cultures, and patronized by the world's most interesting tourists—dynamic, spirited, free-thinking people from around the world who disdain the normal channels of commercial tourism and gravitate to such alternative lodgings.

• Second, by choosing tour operators who expose you to the realities of life at each destination, and not simply to sights gussied up or contrived for the visitor. That, too, is a major theme of this book, and the subject of considerable discussion.

• And finally, by utilizing those many non-profit programs that actually place you in the home of a foreign family, or at least arrange for a social encounter, over tea or at meals.

An Unserved Audience

How many people crave to enjoy this "New World" of vacation experience? Far more than the commercial travel industry realizes. With due apologies to American Express and British Airways, to Russia's Intourist and the Caribbean Travel Association, to Carnival Cruises and all the other travel behemoths, let me suggest that they are overlooking the fastest-growing segment in travel today—one that could account for as many as 40% of all the people who travel. That figure is suggested not only by the success of the first four editions of *The New World of Travel,* but by an important statistical survey conducted by the well-respected Lou Harris organization. In a little-noticed report on vacation motivations, recently issued on behalf of *Travel & Leisure* magazine, Harris concluded from hundreds of interviews that routine travel activities—sunbathing, swimming, visiting relatives—still account for the majority of all vacations. But to his astonishment, he also discovered that a large minority—fully two-fifths of his respondents—cited personal growth as their chief vacation aim: the desire to encounter new ideas, expand horizons, meet new people.

Indeed, among all the several categories of vacation desires, "life enhancement" (with its 40% of the vote) was the single largest.

Alternative travel is thus clearly here to stay, and will henceforth receive a growing amount of attention from travel journalists and travel publications. But when will the standard travel companies awake to these undeniable new trends? How long will the "majors," with their immense resources, continue to cater solely to those 60% of travelers who turn off their minds when they travel, and pay no attention at all to those 40% who do the opposite?

How long, for that matter, will real-estate developers keep opening endlessly duplicated, mindless, cookie-cutter resorts that scarcely differ from one another: rooms, swimming pool, tennis courts? When, in short, will they stop producing hotels in which one expires from boredom?

Imagine the improvement in the vacations of all of us if further resources were applied to learning vacations. Imagine, for example, a resort hotel with all the standard recreational activities, but with two covered walkways leading to two separate buildings. One would be a spa facility, for physical self-improvement. The other would be a complex of classrooms, workshops, and small theaters, for life enhancement.

I'd patronize a resort like that. And I have a feeling that multitudes of other Americans would do so, too.

Pending the awakening of the travel giants, we rely instead on the 1,200-odd smaller entrepreneurs who have created the vacations described in this book. Long may they flourish.

About the Current Edition

This is the fifth successive edition of *The New World of Travel,* expanded in size, broadened in subject matter, and made up-to-date for 1996. But its central theme remains the same. It deals with the growing gap between the vacations mass-produced by standard travel companies and those desired by an increasing number of spirited, intellectually curious Americans. The growth of that audience is shown by the number of persons who purchased the first four editions of *The New World of Travel,* and by the many reviewers who reacted positively to its message, to all of whom I am sincerely grateful.

Some critics dissented. One headlined his article, "Guru of Travel Freaks Out," implying—from the dizzying variety of vacations recommended in this book, each of a radically different sort—that I apparently hold dozens of conflicting philosophies, both spiritual and political. Because that whopping misunderstanding points up the single major advantage of a non-standard, non-conventional vacation, I want to exercise a personal right of reply.

The reason that one travels to visit with people holding exotic or countercultural viewpoints is not because one necessarily agrees with those opinions, but because it is part of the adventure of life to expose yourself to the beliefs of even those with whom you may disagree or doubt. I happen to be intensely skeptical of almost all spiritual beliefs. And also a proud Liberal in my political views. But some of my most memorable vacations have been to places where I have been made to reexamine my assumptions, and to listen with open mind to opinions I normally shun. Though they may not have persuaded me—those optimists with their novel spiritual speculations, those right-wing zealots in country music locales—they have enlivened my life, kept me thinking and excited. And frankly, the people who never do interact with their opposites live—in my opinion—very dull lives. Especially those who have never made a sympathetic effort to consider Eastern theologies or other unfamiliar nostrums of a dozen different types—well, those people have never fully lived, in my view.

One does not choose the unconventional vacation because of any necessary agreement with the theme of those vacations. That's not what travel is about. We travel to free ourselves from the provincial limitations of our accustomed settings and routines. We limit our material possessions to the size of a suitcase, bid goodbye to everything that normally sustains us, then fling ourselves to new and often exotic locations, opposing lifestyles, unfamiliar beliefs. We challenge our minds. And in doing so, we experience a sense of freedom, and of liberation from the ordinary, that is one of the great pleasures of life.

That reward can be made more exhilarating still by choosing a less stereotyped, less commercial, less superficial form of travel.

A wise man once said that Hell consists of being condemned to stay at a different Holiday Inn every night unto eternity. No such fate awaits our readers. With joy and enthusiasm, let's embark now for "The New World of Travel."

Vacation "Resorts" That Stretch Your Mind and Change Your Life

Vacationing at a "Personal Growth Center": Esalen and Others

Their Aim Is to Fulfill the Human Potential, to Expand Consciousness, and Improve Personal Relationships

On a broad lawn leading to a steep cliff, above the rocky surf and sea lions of the Pacific Ocean, couples hugged or stroked each other's arms. Occasionally they reached out to pat the cheek of a passing stranger.

Others raged in response to a trivial slight. Some of them arm-wrestled, grimly, to settle a dispute.

In scenes such as this, flung across the covers of *Life* and *Look,* the Esalen Institute of Big Sur, California, introduced America in the 1960s to "encounter therapy" and related offshoots of the "human potential movement." Drunk with the vision that they could lead humankind into a new era of heightened insight, sensitivity, and understanding, the personalities associated with Esalen—Michael Murphy, Fritz Perls,

Ida Rolf, Abraham Maslow, Will Shutz, Virginia Satir, Rollo May, Gregory Bateson—converted that isolated stretch of seafront heights into a place of unfettered experimentation in psychology, and fired the thought of millions, while offending or frightening legions of others.

Esalen Now

What has happened to Esalen in the ensuing years? Though no longer in the news, it perseveres, even thrives, but at a more measured pace, thoughtful and cautious. And it has spawned over a dozen imitators: residential retreats where hundreds of Americans devote their vacations to exploring a range of psychological subjects so broad as to require college-like catalogs to list them all. Encounter therapy—that almost-instant process of shedding inhibitions and responding to every repressed emotion—is now only one of numerous treatments under study at America's personal growth centers.

For one thing, the early leader of the encounter movement—Michael Murphy, co-founder of Esalen—is no longer certain of the long-term benefits of the art. It is, he believes, only a start—this stripping away of defenses through encounter techniques—which must be succeeded by longer-lasting and less dramatic work. Others have concluded that encounter therapy can be positively dangerous, exposing serious underlying pathologies without providing a trained therapist to deal with what's exposed.

And so the core curriculum of the centers is currently devoted to such multiple emerging sciences as Gestalt therapy, psychosynthesis, Ericksonian hypnosis, shamanic healing, neurolinguistics, Feldenkrais, and Rolfing.

From these basic inquiries emerge, at some centers, more popular discussions: "Intimate Relationships: Keeping the Spark Alive," "Burn-out: Causes and Cures," "Letting Go—Moving On," "Building Community: A Learning Circle," "Exorcising the Demon 'should,'" "From Aging to Sage-ing." All are aimed at expanding human potential, tapping into energies and abilities as yet unknown.

At Esalen, instruction is through seminars or workshops extending over a weekend ($380, including room and board) or five days midweek ($740); a handful of bunk beds, and space for sleeping bags, offer lower-rate possibilities. Many first-timers select the orientation workshop simply known as "Experiencing Esalen" (sensory awareness, group process, guided fantasy, meditation, massage), or the somewhat similar "Gestalt Practice"; others choose from more than 100 other widely varied subjects taught throughout the year.

At Big Sur on the California coast: the model for a dozen other, quite remarkable "resorts."

Studies are combined with exquisite relaxation, in a lush oasis of gardens, birds, and natural hot springs; the springs bring 110° sulfurous water into bathhouses where residents can soak

At Hollyhock Farm. *Courtesy Hollyhock Farm.*

for hours while watching the sun or moon set into the ocean below. Rooms are comfortable and pleasantly decorated, but must be shared with others (usually), and lack telephones, TV sets, or radios; a retreat atmosphere is maintained. Meals are served in a dining hall where dress and decor are casual but the cuisine is gourmet. The Esalen gardens and nearby farm supply the majority of the many options in the daily salad-and-vegetables bar.

When the 100 guest beds are not fully booked (which is common during the winter season and sometimes happens during midweek in summer), it is possible simply to stay at Esalen without enrolling in a seminar. The cost of this varies, but falls into the $75 to $120 range for a night and a day, including dinner, breakfast, and lunch, or for even less than that if you bring a sleeping bag or occupy one of the few bunk beds. Often people come to Esalen simply for a bout of quiet writing, or during a time of life transition. As workshops and bed spaces fill up early (especially in summer), it is important to plan a trip to Esalen well in advance. You may phone for a catalog or to reserve a workshop on your credit card (call 408/667-3000 or 408/644-8476), but the preferred method is to write c/o **Reservations, Esalen Institute, Hwy. 1, Big Sur, CA 93920.** The location is 300 miles north of Los Angeles, 175 miles south of San Francisco, between the spectacular coastal highway and the 100-foot cliffs overlooking crashing waves below.

And how do people respond to that setting? I can best report the reaction of a middle-aged couple from Santa Barbara who come here for a semi-annual "fix," to "feel alive and revitalized." Apart from their interest in Aikido movement/meditation (the subject of their workshop), they feel that Esalen "has the nicest piece of real estate in the world—beach, rocks, surf, sea, air, mountains, hot tubs, good food, and loving people—who could ask for anything more?"

And Farther Afield

Though Esalen was the first, it is now but one of a dozen such "personal growth" retreats on both coasts of the United States and in between.

Their goal? It is again to fulfill the "human potential," to expand consciousness and improve personal relationships, to tap into the same mysterious sources of energy and spirit that enable mystics in other lands and on other levels to enjoy trances and visions, to walk on nails, or fast for days.

Their method? Workshops of a week's or a weekend's duration, attended by vacationing members of the public, who offer up their own psyches to these new therapies or to classroom training.

Unlisted in any directory of which I am aware, and marketed through severely limited mailings or classified ads in magazines of small circulation, they are nonetheless open to all and worthy of far broader dissemination.

East Coast

Omega Institute, 260 Lake Drive, Rhinebeck, NY 12572 (phone 914/266-4444), is—apart from Esalen—the lodestone; it attracts up to 500 people a week during its summer operating period from mid-June to mid-October. On a broad lake flanked by extensive, hilly grounds of forest and clearings, in a joyful atmosphere of kindness and smiles, it presents weekend and weeklong workshops ranging from the clearly lighthearted ("Vocal Joy," "Delicious Movement") to the softly therapeutic ("Working with Dreams," "The Fear of Losing Control," "Choosing to Connect") to the arcane and abstruse ("Oriental Diagnosis," "Interfacing Psychology and Spirituality," "The Tibetan Path of Love and Compassion"); many of the most famous figures in the human potential movement—Ram Dass and Ashley Montagu, Ilana Rubenfeld and Per Vilayat Inayat

Khan—make an appearance, and a great many of the seminars are identical to those presented at Esalen, suggesting a personal growth "circuit" for lecturers. Tuition averages $60 a day; housing and meals (vegetarian) add $50 in campsites or dorms, up to $65 in private cabins. You can contact Omega directly for a copy of their 104-page catalog, which will also alert you to Omega's extensive winter program to St. John (Maho Bay) in the U.S. Virgin Islands, Taos (in New Mexico), St. Augustine (Florida), Phoenicia Center (in New York State) and Warrenton (Virginia).

Aegis, The Abode, R.D. 1, Box 1030D, New Lebanon, NY 12125 (phone 518/ 794-8095): On three-day weekends from May through October, supplemented by five-day mid-week sessions in June and July, and occasional workshops in other seasons, outsiders come to study on this mountain in the Berkshires with a permanent community of "Sufis"—the gentlest of people who have made an eclectic choice from the prophetic messages of all religions, both Western and Eastern. Faculty includes a Benedictine monk, a rabbi, and a Native American. Sample workshops: "Polishing the Mirror of the Heart," "Stages of Spiritual Development," "Breath of Life and Light"; there is much meditation. To weekend tuition costs averaging $125, add room and board charges of about $30 a day in a dorm or cabin, $20 a day in a campsite.

Wainwright House, 260 Stuyvesant Ave., Rye, NY 10580 (phone 914/967-6080): A stately mansion on elegant grounds, just north of New York City, it offers year-round daily workshops—some for only a day in duration—in Jungian studies, spiritual disciplines, "health and wholeness," and other topics of psychology. Themes are far-ranging—"Depth Psychology," "Spiritual Development," "Global Issues," "Sonic Meditation," "The Psychology of Illness"—and speakers more eclectic still: They include Ram Dass, Dr. Bernie Siegel, James Hillman, Barbara Marx Hubbard, and Robert Johnson. One-day tuition ranges from free to $50, and overnight accommodations, including breakfast, run $35 (dorm) to $45 (per person, double room). Other meals are offered in the dining room at additional cost. A catalog of courses is free for the asking.

West Coast

Mount Madonna Center, 445 Summit Road, Watsonville, CA 95076 (phone 408/ 847-0406, or fax 408/847-2683) in the Sierra Mountains of California, overlooking Monterey Bay—you can't imagine a more enthralling location—is another leading retreat facility for the discussion of every psychological issue, every spiritual conundrum, including the latest and hottest topics. Unlike several other such centers, which rent their premises to self-contained groups, Mount Madonna invites the public to every session, and thousands head there each year for long weekends or week long vacations that combine hiking in the redwood forests and cavorting in the open air, with attendance at the weightiest of talks and discussions: "Eros and Spirituality," "A Retreat for Mothers," "Dying—Opportunity of a Lifetime," "Creativity and Success," "Self Hypnosis and Inner Balance"; call in advance to learn the content of the seminars and classes presented during the time of your own desired stay. Though the staff of the center is yoga-trained and yoga-oriented, seminars deal with broader psychological issues. Room and two vegetarian meals daily, supplemented by snacks, range from $33 per person (in a tent supplied with mattress), $44 (in dorms housing four to seven) to $49 (in a triple room) to $55 per person (in a double), or $71 single, per day, to which you add $60 or so for tuition relating to the courses and seminars you've chosen. All this is but an hour from San Jose Airport, an hour and a half from San Francisco Airport.

They will cause you to discover, at the very least, important new aspects of your inner life and relations with others.

Naropa Institute, 2130 Arapahoe Ave., Boulder, CO 80302 (phone 303/444-0202): In a partly urban setting, yet on the slopes of the Rockies, it is serious and intellectual, but with a heavy emphasis on innovative, psychological approaches to music, theater, dance, and creative writing. Nevertheless, workshops also include "Introduction to Buddhist Psychology," "Aging with Awareness," "Human Sexuality: From Birth to Therapy," "Rediscovering the Masculine Soul," "Death as a Spiritual Teacher." Guests find their own housing from a plethora of hotels and motels nearby (rates like those of any other large city), to which average tuition fees of about $250 should be added.

Their goal? To fulfill the "human potential," to expand consciousness, releasing energy and spirit.

Feathered Pipe Ranch, P.O. Box 1682, Helena, MT 59624 (phone 406/442-8196): Open in spring, summer, and fall only, using log-and-stone ranchhouse accommodations in a stunning Rocky Mountain location bordered by a national forest. The program consists of heavily spiritual "holistic life seminars," but also includes standard yoga workshops (presented by Lillias Folen, John Schumacher, and Patricia Walden), studies in holistic health, male/female relationships, and similar subject matter. Frequent lecturers include prominent figures in the personal growth movement, like Jean Shinoda Bolen (author of *Crossing to Avalon*), Dr. Andrew Weil (much-published author on natural health), Brooke Medicine Eagle, and Brent Secunda (teaching courses on Native American shamanism), among others.

Charges start at $900 a week for instruction, meals, and dorm-style lodging, but rates are reduced considerably for individuals participating in a "work retreat" program; inquire.

Ojai Foundation, P.O. Box 1620, Ojai, CA 93024 (phone 805/646-8343): On a 40-acre ridge of semi-wilderness, two hours north of Los Angeles, mainly it offers weekend seminars and workshops in personal growth subjects, with accommodations mainly in tents, and participants receive vegetarian meals. Recent topics have included "The Art of Gender Reconciliation," "Islam: The Garden Beyond the Dragons at the Gate," "Mystery of Eros in Relationship," "Judaism: Seasons of Joy and Contemplation," all characterized by the organization as seeking "to honor the inseparability of learning and living, to heal the split between work in the world and spiritual practice, and to honor traditional wisdom by incorporating it in our present way of being." All programs begin with dinner at 6pm on Friday, and end Sunday at 5pm. Costs average $250 a weekend and are for tented accommodations, vegetarian meals, and all tuition. More standard living arrangements are available for persons seeking to have a (secular) retreat there, for longer periods of time.

Hollyhock, P.O. Box 127, Manson's Landing, Cortes Island, BC, V0P 1K0, Canada (phone 604/935-6465): One hundred miles north of Vancouver, in the Strait of Georgia, this is a warm-weather-only (March through October) facility on an expanse of beach and 48 acres of gardens, orchards, and forest. Workshops are generally five days in duration, average U.S. $600 (and less) for tuition, room, and board, and explore such subjects as "Tibetan Buddhism," "Exploring the World of Alternative Medicine," "Vipassana Meditation," "Jungian Dreamwork," and "Tai-Chi Chu'an." Simple retreats without the workshops, but including morning yoga and meditation, in addition to lodgings and three meals a day, are $100 (Canadian) a day, or $700 (Canadian) for a week. As an added recent attraction, Hollyhock has recently hired a full-time, resident naturalist to teach free courses on ecology, and to lead nature hikes and star-gazing sessions.

Ghost Ranch, HC77 Box 11, Abiquiu, New Mexico, 87510 (phone 505/685-4333): The ranch is owned by the Presbyterian Church, and teaches personal growth, but from a largely religious, though non-denominational, viewpoint. Though much of the subject matter consists of religious education ("Meeting Jesus for the First Time"), at least half the year is devoted to "insights and encounters" ("Body, Mind and Retreat," "What Does the Land Reveal," "Writing with the Heart's Clear Eye" were several recent seminars). For a week-long stay, you'll pay $260 for room and full board, and from $75 to $100 (depending on the course) in tuition.

Personal Growth, New Age–Style

In earlier editions of this book, we followed our chapter on personal growth centers with one on so-called "New Age" hotels and resorts, most of them advocating the philosophies made popular in the 1980s by Shirley Maclaine in a spate of best-selling paperbacks revealing that she had lived past lives, gained strength from crystals, and experienced other cosmic phenomena.

Time has not been kind to the New Age centers, and most of them have either shifted to exploring more realistic, more earthbound issues of personal growth and human relationships, or else to replacing their curriculum with one oriented to environmental matters and sustainable living conditions. Still others have transformed themselves into conference centers rented periodically to outside groups (some of which do

continue to pursue the spiritual speculations and hypotheses of the "New Age"). Such has largely been the course followed by the large **Shenoa Retreat and Learning Center, P.O. Box 3, Philo, CA 95466 (phone 707/895-3156 or fax 707/895-3236)**. Shenoa's activities continue to be impressive, and you'd be well advised to write for its current schedules, which recently devoted a week to the "Findhorn Experience" and invited key members of that Scottish "New Age" center to appear and teach at Shenoa. Though I personally do not react well to New Age teachings, I still find it fascinating and instructive to speculate about them, and to consider the possibility that humankind may someday prove able to understand the nature of mind, the ability to transfer thoughts to another, the ability to communicate with other species, and many more New Age speculations. Shenoa is a large and well-equipped facility in Mendocino County north of San Francisco (but warmer than that sometimes-chilly city).

Each center issues catalogs or other descriptive literature, to be carefully perused before enrolling. From personal experience, I can assure you that a stay will cause you to discover, at the very least, important new aspects of your inner life and relations with others.

A Visit to Famous Findhorn

Thousands Enjoy an "Experience Week" at the World's Most Celebrated "New Age" Community

Fired from his job as a hotel manager, a restless Peter Caddy moved with his wife, three children, and a family friend to a car-trailer parked on a bleak stretch of sandy seacoast in northeastern Scotland, near a village named Findhorn.

And there, in 1962, he grew cabbages weighing 42 pounds. Claiming to tap into a life force that animates the universe, using meditation and "attunement" to feel at one with nature, this rather conventional Englishman (now deceased) created a garden so fertile as to cause dozens of others to join him in building a New Age community on the surrounding site. Its aim: to expand the human consciousness and thus change the world.

Today the cabbages are no more. Residents of the Findhorn Foundation joke about the phenomenon that brought them worldwide attention. "And anyway," said one to a recent guest, "why should anyone want to eat cabbage for a month?"

But what survives is an impressive, sprawling, residential-and-classroom complex of 180 permanent members, another hundred or so visitors pursuing successive, one-week courses of instruction—and a potent tourist attraction. By the thousands each year, adherents of a dozen, radically differing theories of the human potential, joined by others who are simply curious, flock to what has by now become the single most famous utopian community on earth.

The Evolution in Its Function

But Findhorn today is more a learning center than a community. Though the cultivation of its famous garden (books have been written about it) continues to be a major activity, Findhorn is far from self-sufficient in food or other products, and only a handful of its members work at life-sustaining tasks. Rather, the bulk of its population are administrators, publicists, teachers, or loyal volunteers at housekeeping (kitchen, transport, maintenance, accounts). Through those labors they keep the area alive with periodic workshops, seminars, and conferences exploring the spiritual bases of life. And these are attended by guests from around the world.

The goal is a breathtaking one, massively ambitious. "We believe humanity is on the verge of a major evolutionary leap," says one explanatory leaflet, "an expansion of consciousness" creating "new patterns of civilization and a . . . culture infused with spiritual values. . . . We seek [to discover that] new awareness in our own daily lives."

The steps toward the goal are more modest, and pursued in a highly reasonable manner. Findhorn teaches no single creed, explores the principles of all spiritual outlooks, grants total freedom of expression, and tends to ignore exotic dogmas. In its directory of workshop topics, not a single one deals with Shirley MacLaine–type speculations into reincarnation, channeling, or magic crystals. Rather, it is the subconscious and the intuitive,

Its aim: to expand the human consciousness and thus change the world.

the impact of mind upon body, the potential of human imagination, that form the core of discussions listed under such headings as "Meditation as a Way of Life," "Reawakening the Metaphoric Mind," "Dreams and the Spiritual Path," "Learning to Love," "Coming Alive," "A Working Retreat for Managers," "Holistic Healing"—in short, the entire range of the more defensible forms of New Age thinking.

Workshops start at £260 to £280 ($403 to $434) a week, including room and full board, and most are one week in duration.

The Experience Week

The strict prerequisite for attending a workshop, however, is prior participation in a generally less expensive "Experience Week" offered Saturday to Saturday throughout the year, and costing £225 to £315 ($349 to $488), depending on one's ability to pay, for all-inclusive arrangements; that weekly sojourn is the major means for visiting Findhorn on a touristic or temporary basis.

"Experience Week" guests stay for seven nights in two- to six-bedded rooms of Findhorn's Cluny Hill College, a large, old (but well-maintained) former hotel overlooking a golf course; there they also take their meals (vegetarian, fresh, delicious). Throughout the week they tour every part of the Findhorn Foundation, including its work "departments," hear lectures by staff and celebrated theorists, engage in "sharings" (communal social gatherings), "sacred dancing," and innovative games designed to strip away repressions and wasteful defenses. They talk endlessly and lovingly with fellow guests about personal problems and goals.

For each of five weekdays they also work for four hours in Findhorn's garden or kitchens, because work is regarded as a "cement" that brings community members together spiritually, a caring gesture more than a task.

Before each work period, members and guests hold hands in a brief meditation to "attune" to each other and the project ahead. They talk with one another as the work proceeds, express mutual affection, become a close-knit group. Numerous observers (including my daughter Pauline, who visited Findhorn on my behalf) have commented on the energy and enthusiasm that go into such projects, and their impact on Findhorn, where grounds and structures are remarkably well kept and clean. In the kitchen, she reports, "work was done quickly and efficiently, and was more enjoyable than burdensome."

Although Findhorn's "Experience Weeks" have a large capacity, they are always heavily booked, especially in summer, when applications six to nine months ahead are advisable. Write for application forms, and further information, to **Accommodations Secretary, Findhorn Foundation, Cluny Hill College, Forres, Scotland IV 36 ORD (phone 309-673655, or via e-mail to "edudept@findhorn.org").** Another Findhorn number for more general information is 309-690311, which also connects you with the Visitors Centre. E-mail, via the Internet, is sent to "reception@findhorn.org" for the same central information purposes.

Visiting children are not accepted, and have little role at Findhorn, except during occasional "Family Weeks."

Alternative Possibilities

For would-be visitors unable to spend a full week at Findhorn, three lesser and last-minute alternatives are available.

First, you can simply wander through Cullerne, the main gardening area of the foundation, open to the public from sunup to sundown. Some casual visitors have been known to work in that garden; in a large barn on the site, a downstairs coatroom provides raincoats and galoshes to poorly equipped, impromptu volunteers.

Or you can take a guided, but free, two-hour tour of the foundation's grounds, starting daily at 2pm in spring, summer, and fall, but only on Tuesday and Saturday in winter. Tours set out from the Phoenix Shop (a combination bookstore and health-food purveyor) in The Park, which is the large area of trailers where Peter and Eileen Caddy first placed their home. The epochal, small green trailer is still there, but used as an office, and found directly across from the guest reception center. Nearby is the Universal Hall, Findhorn's showplace for conferences and performances; the Sanctuary (for meditation); the Apothecary Shop (for herbal medicines prescribed by holistic physicians who have seen the light); a Community Center with food service; craft studios; pottery and weaving barns; a graphic design shop; a printing plant; and more.

Perhaps the best alternative visit is an unplanned, three-day stay as a "short-term guest." Here, you generally arrange your own accommodations—either pitching a tent or using one of the many £12-a-night ($18.60) B&Bs or guest-accepting farmhouses in the vicinity—but present yourself daily to Findhorn for three hours of work (in your choice of departments, morning or afternoon), supplemented by participation in various gatherings and evening fests to which you'll then be invited. You simply show up unannounced at the Visitors Centre in The Park, or better, write or phone ahead to the **Findorn Foundation (Short Term Guests), The Park, Forres, Scotland IV 36 OTZ (phone 309-30311)**, in which latter case you'll sometimes—but rarely—receive a bed in Cluny Hill College.

Despite your daily three-hour stint of work, you'll pay a "short-term charge" of £12 ($18.60) a day, or whatever you are able to afford (my backpacking daughter offered, and paid, £10 ($15.50), which included lunch and dinner. Unlike Experience Week guests, who are often bused from place to place on the extensive grounds of Findhorn, short-term guests make their own way to and from, and are probably best advised to have a car.

Bear in mind that the Findhorn Foundation is wholly distinct from the adjoining, tiny village of Findhorn—the latter a former fishing town, today a resort whose docks berth pleasure craft. In walking distance from the village's center is a long and lovely beach known as the "Riviera of Scotland" (but normally too cold for swimming).

The nearest larger village is Forres, about five miles away, and nationally acclaimed for its own gardens. In the vicinity is the well-preserved Cawdor Castle, full of armor, traditional furniture, and portraits of the Cawdors.

A larger nearby city is Inverness, 30 minutes by car from Findhorn, and proud possessor of a major airport. But trains stopping at Forres can also bring you to Findhorn.

Elsewhere in this book, I've written about an easily visited rationalist community in Britain, the Centre for Alternative Technology near Machynlleth, Wales, where residents apply logic, science, and egalitarian principles to the conduct of community life. In Findhorn, you

Findhorn teaches no single creed, grants total freedom of expression, and tends to ignore exotic dogmas.

have the contrasting spiritual approach to many of the same concerns, and both communities provide the basis for a profoundly important, endlessly fascinating, vacation trip to the U.K.

On the Road to Utopia

At "Intentional
Communities" across
the U.S.A., Short
Stays and Visits Are a
Mind-Expanding
Experience

Show me a utopian community and I'm soon walking on air. The very thought of people uprooting themselves and reassembling to lead a rational life brings goosepimples to my flesh and awakens youthful dreams of a better world.

Well, wonder of wonders, our nation harbors a hundred and more utopian communities, and some of them accept short-term visitors. Can you think of a more rewarding weekend or week-long stay than at a modern Walden, an Erewhon, a Shangri-La?

None of them, of course, would be so bold as to style themselves by those long-hallowed names. Rather, they are simply "intentional communities"—the modern term for those who have gathered onto a rural site to pursue a carefully planned life of cooperation and sharing.

Some are simply working farms occupied by three or four families, and obviously unsuitable for visiting tourists. Others, a growing number, are elaborate villages, with 60 to 100 residents, that encourage visitors and maintain overnight lodgings for them. From there they take you to classrooms, tour you through the site, lecture and prod you to reexamine your own harshly competitive life.

If all this seems threatening, or against your political grain, you might pause to consider that throughout history, similar intentional communities—both here and abroad—have introduced approaches to life, and forms of social organization, that later became commonplace.

The communal homes of a Denver or Washington, D.C., in which young single people share costs, are outgrowths of the experience of intentional communities. So are the ever-more-frequent platonic households of two singles of the opposite sex sharing an apartment.

The very same intentional communities first launched to a broader audience the current, widespread consumption of health foods, the growing practice of holistic medicine, protection of the environment, energy conservation and the use of nonfossil fuels, the soaring interest in Eastern philosophies and religions (zen, tao, yoga), humane attitudes toward animals.

"We are like laboratories for research into the future," said a member of one community in the course of my own visit. "We are testing the methods that people a hundred years from now will use to improve their lives."

Their Visitor Programs

Care to observe? The most rewarding vacations I know are spent as a guest (or working guest) on the grounds of

a hundred such villages that avidly encourage visitors as a means of spreading their utopian views. They house and feed you for the most nominal charge, because their goal (to put it bluntly) is to change your life—and the life of this planet.

Yet though they proselytize, they do not brainwash. The mildest of people, they fully expect you to recoil initially from such community concepts as "transspecies interaction" (communication with animals, insects, and plants)—and they take no offense at your own disbelief. They are just as accustomed to resistance when first they introduce you to "communal childcare," "planetary citizenship," or "extended families." Instead of arguing, they return calmly to work while you, in dazed confusion, ponder upon an unsettling eruption of new ideas.

And ponder them you will. Just wait until you encounter "variable labor credits" or "flexible work weeks"! Your mind will almost audibly stretch as you learn that, at some communities, members performing desirable work (like childcare) receive fewer hours of credit than

Can you think of a more rewarding weekend or week-long stay than at a modern Walden, an Erewhon, a Shangri-La?

On the grounds of utopia: a frank exchange.
Courtesy Federation of Egalitarian Communities.

members performing undesirable work (like cleaning latrines). By opting for the latter, aspiring artists and writers can reduce their communal labors to two or three days a week—and isn't that sensible?

Among the communities that take visitors are these prominent examples (rich opportunities for your next holiday trip):

Twin Oaks, Virginia

Twin Oaks, near Louisa, Virginia: Nearly 100 people live in this 27-year-old collection of farm buildings on 400 acres of woods, creeks, hilly pastures, and meadows—their goal an eventual community of 200 to 300. To promote both membership and viewpoints, visits are permitted, but only on most (not all) Saturday afternoons from 2 to 5pm (no food is served), for $3 per adult, and only through prior arrangement by phone. Those more seriously interested in joining are then allowed to make a three-week visit, for a total of $40, using self-supplied sleeping bags on the floor of several houses, or a dozen actual beds in the eight rooms of a visitors' building.

Some are elaborate villages, with 60 to 100 residents, that encourage visitors and maintain overnight lodgings for them.

Heavily influenced by the utopian novel of the Harvard psychologist B. F. Skinner, *Walden Two,* the community attempts to be a "model social system" through rational approaches to life that avoid the spiritual emphasis of several other communities. Political solutions are stressed, logic is the tool, and all forms of modern media—books, records, tapes, and magazines, everything except television (because it promotes "those values and products that we are trying to avoid")—are amply available on site.

At Twin Oaks, all labor, property, and resources are held in common, but personal privacy is fiercely protected. Children are raised as in an Israeli kibbutz, occupying their own residence and raised by all adult members. Supervision of economic life is by numerous planner-managers elected to short terms, and the community is self-sufficient through the manufacture of handcrafted hammocks and chairs, other small industries, and the cultivation of extensive organic gardens serving a mostly vegetarian table.

Twin Oaks is easily reached by bus or car from Washington, D.C., but is even closer to Richmond, Charlottesville, or Culpeper. For literature, or to schedule a visit (even the afternoon visit must be booked in advance), contact **Visitor Program, Twin Oaks Community, Louisa, VA 23093 (phone 703/894-5126)**.

East Wind, Missouri

East Wind, near Tecumseh, Missouri, in the Ozark hills, is another kibbutz-like, B. F. Skinner–influenced community of 65 or so members pursuing a "peaceful, cooperative, and egalitarian" life free of "racist, sexist, and competitive behavior." Constantly experimental, open-minded, and diverse, it places a music practice space next to a dairy barn, a trailer-library alongside the inevitable shops for producing hammocks, sandals, and—a proud specialty—"nut butter." Members, each with a full vote, have substantial labor or production quotas, but enjoy weekend rest, plus three weeks of vacation a year, and can earn additional vacation by producing "overquota." Children are raised by "metas"—members who have chosen childcare as their work—but have at least three other "primary people" in their lives: their parents, and one or two others chosen by the parents. Most impressively, the community grows more than half its own food.

Because East Wind is anxious to expand, it encourages visits (costing only $2 a day) for up to three weeks by people who then work the same number of hours as members and spend only the amount of money on site as would equal a member's allowance. Any fears of a spartan life that these rules may evoke are soon overcome by the idyllic natural setting of the site, an area renowned for its swimming, canoeing, hiking, and other outdoor recreation.

Write ahead for a detailed brochure or for reservations (and don't simply drop in) to **East Wind Community, P.O. Box NWT, Tecumseh, MO 65760 (phone 417/679-4682)**.

Sirius, Massachusetts

Sirius, near Amherst, Massachusetts, emphasizes spirituality to the same or even greater extent than its political notions of cooperation and sharing; indeed, it differs from numerous other communities by encouraging members to earn their own incomes, sometimes at jobs in neighboring towns. But most of the members purchase food jointly, take most meals communally, own the 94 acres of their site jointly, reach community decisions by consensus—and meditate until all members acquiesce in the "rightness" of the decisions taken.

Like Thoreau, the Sirius participants have built their homes "in the woods," and there they engage in organic gardening, holistic health practices, and solar design. But it is personal growth to which most attention is paid. Though members are free to pursue varying spiritual disciplines, they believe in the God within each human being and the "interconnectedness" of all nature (animals, plants, humans). Several prominent members are alumni of the famous Findhorn Community in Scotland (we've already visited that magical place in a previous essay) and apply the same loving care to gardens and forests that Findhorn regards as a moral imperative.

Personal growth, so claims the Sirius group, results from the demands of harmonious group living. Members rid themselves of old patterns, become "agents of change," build for themselves and others "a more peaceful, loving world."

Contact **Sirius Community, Baker Road, Shutesbury, MA 01072 (phone 413/ 259-1251)**.

Sunrise Ranch, Colorado

Sunrise Ranch, near Loveland, Colorado, one of the oldest (1940s) and most successful (150 residents) of the alternative communities, places its emphasis almost entirely on personal, spiritual growth, and not on communal, social, or economic practices. Still, a major activity is organic gardening (supplying most of the ranch's foodstuffs), followed closely by the use of personnel in clerical functions supporting the worldwide activities of the Emissaries, the sponsoring organization. The latter's doctrines are a mild, broad, and initially hard-to-comprehend philosophy of "quality living" through "alignment with the rhythms and cycles of life." "Manipulation," says Sunrise teacher Nick Giglio, "as well as hidden agendas and tools of persuasion are unnecessary excess baggage."

Visiting facilities are extensive, cost only $35 to $45 a day (the suggested "donation"), including all three meals (plus the cost of any particular seminar or presentation at the time of your visit), and should be reserved in advance by writing to **Sunrise Ranch, 5569 N. County Rd. 29, Loveland, CO 80538 (phone 303/ 679-4200)**. Loveland is 50 miles north of Denver, and the ranch is seven miles from Loveland.

Stelle, Illinois

Stelle, 90 miles south of Chicago and 30 miles southwest of Kankakee, at the opposite end of the political spectrum from the communal societies described above, is a small (125 residents), planned village (like a miniature Columbia, Md., or Reston, Va.) in which homes are privately owned and incomes privately earned. But various cooperative (not communal) institutions bind the residents together, including bulk purchases of food, joint operation of a local telephone exchange, periodic "celebrations," and a town-hall form of pure democratic government. Residents consider themselves an extended family.

The village is most productively visited for exposure to its library, publications, and audio-visual presentations dealing with subjects that affect the operation of intentional communities. You do this either on a day trip or overnight for $25 single, $40 double, including breakfast, at one of several bed-and-breakfast houses nearby. Or you can arrange a day visit, or have lunch with residents on Tuesday or Friday (at a cost of $3 to $5), by phoning the **Stelle Group Office (phone 815/256-2200)** between 8am and 5pm. Generally, they will have someone available to talk with you and take you on a short tour, occasionally stopping to converse with residents. More detailed, free literature—including a pamphlet called "Visiting the Stelle Group"— is available from the Group Office (see above) and should be read prior to the visit.

> **Throughout history, similar "intentional communities" have introduced approaches to life, and forms of social organization, that later became commonplace.**

Four More Communities

Acorn, in Mineral, Virginia, a seven-mile canoe trip or drive from Twin Oaks, is a 1993 "spin-off" from the latter, but totally independent from the long-established community, and somewhat more spiritual in its approach. Its members are Christian, Buddhist, Jewish, and "Pagan," but they gather together for periodic celebrations; several even host a Jewish Shabbat service for the others on Friday nights.

Growing rapidly (the approach apparently works), Acorn has constructed three large residences from scratch, and currently boasts a big, wood-fired hot tub, a large greenhouse, extensive gardens, and fruit-bearing trees. It welcomes visitors at any time (possibly to gain new members), asks only $5 a day to offset the cost of food and lodging, but asks that reservations be made several weeks in advance. Contact **Acorn, Rte. 3, Box 486A, Mineral, VA 23117 (phone 703/894-0582).**

The Foundation for Feedback Learning, on Staten Island, New York: Minutes from the towers of downtown Manhattan, an 80-member group inhabits 7 large houses and 5 commercial buildings in which they pursue researches so eclectic as to defy generalization: language training, psychodrama, biofeedback, and furniture repair, in addition to multiple new approaches to communal living and personal relationships, the constant exchange of thoughts and feelings. Visitors to New York may stay with them for a day or two at a charge of $30 a day, or for one-month periods for $500 to $650 per person (less per person for couples), including all meals. Contact the **Foundation for Feedback Learning, 135 Corson Ave., Staten Island, NY 10301 (phone 718/720-5378).**

Breitenbush Retreat Center, 60 miles from Salem, Oregon: Here are 14 adults (with 10 children) of widely divergent political and spiritual views, but all with a fierce urge to enjoy a life in nature, and warm, caring relationships. At a 2,500-foot elevation in the western Cascade Mountains, they found and restored this isolated hot-springs resort, where they provide guests with vegetarian meals, holistic health care, meditation, and other such "therapies" for as little as $50 per person per day, cabin and full board. Contact **Breitenbush Community, P.O. Box 578, Detroit, OR 97342 (phone 503/854-3314).**

Green Pastures Estates, in Epping, New Hampshire: A spiritual community in a small New England village. The 50 or so members aged 11 to 85 occupy a compound of period structures clustered around a central dining room where meals (both vegetarian and non) are taken communally. Some members "live in" but "work out" at jobs in neighboring towns, and then pay Green Pastures for their room and board. Others work the adjoining 160-acre farm. All pursue a goal of spiritual growth or maturity that stresses the responsibility of each individual for his/her own emotional state. By attaining that growth (taught, among other topics, at four evening "services" each week), members aid the community to become a joyful, creative, smoothly interacting group. Visitors wishing to participate for a short stay will receive room and board for $60 a day (a suggested donation) by writing in advance to **Green Pastures Estates, 38 Ladd's Lane, Epping, NH 03042 (phone 603/679-8149)**. Epping is about seven miles from Exeter.

And Still Others

Since most intentional communities receive frequent visits by like-minded members of other such communities, members are usually aware of the distinctive features, pros and cons, of several. They share this knowledge with visitors, networking in open, unabashed fashion. Soon you become aware of both the nationwide and international ramifications of the "intentional communities" movement, enriching your knowledge of the contemporary world, and perhaps learning how people will live in future years.

The current-day community members total as many as 200,000 people. In hundreds of small farm settlements or tiny villages, or more frequently in thousands of urban communal households, they have rejected the current forms of society and sought Utopia: a life of cooperation, not competition; of sharing, not owning; of full equality and democracy, without direction or domination from above.

I haven't the space to describe a dozen-or-so other communities known to me (like the visitor-friendly Veiled Cliffs in Scottown, Ohio, phone 614/256-1400; Sandhill Farm, also open to visitors, in Rutledge, Missouri, phone 816/883-5543; or Tekiah, in Check, Virginia, accepting visitors, phone 703/651-3412. But a directory of 400 such communities (costing $16), or a back issue of *Communities Magazine* ($7.50, including postage), is available from "Community Bookshelf," East Wind Community, Tecumseh, Missouri 65760. For still other literature, write the Fellowship for Intentional Community, 615 First Street, Langley, Washington 98260.

America on $35 a Day, Via the Yoga Route

Remarkable Vacations, Rewarding and Cheap, at Ashrams Clustered near Both Coasts

I am not a yogi. And considering my feverish lifestyle, horrendous eating habits, and stubborn rationalism, that's the understatement of the year.

But yogi or not, some of my happiest holidays have been spent at yoga retreats. When it comes to inducing sheer serenity, restoring vigor, flushing toxins from both mind and body, nothing beats these mystical *ashrams* (schools, places of learning) with their vegetarian meals and quiet hillside settings, their twice-daily *asanas* (languid stretching exercises) and moments of meditation, their gentle people.

And when it comes to cost, nothing else in the vacation field even remotely compares. At a score of residential, countryside ashrams clustered near both coasts, the charge for room and all three meals amounts—if you can believe it—to $35 and $45 a day.

Why so cheap? Because the meals are vegetarian, the sites are often donated, and the staff works for free, performing karma yoga (selfless service).

Why, then, aren't they inundated with guests? Because the public, in general, recoils from Eastern thought, equating all such teachings with those of Sun Myung Moon, assuming dreadful acts of brain-washing or abandoned conduct, as at the turbulent Rajneeshpuram in Oregon or the doomed Guyanese community of mad Jim Jones.

As applied to the yoga movement, nothing could be further from the truth. A philosophy of life, not a religion; a questing science, not a dogma—yoga is the most tolerant of creeds, its practitioners good-humored, broad-minded, modest, and non-authoritarian. At the U.S. ashrams, nothing is mandatory other than attendance at the asanas (physical exercises or postures) and silent meditations—and that, only to screen out persons who are simply seeking a cheap crashpad for their vacations.

Apart from those two limited daily sessions, no one cares what you do or where you go, or whether you even attend lectures of the guru. He or she is regarded with affection, called *guruji* or *swamiji* (dear little guru, dear little swami), but treated as fallible, and certainly not as a God-head. Some instructors at the ashrams— even a director or two—will stress their distance from Hindu theology and their pursuit of yoga primarily for its physical and calming benefits.

Though the residential ashrams in North America number far more than a score, not all have guaranteed staying-power. Those that do include:

The Sivananda Retreat

On Paradise Island, the Bahamas: You've heard of Club Med; now meet Club Meditation (at a fifth the price). An ashram that's a 150-bed tropical resort, it sits next to sugary-white sands, across the bay from Nassau on four beachfront acres donated to the Sivananda Vedanta movement by an admirer; the popular, otherworldly complex is now in its 28th year. You arise at dawn to meditate on the beach, proceed immediately (and before breakfast) to a two-hour exercise class (asana), partake at last of a mammoth vegetarian brunch, and are then allowed to do nothing at all (except swim, snorkel, and sun) until 4pm when a second round of meditation and asanas is followed by supper at 6pm, meditation at sunset, and bed. Accommodations range from airy dorms in a colonial building ($45 per person per night, including meals and exercise classes) to double rooms in modern cabins ($50) to "meditation huts" ($60) overlooking the sea, to single rooms affording privacy and great calm ($75). Contact **Sivananda Ashram Yoga Retreat, P.O. Box N7550, Paradise Island, Nassau, Bahamas (phone 809/363-2902)**, for reservations or literature; or you can speak with the New York office: **Sivananda Yoga Center, 243 W. 24th St., New York, NY 10011 (phone 212/255-4560)**.

When it comes to inducing sheer serenity, nothing beats these mystical retreats with their vegetarian meals and quiet hillside settings, their twice-daily asanas (languid stretching exercises) and moments of meditation.

Kripalu Center

Near Lenox, Massachusetts: In the many wings and 400 rooms of a former Jesuit monastery, on a hillside overlooking Lake Mahkeenac in the Berkshire Mountains of western Massachusetts, Kripalu is one of the largest of all ashrams with one of the most varied programs—its brochure resembles a college catalog crammed with courses and options. Soothed by the ministrations of a largely unpaid staff of volunteers, you exercise, meditate, wander, and soak; attend lively seminars; dine in complete silence at both the breakfast and luncheon meal (the latter a vegetarian buffet), but converse at dinner; and hear lectures by a resident guru ("beloved teacher").

Accommodations are comfortable, in spacious dorms (10 to 22 people) of wide-frame, wooden double-deckers, or in pleasant private rooms, and yet the all-inclusive charge—for housing and all three meals, exercise classes, and most other activities—is a reasonable $70 per person in the dormitories, $80 per person in a standard double room. Write or phone **Kripalu Center, P.O. Box 793, Lenox, MA 01240 (phone 413/ 637-3280 Monday through Saturday)**.

Two in New York State

The Yoga Ranch, at Woodbourne, New York: About two hours by bus from New York City, it occupies a stunning setting atop a wooded hill, looking down into a valley and up onto another

At the Kripalu Center. *Courtesy Kripalu Center.*

hill, with the mountains of the Catskills receding into the distance. Dotted about are open areas devoted to organic farming or used by grazing deer. On the extensive grounds is a one-acre pond deep enough for swimming, while nearby stands a stone-faced sauna, wood-fired, rock-heated, and steamed by pure, mountain spring water—one-of-a-kind. "You'll be doing good for a lot of people if you recommend us," said the co-director at the end of our talk. "They come here with jangled nerves, and then leave completely restored." The charge for that revival is an astonishing $35 per person on weekdays, $45 on weekends (half price for children under 12, free for children under 5), including yoga asanas (exercises), meditation, accommodation in twin or triple rooms, and two vegetarian meals. Write or phone **Sivananda Ashram Yoga Ranch, P.O. Box 195, Woodbourne, NY 12788 (phone 914/434-9242)**.

Ananda Ashram, near Monroe, New York: Despite its daily teachings of such classic yoga regimens as *hatha yoga* (stretching) and *pranayama* (breath control), the 31-year-old Ananda Ashram has a far-less-pronounced Eastern orientation than some others: it schedules meditation for as late as 9am on weekends, invites guest teachers from all religious disciplines, and presents classes in creative music, drama, dance, video production, and visual arts. Less than 90 minutes by bus from New York City, at the base of the Catskill Mountains, it occupies 100 wooded acres, including a large private lake, and houses 40 visitors in two main guesthouses, for an all-inclusive room-meals-and-tuition charge (on seven-night stays) of $230 per week. Lesser stays are $50 per person per day in midweek, $58 per day on weekends. Contact the **Ananda Ashram, R.D. 3, Box 141, Monroe, NY 10950 (phone 914/782-5575)**.

Three in California

The Yoga Farm, at Grass Valley, California: Cheapest of the residential ashrams at $35 per person in triple rooms, and from $40 (double) to

$50 (single) in several others, including vegetarian meals, it is the smallest also, with space for just 30 guests. The farm was the personal favorite of the late Swami Vishnu Devananda, founder of the Sivananda movement. Like thousands of others over the years who have driven up the 50 or so miles from Sacramento and then followed dirt roads to the isolated setting, he valued the special simplicity and quiet of this rustic, three-building resort, with its changeless routine of meditation/exercises/free time on weekdays, and its weekend seminars on yoga philosophies and practices, such as vegetarian cooking, *ayurveda,* and *panca karma* (an ancient method of flushing toxins from the body). In the free-time period, as you hike to the top of an adjoining hill and lie daydreaming on its crest, you see the majestic Sierras spread out before you. A very special place. Write or phone **Sivananda Ashram Vrindavan Yoga Farm, 14651 Ballantree Lane, Grass Valley, CA 95949 (phone 916/272-9322).**

The White Lotus Foundation, in elegant Santa Barbara, California: Some 1,800 feet up the mountains just behind the city, overlooking the Pacific Ocean and the Channel Islands, and founded in 1967 and currently directed by Tracey Rich and Ganga White, author of the book *Double Yoga,* its principal emphasis is on yoga and related disciplines (bodywork, shiatsu, acupuncture, acupressure), conveyed to guests through workshops, seminars, and classes throughout the year. A 5,000-square-foot central building provides some of the accommodations, but most guests stay in three- to four-person yurts scattered about the 40 acres of grounds.

A philosophy of life, not a religion; a questing science, not a dogma—yoga is the most tolerant of creeds, its practitioners good-humored, broad-minded, modest, and non-authoritarian.

Personal retreats and classes in yoga can be pursued at any time of the year, at a $35-per-day charge, which does not include meals (participants buy and cook their own food in a central kitchen), but more elaborate one-week and 16-day "intensives" are scheduled at frequent intervals throughout the spring, summer, and fall. These include meals prepared by a noted vegetarian chef, Beatrix Rohlson, as well as morning-till-night classes (in-depth yoga training) at a cost averaging $800 for the one-week sessions, $1,600 for the 16-day "intensives." Since the weather of Santa Barbara is mild even in the winter (daytime temperatures in the upper 60s or low 70s), yoga-inclined travelers might schedule a personal visit at that time of year, at the $35-a-day tariff. To reach this very contemporary, eclectic yoga center, contact: **The White Lotus**

The New World of Travel 1997

The lifeblood of the Arthur Frommer travel guides is the correspondence received from readers, commenting on the establishments recommended in the texts and recommending new establishments. Each such letter is carefully studied, and when a particular lead seems promising, it is followed up and personally checked.

It is hoped that *The New World of Travel* will receive similar assistance from its readers. A yearly publication, issued near the start of each year, *The New World of Travel* will constantly grow. And since much of its content relates to organizations that lack the means to market themselves properly or come to the attention of a travel journalist, your help is invaluable in alerting me to the organizations—hospitality exchanges, alternative resorts, new travel clubs, and the like—that you have discovered.

If you become aware of a new travel organization, program, or development that deserves to be described in our next edition, *The New World of Travel 1997,* won't you please let me know about it? Send your letters to Arthur Frommer, 1841 Broadway, New York, NY 10023. All letters will be acknowledged, and all are warmly appreciated, in advance, by the author.

Foundation, 2500 San Marcos Pass, Santa Barbara, CA 93105 (phone 805/964-1944).

Ananda, The Expanding Light, near Nevada City, California: A strange amalgam of faiths, this yoga ashram is located on the grounds of a larger utopian community known as the Ananda World Brotherhood Village. The "town," 1,000 acres in size, was formed in 1967 by practitioners of yoga from various religious backgrounds, who regard yoga as complementary to other faiths. Today, at "Serenity House" and other scattered structures and (in summer) tents, 200 visitors can engage in a retreat of classic yoga practices—early-morning and late-afternoon asanas and meditations—supplemented by classes and workshops on yogic and meditational themes. For week-long stays, the daily charge is $39 for campers bringing their own tents, $44 in shared tents, $58 per person in a double room, $80 for a private single room, including all three vegetarian meals and classes. Guests volunteering for a "work exchange" program, doing some cooking or cleaning, pay only $20 a day. Ananda is 15 miles from Nevada City; the latter is 70 miles north of Sacramento. Contact **The Expanding Light, c/o Ananda World Brotherhood Village, 14618 Tyler Foote, Nevada City, CA 95959 (phone 916/292-3494, or toll free 800/346-5350).**

Still Other Possibilities

The large, 25-year-old Himalayan Institute of Pennsylvania is yet another major center of yoga practice and studies, yet so diverse in its programs that it is practically impossible to describe. A 24-page catalog lists all its weekend, week-long, 10-day, and month-long investigations throughout the year into every aspect and theory—sometimes conflicting—of the yoga literature; it is for serious students of the art, and beginners may feel "in over their heads"! Figure $50 a day, all inclusive, for most week-long and longer programs, which do include beginners' classes in hatha yoga (physical exercises) and meditation, of which those for beginners in meditation are especially popular. If you do attend, you'll be housed on a 422-acre campus in the hills of the Pocono Mountains region of northeastern Pennsylvania, six miles north of the town of Honesdale, overlooking spectacular wooded hills and valleys. Contact **The Himalayan Institute, R.R. 1, Box 400, Honesdale, PA 18431 (phone toll free 800/822-4547).**

I have not described the important 2,000-bed Muktananda Center (the "Syda Foundation") in South Fallsburg, New York (phone 914/434-2000), because of its heavy (and somewhat atypical) theological emphasis, which stresses chanting and meditation to a far greater extent than hatha (physical) yoga and exercises. The Syda Foundation discourages casual visitors but is happy to accept potential acolytes.

Nor have I mentioned large retreats in Canada and Baja California.

To find other residential ashrams, phone the in-city centers listed under "Yoga Instruction" in the *Yellow Pages,* and ask the personnel to name the countryside location, if any, to which they go for an occasional retreat. I'd be grateful if you'd also pass on the information to me, at the address listed in the Preface; and in gratitude, I press my hands together beneath my lips, and intone: "Jai Bhagwan" ("I honor the spirit within you").

II

Political Travel, to See for Yourself, to Widen Your View

Meet the Political Travel Agent, a New Breed

Their Trips and Tours Are Sharply Different from the Usual Variety—Profound and Stimulating

They are fed up and furious with the Changing of the Guard, the beach at Copacabana, the Golden Gate Bridge. Though they are travel professionals, they are grieved by the often trivial content of their profession. Unlike the usual travel agent—who tends to be a rather conservative retail merchant, glued to the bottom line—they are passionate idealists out to change the world.

Travel, they believe—properly conducted and serious in content—can change the consciousness of the traveler, and thereby alter the United States. Whether to the right, left, or center, and in however small a way, they feel they can make a difference.

Meet three examples of the "political travel agent" or "public affairs travel agent":

Gate (Global Awareness Through Experience)

Though it's been far less strident in recent years, more conciliatory and subject to church discipline, this organization was once the reflection in travel of the surging and controversial "Liberation Theology" movement in the Catholic Church. Determined to expose a wider public to the realities and sufferings of Emerging World nations, nuns of the Sisters of Charity founded the odd travel agency in 1981 in Mount St. Joseph, Ohio, then moved its offices in the early '90s to the Abbey of the Franciscan Sisters of Perpetual Adoration in LaCrosse, Wisconsin, for greater effectiveness. From there, each month, simple, unadorned, one-color leaflets—like none you've ever seen—go cascading forth to every part of the nation, advertising GATE-led tours to Guatemala and the barrios of El Salvador, or to "base communities" in Mexico.

In place of "today we journey to the famous waterfall," GATE's literature talks of "dialogues with ministers, professors, and the poor," attendance at "meetings of popular movements . . . supporting their search and struggle for freedom in their country." Tour rates (and amenities) are moderate in level; participation is ecumenical and increasingly promoted also by Protestant groups; tour leaders and destination representatives (some of them on-the-spot missionaries) are opinionated but noncontrolling. Some tours go to countries of Eastern Europe.

Despite its recent move to the center (politically), there still remains a hint, in GATE's approach, of "liberation theology." That, as one of GATE's officials once described it to me, is "a theology in which we are all brothers and sisters, achieving equality, freeing and then empowering the oppressed to achieve their full dignity, enabling them not always to be dominated by some white-faced person."

Most GATE tours (some go to Eastern Europe, in addition to Mexico, Guatemala, and El Salvador) are 10 days in length, and consist of visits to un-touristed local communities and homes, as well as daily seminars attended by persons representing every stripe of political thinking at the destination. Tour members learn, says GATE, "from the poor, as well as from social and political analysts, theologians, and economists."

Travel, they believe, can change the consciousness of the traveler, and thereby alter the United States.

GATE tours are among the least expensive to anywhere, generally costing $550 plus air fare for 10 days of all-inclusive arrangements (all lodgings, meals, and transportation to program events), in addition to a $50 nonrefundable registration fee. On trips to Mexico several times a year, participants meet in Mexico City and travel to "rural, indigenous communities, marginal settlements and the megalopolis . . . to grow in global awareness of the social, religious, economic and political challenges of the mid-1990s." In Guatemala, GATE travelers "explore human rights issues with a people whose tradition spans centuries of development—ancient, colonial and

Housing in the developing world.
Courtesy Global Awareness Through Experience.

modern." In El Salvador, a nation "struggling for peace after years of civil war," participants hear the views of "campesinos, church leaders, teachers" and others. In Central Europe (Czech Republic, Slovakia, the former East Germany), during a two-week trip costing $1,425 per person, participants "dialogue with Christians and non-Christians about health, education, church, political, social and cultural life" and explore "dynamic changes in those countries."

For literature, you contact **Marilynn Hammes Meier, GATE, 912 Market Street, La Crosse, WI 54601 (or phone 608/791-5283)**, enclosing the postage (or, better yet, a stamped and self-addressed envelope) that these dedicated, cash-poor church workers will need to respond to your requests. May I suggest that no better use could be made of our vacation time than to travel with them?

People to People International

This is the "centrist" of the political travel agencies, more heavily involved in broad public affairs than in special-interest advocacy or politics, and so prestigious as to be frequently mistaken for a U.S. government agency.

It once was. President Dwight D. Eisenhower founded it in 1956 out of a belief that people-to-people contacts across national boundaries were as vital as government efforts to maintain world peace. He initially made the organization a part of the U.S. Information Agency, then in 1961 persuaded his friend, Joyce Hall, of Hallmark Cards in Kansas City, to fund the transition to a private, nonprofit corporation, for which the then-former President Eisenhower was the first chairman of the board. Today, in addition to its many Student Ambassador Programs sending teenagers abroad, its collegiate study

> The goal of People to People International: to "unleash the common interests among citizens of all countries and avoid the difference of national self-interest."

programs abroad, and American homestay plans for foreign visitors to the U.S., PTP organizes trips by several thousands of adult Americans each year to visit with their counterparts overseas: lawyers with lawyers, teachers with teachers, scientists with other scientists in their field. The goal: to "unleash the common interests among citizens of all countries and avoid the difference of national self-interest." More than 180 overseas chapters in 34 countries make the arrangements for personal contacts; several prestigious U.S. tour operators handle the technical arrangements. Because itineraries involve an intricate schedule of meetings, briefings, speeches, and seminars, the trips aren't cheap. Contact **People to People International, 501 E. Armour Blvd., Kansas City, MO 64109 (phone 816/531-4701)**.

A Third Example

Forum Travel, of Pittsburgh, Pennsylvania: A traditional, full-service travel agency, Forum nevertheless specializes in study tours of China, Nicaragua, and especially the Middle East, devoting special attention to issues between Israel and the P.L.O. (Palestine Liberation Organization). Tours go to Israel, Jordan, Egypt, and Syria; to kibbutzim, West Bank settlements, and Arab villages; and to the homes of both Israeli and Arab families. Though most groups desiring such tours are already organized before they come to Forum for assistance and arrangements, Forum can occasionally place individual applicants with groups already created and scheduled to depart. Contact **Forum Travel, 4608 Winthrop St., Pittsburgh, PA 15213 (phone 412/681-4099, or toll free 800/888-4099)**.

Although the bulk of the new "political travel agents" send their clients to all parts of the world, a number focus solely on problems of the Emerging World. Because the latter approach is somewhat different, I've split off the Emerging World specialists from the preceding discussion and dealt with them mainly in the very next essay. Please read on.

Reality Tours to the Emerging World

On "Travel Seminars," in Nations with Two-Thirds of the World's Population, Americans Are Exploring the Most Important Issues of Our Time

How many "worlds" do you know? To how many "worlds" have you traveled? Apart from a periodic jaunt to Mexico or the Caribbean, have you traveled to the "Emerging World," the "Third World"? And can those beach vacations at a Club Med in Cancún, or a casino-resort in Curaçao, really be regarded as equivalents to the real thing?

Five organizations outside the bounds of the normal travel industry have set about operating "reality tours" to the true Emerging World. Their aim is enlightenment rather than recreation or rest. Their area of activity is the poorest part of what is also called the "developing world": most of Central and South America, most of Africa, some of Asia,

Touring a slum in South America. *Courtesy The Center for Global Education.*

a cauldron of struggle and promise. Their method is to stress contact with ordinary people of the Emerging World, to expose tour passengers to conditions experienced by residents of that "world" (who make up three-quarters of the population of the earth). And their search is for solutions: to poverty and debt, domestic instability and disease, the unequal allocation of income and resources.

So is the trip a chore, an exercise in self-flagellation? Far from it, say the backers of these odd travel ventures. For this, it is claimed, is "transformative travel" that irrevocably broadens the mind and liberates the spirit of those who engage in it, makes them clear-headed and emphatic in their public judgments, enhances their love for humankind, gives them goals and purpose. And some concessions are made to personal comfort: the use of modest hotels in place of mud huts, an occasional stay in modern dormitories or pleasant private homes.

Largest of All

The Center for Global Education, Augsburg College, 2211 Riverside Avenue, Minneapolis, MN 55454 (phone 612/330-1159, fax 612/330-1695, e-mail globaled@augsburg.

edu), is the largest of the Emerging World tour operators. Though its base is that of a small Lutheran school with limited funds, it successfully sends out more than 30 groups a year—more than twice a month—to Mexico, Central America, and Africa for the most part, but occasionally to the Philippines, Vietnam, and islands of the Caribbean, and rarer still, to the Middle East. Most tours are planned to visit combinations of two and three countries—say, Guatemala and El Salvador, or Mexico, Honduras, and Nicaragua—for 10 to 14 days, at total tour costs of $900 to $2,200 per person, including air fare, accommodations, and all meals.

Heavily influenced by the Brazilian educator Paulo Freire, the center's officials take pains to emphasize their use of his theories: that "experiential education" (here, a short-term immersion in travel) is the most potent form of self-education; that dialogue, in which people critically assess their own situation, can liberate them from prejudice and lead to beneficial social action; that even the illiterate can gain from such dialogue; and that communication can be achieved between the poor and nonpoor, greatly benefiting both.

Accordingly, the center stresses advance preparation for travel, which "helps people recognize their biases and provides them with tools to discern the truth in the voices they will hear." En route, it exposes passengers to "a variety of political points of view so that they can reflect more critically on all the voices they hear." And though it seeks to meet with leaders and decision-makers in the countries it visits, it "places emphasis on learning from the victims of poverty and oppression—those who do not often have any opportunity to speak."

Accommodations in most nations are in modest hotels or in the organization's own dormitory-style residences in Mexico and Nicaragua. For literature, contact the center at the address above.

Plowshares Institute, P.O. Box 243, Simsbury, CT 06070 (phone 203/651-4304), operates a similar if smaller program, but to a broader array of geographical areas—Africa, Asia, India, South America—and with a particular emphasis on critical issues of U.S. foreign policy toward the Third World, debt and human rights issues among them. The organization was founded in 1982 by a Protestant minister, the Rev. Robert Evans, whose life and outlook were profoundly changed by a stint as visiting professor in the African nation of Uganda; he resolved soon after to use travel as a means of "transformative education," and has since co-authored an important book often cited by others in the field, *Pedagogies for the Non-Poor* (Maryknoll, N.Y.: Orbis Books, 1987; $13.95).

The strategy of Plowshares is to visit areas and organizations of the Third World where active solutions are afoot to the area's classic problems; the group feels it is nonproductive simply to dwell upon festering conditions or to feel rage without hope. Once at the destination, according to program director Hugh McLean, "we find articulate voices on all sides of each issue; the goal is to listen to as many voices as possible." On a recent visit to Mexico, Plowshares travelers met with officials of IBM, but then with landless peasants; with members of the "PRI" (Mexico's ruling political party), but then with social workers and "base Christian communities in the barrios"; they lived in a dormitory of the Lutheran Theological Seminary in Mexico City, but then traveled to the poor and rural province of Hildalgo in the north to visit creative development projects.

Tours are frequently co-sponsored by a variety of other religious organizations, including New York's Union Theological Seminary, but also by a host organization at the destination.

A Major New Source

Global Exchange, 2017 Mission Street, #303, San Francisco, CA 94110 (phone 415/255-7296), headed by the dynamic Medea Benjamin, is among the "newer" reality tour organizations, but since 1988 has rivaled The Center for Global Education in the size of its following and frequency of its tours—possibly because it is a strongly activist organization. In 1994 and 1995, they have maintained a major presence in Haiti, and more recently in the state of Chiapas, Mexico, monitoring the uprising of the so-called "Zapatistas." Their groups going to Chiapas meet with coffee producers, *campesinos,* human rights workers, church leaders, both government and non-government organizations, including (it's rumored) the Zapatistas themselves. The 10-day trip to Chiapas is priced at $1,300, including air fare, lodgings, interior transportation, reading materials, translator, and two meals a day. Planned for 1996: trips to Vietnam, Cambodia, South Africa, Senegal, the Gaza Strip and West Bank in the Middle East, and many others. Prices are kept low ($960 to $2,300), but include air fare, all three meals daily (mostly local fare), and clean, proper accommodations (but don't expect five-star hotels). And daily schedules consist almost entirely of constant dialogue—seminars—with religious leaders, peasant farmers, government officials, labor organizers, peace activists, environmentalists, and scholars.

Other Important Groups

Marazul, 250 West 57th Street, New York, NY 10107 (phone 212/582-9570 or 800/223-5334). Its programs to Cuba (once its mainstay) severely reduced by government restrictions on travel there, Marazul nonetheless manages to send out more than 150 groups a year to Guatemala, Honduras, Haiti, Vietnam, and Nicaragua (the latter consisting of visits with representatives of all major political parties, trade union and cultural figures, women's organizations). A week in Managua, typical of their trips, costs $990 per person, including roundtrip air fare, accommodations, three meals daily, a guide/translator, and their own tour leader. Most trips pursue a specific theme: "Guatemalan Women Today," "Health Care in Nicaragua." They also assist persons legally entitled to visit Cuba in making their travel arrangements. Intensely political, some of their literature refers to their trips as "progressive travel for progressive people."

Their search is for solutions: to poverty and debt, domestic instability and disease, the unequal allocation of income and resources.

CHRICA (Committee for Health Rates in Central America), 347 Delores Street #210, San Francisco, CA 94110 (phone 415/ 431-7760), currently operates only one tour each year, in August, to Nicaragua. While most participants are health professionals, interested members of the general public are permitted to join, paying about $950 for 10 days of visits to hospitals, clinics, and community organizations; the price includes all transportation from the U.S., accommodations, all meals, guides, and extensive pre-trip reading matter.

Our Developing World, 13004 Paseo Presada, Saratoga, CA 95070-4125 (phone 408/379-4431), is another secular West Coast heavyweight in the Emerging World field. A nonprofit group whose directors are mainly educators from cities in northern California, it schedules its departures primarily from Los Angeles and San Francisco, but also permits participants to join up in Miami on those of its tours that go to Central America, and uses New York as its gateway to Africa. A major focus is on problems of development in southern Africa (Zimbabwe, Mozambique, and South Africa); a frequent practice is to "theme" each tour to concentrate on one particular subject matter per destination: "Women's Role in Development," "Appropriate Technology," "Education and Health Care," and so on. Except for the occasional one-month trip to Africa from New York (costing a high $4,000, all inclusive), trips are two to three weeks in duration, usually range from $1,700 (for two weeks) to $2,399 (for three weeks), use West Coast departure points, are also all inclusive, and (in the words of co-director Vic Ulmer) "bring the realities of the Third World into the consciousness of North Americans through direct contact with the people of those areas." Thus a three-week summer tour to study "Human Services in Honduras and Nicaragua" will meet with peasants, social workers, church leaders, "members of Christian base communities," trade unionists, and government officials, and will visit facilities ranging from medical clinics to day-care centers. U.S. participants are particularly sought from among teachers, social workers, and health-care professionals, but any concerned member of the public can come.

The Third World. The Developing or Emerging World. Our understanding of the human condition is stunted so long as we delete it from our travel plans. Thanks to the efforts of six unusual "tour operators," that needn't be the case.

The Bold, New World of the Feminist Tour Operator

Organized Travel

for Women Only

Should women travel only with other women? Should they do so on occasion?

If the trip is one of outdoor adventure, involving physical challenge, should they travel only with other women? Should they agree to include men on a group tour only if the group is led by a woman?

Because so many women are responding to one or more of the above questions with a resounding "Yes," a sizable new segment of the travel industry has emerged to serve their wants. As surprising as it may seem, more than 50 tour companies in a dozen major states are now openly feminist in their orientation, and limit their clients or leadership to women only.

The reason is unrelated to sexual proclivities or the lack of them. From a review of their literature, not one of the 50 new firms seems operated for homosexuals, and most stand carefully apart from a wholly separate group of tour companies openly appealing to gay men or gay women.

The Premise of Feminist Travel

Rather, the move to feminist travel seems motivated by a combined goal of consciousness-raising and female solidarity, and by the belief that women enjoy a holiday change of pace (stress-free, relaxing) when they travel only with other women. Though the philosophy is rarely articulated in the feminists' tour brochures, and is obtained with difficulty even in conversations with feminist tour operators (I've now spoken with several), the gist of it seems as follows:

A sizable, new segment of the travel industry has emerged to serve the feminist cause.

When women travel with men, and especially on outdoor trips, both they

and the men, say the feminists, tend to fall into predetermined gender roles: the men do the heavy work, the women putter about and cook. Traveling only with other women, women accept greater challenges, court greater responsibility, acquire new skills, gain confidence and a heightened sense of worth.

Male travelers are conditioned by society to be excessively goal-oriented: they must conquer this or that mountain, show prowess and strength, domineer. Most women, by contrast, enjoy the mere experience of travel, the joy of encountering nature, all without stressful competition or expectations. They have less need to boast and strut; they lack the male's inner urge (from early upbringing) to seem always skillful, strong, serene, and protecting. "I don't want to be protected on vacation," say many women; "I want to be myself."

In the presence of the other sex, so goes the argument, both sexes find it difficult to "let down their hair." On a tour limited to women, say the feminists, these tensions subside. Women spend less time on personal appearance and grooming, dispense with sexual role-playing, and care only for themselves.

"And why should men feel threatened by that need?" asks one prominent female tour operator. "Why should an all-female tour be the subject of sneers? Men have been going off to hike or fish 'with the boys' for centuries."

Practical considerations: Since everyone on a woman-only trip is "single," participants pay no single supplement, but instead share rooms and costs. Since some male spouses don't care for outdoor trips, feminist tours often provide the only vacation outlet for women who genuinely enjoy the attractions of nature. Then, too, women who are recently widowed or divorced are enabled by such tours to meet others in the same situation; the experience is healing,

Fishing on a feminist tour. *Courtesy Outdoor Vacations for Women over 40, photo by Marion Stoddart.*

restorative. But mainly, the women "take charge" of their holiday, free from the customary domination of men.

Hub of the Movement

The largest (70 departures a year) and oldest (18 years) of the feminist tour operators, and a clearinghouse for all the rest, is Woodswomen, of Minneapolis. Nonprofit, and eager to promote the offerings even of its competitors, its quarterly publication, *Woodswomen News,* is replete with the ads of dozens of widely scattered feminist travel firms. Most of the latter are engaged in purely local operations.

While Woodswomen is also heavily oriented toward its own state of Minnesota (and the nearby Northwest), it supplements that emphasis with expeditions to California, Alaska, Hawaii, Massachusetts, and France (for biking), the Swiss Alps (for hiking), and Nepal (for trekking, an organized walk along the lower slopes of the Himalayas). Send either $2 (for postage and handling) for a copy of the organization's 12-page *Woodswomen News,* or else $20 for a year's membership (including all publications and related services), to **Woodswomen, 25 W. Diamond Lake Rd., Minneapolis, MN 55419 (phone 800/279-0555 or 612/822-3809).**

Active and Thriving

Runners-up to the leader? Marion Stoddart's Outdoor Vacations for Women over 40 (of Groton, Massachusetts), and Rainbow Adventures (of Bozeman, Montana), vie for the No. 2 spot. The first is best known for its weekend outings in the northeast, hiking tours of Mexico's Copper Canyon, its windsail cruises down the coast of Turkey. The second was founded 14 years ago by Suzanne Eckert to promote adventure travel for women over 30, in areas which she had herself traveled while in the Peace Corps. Today, along with standard, mild safaris, cruises, treks,

and ski trips limited to women, she also deals in challenges of considerably greater daring: camel expeditions in Kenya, helicopter skiing over the highest peaks of the Rockies, even—and are you ready for this?—the first, all-female dog sled and ski expedition to the North Pole (in 1994). Contact **Outdoor Vacations for Women over 40 at P.O. Box 200, Groton, MA 01450, phone 508/448-3331; contact Rainbow Adventures (for women over 30) at 15033 Kelly Canyon Road, Bozeman, MT 59715 (phone 800/804-8686 or 406/587-3883).**

Still another relatively large firm is Womanship, of Annapolis, Maryland, offering a learn-to-sail program in a field of sport heavily dominated by men. Because (according to founder Suzanne Pogell) men tend to handle the main tasks on sailing expeditions, women are rarely able to do more than prepare the sandwiches; certainly they never "take charge" of the vessel. With Womanship, they do, gaining confidence, achieving independence.

Male travelers, they believe, are excessively goal-oriented; most women, by contrast, enjoy the mere experience of travel, the joy of encountering nature, all without stressful competition or expectations.

Weekend, weekday, and week-long cruises are offered for both beginners and advanced sailors aged 20 to 70, in locations ranging from Chesapeake Bay, New England, and Long Island Sound, the west coast of Florida, and the Pacific Northwest (San Juan and the Gulf Islands) to the U.S. and British Virgin Islands. Contact **Womanship, Inc., The Boathouse, 410 Severn Avenue, Annapolis, MD 21403 (phone 800/342-9295 or 410/269-0784).**

Other major feminist tour operators include **New Dawn Adventures, P.O. Box 1512, Vieques, PR 00765 (phone 809/741-0495),** heavily emphasizing camping retreats at their bunkhouse on the island of Vieques, Puerto Rico; **Mariah Wilderness Expeditions, P.O. Box 248, Point Richmond, CA 94807 (phone 510/233-2303 or toll free 800/4-MARIAH)**, with an impressive four-color catalog featuring white-water rafting, kayaking, and ballooning; **Adventures for Women, P.O. Box 515, Montvale, NJ 07645 (phone 201/930-0557)**, for its hiking trips in New Jersey and New York; and **Alaska Women of the Wilderness, P.O. Box 773556, Eagle River, AK 99577 (phone 907/688-2226)**, which has thus far provided confidence-building programs to several thousands of women; in the words of manager Rochelle Wagner, they provide a "safe, supportive, non-competitive atmosphere in which women can explore the wilderness within and around them"; highly recommended. When the Alaskan weather makes it too difficult to conduct tours there, they switch to kayaking and other adventures near Bali and Hawaii.

A Special Word About "New Dawn"

Because she has overcome such special problems to operate "New Dawn," Gail Burchard deserves an expanded treatment.

Hers is probably the cheapest vacation resort in all the Caribbean (see its address and number earlier in this chapter). It is a complex of wooden bunkhouses and platformed tent sites surrounding a six-bedroom guesthouse on a high hillside overlooking the Caribbean (but three miles from the beach) on the sleepy island of Vieques, off the east coast of Puerto Rico. You get there either by plane ("Sun Air Express") from San Juan Airport (15 minutes) or by ferry (one hour) from Fajardo. In high season (December 15 to April 15), rooms in the dramatic, two-story guesthouse are $35 for a single, $45 for a double, $55 for a triple, while bunkhouse beds are $15 a night, and tent sites are $10 per person (you bring your own tent); total capacity of the entire complex is a maximum of 30 persons. In the guesthouse restaurant, a full breakfast is $3.50, a full buffet dinner is $12.50. The decor? Pure tropics, with Guatemalan textiles, woven palm lampshades, and numerous windows open to the trade winds; the house is surrounded by open verandahs, on which there are today 10 hammocks for gazing out onto a hillside dotted with hibiscus, bougainvillaea, and grazing horses.

Gail Burchard is a registered nurse from New England. A divorced single mother, and painfully conscious of vacationing costs, she purchased this five-acre plot of hillside, on this inexpensive island, and then induced several friends to join her in, first, a carpentry course, and then in the actual construction of the "New Dawn" complex.

But no sooner was it completed than Hurricane Hugo—which went straight as an arrow to the island of Vieques—completely demolished the structure. Recently, she began all over again, took a refresher course in carpentry, and today "New Dawn" has reopened as a a proud and unvanquished Caribbean retreat and guesthouse.

I recently interviewed her by phone, and her story is so colorful and her ideals so worthy that you'll want to obtain the literature she's created for inquiring would-be guests. And you'll want to pay particular attention to the off-season values at "New Dawn," when the entire guesthouse can be rented for the week by up to 12 women for a total of $1,000 (that's $83 per person per week) or by a family of six for $126 per person per week. (When one family or group occupies the entire house, a Viequan cook is hired for an additional charge to prepare especially elaborate group meals.) The restaurant is maintained for individual guests in high season.

A Visit to the World of "Small Is Beautiful"

At the Centre for Alternative Technology in Wales, the Most Basic Assumptions of the Industrial West Are Attacked and Derided

What do we really seek on a holiday abroad? Should we travel simply to feel pleasure? Or should we travel sometimes to get mad? I opt for the brand of travel that disturbs mental calm, compels you to think, challenges your most cherished beliefs, supplies new ideas and comparative lessons, leaves you a bit different from when you began.

In the alpine-like center of Wales, near the dreamy little town of Machynlleth (pronounced "mah-hun-lith"), Britain's Centre for Alternative Technology does just that. It disputes the very need for industrial development, rejects all arguments for large-scale commercial growth, condemns the activities to which the greater number of Americans have devoted their lives. In so doing, it acts as the cutting edge for an ideological movement that has won the loyalty of millions of Europeans, and even achieved a semblance of political power in Germany. To the "Greens" of Europe, the extreme ecologists, the fierce, anti-nuclear-power activists, the advocates of "Small Is Beautiful," and to similar groups in 21 European nations, the Centre has become a secular Mecca to which more than 80,000 people make visits each year. No one understands contemporary Europe who does not understand the movement the Centre represents.

You reach Machynlleth by British Rail in four comfortable hours from London's Euston Station, changing at Shrewsbury (pronounced "shrozeberry") and proceeding from there through the "harp-shaped hills" of Wales (Dylan Thomas's phrase) into one of the least populated areas of the British Isles—a scene of rocky heights dotted with patches of dark-green outcroppings. At Machynlleth, a three-mile ride by taxi or bus takes you to the bottom of a soaring but thoroughly exhausted slate quarry where

signs advise you, in Dante-esque fashion, to abandon your car and ascend the steep hill by other means (an ecologically correct, water-powered cliff railway).

You are leaving behind civilization as we know it (or "crossing the green line," as the staff sometimes puts it). The Centre—a tiny, working village—is unconnected to the electric grid of Britain, or to water mains. It provides its own power from wind, solar, or hydro sources; produces much of its own food from organic gardens, fish ponds, and poultry yards on the site; replaces worn-out machinery with parts forged by its own blacksmith. Within its bounds, nothing is wasted: organic refuse is recycled into compost-created fertilizers; metal is fired down and reused; sludge is collected from septic tanks and placed into methane digesters for the production of combustible gas and fertilizer by-products; homes are insulated to an extraordinary degree; even human urine is preserved for soil fertilization via amusing, odorless "pee collectors" discreetly placed at convenience stops. On the grounds, past a forest of solar panels, near a grove of modern metal windmills of every shape and size, runs an electric truck recharged by on-site water turbines powered by rushing streams. Using and displaying such "alternative technology," a utopian community enters its 22nd year in mid-1996, locked in combat with the enemies that its chief theorist, the late E. F. Schumacher, succinctly ticked off as "urbanization, industrialization, centralization, efficiency, quantity, speed."

The combatants in this awesome battle, permanent residents of the Centre, are a slowly changing group of 32 young Britons whose average tenure here is about four years. A highly attractive lot, neatly if simply dressed in work clothes, well-educated and articulate, they defy the stereotyped image of the "eco-freak," and

Ascending hill, the Centre for Alternative Technology. *Courtesy Centre for Alternative Technology.*

emerge from a broad mix of schools and skills. Some are Ph.D.s in electrical and mechanical engineering; three are registered architects. All receive the same subsistence-level salary, except those with dependent children, to whom a "need-related" supplement is given. They eat communally (of a largely vegetarian diet), govern themselves by consensus reached at fortnightly meetings, confront daily decisions in 15-or-so, four-member "topic groups," each dealing with specialized work areas. They receive no major government support, and are a nonprofit organization subsisting almost entirely on the admission and study-course fees paid by members of the public.

Going Beyond Conservation

Why have they come together at the Centre to lead lives that, to the outsider, seem so harsh and confined? It is because they share a common vision that goes far beyond the well-publicized conservationist goals of preserving natural beauty and reducing harmful pollution. To the European ecological movement, simple technology and decentralized economic organization are part of a happier, healthier approach to life, as well as a moral imperative. By using renewable sources of energy present in nature, by keeping technology simple and small, one preserves meaningful work opportunities for more and more people, they argue; one spreads the activity of production over broad rural areas, slows the movement to cities and the creation of inhumanly large industrial complexes, keeps nations democratic and people healthy, promotes nonviolence in all spheres of life, teaches personal responsibility, and—most important—shares the dwindling supply of finite fossil resources more equitably among all the people of the earth.

To these ends, all 32 of "The People," as the Centre styles its staff, are researchers relying for their daily existence almost entirely on small machines and devices that make use of wind, sun, water, and biomass for their energizing forces. Though the technology itself emerges from universities and laboratories around the world, it is the Centre's task, the People believe, to "live with" the machines, discovering the necessary modifications and improvements that only actual experience can provide.

School and Laboratory

Are they, then, simply a test-tube community? They are more. Though officials of the Walt Disney organization would blanch at the comparison, they are perhaps a tiny version of what the late Walt Disney once envisioned as his EPCOT Center in Orlando, Florida: an actual working city that would, at the same time,

The Centre is a working city meant to be visited and observed by a steady stream of tourists—a teaching device as much as a laboratory.

be visited and observed by a steady stream of tourists—a teaching device as much as a laboratory. While Disney obviously failed to pull off the feat of combining two such antagonistic functions, the Centre quite demonstrably does.

It teaches. Its staff supplies a running commentary as they go about their tasks. You compliment a chef on the beansprout salad served in the Centre's superb vegetarian restaurant and he runs into the kitchen to extract a large bell jar in which the sprouts are grown, explaining how you, too, can enjoy such daily treats from the moistened seeds of simple alfalfa. You gaze over the shoulder of an engineer adjusting a "biomass gasifier" and she hastily explains how a renewable supply of wood, burned in a near vacuum, will result in a combustible gas capable of powering an electric generator. Everywhere are colorful, cartoon-illustrated explanations and exhortations, such as: "Use Less/Build to Last/Reuse/Repair/Recycle." "What good is efficiency if it puts people out of work and uses up resources?" "Gross product per head measures only the quantity of our wealth, not the quality of our lives. Are we happier?"

Have We Anything Comparable in the U.S.A. to the "Centre for Alternative Technology"?

Except for the unrealized dream of the late Walt Disney to make "EPCOT" (the "Experimental Prototype Community of Tomorrow") into a teaching mechanism of new, technological approaches to daily life, no one else in the United States—to my knowledge—has ever attempted a project similar in scope and ambition to Britain's "Centre for Alternative Technology." Bear in mind that the Centre is meant not only to experiment in new technologies, but to simultaneously and dramatically convey the lessons resulting from those tests to the public. Upwards of eighty thousand people now visit it each year.

But three U.S. institutions come close.

- First and foremost is Stanley Selengut's *Maho Bay Camps,* and *"Harmony,"* two ecological vacation resorts on the tiny island of St. John in the U.S. Virgin Islands. Employing the most resourceful methods, materials, and machines—roof panels for solar energy, recycled building materials, computer monitoring of energy use, wooden walkways for preserving the environment—these are classrooms as much as they are resorts. For more information on them, see the discussion in "Camping in the Caribbean" on page 124.

- The one-week workshops of *"Real Goods,"* a mail-order outlet of "alternative energy products," are somewhat similar. Held at scattered sites around the country in the summer months, and (sometimes) at Maho Bay in fall, it teaches the use of solar, wind, and hydro energy in one's own daily life, as well as build-it-yourself housing, retrofitting existing homes, managing water resources, gardening, and making proper use of electricity. In 1995, courses were presented at countryside locations ranging from a country inn near the Yestermorrow Institute at Warren, Vermont, to an "environmental station" near Amherst Junction, Wisconsin, at a six-night charge, for all tuition, accommodations, and meals, of $775. "I can't decide," wrote one recent participant, "if I've just had the best short vacation of my life or the best learning experience." Sites for the same program in 1996 and thereafter, known as the "Institute for Independent Living," had not yet been announced as we go to press, but can be ascertained by contacting Real Goods, at 966 Mazzoni Street, Ukiah, CA 95482-3471, phone 800/762-7325.

- *"High Wind,"* an impressive "eco-village" near Plymouth, Wisconsin, is a third possibility—a community of highly skilled individuals, most in their thirties and forties, who have come together to achieve "sustainable living" through the proper use of new, non-destructive technologies. Expanding from their original complex of farm buildings into futuristic lodges and "bio-shelters," they have recently acquired 144 adjacent acres for artesian wells, a fishery, several farm areas, and rental chalets. You can visit on your own ($30 single, $40 double, with kitchen privileges for making your own meals), although the staff warns that "villagers tend to be too busy at their own enterprises to interact much with visitors." In that regard, High Wind is unlike Britain's Centre for Alternative Technology. But from spring through fall, formal week-long and weekend workshops and other special educational events are scheduled, which better fit the needs of most visitors ("Small Head Hydro," "Sustainable Development," and "Solar Houses and Sustainable Energy" are recent themes). Meals (vegetarian) are then supplied by High Wind, rates are generally $45 a day for room and all three meals, and much interaction occurs between staff and guests. Phone Lisa Paulson, Outreach Coordinator, at 414/528-8488, to learn about the programs and their schedules; and Karen Jacobson, Bookings Coordinator, at 414/893-0969, to book space for both private retreats and workshop attendance (her fax is 414/892-4992). High Wind is at W7136 County Road U, Plymouth, WI 53073, about 55 miles north of Milwaukee, 6 miles west of Highway 57, which in turn is 7 miles southwest of Plymouth and 18 miles west of Sheboygan.

The Centre's staff heatedly deny that their work is of exclusive relevance to the Emerging World, responding to a frequent comment. It is morally and politically indefensible, they affirm, that the advanced West should make such a lavish, disproportionate use of the world's resources, especially fossil fuels (America, with 6% of the earth's population, uses 40% of the world's primary resources). And there are insufficient such resources for the entire world to follow the wasteful, indulgent course of the West; consequently, that course must change—in all areas.

They also deny that a recent glut in the supply of oil is at all significant; it is a brief lull in the crisis, a fool's paradise. Even were those supplies sufficient, their use exacts too high a human toll in acid rain, pollution, industrial blight, ruined lives; and fossil sources can, in any event, be put to better use than as energy. So goes the argument of Wales's Centre for Alternative Technology, in seminar presentations, group discussions, gardenside chats, and quiet admonitions from engineers tinkering with a solar roof, a waterless toilet, a compost heap, or an "aerogenerator" manufactured at the Centre and sent around the world.

Planning a Visit

Two days set aside from the normal routines of a British vacation, or added to it, suffice for a thorough visit to the Centre. After traveling there by train from London (£30, approximately $48, roundtrip), most visitors base themselves in Machynlleth (where the Wynnstay Hotel, phone 70/2289, is your best bet, followed in distant second place by the Glyndwr, phone 70/2082), or in Corris, two miles from the Centre (Hotel Braich Goch, phone 73/229), or in several guesthouses in the area.

The Centre is open to visitors every day of the year except Christmas, for an admission charge of £4 ($6.40) for adults, less for seniors, students, and children. Two weekends a month from October to June it offers two-day courses in which you pursue one topic per weekend: blacksmithing, low-energy buildings, solar collectors and systems, organic gardening, wind power, etc. Free time involves explorations of Machynlleth, mid-Wales, and the Cambrian Coast. For specific dates, subjects, and application forms, contact the **Courses Coordinator, Centre for Alternative Technology, Machynlleth, Powys, Wales, U.K. SY20 9AZ (phone 0654/ 703743, or fax 0654/ 702782)**. The Centre's main number is 0654/ 702400.

Visits of lesser duration are best followed by a driving tour through awesome Wales, perhaps starting at the nearby small (but active) seaside town of Aberystwyth, heading north from there to Snowdon, highest mountain in Wales, visiting abandoned lead mines en route. Richard Llewellyn's Welsh classic, *How Green Was My Valley,* is your best preparatory reading.

But now it is dusk, at the end of a day of "alternative technology," and you are coming down from the mountain, perhaps jarred and disquieted, perhaps exhilarated, always alive with new ideas. This new approach—this confrontational approach—to travel has converted a routine British vacation into a memorable one, of lasting value.

The Centre disputes the very need for industrial development, rejects all arguments for large-scale commercial growth, condemns the activities to which the greater number of Americans have devoted their lives.

Cerebral Vacations, in the Summertime

Summer Camps for Adults

Audubon Camps, Sierra Camps, Unitarian Camps, and Political Camps Use "Sleepaway Camps" for Grownup Needs

ou approached it through a forest, on a dirt road, beneath a canopy of leafy boughs. You slept there in a rustic cabin or a lean-to made of logs. You ate in a wooden mess hall, at long, communal tables; swam in a lake; sat around an open fire at night.

And paid very little.

Sleepaway camp. Was there ever a better vacation? A more treasured time of childhood? And can those joyful, vibrant, inexpensive holidays be reexperienced at a later time, as an adult?

The answer is a limited yes. Provided you apply soon enough—say, by early spring, before the rolls are filled and closed—you can stay at one of nearly 50 widely scattered camps that operate for people of all ages, 18 to 80, in a setting almost identical to those cherished memories of youth.

Audubon Ecology Camps

These have existed for 58 years. On a thickly wooded 300-acre island off the mid-coast of Maine, at a lofty ranch in the Wind River Mountains of northwestern Wyoming, and in a large nature sanctuary near Greenwich, Connecticut, the National Audubon Society has enabled adults from all over the nation to enjoy an intense, camp-style experience, for one or two summer weeks, with all forms of plant and animal life: birds and marine mammals, insects, herbs and wildflowers, mink, beaver, otter, and eagles. You go birding or canoeing at 7am, take leisurely hikes through open meadows or on mountain trails, make field trips to a hemlock gorge, and alternate all the outdoor activity with attendance at classroom lectures by expert naturalists. The simple aim is to reintroduce you to nature and its delicate balancing act; to show how all life is interdependent, and what you can do to protect it.

You are in a setting almost identical to those cherished memories of youth.

In the undeveloped wilderness settings of all three camps, you quickly forget all urban concerns, but enjoy a reasonable standard of comfort at the same time: original homestead cabins in Wyoming (mostly dormitory in style, but with some facilities for couples), wood-frame dormitories and a restored 19th-century farmhouse on Hog Island in Maine, slightly more modern facilities and private rooms in Connecticut. Hearty meals are served buffet style, three times a day.

Connecticut camp sessions, from late June to mid-August 1996, are run for one week and cost a flat $695 per person, including all instruction, room and board, all field trips and recreation.

Wyoming's camp is also operated from late June through the middle of August, and consists of both one-week and two-week sessions in "field ecology" and "field ornithology," also costing approximately $695 for one week, again all inclusive.

The camp in Maine is open in June and July, specializing again in "field ecology" and "field ornithology," for periods of 7 to 10 days, for charges of $650 and $705, respectively.

There's not another cent to pay (except your transportation to the camp), nowhere at all to spend additional money, and no supplement for single persons traveling alone.

Who attends the Audubon camps? Adults of all ages and backgrounds: an accountant from Atlanta alongside a professional educator from San Francisco, college students, firemen, and retired senior citizens—their common tie, the urge for a vacation "with more substance to it than sitting on a beach," in the words of Philip Schaefer, Audubon's former director of camps and summer programs. Returning to nature, he adds, is an "emotional as well as a learning experience," and at the final campfire, "there isn't a dry eye."

For extensive, colorful literature and application forms relating to all three camps, contact the **National Audubon Society, Audubon Camps and Workshops, 613 Riversville Rd., Greenwich, CT 06831 (phone 203/869-2017).**

Sierra Club "Base Camps"

Here's an even older program of adult summer camps, a small part of the much broader year-round schedule of "outings" operated since 1901 by the fierce and powerful (500,000 members) environmental organization called the Sierra Club. In "wild places" of the United States, at least a dozen times each summer, experienced Sierra volunteers establish "base camps" at small cabins or lodges, or at tented camp areas, to which other participants then usually hike in from a road several miles away. Once established at the base camp, to which supplies have been brought by mule or vehicle, campers make day hikes into the surrounding countryside, or simply enjoy the outdoor pleasures of their wilderness base. Most of the base camps are in California, Utah, and Arizona, or the Sierra Mountains of California/Nevada; a few are in the Virgin Islands, Florida, Virginia, and the Great Smoky Mountain Park of Tennessee/North Carolina.

With a minor exception or two, charges are remarkably low, even though all inclusive: as little as $400 for some one-week stays, an average of $600, a top of $800. That's because all campers pitch in to perform camp tasks, including cooking, supervised by the camp staff.

Sample base camp stays planned for 1996: in the Tahoe Forest of California/Nevada, near early Native American habitats, abandoned mines, and ghost towns; near the Donner Pass amid majestic rock cathedrals and trout-stocked lakes; on a Navajo reservation near Canyon de Chelly National Monument of Arizona; in a nationally protected area of fossil beds in Oregon; in the densely wooded Monongahela Forest of West Virginia. Though the accent throughout is on fun—the sheer pleasure of removing oneself for a week or two to an untouched, untrammeled wilderness—participants (of all ages, and including families) have the added opportunity to "network" with other kindred sorts, the dedicated environmentalists of our nation.

The full list of base camps appears in a larger directory of club outings bound each year into the January/February edition of *Sierra,* the club's magazine. For a copy, send $2.50 to **Sierra Club, 730 Polk St., San Francisco, CA 94109;** and for other specific information or longer leaflets on individual base camps, contact the **Sierra Club Outing Department, 730 Polk St., San Francisco, CA 94109 (phone 415/923-5522).** Since base camps are open only to Sierra members or "applicants for membership," you'll eventually need to include your membership application and fee ($15 for seniors, students, and people of limited income, $35 for all others) with your reservation request.

Unitarian Camps

And then you have the often more comfortable and more numerous adult summer camps of the merged Unitarian/Universalist church, each one of which is open—as a matter of firm church policy—to Americans of all religious persuasions, and of none at all. Acting from the same tolerant impulses that

In undeveloped wilderness, campers quickly forget all urban concerns.

led them to found the American Red Cross, the ASPCA, and much of the public school movement, Unitarian/Universalists have created a major travel/vacation resource, yet one that is unknown to much of the traveling public.

Why do they invite people of all religious persuasions to make use of their summer camps? Certainly not to proselytize or seek converts—they don't believe in that. Rather, as it's been explained to me, they do it because they seek to discover common bonds among all humankind, and common spiritual truths; because their creed is without dogma and broadly compatible with all other faiths. What better place to experience such unity, they theorize, than at a summer gathering, in a pleasant, unstressed, cooperative camp?

Because some of the Unitarian/Universalist camps fill up by summer, you'd be well advised to apply quickly to one of the following:

Star Island Camp, New Hampshire: A rustic, rocky, sea-enclosed marsh connected to the mainland by a single telephone line, Star Island is one of the historic "Isles of Shoals" off the New England coast (reached by ferry from Portsmouth, N.H.). A naturalist's dream, a photographer's vision, it has been owned by the Unitarians since 1915, and used as an adult summer camp (swimming, boating, fishing, hiking, tennis, softball) open to all, but mainly patronized by Unitarian/Universalists. From mid-June to early September, singles, couples, and families can opt for "theme weeks" focused on the arts, natural history, international affairs, psychology, and the like. They stay either in a wooden main building or a number of cottages (comfortable but not modern) at charges averaging $290 per adult per week for room, full board, and all activities. Prior to summer, contact **Star Island Corporation, 110 Arlington St., Boston, MA 02116 (phone 617/426-7988)**: thereafter, **P.O. Box 178, Portsmouth, NH 03802 (phone 603/964-7252)**.

De Benneville Pines Camp, near Angelus Oaks, California: Half an hour from the better-known town of Redland, in a heavily wooded area laced with hiking trails, is De Benneville Pines Camp. Its Unitarian programs—usually open to all—consist primarily of a "family week" in August, several singles weeks in April and October, and a "theme week" (which was chamber music in recent years) in late November. Family week is devoted to classic summer recreations, with the Unitarian theme largely limited to evening campfire discussions of broad ethical themes. Accommodation is in cabins; meals, according to staff, are "honest-to-goodness homemade—i.e., bread done from scratch"; all-inclusive weekly charges average $255 per adult for family weeks, much less for children; under $355 per adult for the theme-week session (which is occasionally, but not always, closed to the general public). Contact **De Benneville Pines, 41750 West Jenks Lake Road, Angelus Oaks, CA 92305 (phone 714/794-2928)**.

> **T**hough sponsored by a church, they seek to discover common bonds among all humankind, and common spiritual truths.

The Hersey Retreat, on Penobscot Bay, Maine: A small "resort" off the mid-coast of Maine, this shingle-style lodge (built in 1909) and adjoining farmhouse are owned by the Universalist church, but open to all—including families—from late May to mid-October. "In keeping with our liberal tradition," says the group's brochure, "we invite others to share our facility in summer." Afternoons make use of broad recreational opportunities in a superb, beach-lined setting; mornings are given over to discussion of such typical recent themes as: "Religious Education: Spirit Quest," "Family Dynamics," and "Music Week." August sessions are known as "family camps" and average $180 per adult, $90 for children 3 to 18, free for children 2 and under. Write **Hersey Retreat, P.O. Box 1183, Stockton Springs, ME 04981.** Or phone the director of Hersey, David Greeley, at 207/567-3420.

Ferry Beach Center, on the coast of Maine: For its summer-long, 10-week program of adult activities, open to all without question, Ferry Beach makes use of 30 woodland acres on Saco Bay, and adjoining sand dunes and pine groves, with access to bike paths and walking trails in a state park. Though participants are free to romp and relax, they can also attend week-long conferences from the end of June through the Labor Day weekend. Conference themes will be in the spirit of these from the 1995 season: "Exploring the Maine Coast," "Creative Leisure," "Single Parents," "Gay Week," "Tai-Chi and Fine Arts." Expect to pay about $325 per adult for a week's room, board, registration, and activities, slightly less for children, much less for those occupying tented campsites. Contact **Ferry Beach Park Association, 5 Morris Ave., Saco, ME 04072 (phone 207/282-4489)**.

Camp UniStar, in northern Minnesota: A Unitarian camp maintained, this time, exclusively for adults and families through all of June, July, and August. On the northeast tip of isolated Star Island in Cass Lake, accessible only by pontoon boat, Unitarians and "like-minded individuals" occupy cabins and lodges of a simple nature, but all with private facilities. They take meals communally in a nearby dining hall from which smoking has been banished. While the key aim is relaxation, pursued in unstructured fashion,

Evening fun at the World Fellowship Center. *Courtesy World Fellowship.*

lecture/discussions are conducted from 10am to noon daily on such weekly themes as "Writing and Reading Fiction," "Sailing and Shiatsu," "Israeli/Palestinian Tensions," "Philosophy and Fishing," "An Examination of American Identity." Charges run to approximately $225 per adult for the week (including the boat over and back), as little as $125 per child. Prior to June 1, contact **Judy Burtis, 7325 Fremont Ave. South, Richfield, MN 55423 (phone 612/866-8248); thereafter, Camp UniStar, Star Island Water Rte. 51, Cass Lake, MN 56633 (phone 218/335-2692).**

Rowe Camp, in the Berkshires of northwestern Massachusetts: A Unitarian children's camp for much of the summer, Rowe largely replaces the youngsters with adults during three warm-weather periods: for a week in July ("Recovery Camp," for adult children of alcoholic parents), a week in early August ("Women's Week"), and a week in late August ("Liberation Camp"); the second is a consciousness-raising program for females only, while the third attempts to free all participants—singles, couples, families— "from whatever confines their spirits." In all three, daily workshops deal with growth in the physical, emotional, spiritual, and political realms, and are combined with swimming, dancing, canoeing, silk-screening, and picnics—a joyful, dynamic, but intensely spiritual atmosphere. Scattered wooden cabins and main lodges resemble the camps of your own youth. The all-inclusive cost for a week averages $395 per adult, $260 to $280 per accompanying child, depending on age. Contact **Rowe Camp, Kings Highway Road, Box 273, Rowe, MA 01367 (phone 413/339-4216).**

A Political Summer Camp

Finally, a group of proud and unrepentant, happy and defiant liberals from all over the nation (of all ages, families and singles) converges each summer on the World Fellowship Center in the White Mountains of New Hampshire for a special vacation.

With its 300 acres of forest, mile-long Whitton Pond for swimming and boating, cookouts, campsites, and rustic lodge buildings, WFC would seem at first to be a standard resort for standard, warm-weather relaxation.

But from mid-June to early September, every week of the summer is devoted to such atypical, even unsettling, "resort" themes as "Care for the Poor," "Central America—Witness to War," "Multi-Cultural Families," "Ethnicity," "Confrontation in the Emerging World," "A Women's Movement for the '90s," "Bretton Woods Revisited," "Peace Priorities." Noted lecturers take to the stump on each week's topics, and twice-daily discussions, at 10:30am and after dinner at 8pm, alternate with lighthearted blueberry-picking, exercise sessions, swimming, and boating.

All three meals are included in the room rates, and yet those charges amounted last season to only $260 to $399 per person per week (depending on room category) or to only $180 per week for people bringing a tent. At those price levels, space fills up fast.

To apply, contact **World Fellowship Center, c/o Christoph and Kathryn Schmauch, 46 Ash, North Conway, NH 03860 until June 1, and thereafter R.D. Box 136, Conway, NH 03818 (phone 603/447-2280) all other times**.

Campus Vacations

Like the TV Hosts of "Fantasy Island," They Enable You to Briefly Re-experience the "Shortest, Gladdest Years of Life"

Remember them? Those wondrous years? You lived in a dorm, next door to a dining hall. Your days stretched on without limit, it seemed, and there was time for everything: discussions lasting hour after hour, a movie at night, the stillness of library and lab, your mind pulsing with new ideas and challenging thoughts.

"Bright college years"—through a wise use of vacation time, you can touch them again, feel the glow, recharge the spirit. At scattered colleges and universities, a number of short-term summer programs enable adults of all ages to briefly re-experience "the shortest, gladdest years of life."

There are, by my reckoning, 11 such schools. For a week in summer, when the campus blooms, they open their residences, dining halls, and classrooms to every sort of student from around the nation, without conducting tests or issuing grades, and at wonderfully low costs. Few other short vacations offer so much pleasure, and yet such mental growth.

And how do these programs differ from the "learning vacations"—an exotic cruise, an archaeological dig—that we, as alumni, are so often offered in the mails? First, because they are offered to alumni and non-alumni alike. Second, because they are operated by the university itself, on a nonprofit basis, and not by a commercial tour operator or professor-turned-entrepreneur. Third, because they take place on campus. Fourth, because, unlike other classier, costlier seminars conducted on campus, these place you not in nearby hotels but in simple college dorms, from which you take your meals in adjacent student cafeterias, exactly as you did at the ages of 19, 20, and 21. And last, because, unlike the somewhat similar Elderhostel programs, they are available to youngsters in their thirties, forties, and fifties as well.

Unlike other classier, costlier seminars, these place you not in nearby hotels but in simple dorms.

11 Campus Choices

Cornell's Adult University is the most ambitious of the lot: It hosted four one-week sessions in July 1995. At least 300 people attend each week, enjoying comfortable student lodgings and highly regarded food, eminent professors, bright fellow "students," the verdant surroundings of Cornell's famous hillside campus ("far above Cayuga's waters"), and sensible prices: $740 to $800 per week per adult, including tuition and full room and board; $280 per child, depending on age. Most adults opt for a single one-week topic, taught in daily sessions (they let out in midafternoon) throughout the week: "Archaeology of the Ancient Worlds," "Decadence and Creativity in Nero's Rome," "Frontiers of Technology," "Louis XIV and Versailles," "The Physics of Everyday Things," "Poets and Prophets: The Heritage of the Greeks and Hebrews," and "Figaro and Don Juan," are highly illustrative samples from previous years' curricula. The quality of instruction, and convivial afternoon and evening recreation, create a setting so compelling that some guests need almost to be evicted after their week in "Brigadoon"; though the literature doesn't say so, guests are encouraged to stay for only a single week (but may add another), and early applications are advisable. Contact **Cornell's Adult University, 626 Thurston Ave., Ithaca, NY 14850 (phone 607/255-6260)**.

Brown's "Summer College" invites both alumni and "friends" of the university to enjoy a remarkable week (mid- to late June) of high-quality lectures and discussions by eminent Ivy League professors. Each year's program pursues one common topic in morning sessions throughout the week, which are then followed by one's choice of varying afternoon subjects: a recent theme was the pre-Columbian civilization of the Aztecs, Maya, and Incas; another program explored the difficult task of American secondary education in building both competence and character, both "cleverness" and "goodness"; in still another, participants explored the "European Shuffle from the Atlantic to the Urals," led by former national security adviser to President John F. Kennedy, McGeorge Bundy; 1996's theme hasn't been chosen as we go to press, but may deal with "America in the Gilded Age" (the period immediately following the Civil War). Brown University, along with Dartmouth (discussed below), was the grandparent of continuing education in America and one of the earliest operators of short-term, residential, summer courses for adults. With room, board, and tuition included, expect to pay about $800 per person. Contact **Brown's Continuing College, c/o William J. Slack, P.O. Box 1920, Brown University, Providence, RI 02906 (phone 401/863-2474)**.

"Summer of '96" at the College of Wooster, Ohio, consists of lectures from 8:30am to noon, followed by buffet luncheons and afternoon excursions to attractions in the area, followed by films or light opera *(H.M.S. Pinafore, Wiener Blut)* at night, and gala dinners consisting occasionally of barbecues in a giant tent. All this occurs in June, with academic matters pursued for six straight days, through noon of Saturday. One typical theme topic of an earlier year was "Paris and Vienna 1889," as presented by eminent faculty members; 1996's discussion will range from architecture to cyberspace, from history to marital relations in the medieval world. Although organized by the Office of Alumni Relations, its staff members assure me that mere "friends" of the college are admitted to the program and to use the near-pastoral setting of a 300-acre campus and its many recreational facilities. Room, full board, and tuition total $470 per person for the entire week, using university dorms and the Lowry Center Dining Hall. Contact **Summer of '96, Office of Alumni Relations, The College of Wooster, Wooster, OH 44691 (phone 216/263-2324)**.

"The Mini University" of Indiana University takes place for a week in late June (not yet known as we go to press), and consists of 112 lectures on 112 separate subjects delivered by 114 faculty members of the great Hoosier center of learning; you are encouraged to attend as many as you can manage in the course of a six-day, five-night stay in Halls of Residence costing an average of $300 per adult for a week's room, board, tuition, and registration. Children coming along are sent to a separate campus "gym camp," but stay with their parents at an average cost of $180 per week, including registration and all meals. Costs are kept low by the fact that all profs donate their services free, as they speak on topics clustered under such headings as "Humanities," "Sciences," "International Affairs," "Arts," "Business," "Domestic Issues," "Health, Fitness, and Leisure," "Human Growth and Development." Contact **Mini-University '96, Indiana University Alumni Association, Fountain Square 219, P.O. Box 4822, Bloomington, IN 47402-4822 (phone 800/824-3044)**.

The Vacation College of the University of North Carolina at Chapel Hill draws its faculty from the several noted universities in the area (including Duke), a resource so rich that two separate weeks are offered and two alternative subjects per week are taught throughout the day. Dates in 1996 will be in both June and July, and lecturers will explore—in the university's words—"important cultural, moral and social topics from the perspective of the humanities"; in 1995, these included "What Makes the South Southern," "A Room of Their Own: Modern Women Writers," and "Roots: Searching the Ancient World for Our Origins." Musical programs or appropriate films are the relaxing evening activity. Tuition for the week is $240 per person, but meals and lodging in campus dormitories are billed separately, at a yet-to-be-determined (but moderate) charge. Contact **Humanities Program, CB#3425, 3 Bolin Heights, University of North Carolina, Chapel Hill, NC 27599 (phone 919/962-1544)**.

Smith College Adult Sports and Fitness Camp, for both men and women, is a highly active week of classroom instruction in fitness, nutrition, and stress management, alternating with active participation in yoga, cycling, hiking, swimming, windsurfing, tai-chi, canoeing, badminton, squash, tennis, and other forms of aerobics. The college's facilities for all this are among the best in the nation, and applications (from adults of all

They are operated by the university itself, on a nonprofit basis.

The New World of Travel 1997

The lifeblood of the Arthur Frommer travel guides is the correspondence received from readers, commenting on the establishments recommended in the texts and recommending new establishments. Each such letter is carefully studied, and when a particular lead seems promising, it is followed up and personally checked.

It is hoped that *The New World of Travel* will receive similar assistance from its readers. A yearly publication, issued near the start of each year, *The New World of Travel* will constantly grow. And since much of its content relates to organizations that lack the means to market themselves properly or come to the attention of a travel journalist, your help is invaluable in alerting me to the organizations—hospitality exchanges, alternative resorts, new travel clubs, and the like—that you have discovered.

If you become aware of a new travel organization, program, or development that deserves to be described in our next edition, *The New World of Travel 1997,* won't you please let me know about it? Send your letters to Arthur Frommer, *The New World of Travel,* 1841 Broadway, New York, NY 10023. All letters will be acknowledged, and all are warmly appreciated, in advance, by the author.

ages) are so heavy that two separate sessions have been scheduled for 1996, in the second and third weeks of June. A single fee of $650 per person covers sports, instruction, and room and board (single or double rooms) from dinner Saturday through breakfast the following Sunday. Contact **Jim Johnson, Adult Sports and Fitness Camp, Scott Gymnasium, Smith College, Northampton, MA 01063 (phone 413/584-2700, ext. 3975).**

The Dartmouth Alumni College, in Hanover, New Hampshire, operating for 12 consecutive days in mid-August of 1996, is among the oldest and most serious of summer campus sessions for adults, and assures me it is open to non-alumni. Each morning of the nearly two-week period, two lectures are followed by small-group discussions with faculty, but afternoons are left mostly free for tennis or golf on campus, boating, or hiking in the White Mountains. Evenings are devoted to films, special lectures, concerts, or plays related to that summer's theme, which in recent years has been "Riddles of Creation" and "Great Literature Reinterpreted." Professor Robert Henricks presided over a program of "major national names" as guest speakers, in addition to eminent faculty members from all departments of the college, including even the physical sciences. Participants pay $800 for the two weeks (that's per person, double occupancy, for those out of college for more than 10 years; younger grads get a discount of about $250 per person), including accommodation in Dartmouth dorms, books, instruction, and all meals (of which two are festive banquets). Contact **Dartmouth Alumni College, Dartmouth Continuing Education, 6068 Blunt Alumni Center, Hanover, NH 03755 (phone 603/646-2454).**

The Alumni College of Penn State is yet another of those mistitled programs meant mainly for alumni, but firmly open to all. It is also somewhat less of an academically rigorous program than a partly recreational week for the entire family. Thus, a recent classroom discussion pursued the theme "The World Around Us: An American Perspective," and included lectures on the "Greenhouse Effect," AIDS, nutrition, hydrofarming, and other current topics. Oxford it's not, but rather a type of "cruise with faculty," according to one staff member. A fee of approximately $70 a day covers your accommodation in university residence halls (bath down the corridor), all meals, and all tuition. Sessions are usually scheduled for mid-July, and you can contact **Mary Jane Stout, Alumni Vacation College, 105 Old Main, Penn State University, University Park, PA 16802 (phone 814/865-6517).**

Skidmore College's Summer Special Programs, near Saratoga Springs, New York, invites several different groups to use its campus in summer for residential adult study programs, and some of the latter are open to the public at large. I'm particularly impressed by the four-week creative-writing course of the New York State Writers Institute (mid-July of 1996: $2,000, all inclusive), and by the nine-day conference and workshops of the International Women's Writing Guild (early August of 1996: approximately $650 for tuition, room, and board). Contact **Prof. R. Boyers, N.Y. State Summer Writers Institute, Skidmore College, Saratoga Springs, NY 12866; International Women's Writing Guild, P.O. Box 810, Gracie Station, New York, NY 10028; or Office of the Dean of Special Programs, Skidmore College, Saratoga Springs, NY 12866 (phone 518/584-5000, ext. 2264).**

Next, Colby College of Waterville, Maine, plays host each August to the Great Books Summer Institute, an intensive discussion and analysis of four outstanding books that participants (up to 250 of them) have already read and pondered prior to arriving for their one-week stay. This year's session is in mid-August, 1996; this year's fee is $408, either single or double occupancy, including all lodging in college residence halls, all meals, and all tuition, as well as the four books sent to you via U.P.S. about four months in advance. During the session attended several years back by a friend of mine, books for discussion included Thomas Mann's *The Magic Mountain,* Frijthof Capra's *The Tao of Physics,* and William Barrett's *Irrational Man;* participants discussed the interrelationship of the books and their themes, in a week that was described to me as quite remarkably stimulating and satisfying. More recently, selections were: De Tocqueville's *Democracy in America, What to Believe* by E.M. Forster, *The Aquarian Conspiracy, Wholeness and the Implicate Order, The Universe Is a Green Dragon,* and Thornton Wilder's *The Skin of Our Teeth.* One note: Discussions are led by a lay "moderator," not a professor, whose role is to elicit student comments and not to hand down scholarly judgments from above. For information, contact **Great Books Summer Institute, 680 Elton St., Riverhead, NY 11901, Attn: Bill Thurston (phone 516/727-8600).**

And finally, from its mountainside campus overlooking the adobe-and-earth colors of stunning Santa Fe, New Mexico, St. John's College ("the Great Books school"), whose undergraduate education consists of reading 100 Western classics, sequentially, in the course of four years, will be operating week-long residential seminars (no examinations, no grades) for adults of all ages, in major classics of Western culture: Plato, Homer, Darwin, Shakespeare, Arthurian legends (Tristan & Isolde), and others. Living in a St. John's dorm, taking all three meals daily at a student dining hall, instructed by the college's famed tutors (akin to the dons of Oxford), you'll pay only $950 for one week, $1,900 for two weeks, all-inclusive except for the transportation that brings you there. There is no single supplement. Sessions in 1996 run from mid-July to mid-August. Write for literature to: **Summer Classics, St. John's College, 1160 Camino Cruz Blanca, Santa Fe, NM 87501-4599.**

At all such schools: When the week is over and "students" depart, what usually is their appraisal of the experience? "It was a stimulating relief from my day-to-day office routine that I do not find lying on a beach," said one. "It was good to talk ideas with my spouse," said another, "and know both of our heads were still very much alive."

Vacationing at a Cultural Folkdance Camp

With an Intensity That Must Be Seen to Be Believed, Some Americans Devote Their Holidays to Exploring the Folkways of Ethnic Cultures

On winter evenings in deserted gyms, they dance to the music of a dozen cultures, learning the steps as they go along, helping their partners, uncritical of the efforts of a sheer beginner.

Summers, from late June to early September, they repair to wooded settings near lakes or mountains to dance the entire day and evening. For a full week, or at least a long weekend, residential, rural folkdance camps provide an increasingly popular holiday/vacation alternative to tens of thousands of Americans.

Their atmosphere is among the most democratic of all our holiday institutions. Participants are wholly intergenerational and range from college sophomores to dynamic seniors in their seventies—some bearded, some in bold gypsy skirts or country dirndls. Without introduction, they take your hand to start a dance, then hand you off without skipping a beat to the next in a circle or line of whirling, or foot-stomping, or waltzing, dancers. There are no awkward social barriers, no inquiries into background or tastes, no attention paid to beauty or dress.

The music to which you dance, and the steps, are those that descend not from a paid composer or choreographer, but from the people, mainly poor people, and have been handed down from decade to decade by oral tradition or direct demonstration. It is intensely ethnic music and dance, and usually jumps from country American to Balkan to Greek and Israeli in the course of a single set.

It is also soul-stirring, insistent, pulsating music and dance that makes you joyous to be alive, and exercises every faculty of mind and limb. If you've never been to a folkdance camp or even folkdanced, you might think of taking the plunge, because the steps are easily learned and sheer beginners are accepted at every camp.

The major camps—as best as I've been able to determine—are the following:

On Both Coasts

Pinewoods Camp, near historic Plymouth, Massachusetts: Here is perhaps the most extensive of the residential folkdance programs, a series of eight one-week sessions running from early July to early September. But all are focused on English, Scottish, and American forms of the art, without the enlivening digressions (in my opinion) into the Balkan or Mexican varieties that mark so many other camps. Still, for lovers of those familiar steps, here are several hours daily of dancing paradise, in spacious and airy wood pavilions scattered over 24 acres of pine groves. Housing, almost always double occupancy, is in rustic, screened cabins located among the trees, but none far from two clear-water lakes for swimming and boating. Seven of the weeks are sponsored by the Country Dance and Song Society,

and cost about $475 a week (in all but one instance) for room, full board, and dancing; inquiries should be sent, prior to around June 30, to **CDSS, 17 New South St., Northampton, MA 01060 (phone 413/584-9913)**, and thereafter to **CDSS, Pinewoods Camp, Off West Long Pond Road, Plymouth, MA 02360 (phone 508/224-4858)**. One session (early July, and usually $450, all inclusive) is sponsored by the Royal Scottish Country Dance Society, and features the three or so basic steps of Scottish folkdancing in endless combinations. A bagpiper wakes you in the morning! Contact **RSCDS, c/o Ken Launie, 15 Salem St., Cambridge, MA 02139 (phone 617/491-6855)**.

Stockton Folk Dance Camp, in Stockton, California: One of the nation's oldest, in its 48th year, it always takes place the last week of July and the first week of August, Sunday through Saturday. With several two-hour classes running simultaneously, it isn't possible to sample everything, and many people therefore go for both weeks. According to one teacher, Stockton is not well suited for beginners, but is rather a skilled "work camp" for learning new dances. Accommodation is in University of the Pacific

Participants are wholly intergenerational and unconcerned with your own background, appearance, or dress.

dorms, and fees for tuition, room, and board run about $450 per week. In winter, write for further information or for applications to: **Cookie Brakebill, 3005 Montclaire Street, Sacramento, CA 95821.** In summer, contact: **Stockton Folk Dance Camp, c/o Bruce Mitchell, Director, University of the Pacific, Stockton, CA 95211 (phone 916/488-7637)**.

And Elsewhere

Lady of the Lake, of northern Idaho: In the popular resort area of Lake Coeur d'Alene, an hour from Spokane, Washington, this is an almost frantically intense week (the last full week of June) of folkdancing that starts at 9am each day and roars on till 11pm. You do "contras," squares, clogging, "swing," and "vintage" (turn-of-the-century) dancing, aided by accomplished instructors and musicians, all for the remarkably low weekly charge of $335, including meals and accommodations in rustic cabins housing 6 to 10 people. Children aren't encouraged to come in June, but are eagerly accepted at "family camp" in late August, for a charge of $300 per adult for the week, $100 to $200 per child (depending on age). Contact **Lady of the Lake, c/o Penn Fix, 703 W. Shoshone, Spokane, WA 99203 (phone 509/838-2160).**

Buffalo Gap Camp, near Capon Bridge, West Virginia: A 2½-hour drive from Washington, D.C., Buffalo Gap Camp (on a spring-fed, clear-water lake) becomes an international dance camp on the three-day Memorial Day and Labor Day weekends, charging $240 per weekend for dancing, ethnic meals, and lodging in dorm-style cabins. Teachers are brought in from around the world to supervise exotic, foreign folkdances from 9am to 5pm (repeated at evening dance parties), and yet total beginners are invited to the camp. In between the opening and closing dates for summer the camp is rented to outside groups for week-long sessions of specialized dancing ("Scandinavian Week," "Balkan Week"). For information on the full summer program, contact **Buffalo Gap Camp, c/o Phyllis Diamond, 2414 E. Gate Dr., Silver Spring, MD 20906 (phone 301/589-9212 during office hours, 301/871-8788 evenings and weekends).**

Christmas Country Dance School, at Berea College in Berea, Kentucky: Always from the day after Christmas to New Year's Day, a joyous week of folk-dancing ("it's a pleasant alternative to jogging alone," says the college's brochure), in a sylvan place—a historic small town set in the foothills of the western Appalachians, at a college noted for its support of the folk arts. The music is live, the faculty comprises nearly 25 teachers from around the world, and the

folkdancing itself is Anglo-American and Danish in origin. Cost for the entire week: $115 for the folk dancing and instruction, $45 for the dorm, $80 more for a campus meal plan. Ask, too, about the March, 1996 weekend of dancing to the music of the well-known folk band, "Bare Necessities." Contact **John Ramsey, Director, Folk Dancing Programs, Berea College, Box 287, Berea, KY 40404 (phone 606/986-9341, ext. 5143).**

Augusta Heritage Arts Workshops, at Davis & Elkins College, West Virginia: In the context of a much broader, summer-long program delving into every conceivable folk art and craft, specialized dance weeks take place in mid-July (for Appalachian Buckdancing, clogging, and "step dancing" only) and in early August (for southern squares, contras, swing dances, Cajun dances, clogging, and callers' workshops). Work is intense but open to all levels of expertise; lodging is in college residence halls, on the hilly, 170-acre campus of Davis & Elkins in the highlands (2,000 feet) of central West Virginia. Cost for a week: just over $455 for tuition, meals, and semiprivate room. Contact **Augusta Heritage Center, Davis & Elkins College, 100 Sycamore St., Elkins, WV 26241 (phone 304/636-1903).**

John C. Campbell Folk School of Brasstown, North Carolina: "Dance Weeks" at this noted, long-active school for folk arts and crafts take place on scattered dates throughout the year, and are almost wholly devoted to steps and formations of the home-grown variety, thoroughly American. Grounds are a 365-acre campus nestled between the Smokies and the Blue Ridge Mountains, a 2- to 2½-hour drive from such cities as Atlanta, Chattanooga, Knoxville, Asheville, and Greenville. Meals, as you'd expect, are southern, homestyle, and accompanied by home-baked bread. And weekly charges average $418 in dorms, slightly more per person in double rooms, for tuition, meals, and lodging. Contact **The Registrar, John C. Campbell Folk School, Brasstown, NC 28902 (phone 704/837-2775 or 704/837-7329).**

Fiddle and Dance Workshops, in the Catskill Mountains of New York State: The camp is Ashokan, along a lake at the base of heavily forested hills, $2^1/_2$ hours north of New York City by car. And there, for three weeks in July and August, dedicated folkdancers (including beginners) attend either the "Northern Week" (squares, contras, and couple dances of New England, Britain, France, Sweden, and Canada), the "Southern Week" (Appalachian, Cajun, and "old-time," plus buckdancing, clogging, and "flat-footing"), the "Celtic Week" (Irish, Scottish, and Cape Breton), or the "Western and Swing Week" (country, western, cowboy, Texas two-step, jitterbug, and lindy). Just $435 a week covers tuition, meals, and lodging in bunkhouse dorms, 15 to 20 people per room; less than that if you camp out in your own tent or trailer. Contact **Fiddle and Dance, R.D. 1, Box 489, West Hurley, NY 12491 (phone 914/ 338-2996)**.

Oglebay Dance Institute of Wheeling, West Virginia: This dance camp, the oldest in the country, schedules three-day/two-night camps each year for the Memorial Day and Labor Day weekends in a 1,400-acre park outside the city limits, on the landscaped grounds of a former farm set in rolling hills. Participants sleep in bunk beds like those of a children's summer camp, and spend their days and evenings in ethnic-dance classes supervised by three specialist instructors. Total cost: $135, including meals, lodging, and instruction. Contact **Oglebay Dance Camp, 1330 National Rd., Wheeling, WV 26003 (phone 304/242-7700)**.

Camp Olin Sang Ruby, near Chicago: A once-a-year weekend (usually in October) of Israeli folk-dancing taught by well-known figures from both Israel and the U.S., at the organization's 180-acre residential, rural retreat (wildlife and trails) along the shores of Lake LaBelle. More than 200 persons attend. While prices for 1996 room, board, and dancing haven't yet been set as we go to press, write or phone: **Camp Olin Sang Ruby, 100 West Monroe Street, Chicago, IL 60603 (phone 312/782-1477)** for the latest figures.

Folk-Dancing Tours with Karl Finger: America's leading operator of folk-dancing tours around the world, 19 years in the field, he accompanies groups of avid beginners and intermediates on moderately priced, one-week, two-week, and three-week expeditions to folk-dancing festivals in locations ranging from Bulgaria to Turkey and Greece to Alaska and the Caribbean; European trips cost about $2,400 per person (double occupancy, but with "shares" guaranteed), including round-trip air fare from New York. Participants travel by bus, and then fling themselves out of the bus to join whatever streetside or roadside folk dancing is in progress (according to my wife, Roberta, who took one of Karl Finger's tours to Eastern Europe several years ago; she rates the experience outstanding). More recently, Karl has added long-weekend, holiday (New Year's, President's Week, Easter, Memorial Day)

The world of folk life and art is a vast one, yet largely "underground" and little known.

At the Oglebay Institute. *Courtesy Oglebay Dance Institute.*

gatherings at the Solway House Resort in Saugerties, New York, for intensive folk-dancing; costs range from $185 to $379 (all-inclusive), depending on date and accommodation. For information on international trips, contact **Karl Finger, Hupi Road, P.O. Box 933, Monterey, MA 01245 (phone 413 528-2963)**; for details on the holiday weekends, contact **Rebecka Peters, P.O. Box 419, Saugerties, NY 12477 (phone 914/246-4021)**.

But Are You Up to It?

A word of warning before you enroll in any program: Be sure you can take the pace. Sessions involve as many as nine hours of movement per day—the most protracted "aerobic exercise" in America—beginning with up to six hours daily of workshops, followed frequently by three hours of "partying" (continual dancing) at night. And be sure you can move in rhythm to music. Some retirees looking for a new vacation experience, but physically awkward or unable to last on the floor for more than an hour, have had a miserable time at dance camps. Try looking up a local teacher before you leave. Despite this caution, most dance camps are open to sheer beginners, although some are more attuned to them than others.

Finally, bear in mind that the world of folk life and art, represented in part by the folkdance movement, is a vast one, yet largely "underground" and little known. Though I've mentioned the major camps, dozens of smaller ones have been necessarily overlooked. Once you tap into the rich folklife culture, you'll quickly discover many other such opportunities, and add new dimensions to your life.

Brainy Tours for High IQs

Vacations That Turn Your Mind On, Not Off

ow can you safely book onto an organized tour if you can't stand the company of people less intelligent than yourself? How can you ensure that other tour members will be congenial companions, alive to new discoveries, thoughtful and bright?

For years, brainy tourists have sought to solve that conundrum by confining their choices to tours that were advertised as having a serious theme, or a scholarly content, or a famous professor to provide the lecture commentary. The theory was that tours described in lugubrious tones would scare off the sluggards and the philistines, and attract instead the readers of books, the lovers of art, the collectors of degrees—all like a form of Darwinian selection.

The trouble was, and is: such tours are few and scattered. They come to your attention only by chance, in random mailings from alumni groups or museums to which you may or may not belong. Rather than appearing in a year-long catalog of departures, to be consulted when the travel urge hits, they materialize at odd and inopportune times when you're simply unable to go.

With seven major exceptions:

Swan Hellenic Cruises, represented by Esplanade Tours of Boston, is the oldest of the brainy tour companies operating year round. Owned for half a century by the prestigious P&O Lines of Britain, and largely booked by British vacationers, it places not one but several guest lecturers—each a noted historian or archaeologist—on each of its cruises to the eastern Mediterranean and motorcoach tours to other important destinations around the world. Thus you travel with the likes of Oxford "dons" (teaching masters), Egyptologists and Greek classicists of renowned museums, authors of encyclopedic works—all in an atmosphere of high erudition, sharing the experience with other well-read travelers. Possibly because the clientele is mainly British, rates are moderate: an average of $250 a day for air/sea/land arrangements so comprehensive that they include all shore excursions and even tipping on the particularly popular journeys to classical sights in the Aegean (on a ship limited to fewer than 250 passengers). They thus attract a cross-section of thoughtful, intelligent people from all walks of life. For literature and reservations, contact **Swan Hellenic Cruises, c/o Esplanade Tours, 581 Boylston St., Boston, MA 02116 (phone 617/266-7465).**

Often, tours described in lugubrious terms scare off the sluggards and the philistines, and attract the readers of books, the lovers of art.

Prospect Ltd., of England, is a more recent entrant, another British company that markets its tours in the U.S., and with such early success that its large catalogs are already three in number—"Art Tours of Europe, Africa, and the Middle East," "Opera and Music Tours of Europe" and "Music and Art Tours of Great Britain"—and nearly 200 year-round departures in scope. For each tour a specific tour leader is listed, and biographies at the back identify each as a noted academic with impressive credentials. These are no glib "personality kids" of the sort encountered on a standard tour, but—in one example—a scholar who "obtained his doctorate on Gothic architecture in Spain before becoming curator for Spanish and late Italian art at the National Gallery." Their commentary is not for the viewers of TV sitcoms. Tours explore history, art, music, and architecture for the most part; are one to three weeks in length and usually limited to 20 or 25 people apiece; and cost an average of only $100 to $140 per day in Britain, $225 per day in Europe, including (in the latter case) round-trip air fare from London to the jumping-off point for each tour. (Prospect will make alternate arrangements for non-British tour passengers.) For literature and reservations, go directly to **Prospect Music & Art Tours Ltd., 454 Chiswick High Rd., London W4 5TT, England (phone 081/995-2151).**

The Smithsonian Study Tours, of Washington, D.C.'s famed Smithsonian Institution, offers 150 different "study trips" throughout the year, as an educational benefit of membership in the parent organization (which costs $22 a year). Each tour is led by either an art historian, ethnologist, marine biologist, ornithologist, or astronomer; those specialties reflect the broad categories of the program. Small Smithsonian tour groups rove the world over from Soviet Central Asia to Zapotec and Mayan Mexico, for periods of widely differing durations, and pay from $1,200 to $4,000 for varying trips, or an average of $175 per day for domestic tours, $275 per day for foreign ones. Surprisingly, according to deputy manager Prudence Clendenning, two-thirds of all tour passengers are single, despite the fact that the median age of participants is a fairly low 50. "Single travelers make a point of commenting how welcome they are in our tour groups. . . . Our participants are bright, thoughtful people who don't fit the stereotype of the 'casual tourist,'" she adds. Contact **Smithsonian Institution Study Tours, 1100 Jefferson Dr. SW, Room 3045, Washington, D.C. 20560 (phone 202/357-4700)**.

Citisights of London is for serious, short tours of Britain—one to three days in length—guided by professional archaeologists and historians, and meant to be mixed and matched with standard touring or stays in the British Isles; they are also heavily booked by intellectually curious residents of Britain. Though touring is done by motorcoach, there all resemblance ends to the ordinary "once-over-lightly" approach of the usual programs. Three-day tours, leaving on Friday or Saturday, explore such weighty themes as "Wessex—Its History, Legends, and Thomas Hardy," or "Saxon Churches: The Arrival of Christianity in the North." One-day tours, from February through October, delve into "The Peasants Revolt," "A Bronze Age Lake Village," "Chaucer's Canterbury Trail," and "Inside Roman and Medieval Colchester." Originally an operator of London walking tours, and still heavily into that worthy activity, Citisights is fast expanding into intellectual vehicular sightseeing and is gaining acclaim not only for its refusal to pander to superficial touring attitudes but also for the moderate price level of its program: $50 for the average one-day tour, $275 for the average three-day variety. Contact **Citisights of London, 213 Brooke Rd., London E5 8AB (phone 71/739-2372)**.

Biological Journeys of McKinleyville, California, operates whale-watching and other natural-history expeditions of serious scientific content but open to the public at large. Departures, nearly 50 of them, are for one and two weeks during seven months of the year; go mainly to the waters of Baja California, the Canadian Arctic, the Caribbean, and South America; average $280 a day, all inclusive; and are each led by a prominent naturalist. You can be fairly certain that your fellow passengers— usually limited to 10 or 20 per trip—will have outlooks and imaginations similar to yours. Contact **Biological Journeys, 1696 Ocean Dr., McKinleyville, CA 95521 (phone 707/ 839-0178, or toll free 800/548-7555 outside Calif.)**.

Dolphin Charters of El Cerrito, California, is primarily for "high level educational tours" (their words) to Alaska and British Columbia (mainly cruises), May through September. Groups are kept small (8 to 10 tourists, a naturalist, and crew) and explore the wilderness and wildlife, along with native culture, arts, and outpost communities. Figure $300 a day for most 8-to-10-day cruises. Contact **Dolphin Charters,**

Exploring Anasazi ruins. *Courtesy Four Corners School, Smithsonian Study Tours & Seminars.*

1007 Leneve Place, El Cerrito, CA 94530 (phone 510/527-9622).

Discovery Cruises and Tours, of New York City, is a rather high-priced but extensive (40 departures a year, of which half are cruises) program of nature tours, each accompanied by as many as three lecturers (curators, researchers) from New York's natural history museum. Contact **American Museum of Natural History, Central Park West at 79th Street, New York, NY, (phone 800/ 462-8687 or 212/769-5700).**

And finally, Dailey-Thorp Travel, of New York City, is the nation's leading operator of year-round opera and music tours to music festivals in the United States, Britain, and at sea,

> **S**wan Hellenic places not one but several guest lecturers — each a noted historian or archeologist — on each of its cruises.

also offering massive doses of opera-going in Europe, and opera and concerts in New York. These attract the dedicated music-lover, but the fairly affluent one, as tours—with their expensive admission tickets included—sometimes range as high as $300 to $400 per day. Contact **Dailey-Thorp Travel, 330 West 58th Street, New York, NY 10019 (phone 212/307-1555).**

To repeat a point: I am of course aware of the scores and scores of serious university, alumni, and museum tours that are sponsored by different institutions, and largely marketed to their members or mailing lists on a local basis, but here I've tried to identify the nationwide operators of intellectual tours that offer these on a consistent basis throughout the year, and reliably year after year. If I've omitted any major players, please advise me, by writing to Arthur Frommer, 1841 Broadway, New York, NY 10023, and we'll remedy the omission.

The Religious Retreat As a Form of Vacation

More Than a Million Americans Each Year Devote Large Portions of Their Leisure Time to Sojourns in Retreat Houses

The religious retreat is a form of vacation activity that most professional travel observers seem to have overlooked. Yet more than a million Americans each year—the figure could amount to 1,500,000—devote large portions of their leisure time to sojourns in retreat houses. And while the greater part of them limit the stays to weekends, and to locations close at hand, a large number go for a week or two and many hundreds of miles away to centers whose broad range of subject matter and activities go well beyond the normal conception of a personal retreat.

As best as I can determine, there exist slightly more than 500 Catholic retreat centers and houses throughout the U.S. and Canada, about 150 Protestant centers, a dozen or so Jewish ones, and an emerging handful of Buddhist retreats. For a near-comprehensive listing of the Christian retreats, send $25 to **Retreats International, P.O. Box 1067, Notre Dame, IN 46556 (phone 219/631-5320)**, for the most recent edition of their extensive "Directory of Retreat Centers," which lists several hundred such locations, of which the great majority are Catholic retreats, others Protestant, all set forth state-by-state in pared-down fashion: addresses and phone numbers, name of director, months of operation, number of rooms, heavily abbreviated references to basic approaches and programs. You'll really need to phone the centers listed for your area to determine which best meet your needs.

> The experience is largely a personal one, and guests take advantage of the stressless atmosphere and freedom from business/family pressures to ponder the eternal verities.

For a more complete list of Protestant retreat houses (totaling about 150 in all), contact the **North American Retreat Directors Association, Olmsted Manor, Ludlow, PA 16333 (phone 814/945-6512)**. While theirs is simply a mailing list, not a directory with descriptions, they'll be pleased to furnish a copy free (after which you can phone the houses in your state for more details). Despite that kind offer, it would be a nice gesture to enclose $2 for postage and handling.

Upward of a hundred retreat houses have from 50 to 100 or more rooms apiece, while the remainder average 20 to 40 rooms. At the smaller houses, you obviously can't expect a complete activities program. Rather, in the monastic tradition of some (especially Catholic) retreats, the experience is largely a personal one, and guests take advantage of the stressless atmosphere and freedom from business and family pressures to ponder the eternal verities. For people of all religions, and of none, it is a refreshing interlude that places more petty concerns into perspective.

The larger retreats have elaborate programs, often on major religious, social, or political issues. Probably the most extensive program (35 separate instructors, including widely known theologians, therapists, and authors) is the month-long summer institute conducted every July on the campus of Notre Dame University by the before-mentioned Retreats International. Here, in the casual setting of summertime, nearly 400 people (teachers, counselors, clergy, nurses, social workers, and other concerned adults) are in attendance each week (and one week is all you need stay), auditing courses and seminars in spiritual and other church-related issues, but also dealing with family and youth problems, intimate relationships, morality and self-healing, community needs. Housing for the entire week amounts to only $55 to $75 per person (depending on the room), meals add about $10 to $15 a day, and week-long courses (five two-hour sessions) are $100 for tuition, in addition to an overall $30 registration fee. Write for literature to the address earlier given.

Genesis Spiritual Life Center, in the Berkshire Mountains of western Massachusetts, is a far less typical example of the large retreat center, in that it is purposefully ecumenical in nature, appealing to people of all religious beliefs, even though it is administered by the Sisters of Providence, a Catholic order. "We believe," says their credo, "that when persons of differing lifestyles and spiritualities connect, God's creative and healing energies are released. . . . We give preference to those who often feel alienated from their church or society." Heavily influenced by theories of the "New Age," the center's theme retreats include courses ranging from "Meditation Techniques" to "Guided Imagery and Music" to "A Jungian Look at the Christian Message," as taught by an equally ecumenical faculty that at times has included Lutherans, followers of Joseph Campbell, massage therapists, and psychoanalysts. Programs are offered throughout the year, as are "private retreats" ($40 a day for room, board, and the spiritual assistance of a Genesis staff member). All this in a peaceful wooded setting dotted with flower and vegetable gardens, an old restored carriage house, a chapel, a library, and two dining rooms. For their fascinating literature, contact **Genesis Spiritual Life Center, 53 Mill St., Westfield, MA 01085 (phone 413/562-3627).**

The Maryknoll Sisters Center in upstate New York, welcoming people of all churches and cultures, is the site for year-round group retreats that often deal with social change and other partly political issues, in the context of the intense religious missions for which the Maryknoll order is so well known. Six-day retreats range in subject matter from "How the Church was Born," "Sacraments and Liturgy," and "Eucharist/Evangelization in the New Testament" to "An African View of Morality," "Human Sexuality and Justice Making," "Ethics for the Twentieth Century," and "Evangelization Today: Tribal/Peasant/ Metropolitan Societies." Die-hard conservatives will not feel at ease here, although they will like the rates: $30 a day for room and full board, $65 to $150 for registration and week-long tuition. Contact the **Maryknoll Mission Institute, Maryknoll Sisters Center, P.O. Box 529, Maryknoll, NY 10545 (phone 914/941-7575).** Maryknoll is at Ossining, New York, about 35 miles north of New York City.

In other areas of the country, the key, larger retreats include Covecrest Christian Renewal Center, in northern Georgia, a year-round Methodist complex with extensive program and facilities, and low rates of from $25 a day per person for a couple staying in a cabin with kitchen facilities to $50 a day for a single individual living in Covecrest's motel-like structure of rooms; meals are not included or provided, but must be taken in nearby diners or restaurants. Rates go down considerably for recreational vehicles and tent campers parked alongside the sweeping lawns. Write or phone **Covecrest, Rte. 1, Box 3117, Tiger, GA 30576 (phone 706/782-5961).**

On the West Coast, but much smaller and radically different in atmosphere, is the highly regarded, Anglican-run Mount Calvary Retreat House near Santa Barbara, California, overlooking the Pacific from a high vantage point. In the quiet atmosphere of this Protestant monastic community, in a large Spanish home with a well-stocked library, individuals enjoy the essence of the retreat experience for a suggested daily donation of $50 for room and board. Write or phone **Mount Calvary Retreat House, P.O. Box 1296, Santa Barbara, CA 93102 (phone 805/962-9855).**

The available Jewish retreats are almost all long weekends in nature, and include, most prominently:

The Brandeis-Bardin Institute, 1101 Peppertree Lane, Brandeis, CA 93064 (phone 818/348-7201), has cottages amid rolling hills 45 minutes from Los Angeles, and offers a wide variety of themed programs on religious practices in the tradition of Reform Judaism. Cost is $150 to $235 per weekend, including full board.

Hadassah, the well-known Jewish organization, sponsors two broad categories of retreats, of which the first is perhaps the most serious. It is a week-long "Adventure in Learning Study Program," which focuses on spiritual studies supplemented by some recreational activities. The second, a "Singles Retreat" held across the country, is heavily patronized by persons seeking a mate of similar background and values, but has a strong religious and spiritual—

The larger retreats have elaborate programs that go far beyond the normal perception of their functions.

as well as social—content, I am assured by Hadassah's national office. For the many dates, locations and prices, write or call **Hadassah Outreach Department, 50 West 58th Street, New York, NY 10019 (phone 212/ 303-8140),** which operates these programs for the public at large, and does not require that participants be members of Hadassah. More traditional retreats ("Kallahs"), for members only, are offered on summer weekends at locations around the country, and are led by distinguished biblical scholars: write to Hadassah's Jewish Education Department at the above address.

Discovery Seminar's 2½-day presentations, Friday evening to Sunday afternoon, of basic elements in the Jewish heritage, are offered mainly to those with little background, in several locations throughout the country, from September through early summer. Cost is $150 per person for tuition, room, and board. For information, write or phone **Discovery Seminars, 1388 Coney Island Avenue, Brooklyn, NY 11230 (phone 718/377-8819)**.

Jacobs Camp, in Mississippi, has three large weekend retreats each year, September through May, discussing Jewish issues in a countryside setting that now also contains an 8,000-square-foot Museum of the Southern Jewish Experience, operated by the Union of American Hebrew Congregations. The all-inclusive charge is only $65 per person from Friday evening to Sunday evening. Contact **Jacobs Camp, P.O. Box C, Utica, MS 39175 (phone 601/885-6042)**.

Camp Olin-Sang-Ruby, in Oconomowoc, Wisconsin, hosts a variety of midweek and weekend retreats—some for adults only, others for families or mature adults only—on themes such as "Spirituality and the High Holidays" and "Jewish Literature and the Arts." The all-inclusive charge is $80 a day per person for lodgings and meals, in an extensive complex of 180 acres along the shores of Lake LaBelle. For information, write or phone **Camp Olin-Sang-Ruby, 100 W. Monroe St., Chicago, IL 60603 (phone 312/782-1477)**.

Volunteer Vacations, for Free or Almost for Free

CAESAREA MARITIMA 80
AREA C-28
LOCUS
DATE 6-26
FvD SESSION I 2M

Volunteer Vacations for Vital Adults

At Locations Ranging from Wilderness Lands in the U.S. to Collective Farms in Israel, the Donation of Your Labors Can Result in a Free or Almost-Free Stay

ome of us devote our vacations to frantic aerobics—jogging, jumping, straining, pulling, and clamping on Sony Walkmen to ease the crushing boredom of the aimless sport.

Other, more enlightened sorts gain the very same aerobic benefits—and personal fulfillment of the highest order—by engaging in voluntary physical labor at a socially useful project, in mountains and deserts, forests and farms. Though most such "workcamp" activity is designed for the vacations of young people, a number of other major programs are intended for adults of all ages, or—in some instances—for adults up to the age of 40.

A Hundred Holiday "Digs"

All over the world, but at home as well, archaeo-logical excavations utilize volunteer labor by adults with no previous experience in the art. In many cases the projects pick up all expenses of your stay (other than transportation to the site); in some instances they also pay you a small sal-ary; in most, they charge a fairly nominal fee for your spartan room and board.

And though the work is often limited to the painfully slow removal of earth from fragile fos-sils—with a toothbrush, no less, delicately, as you crouch over a slit trench in the baking sum-mer sun—it leaves you full of fatigue, drenched with sweat, and pounds lighter, at the end of each day's stint. Who needs the Golden Door?

Minimum stays range from three days to the entire summer. Examples (some from past pro-grams)? In Arizona, California, and Oregon, in the warm-weather months, a government-sponsored archaeological survey has used summer-long volunteers to "identify and record prehistoric and historic sites . . . in rough terrain. . . . Volunteers received partial insurance coverage, on-the-job transportation, training, room, and board." At the east Karnak site of Luxor, Egypt, volunteers for six weeks devote the months of May and June of each year to unearthing building blocks used for the sun temples of the Pha-raoh Akhenaten; "lodging and meals on site are provided without charge, except on Fridays (the day off)." In York, England, volunteers through-out the year pay $120 a week for the experience of participating for as little or long as they like in excavating stratified Roman, Anglo-Saxon, Viking, and medieval ruins of that historic city. Near Pisa, Italy, two-week volunteers are cur-rently being sought this summer for excavations of 12th- to 15th-century structures in the Ripafratta area; volunteers pay $130 a week for room and board.

The chief source of information is the 124-page *Archaeological Fieldwork Opportunities Bulletin,* listing more than 200 domestic and for-eign "digs," issued each January by the Archaeo-logical Institute of America. (Some listings, you should be warned, are of "field schools" rather than "fieldwork," and involve substantial tuition charges.) Send $15 for a copy to **Archaeologi-cal Institute of America, 656 Beacon Street, Boston, MA 02215-2010 (phone 617/353-9361)**. Add $2.50 more if you wish it sent by first-class mail.

A Stint As a Stone Mason

La Sabranenque is the strange but melodious source of this next volunteer vacation; it sends you to labor in the summer months in what many consider to be the most attractive areas in all of Europe: southern France and northern Italy. Nonprofit, and international, its goal is to restore

Restoring a Romanesque chapel.
Courtesy La Sabranenque.

a host of decaying, crumbled medieval villages at hillside locations throughout the historic area.

La Sabranenque's goal is to restore a host of decaying, crumbled medieval villages at hillside locations throughout southern France and northern Italy.

It did so first in the early 1970s, with spectacular success, in the village of St.-Victor-la-Coste, France, returning to their original form the 14th- and 15th-century stone farm buildings, chapels, and other community structures that had become heaps of rubble in the ensuing centuries. So favorable was the reaction of historians (and the French government), and so improved was the life of the village, that several other French and Italian villages immediately invited the group to attempt similar reconstructions of their own medieval ruins. Today, a half dozen such projects are pursued each summer, all utilizing international volunteers to set the stones and trowel the mortar for fences and walls.

Because the ancient structures of a European rural village are rarely more than two stories high, the work requires no special construction or engineering skills; stone-laying is quickly taught at the start of each two-week or three-week session. Charges to the volunteers for housing, full board, and all activities are $535 for two weeks (spent in France only, at St. Victor-la-Coste) and $930 to $990 for three weeks (spent in both France and Italy; round-trip transportation between France and Italy is included). For more detailed information, contact **La Sabranenque Restoration Projects, c/o Jacqueline C. Simon, 217 High Park Blvd., Buffalo, NY 14226 (phone 716/836-8698)**.

Maintaining the "Wild Lands"

You achieve this next worthy end by participating in a Sierra Club Service Trip operated in nearly 20 U.S. states by the mighty conservationist organization called the Sierra Club, now 500,000 members strong. Because many of the trips are subsidized by corporate donations, fees are low: as little as $250 for all the expenses of a seven-day tour of duty, except for transportation to the site—and that's a fairly average charge for the 50-odd service trips offered from April through late September.

You perform your "service" in some of the most enchanting places in all of America—not the standard, popular national and state parks, but the remote and less accessible ones, like the Gila Wilderness of New Mexico, the Washakie Wilderness of Wyoming, the Adirondack Forest Preserve of New York. Though most of the work is related to trail maintenance—by encouraging visitors to use well-marked trails, and limit their wanderings to them, the Sierra Club protects the delicate ecosystems of the park—projects extend to numerous other matters. "Workdays," says one description of a Sierra Club project, "will be divided between cleaning up nearby abandoned mining towns and reconstructing part of the Brown Basin Trail." Says another: "We will re-vegetate campsites." Or "our work will include cleanup and maintenance in and around the most imposing prehistoric ruins of the Southwest"; "we will cut and clear downed trees and underbrush from . . . around Chub Pond north of Old Forge."

Half the days of every trip are devoted to simple enjoyment of the wilderness; half are workdays. Lodging is in rustic cabins, lodges, or tents; cooking is done cooperatively by all participants; companionship is provided by vital, dynamic Americans of all ages. Complete descriptions of each service trip are set forth annually in the January/February edition (occasionally in other months as well) of *Sierra,* official magazine of the club. For a copy of that listing, send a $4 check to **Sierra Club Outing Department, 730 Polk St., San Francisco, CA 94109.**

Preserving the Trails

Slightly different in character is the even more extensive program of volunteer work projects in national and state parks, and national forests, for which the American Hiking Society serves as clearinghouse. Each year it lists several hundred such opportunities, for which food and lodging costs are either nil or nominal; volunteers provide the open-air parks with services that tight budgets will not allow the government agencies themselves to supply. Thus, for two to six weeks people act as unpaid, or nominally paid, "hosts" of campgrounds, build suspension bridges in Yellowstone National Park, weed out non-native plants from Haleakala National Park in Hawaii, spot and record the movements of bald eagles, act as deputy forest rangers or fire lookouts, even help out in the on-site offices of parks and forests. But mainly, in keeping with the core function of the nation's major hiking club, they maintain forest trails—and what "aerobics" that entails! "We clear brush, grub out stumps, trim vegetation, remove downed trees, repair erosion damage, and generally keep trails open . . . using hand tools like shovel, pick, pulaski, and saw. . . . It's strenuous," says an A.H.S. publication.

For information, write to **P.O. Box 20160, Washington, D.C. 20041-2061** for a copy of *Helping Out in the Outdoors: Volunteer Opportunities on Public Lands;* enclose $7 to cover costs.

Replacing a Reservist

Far less traditional, but fully as vital, is an unusual three-week stint of voluntary effort in the state of Israel, at any time of the year, and free of expense except for air fare (which, on this subsidized program, costs as little as $599 for a student traveling from New York to Israel and $629 for adults). But once there, "they" take care of everything else: room and board, even a set of boots and khaki fatigues.

"They" are the Israeli army. As a "Volunteer for Israel"—aged 18 to 70, male or female, Jew or gentile—you're housed at an Israeli military base, working at light, unskilled chores for $5^1/_2$ days a week (for three weeks) to free up Israeli reservists for actual military training.

At an armored camp near Ashkelon, you grease or paint tanks, tighten the screws on howitzers, make careful inventories of spare parts. At an infantry bivouac in the Negev, you cook for the troops or serve in the mess hall. At a supply depot near Jerusalem, you sort uniforms, pack kit bags, clean rifles, or cut grass.

> **A**t an armored camp in Israel near Ashkelon, you grease or paint tanks, tighten the screws on howitzers, make careful inventories of spare parts.

The working day is from 8am to 4pm. In the evenings, there's a "rec room" and subtitled movies or an Israeli professor (doing reserve duty) happy to deliver a lecture (in English) on the Dead Sea Scrolls. You sleep in barracks segregated by sex, but take your meals with both male and female soldiers, enjoying mammoth Israeli breakfasts of yogurt and fresh vegetable salads, eggs, bread, and black coffee.

If, following your stint, you wish to stay on for extra weeks in Israel (this time, at your expense), your air ticket is easily extended for up to 180 days.

Some Americans devote every one of their yearly vacations to the work I've just described—and then can't wait to return. Some older Americans go several times a year.

"It can be tedious," wrote one volunteer grandmother in her sixties, in a newsletter for alumni of the program. "I packaged coffee beans for distribution to the troops. But I was happy to do it."

"Some grandmothers take their grandchildren to the park—and some grandmothers volunteer for the Israeli army." (Incidentally, though you assist that army, you do not join it, or otherwise endanger your U.S. citizenship.)

Groups depart on three-week programs as often as eight times a month in the busy summer season, four times a month in the winter. Participants apply either to the New York office of Volunteers for Israel or to volunteer representatives. Recently, the organization has begun offering civilian projects as well (like tending plants in the Jerusalem Botanical Gardens, or archaeological excavations at Beit Shean), about which you might inquire when you write or phone. Unlike the military program, these tamer civilian projects require a small payment, from $12 to $25 a night, for housing and meals).

Contact **Volunteers for Israel, 330 W. 42nd St., Suite 1818, New York, NY 10036-6092 (phone 212/643-4848)**.

Alleviating World Poverty

You perform this next voluntary deed with a highly impressive group. Like the fictitious priest who lived among the lepers, beggars, and cart-pullers of *The City of Joy,* permanent members of the Fourth World Movement share the actual lives of the most abject poor in shantytown communities all over the world. Without making quite the same commitment, nonpermanent "volunteers" spend two weeks each summer in workcamps at the movement's international headquarters in Pierrelaye, France, held late June to mid-July, mid-July to early August, and early to late September. No knowledge of French is needed; total cost for the two-week stay is 420 francs (around $80); work includes carpentry, painting, masonry, cooking, followed by evening discussions and readings—until recently, with the movement's much-revered founder, the late Fr. Josef Wresinski.

Other volunteers devote two months, at any time of the year, to an internship at the movement's Washington, D.C., headquarters, or

The kibbutz movement currently permits young Americans of any religion to join their ranks for a two-month (or longer) "workcamp vacation."

at the New York City branch office, again working with families living in extreme poverty on projects designed to draw them back into society: street libraries, literacy and computer programs, family vacations. Interns share housing (free) and housing duties with permanent Fourth World members, but are asked to make a small contribution to food costs during the first month only.

Because the movement is painfully strapped for funds, be sure to enclose an already-stamped, self-addressed envelope (and perhaps a contribution, too) when requesting further information and literature: **Fourth World Movement, 7600 Willow Hill Dr., Landover, MD 20785 (phone 301/336-9489), or to the New York branch office at 172 First Ave., New York, NY 10009 (phone 212/228-1339)**.

Working on a Kibbutz

Finally, a 30-day overseas opportunity for young adults (up to 35 or 40 years of age; see below). That's the minimum stay required to share the life of an Israeli kibbutz, one of the communal societies that contain only 3% of the Israeli population, but produce 50% of its food and none of its crime. A type of collective farm in which property is held in common and children are raised as a group, the kibbutz has long held a strong fascination for Americans, both Jewish and gentile. Responding to a heavy demand, the kibbutz movement currently permits young Americans (18 to 35) of any religion to join their ranks for a two-month (or longer) "workcamp vacation" for a total fee of $95, not including air fare to Israel or mandatory insurance. For a slightly older age group (18 to 40), and one that doesn't want to work quite that hard, they offer a five-week summer program called "Project Discovery," which consists of only three weeks at a kibbutz, one week of archaeological digs, and one week simply visiting biblical sites. This one costs $2,400 for everything, and this time *includes* round-trip air fare to Israel, and insurance—quite a value for a five-week, totally all-inclusive trip. And what sort of work do you perform while actually "on" the kibbutz? You either labor in the fields, do laundry or cooking, or even work in small kibbutz "factories" for six to eight hours a day, six days a week, receiving all meals daily and lodgings with a kibbutz family. For all the alternatives and more, write **Kibbutz Program Center, 110 East 59th Street, 4th floor, New York, NY 10022 (phone 212/318-6130)**.

What About "Earthwatch"?

You may have noticed that I haven't included the Earthwatch organization in this listing because I sought out vacations that are either free of charge (except for air fare) or available at a nominal cost. Earthwatch enlists volunteers to assist noted university professors in their research efforts around the globe but charges the volunteer what seems to be an average of about $1,500 for a two-week stay (and volunteers, of course, secure their own air transportation). That figure, true, works out to considerably less if volunteers treat their costs as a tax-deductible contribution to a non-profit organization (Earthwatch takes no stand on whether or not they are entitled to do so). But even considering a possible tax saving, an Earthwatch trip is not the free or nominally priced activity that I consider a "volunteer vacation."

Having said that, the non-profit Earthwatch trips are among the most impressive, fascinating, and socially beneficial of all such volunteer efforts, to remote locations where serious work is performed; they also attract well-read and highly-dedicated volunteers, whose company is alone a reward of working with Earthwatch. Examples of their projects? "In an Indonesian village of fewer than a thousand people, you will interview villagers to determine their preferences in solar ovens, and then work with residents to construct about 100 solar ovens and assist in oven maintenance training." . . . "Volunteers will assist Professor S— in documenting celebrations, musicians and instrument builders in Senegal." . . . "You will help capture small sharks, fit them with ultrasonic transmitters, then follow their movements." . . . "In the lovely Mallorcan countryside, volunteers able to ride bicycles are needed to carry out ground-truth studies related to remote sensing, including mist netting birds, pond-dipping for freshwater invertebrates, preparing reed-bed specimens, recoding rare orchids and other wildflowers, and observing the effects of new water-management."

For more information, contact **Earthwatch, 680 Mount Auburn Street, P.O. Box 403, Watertown, MA 02272 (phone 617/ 926-8200)**.

Send Your Child to an International Workcamp!

They Bear No Resemblance to the "Gulag," but Rather to the Best Form of Residential Education, Among Other Young People from Around the World

This summer, many thousands of American teenagers will be hurtling through Europe by escorted motor-coach, isolated from the life of that continent by the steel-and-glass enclosure of their buses. They will socialize with one another, speak and hear English throughout, eat in segregated portions of hotel dining rooms, and regard themselves—subconsciously but firmly—as a privileged elite.

A better-informed segment of our youth will be sent by their parents, out of motives of the purest love, to international workcamps. Several hundred such places are found in countries of both Western and Eastern Europe.

There they will perform socially useful projects in the full midst of the European population. They will mix with other international young people, attempt foreign languages, make lifelong friendships, enjoy the satisfaction of contributing to worthy efforts, gain an appreciation for the realities of life abroad, and feel their minds stretch and grow.

And having paid only their air fare to reach the workcamp, they will receive free room and board once there.

Workcamp—Really a Misnomer

"International workcamps"—a horrid term unrelated to the happy atmosphere of the sites—were first formed at the end of World War I. A Swiss pacifist, Pierre Ceresole, conceived of projects in which youth of the former combatants—France and Germany—would work together to clear the wreckage of war. Fittingly, he chose the battlefield of Verdun for the first voluntary "workcamp."

In the several decades since, many hundreds of communities have sponsored similar efforts at other sites in Europe or, in a few instances, in North America. People in each locality propose a socially significant task to be performed by international volunteers, and raise the funds to pay for the modest local lodgings and meals required by the participants. Then, by various means of publicity, for which UNESCO has been the most effective channel in recent times, they invite young people of the world to travel at their own expense to the workcamp site. Once there, on stays averaging three weeks, the volunteers receive free room and board (and sometimes a bit of pocket money) in exchange for a few hours of enthusiastic effort each day.

While no one would denigrate their ensuing accomplishments, it becomes clear that the camaraderie of shared work, and the international understanding it brings about, are as important as the structures they build or the services they render.

What do the young volunteers do? In the midlands of England, they take underprivileged children on summer excursions to the sea. On the outskirts of Paris, they fill in for vacationing orderlies at centers for the aged. In the national parks of Germany, they restore hiking trails or clear away debris. And in the slums of Boston, they help to refurbish low-cost housing for the poor.

There, young people will enjoy the satisfaction of worthy efforts, gain an appreciation for the realities of life abroad, and feel their minds stretch and grow.

As many as 1,500 workcamps are operated throughout the year, although the great bulk take place in the summer months.

Hard work at a rural construction site. *Courtesy VFP International Workcamps.*

The Major Sources

Here in the United States, the two major clearinghouses for information on nearly 1,000 international workcamps (they will also book you into them) are: **Service Civil International (SCI/USA), c/o Innisfree Village, Rte. 2, Box 506, Crozet, VA 22932 (phone 804/ 823-1826); and Volunteers for Peace International Workcamps (VFP), Tiffany Road, Belmont, VT 05730 (phone 802/ 259-2759).** SCI requires its overseas volunteers to be at least 18 years of age, and will accept 16- and 17-year-olds only into its several domestic workcamps scattered around the country. VFP will accept 16- and 17-year-olds at more than 200 workcamps in France, Germany, and Spain, in addition to its U.S. workcamps, and enforces an 18-year-old minimum only for the remainder of them.

SCI, with branches ranging from the U.S. to India, is the more strongly ideological of the two; many of its workcamps stress liberal political values or ecological concerns. Recent workcamps have included construction of energy-efficient "hogans" (dwellings) and aid to elderly people on Navajo reservations in the Far West; gardening and outdoor activities in Los Angeles with young people otherwise in danger of recruitment into youth gangs; staffing of refugee camps in Croatia; renovating a home for AIDS patients in Matera, Italy.

VFP is less political in its approach. "We believe that any opportunity to come into contact with other cultures is worthwhile" is how a recent official once put it. Sample activities include

> **While no one would denigrate their accomplishments, the international understanding they achieve is as important as the structures they build or the services they render.**

coordinating activities in a center for the homeless of Vienna, repairing a Belgian Red Cross shelter for political refugees, and path clearing and fire prevention work in Italian wildlife parks.

Interestingly, both programs include numerous camps in Central and Eastern Europe (working with newly settled gypsies in Slovenia, organizing educational activities for refugees in Croatia); and VFP is particularly proud of its 16-year record of sending youthful American participants to several different workcamps in Russia. For three- and four-week periods in the summer of 1995, international volunteers helped an equal number of Russians to build a children's sanatorium on the west bank of the Volga, assisted scientists in identifying and tracking wildlife in various nature preserves of the Western Urals, and worked in two children's hospitals in Moscow. On similar programs planned for 1996, work fills half a day, discussions and debates the other half, and U.S. kids do more than hold their own in the lively afternoon discussions. Unlike other European workcamps, those in the former Soviet Union require a payment of $700 to $850 for three to four weeks by foreign participants.

What does it all amount to? Listen to the returning three-week volunteers. "It was wonderful," said a youngster from Michigan, "to see people working toward a common goal, not as 'Americans' or 'Czechs' or 'Germans' or 'Catholics' or 'Protestants' or 'Jews,' but as people." "I felt so lucky to have befriended people from around the world and across the political spectrum," said another. "There were 60 of us, from 14 nations, and after work we would sit around a campfire. What followed were conversations and arguments, some dancing, and also some people sitting quietly, reflecting. It was during those informal times that I learned the most."

Both the SCI and VFP directories for the coming summer are published in April. SCI charges $30 for membership, newsletters, and a periodic list of opportunities; VFP asks a mere $10 (and the latter charge also includes subscription to a newsletter and is deducted from any later registration fee). After perusing the several hundred descriptions of workcamps, applicants pay (to SCI) $35 for a U.S. workcamp assignment, $75 for one abroad; and (to VFP) $90 per workcamp in Western Europe, $100 per workcamp in Eastern Europe.

A Similar Program

A similar but much smaller workcamp program is offered by the official U.S. student travel organization, the **Council on International Educational Exchange (C.I.E.E.), 205 E. 42nd St., New York, NY 10017 (phone 212/661-1414)**. Here the literature is free, but a later application costs $165.

Selfless Vacations, the Jimmy Carter Way

The Rewards of Undertaking an Uncommon Series of "Outer-Directed" Trips

His life—comparatively speaking—was in ruins. He had been defeated for reelection to the presidency. His family business was in debt. Prematurely retired, shaken and adrift, he faced a midlife crisis more intense than most, but similar in essence to that confronting millions of middle-aged Americans.

And so he and his wife traveled. But in a different way. What restored the spirits of Jimmy and Rosalynn Carter, among several major steps, was an uncommon series of selfless, "outer-directed" trips. For them, travel was undertaken to discover new world issues and social needs, and—equally important—to be involved in curing the ills that travel revealed.

The vacation challenge, writes the former president, "lies in figuring out how to combine further education with the pleasures of traveling in distant places, and, on occasion, helping to make the lives of the people you visit a little better." Having done both, the Carters leave little doubt that the activity has launched them on a second, rewarding phase of life.

In a remarkable book published by Random House—*Everything to Gain: Making the Most of the Rest of Your Life*—Jimmy and Rosalynn Carter tell, among other things, of the several life-enhancing travel or travel-related organizations with which they have associated their names, or which they recommend to others. These are: the Friendship Force, Habitat for Humanity, GATE (Global Awareness Through Experience), the Citizen Exchange Council, and the International Executive Service Corps.

The Friendship Force

This is already known to many Americans. It is the 18-year-old, nonprofit, Atlanta-based organization founded by the Carters and the Rev. Wayne Smith, which each year sends thousands of adult travelers ("citizen ambassadors") to live for two weeks in foreign homes found in 45 countries, on several continents. Subsequently, the foreign hosts come here to live in American homes. Since the stay in each case is basically without charge (except for transportation and administration), the cost of a Friendship Force holiday is considerably less than for standard trips to the same destination, and upward of 400,000 people have thus far participated. Upon returning, they continue to exchange correspondence or privately arrange visits with the families they have met. In this way, writes Rosalynn Carter, "friendships are . . . made that can only lead to a more peaceful world."

For information on membership in the Friendship Force, and on the 1996 exchanges planned from dozens of U.S. cities, contact **Friendship Force, 57 Forsyth Street NW, Suite 900, Atlanta, GA 30303 (phone 404/522-9490)**.

Habitat for Humanity

This is a less obvious travel resource. Based in Americus, Georgia, near the Carter household in Plains, it was created some 20 years ago (before the Carters' involvement in it) to work for the elimination of poverty housing (namely, shacks) from the U.S. and the world. Its founder, a fierce Christian crusader named Millard Fuller, enlisted

For them, travel was undertaken to discover new world issues and social needs.

the assistance of Jimmy Carter in the period immediately following Carter's defeat for reelection.

At Fuller's urging, the Carters traveled by bus to Manhattan, lived in a spartan, church-operated hostel, and worked each day for a week as carpenters in the rehabilitation of a 19-unit slum tenement in New York's poverty-ridden Lower East Side. The worldwide publicity from that volunteer effort made Habitat into a powerful organization that built more than 14,000 homes in 1995 (and projects even more in 1996) in a thousand locations in the United States and Canada, and in scores of countries worldwide.

Jimmy and Rosalynn Carter continue to travel periodically to workcamps at these locations.

Though others may recoil from the suggestion that arduous, physical labor on a construction site can be a "vacation" activity, hundreds of Habitat volunteers disagree. To cast their lot with the poor is, for them, many times more refreshing than lazing at a tropical resort. If they have one to three weeks off, they travel to work at scores of Habitat locations in the U.S. and Canada, paying for their own transportation and food, and often receiving accommodations—rather basic—at the site. No prior construction experience is required.

Similar opportunities are now available overseas—in Central and South America, Brazil, India, Zaire, and Malawi—under Habitat's recently instituted "Global Village" program. For one or two weeks, volunteers build housing in those

Raising the wall of a modest home.
Courtesy Habitat for Humanity International, photo by Julie Lopez.

countries under conditions similar to those of the domestic program: they pay for their own transportation there, and for food, although it is sometimes also necessary to pay the cost of simple accommodations as well. Mainly they work alongside the Emerging World people who will eventually occupy the houses under construction.

For information on how you can devote your vacations to building a "habitat for humanity," or for application forms, contact **Habitat for Humanity, 121 Habitat Street, Americus, GA 31709 (phone 912/924-6935)**.

A "Habitat" Project in Tropical Winter Weather

The idea of embarking on a "Jimmy Carter-style" volunteer vacation is made more compelling still

What results is not a mere vacation, but the most rewarding interludes of life.

by an ongoing (winter, too) Habitat for Humanity project in South Dade County, about 20 miles south of Miami, Florida. This was the area devastated by Hurricane Andrew on August 24, 1992, and Habitat is currently building a 90-home community there

for people in poverty. The work proceeds throughout the year, on a 15-acre work site, and up to 250 volunteers a day can be accommodated—including totally unskilled persons of all ages who can haul lumber, paint, and landscape.

I've received a remarkable letter addressed to "The New World of Travel" by David G. Tilden, "Director of Work Camps" of Habitat in Miami. "We would like to let your readers know," he wrote, "that we can provide food and lodging for individuals at the rate of $10 per person per day. And persons interested in a longer term stay (three weeks or more) are eligible for complimentary food and lodging. Our program of construction is open year round to anyone over the age of 14, regardless of experience or religious affiliation. No minimum stay or compulsory donation is required."

Each weekday at 7:15am, after a group breakfast served from 6:15 to 7, according to Tilden, volunteers are transported from their dorm-type lodgings to the construction site half an hour away, where they work (with a lunch break) until 3pm, returning to camp by 3:30pm. Dinner is served from 5:30 to 6pm, and volunteers enjoy planned evening activities, as well as free time on Saturdays and Sundays. All for $10 a day. For copious literature that will set off turmoil in your mind, write or call **Habitat for Humanity Volunteer Center Office, 17300 S.W. 177 Avenue, Miami, Florida 33187 (phone 305/252-8606** or **fax 305/252-2806)**. And refer to the "South Florida Work Camp." There you may learn that a change is a vacation; that working at some socially beneficial task is ultimately more refreshing than all the golf courses and tennis courts ever built.

Gate, C.E.C., and I.E.S.C.

Other Carter-approved travel programs include the **International Executive Service Corps, P.O. Box 10005, Stamford, CT 06904 (phone 203/967-6000)**, arranging trips by retired business executives to lend their expertise to would-be entrepreneurs in developing nations; and **GATE (Global Awareness Through Experience), 912 Market Street, LaCrosse, WI 54601 (phone 608/791-5283)**, operated by an order of Catholic nuns, the Sisters of Charity. For more on "GATE," see our Chapter II.

For the Carters, as for so many other Americans, simply to lie on a beach, or otherwise turn off the mind, is no longer the sole—or even the wisest—approach to vacationing. Using the mind is a far happier leisure activity. Seeking challenge and new ideas is the way to travel pleasure. A change can help us, in Allan Fromme's words, "become more alive again."

And when the changes achieved through travel are combined with selfless activity—work designed to help others or advance world understanding—then what results is not a mere vacation, but some of the most rewarding interludes of life.

A "Mini Peace Corps," Now in the Reach of Everyone

"Working Vacations" to "Host Communities" in America and Around the World

Our families, our jobs, the need to earn a living, carry a mortgage, repay a college debt—all these are reasons, imagined or real, that have dissuaded multitudes of Americans from joining the Peace Corps, though they longed to do so. Here was the "ultimate trip," the chance to experience the village life that half of humankind leads, but one unattainable to those of us who can't lightly abandon obligations at home.

Well, now there's a way, and it's a breathtaking, breakthrough travel opportunity achieved after eleven years of preparatory work by a Minneapolis/St. Paul organization called Global Volunteers. In 1996, they will be offering some 70 varied departures of a "working vacation" to host communities in Mexico, Costa Rica, Jamaica, Tanzania, Indonesia, Vietnam, Spain, Russia, Poland, and within the U.S.—each lasting a manageable two or three weeks. And each will be available to those with no particular engineering or agricultural skills—like lawyers, let's say, or homemakers from Memphis or Chattanooga.

If all this seems a bit of radical chic, a patronizing, quick trip by dilettantes (as it initially appeared to me), then you'll want to know the following:

Each trip is undertaken at the specific request of the host community, for projects they eagerly wish to complete. The long and laborious task of soliciting such invitations has largely occupied the time of the organization over the past several years, and is now complete. No one arrives uninvited, and villagers give a warm welcome to the volunteers who will assist them in programs of education (teaching English, math, or science), health care (building clinics and community centers), and natural resources (securing potable water supplies, reforestation)—all as mapped out by the villagers themselves.

Though each participant stays for only two or three weeks, the projects go on for a much longer time, and are worked on by successive groups averaging 8 to 12 volunteers apiece. As one group leaves, another arrives, and the work continues unabated.

On some trips to the less developed countries, so great is the gap in formal education between the villagers (many of them illiterate and thus unable to read instructions) and their guests (mostly college graduates) that even the most technically untrained of those volunteers can make a substantial contribution. "I never knew I had these skills," said one middle-aged matron, "but mixing concrete is like baking a cake: you simply follow the recipe."

The initial four or five visits to each of the destinations (a total of thirty-nine preparatory trips) were immensely successful. "We built a relationship of trust," says Burnham (Bud) Philbrook, a lawyer and former member of the Minnesota House of Representatives who is president of Global Volunteers. "We showed them that not all Americans were like characters from 'Dallas.'" Currently, the requests for further visits arriving from villages around the world are far greater than the number of volunteers on hand to make the trips.

If all this seems a bit of radical chic, relax; each trip is undertaken at the specific request of the village, for projects they eagerly wish to complete.

In the early 1990s, the organization made frequent visits to such locations as the following:

• **Pommern,** in Tanzania, a remote rural community of 3,000 people, to which Global Volunteers was invited by the Tanzanian Lutheran church. There, participants lived for three weeks in an old German mission house built of red clay in 1912, sleeping in separate men's dorms, women's dorms, and a few private rooms for couples, and consuming meals carefully prepared for them by local women. Daytimes, they expanded a woefully inadequate 16-bed clinic currently serving a dozen surrounding villages, created a secondary school and taught the English-language skills so vital to commercial success in Tanzania, and

Helping a young Jamaican to build a school chair. *Courtesy Global Volunteers.*

assisted villagers in several water-supply projects.

• **Llanos de Morales,** in Guatemala, at the invitation of a nonprofit, secular Guatemalan foundation. Members stayed for two weeks at a time in the annex to a Catholic church, eating in the back room of a nearby small *tienda* (store). In a country whose government provides its poverty-stricken villagers with scarcely any training or resources at all, Global Volunteers ran the gamut of development efforts, from renovating an old building into a preschool, teaching English, helping preschoolers to use toothbrushes, coaching volleyball, constructing a community center, and providing assistance in the start-up of small businesses.

> "**I** never knew I had these skills," said one middle-aged matron, "but mixing concrete is like baking a cake; you simply follow the recipe."

• **Leabuu,** in Western Samoa, the independent nation that is far poorer but far lovelier (say several volunteers) than nearby American Samoa. At the invitation of Roman Catholic Cardinal Pio Tafinuu, a native Samoan who wears the traditional "lava lava" skirt, they stayed for three weeks at a time in a church retreat center 20 yards from the Pacific Ocean. Their task: to renovate a large community center that will then serve as the catalyst for a broad range of development projects.

• **Adjuntas,** in Mexico, south of Guanajuato, the poorest of the villages served by Global Volunteers and also the nearest, and typical of literally thousands of Mexican villages that lack both electricity and running water, requiring villagers to place large buckets on their burros to carry water from locations miles away. And yet, says Philbrook, the village is rich in both culture and a sense of community, and determined to make progress. There are now latrines in Adjuntas (Global Volunteers built them), and a host of other energizing communal activities, most of them sponsored by the University of Guanajuato, which also coordinated the villagers' invitation to Global Volunteers.

Trips more recently operated, or planned for 1996, include (and there are many more): *Dobczyce, Poland (outside Cracow),* where volunteers will teach English in classrooms to both elementary and secondary students; *Ho Chi Minh City* (the former Saigon) in Vietnam, and to *Rota, Spain,* near Cadiz, again for the teaching of conversational English; to *Santa Elena, Costa Rica,* working outdoors on construction projects in nature reserves; and to the *Blue Mountains of Jamaica,* working in three mountain villages on water systems, or in the construction or renovation of community buildings.

The New World of Travel 1997

The lifeblood of the Arthur Frommer travel guides is the correspondence received from readers, commenting on the establishments recommended in the texts and recommending new establishments. Each such letter is carefully studied, and when a particular lead seems promising, it is followed up and personally checked.

It is hoped that *The New World of Travel* will receive similar assistance from its readers. A yearly publication, issued near the start of each year, *The New World of Travel* will constantly grow. And since much of its content relates to organizations that lack the means to market themselves properly, or come to the attention of a travel journalist, your help is invaluable in alerting me to the organizations—hospitality exchanges, alternative resorts, new travel clubs, and the like—that you have discovered.

If you become aware of a new travel organization, program, or development that deserves to be described in our next edition, *The New World of Travel 1997,* won't you please let me know about it? Send your letters to Arthur Frommer, *The New World of Travel,* 1841 Broadway, New York, NY 10023. All letters will be acknowledged, and all are warmly appreciated, in advance, by the author.

In every village, the organization insists that the ultimate responsibility for development be on the local people, who initiate and supervise every project, using resources on hand and tools they are familiar with. In total agreement with the teachings of the late British economist E. F. Schumacher ("Small Is Beautiful"), Global Volunteers imports no complex devices or machines; if shovels are lacking to dig a well, they send out no urgent orders for a shovel, but use local implements. While providing assistance, the volunteers learn about community structures, family loyalties, and courage in the face of adversity, "receiving far more than we contribute," according to Philbrook.

As one volunteer put it: "I expected to find a sense of futility and hopelessness. I discovered instead a determination of the human spirit to carry on in spite of limited circumstances, an attitude of innovation and make-do, an eagerness to learn new ideas, and hope for their children to have a better life than they've had."

And lest the group be accused of overlooking widespread poverty and development needs here at home, the organization is planning future projects in American "villages": Native American reservations in several southwestern states, rural towns in the Mississippi Delta or southern Appalachia. "We couldn't have operated domestically before we had acquired global experience," says one officer. Careful to operate frugally and within their means, the organization claims to be on a firm financial footing, issues impressive literature, and has ambitious plans for the future, of which the most recent "breakout" program (as many departures as in several previous years) provides a glimpse.

Because Global Volunteers is a registered, nonprofit organization, contributions to it are tax deductible; and because the expenses incurred by each volunteer are deemed to be contributions by them, they, too, are deductible (provided you don't take any additional vacation immediately before or after the scheduled trip). Keep that in mind when considering the modest cost of participating: from $300 for one week in the United States, $1,300 for two weeks in Jamaica, $1,500 for two weeks in Costa Rica, $1,690 for 15 or 19 days in Vietnam or two weeks in Spain, or $1,825 for three weeks in Poland, not including air fares, but otherwise all-inclusive. Each of these prices is reduced by federal and state tax savings of as much as 38% for some Americans. And each price includes the services of a trained tour leader, and about $100 per person for project materials (concrete, nails, other construction aids). Accommodations? Hotels (double occupancy rooms) in Spain, Poland, Russia, Mexico, Vietnam; community housing, dormitory style, in the developing countries. In the U.S., homestays with local people. The emphasis in each case is on experiencing local life from a non-tourist perspective.

To join a "private" Peace Corps sponsoring short-term working vacations, one that has gained my own excited attention to the same extent as the original Peace Corps, contact: **Global Volunteers, 375 Little Canada Rd., St. Paul, MN 55117 (phone 800/487-1074 or 612/482-0295)**.

V

Living with a Private Family, Both Here and Abroad

Inexpensive, Short-Term "Homestays" for Two Nights to a Week

A Travel Experience That Widens Your Horizons As No Commercial Lodging Could

In 12 scattered weeks of the year, Hans and Ilse Sternhagen of Salzburg, Austria, take paying guests into the single spare bedroom of their chalet home.

They do so as much for pleasure as for profit. Though they value the income from that activity, they are far more excited by the chance to converse with exotic visitors, like people from Albuquerque or Santa Fe. They like to linger over a brandy, after a home-cooked dinner of *Beuscherl mit Knödel* (calves' liver with dumplings), and exchange opinions and outlooks with their new overseas friends.

Instead of merely providing a bed, the Sternhagens are sharing their lives.

And that is the essence of a "homestay." It can never be adequately stressed that in the world of travel a homestay is radically different from, and usually infinitely superior to, a guesthouse stay or a bed-and-breakfast stay.

The latter is often supplied by rather jaded individuals who make their living from the rental of multiple rooms in a residence each night of the year. While they may be warm and generous people, their behavior has frequently been affected by too much continual contact with international tourists; they no longer reflect the national attitudes of their nation. In their multibedded guest homes, you receive a room for the night, breakfast the next morning—and little more. You save money, but gain no worthier rewards.

Instead of merely providing a bed, the hosts are sharing their lives. And that is the essence of a "homestay."

A homestay, by contrast, takes place in the dwelling of a private family with only a room or two to rent, and then only on occasion, simply to supplement their income but not to provide the major portion of it. Here the arrival of a tourist is still an event. After breakfast, the guest stays on to converse, and often to share in daily activities, and returns at the end of the day for dinner. The inclusion of two meals a day, or at least the option for it, is a hallmark of a homestay.

Of the many organizations placing tourists in bed-and-breakfast situations, only a portion offer true "homestays" (single-unit rooms, two meals a day, contact with the family) to people of all ages. The following are typical for:

Homestays in Britain and Europe

Though several agencies on the continent provide these arrangements in their own countries (I'll supply an example farther on), a great many travelers prefer using the British firm known as Home & Guest Service, which places homestaying tourists not simply in Britain, but in France, Germany, Italy, Spain, Portugal, Greece, and the Benelux nations as well. You are thus generally assured that your hosts will be English-speaking. The long-established Home & Guest claims to have chosen only such hosts as will pledge "to introduce the guest to family and friends."

"Our kind of tourism," they say, "is the dynamic kind where you get to know the country you are visiting thanks to the people who live there." It differs, they add, "from the sad kind of tourism where you travel abroad and hardly see anything of the life of the country and never meet any worthwhile resident in that country."

Though Home & Guest's charges differ from country to country, they average the equivalent of £12 ($18) per person for "budget-category" lodgings (even in London), £15 ($22.50) in "standard" rooms, £18.50 ($27.75) per person in "superior" ones, £25 ($37.50)—still reasonable—in what proprietress Mrs. Rutter calls the "deluxe" variety.

In recent months, Home & Guest has branched out to represent working farms all over the British Isles at rates similar to those of the homes, and can even enable you to camp out on the grounds of farms, with use of their water and kitchens, for £6 to £9 ($9 to $13.50) a night. Write: **Home & Guest Service, Harwood House, 27 Effie Road, London SWGIEN, U.K., or phone 011- 44-171-731-5340.**

An example of the several national agencies arranging English-language European homestays is the Belgian firm known as La Rose des Vents ("The Windrose"), whose per-person-per-night charge of $34 covers a double room and breakfast (dinner is optional) in scores of homes scattered about the tiny country. Descriptions of hosts are especially fulsome: in one location 10 minutes from downtown Brussels, the lady of the house is said to be "a most pleasant woman of style and polish, in her 50s. Her former profession of social worker has developed her natural grace in human contact and in being helpful. . . . Monsieur . . . is a chemical engineer who speaks English." Contact **La Rose des Vents, Avenue des Quatre-Vents 9, 1810 Wemmel, Brussels, Belgium (phone 02/460-34-59)**.

A larger (and somewhat costlier) source of budget-priced homestays in Britain is Wolsey Lodges, a loose marketing association of independently owned country houses clustered in the southern half of England, heavily in the Cotswolds and East Anglia, but throughout Scotland and Wales as well. They have a few properties in France and Spain, too. Though some resemble the more commercial variety of bed-and-breakfast, they are all a cut above, and by studying the Wolsey literature carefully, one can find homes owned by Oxford graduates, retired lieutenant-colonels of the Royal Air Force, people actively engaged in demanding professions and business activities. Their charges range from as little as £20 ($30) per person to rarely more than £44 ($66) per person, a cooked breakfast included, and although they engage in none of the elaborate screening and matching of guests with hosts of the sort promised by the other firms, they offer the opportunity (through careful selection of homes, this time by yourself) to socialize with English people of above-average intelligence and tastes. Contact **Wolsey Lodges, 17 Chapel St., Bildeston, Suffolk IP7 7EP, England (phone 0449/ 741-297)**.

Homestays in Ireland

A 27-year-old school for the teaching of English as a foreign language, whose students stay with private families, the Dublin School of English quickly realized that its homestay arrangements would also be suitable for tourists. It currently services a great number of them. Homes are provided throughout the Republic of Ireland, and in Northern Ireland, but travelers using these arrangements in Dublin have the added bonus of enjoying the school's social and touring activities as well. Rates per person per week, for room and "part board" (breakfast and evening meal), in Irish pounds, are IR£160 ($240) in the Dublin area, IR£145 ($217) outside Dublin, IR£185 ($277) in Northern Ireland. Contact the **Dublin School of English Ltd., 10-12 Westmoreland St., Dublin 2, Ireland (phone 773322)**.

> **A** homestay is radically different from, and usually infinitely superior to, a guesthouse stay or a bed-and-breakfast stay.

Homestays in Indonesia

Founded by Mrs. B. Moerdiyono in 1970, when she first welcomed travelers to her own home in Yogyakarta, on the big island of Java, Indraloka Home Stays has become a thriving organization that places tourists with English-speaking private families in every major Javanese location: Djakarta, Yogyakarta, Bandung, Surabaya, Malang, and others. Hosts include university lecturers, teachers, physicians, businesspeople; guest rooms are invariably large and comfortable, with ceiling fans; and Indonesian home-cooking, according to Mrs. Moerdiyono, "far surpasses most restaurant food." Her lodgings, she adds, are particularly popular with "single women traveling alone, and businesspeople tired of the impersonality of a conventional hotel." Rates for 1995 (they may be a bit higher in 1996) were a remarkable $15 per person for room and breakfast, double occupancy, $25 for single people traveling alone. Other meals—lunch for $4, dinner for $5—are available as options. Contact **Indraloka Home Stays, c/o Mrs. B. Moerdiyono, 14 Cik Di Tiro, Yogyakarta 55223, Indonesia (phone 0274/3614)**.

Inexpensive, Long-Term "Homestays" for Three Weeks and More

At Last, the Famed "World Learning, Inc." Has Extended Its Facilities for Placing Teenagers with Foreign Families, to Permit Adults of All Ages to Enjoy the Same Remarkable Benefits

Every autumn for three of the last five or so years, Earlene Richards—a 48-year-old nurse from Milwaukee—has traveled abroad to spend two weeks with a foreign family: a different family, in a different nation, each time. On one occasion, Sri Lanka; on another, Japan; most recently, a more familiar stay, in the midlands of England. Each time, the cost of her visit was a modest $475, plus air fare. But the experience was priceless.

"When you live abroad as a tourist," she says, "you see the world from your own point of view. When you live with a family, you see things from *their* point of view, and you are never the same again."

Such is the classic "homestay vacation," as operated by the "Federation" division of World Learning, Inc. (formerly, the Experiment in International Living, Inc.). It will come as a surprise to many that the famous Brattleboro, Vermont, organization, long known for its live-with-a-family programs offered to teenagers in summer, or to college students for a semester, is now making the same experience available, for one to four weeks, to adults of all ages and throughout the year.

It was inevitable, in my view, that such expansion of its activities would come about. For nearly 64 years, since its founding in 1932 by educator Donald Watt, World Learning, Inc., has argued that the family is the finest of all laboratories for learning; that travelers living for a week and more with a foreign family, as unpaid houseguests, would receive unique rewards; that sharing the family's daily activities, its values, its circle of friends, would enhance their understanding of the human condition, of cultural differences and human similarities, all in the course of an immensely pleasurable and invigorating vacation experience. Why, then, limit such rewards to youngsters?

Quietly, and without the publication of a single brochure, World Learning has now made its international homestays available to people of all ages, as part of any overseas trip; and it is anxious, as recently confirmed to me, to increase the number of adult participants. The sponsor of these "Individual Homestay Programs" is the organization's separate "Federation" office in Putney, Vermont, eight miles from the student-and-teenager doings in Brattleboro.

The separate office results from the fact that World Learning is now part of an association— a "Federation"—of 27

> **"World Learning" has contended for years that the family is the finest laboratory for learning.**

wholly autonomous organizations in as many countries on six continents. Each sends travelers of its own nation to enjoy homestays in other member nations, and each has enlisted scores of volunteer host families who—largely without payment of any sort to themselves—accept adult guests for stays of one to four weeks as members of their family, taking all meals and enjoying all family activities. They do so, according to the Federation, to enjoy a cross-cultural experience that also furthers the cause of world peace.

To apply for a foreign homestay, adults should contact **Federation EIL, P.O. Box 595, Putney, VT 05346 phone (802/387-4210)**, advising the dates and length of stay you desire, and the preferred country. Federation organizations accepting U.S. adults are in 5 European nations, 5 Latin American republics, and 8 countries in Asia and the South Pacific. Each sets its own policies and conditions. Some permit participation by people of any age, while others stipulate ages 18 to 60; others, 17 to 50, 18 to 40, and so on. Some print their own descriptive literature on adult homestays, which the Federation office will pass on to you.

On a long-term homestay abroad.
Courtesy Federation of National Representatives of the Experiment in International Living, photo by Kim Luce.

A consciousness-changing homestay abroad. *Courtesy Elderhostel, photo by Nanci Leitch/The Experiment.*

instead of being content with 'doing' us, you want to make an effort at understanding us. . . . We also presume you are free of Western misconceptions about our country, [including] those of Oriental splendor (or squalor, as the case may be) . . . and whatnot."

In most countries, the homestay is offered in locations remote from tourist-filled capital cities; you cannot choose New Delhi, but rather Hyderabad, or Madras, or Varanasi; not Tokyo, but Nagoya, or Kagoshima, or Niigata. You write a "Dear Family" letter in advance of arrival, bring a token gift, and thereafter share the home as a relative would, conversing, relating experiences, enjoying cross-cultural learning.

Bear in mind that the experience is wholly unlike the free two-night or three-night stays available from the Servas organization (11 John St., New York City) as part of a broad, city-hopping tour; here, the stay is a sustained one, and the major—if not the sole—purpose of the overseas trip. The experience is also wholly unlike that of a bed-and-breakfast stay in a foreign guesthouse or pension; the latter is often just that—bed and breakfast—in a structure usually run by a commercial entrepreneur grown jaded by overexposure to a constant daily volume of foreign guests.

While the Federation office arranges the homestay, participants make their own travel arrangements. Generally, you will be met by your hosts at the railroad station of their town or city.

Although most host families receive either nothing, or at best a small sum, for your stay with them, each national organization imposes a charge designed to offset the considerable expense of administering the program (and including the small fee to the hosts). Charges vary from country to country, but generally average $475 for a two-week stay by one person, $700 to $800 for a two-week stay by two people, with small additional sums for extra weeks and slight reductions for a one-week stay. New Zealand, Germany, and Turkey are among the cheapest nations for a Federation homestay.

> "**A**s a tourist, you see the world through your own eyes; as a homestay guest, you see things through their eyes, and you are never the same again."

Each such country publishes an explanatory leaflet, and one of them is especially appealing: "We are all the happier to receive you," it says, "because you do not come as the ubiquitous tourist, and

"It's unique," said a professor of English whom I interviewed, "a remarkable welcome." He had arranged a Mexican homestay through Federation "to see what life was like within the culture and not as an outside observer. I experienced viewpoints and dealt with people in a way that would have been impossible through traditional tourism."

"The whole community accepted us," said a middle-aged couple who had enjoyed a three-week homestay in Cesme, Turkey, arranged by the Federation. "They shared everything and answered every question we put to them."

The Federation also cooperates with the well-known Elderhostel organization to provide Americans over the age of 60 with a one-week homestay program abroad, but this time sandwiched between two weeks of group travel (and classroom instruction) in the same overseas area. For details, contact **Elderhostel Homestays** at the Elderhostel headquarters in Boston (see elsewhere in this book).

But simply to enjoy a remarkably inexpensive individual homestay of one to four weeks, write to the Putney, Vermont, address given elsewhere in this essay. That's the first step of a cerebral travel adventure designed to observe a different system of values and beliefs; to feel part of a family abroad, not simply a tourist; to become directly involved in the community life of another culture; to acquire ease in a foreign language (though English is often spoken); to form an enduring international friendship.

How many of us ever have such an opportunity?

Join a "Hospitality Exchange" and Stay for Free Whenever You Travel

It's the Most Logical Idea in All of Travel, and Increasingly Utilized by a Broad Range of People

In theory, at least, it's a simple idea. We all have spare rooms, spare beds, a cot or a couch. Why not make them available to congenial people when they travel to your home city, in exchange for their doing the same for you upon a visit to their home city—or to the city of another congenial person?

Unlike a "vacation exchange," which involves a meticulously scheduled, simultaneous swapping of homes or apartments, the "hospitality exchange" is a far more casual facility, available at any time. On the eve of a trip, members—in the usual instance—consult a directory of other members, and then phone or write to learn if they can be accommodated. The others—the hosts—do the same when it's their time to travel.

Each is received in another's home as a relative would be, either for free, or at most for a simple reimbursement of out-of-pocket expenses.

Sensible? Logical? It's more than that. It's like a perfect world, this cooperation among people, like enjoying an extended family all over the world.

But there's a problem: the considerable amount of time required of an organizer. The practice involves, at least, the periodic publication and distribution of a members' directory, sometimes even direct assistance from the central organization in making reservations. Because membership fees must be kept modest, and no one earns a living from them, the idealistic founders of many a "hospitality exchange" have eventually been forced by hard reality to give up the effort.

That's what happened in 1986 to Tom Lynn's "Travelers Directory," a 27-year-old, nationwide "hospitality exchange" that was both the "giant" (several hundred members) and pioneer in the field.

But five other groups continue to carry the torch, and deserve our attention. Each caters to a different type of American:

The Hospitality Exchange of Helena, Montana, is the direct successor to the Travelers Directory, a five-year-old project by several of the latter's members to perpetuate its membership list, policies, and ideals. About half the current 400 hosts are over the age of 40; the other half tend to be young, enthusiastic and low-income, with some stressing that they are able to offer only floor space (presumably for sleeping bags) to would-be guests (picture a "personals ad" in New York's *Village Voice,* and you have an image of some members). "They come from all income brackets and all occupations, but share one ideal: an enthusiasm

for travel and travelers," says founder Joy Lily. As potential hosts, members all retain the right to say no to a prospective stay; "but if they always say no," says Ms. Lily, "we phone and ask what's the problem." Bookings are made via a twice-yearly directory sent to all members, but only persons willing to appear in it are entitled to receive a copy. Membership: $15 a year, which brings you an immediate March edition of over 150 members (again, only if you're willing to be listed in it). For an application form, contact: **The Hospitality Exchange, 704 Birch Street, Helena, MT 59601, phone 406/449-2103.**

Unlike the "vacation exchange," which involves a meticulously scheduled, simultaneous swapping of homes or apartments, the "hospitality exchange" is a far more casual facility, available at any time.

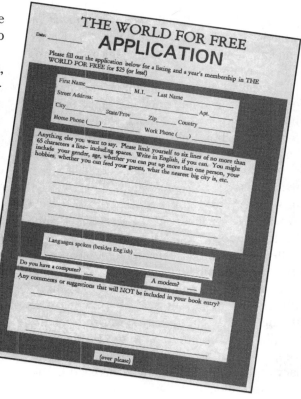

The World for Free. *Courtesy The World for Free/Seidboard World Enterprises.*

The World For Free, of New York, is another long-established exchange, and the possessor of 300 names and addresses, of which nearly half are found in Europe, including Eastern Europe (Poland especially), half in the U.S., and one apiece in Australia, Peru, Kenya, and Japan. Founded by a former musician, and thus partly oriented to creative people in the arts, it uses a biannual directory to convey offers of hospitality. Sample listings: "We are a politically sensitive collective of artists and writers living on the top floor of an old Chicago department store, where we have a gallery/performance space, studios, and living areas. We have futons, couches, and hammocks for four people and floor space for a small army. We don't get to travel much, so we appreciate the world coming to our house."

Five groups carry the torch, alerting the rest of us to offers of hospitality.

"San Francisco: Middle-aged woman with a wide variety of interests limited only by a slight physical handicap. Small guestroom and cat, on a hill in San Francisco, love to travel in France and Italy, especially enjoy company in the house, though I'll leave them on their own a lot . . . "

"Lincoln, England: I live together with three other people and four cats, in a small terraced house on a quiet street in a town famous only for its cathedral. But there are friendly people and nice pubs. We are vegetarians, dancers, musicians, artists, TV watchers, and apart from that, teachers . . . " Membership: $25 a year. Contact: **The World for Free, c/o Seidboard World Enterprises, P.O. Box 137, Prince Street Station, New York, NY 10012,** or—better yet—send an e-mail communication to: **mykel@wps.com,** or a fax to **212/979-8167.**

Evergreen Bed and Breakfast Club, of Dixon, Illinois, limits its services to persons over the age of 50—the theory being that mature people prefer accommodating other mature people in their homes. A 1,000-member subsidiary of the powerful American Bed and Breakfast Association, it charges $44 a year for single membership, $50 for a couple, for which members receive a yearly directory (in which they also must be listed) and the right to enjoy the hospitality of other members for a fee of $10 a night for a single room, $15 a night for a twin. Considering that the charge includes a full American breakfast, these must be the lowest bed-and-breakfast rates in the world. Why the fee at all? Club officials think that the $10 and $15, in addition to offsetting out-of-pocket costs, add a businesslike quality to normal attitudes of hospitality. Enclose a self-addressed, stamped envelope in contacting: **Evergreen Bed and Breakfast Club, 404 N. Galena, L20, Dixon, IL 61021, or phone 815/288-8207 or 800/374-9392 on weekdays between 3 and 6pm.**

Globetrotters, of London, is a worldwide organization of largely young, but always-intrepid and usually impecunious travelers—the kind that hitchhike across Emerging World countries, sleeping in village huts and cadging meals; an "anemic wallet" is actually cited as a prerequisite for membership. Membership fees of $14 per year, $24 for two years, enable you to receive the group's six-times-a-year newsletter, "The Globe," and the "Globetrotters Directory" listing names, addresses, ages, and travel experience of members, as well as purely optional offers by them of free accommodations. Because a great many members do, in fact, make such offers of lodging (in spare beds or cots of their living rooms or dens), the Directory is a rich source of free travel opportunities, although not primarily designed as such. Contact: **Globetrotters Club, c/o BCM Roving, London WC1N 3XX, England.**

And finally, there's *Servas,* of New York City, similar to a "hospitality exchange," but not really so, because members are entitled to receive hospitality without being obligated to provide it; as a Servas member, you can be a "taker," not a "giver," all because thousands of other Servas members around the world are willing to put you up without expecting anything in return; they do so because they enjoy having foreigners in their homes and because they believe the activity furthers the cause of world peace. Applicants pay a fee of $55 and are then screened for membership by a Servas interviewer in their locality; being accepted for membership, they are then entitled, on the eve of a trip, to receive the names and addresses of hosts in the cities to which they will be traveling. The normal stay with a Servas host is three days and two nights, which may be extended at the discretion of the host. Contact: **U.S. Servas Committee, 11 John Street, Suite 706, New York, NY 10038 (phone 212/267-0252).**

I haven't described "Mennonite Your Way" because the church-sponsored hospitality exchange of that name, with several hundred members, is a rather restricted organization anxious to confine its services to intensely religious Christians. It shuns publicity, and should be approached, if at all, through your local Mennonite congregation.

But all the rest are anxious to grow, anxious to serve. By simply providing occasional hospitality to their members—an enriching experience—you can then receive hospitality from their members, traveling cheaper and better.

Bed-and-Breakfast in a Private U.S. Home

The Use of "RSOs"

Has Now Become the

Key to Finding a

Proper "B&B"

Clint Eastwood's Carmel, California, has banned them altogether. So has trendy Santa Fe. The once-burgeoning bed-and-breakfast industry—a source of livelihood for more than 20,000 American households—is currently beleaguered with threats from zoning officials, angry hoteliers, and frightened neighbors of the B&B proprietors.

To make things worse, numerous Americans are badmouthing these unpretentious, overnight lodgings, claiming them to be more expensive, on occasion, than comparable hotels.

What has happened to the B & B movement? In my view, simple growing pains, basic misunderstandings, and nothing more. An activity less than 20 years old (for all practical purposes) is moving into maturity, achieving importance, and setting off understandable—if flawed—reactions.

The B&B Boom

Although people from time immemorial have been renting spare rooms in their homes to transient visitors, the activity came of age in the United States only with the creation of large-scale "reservations service organizations" (RSOs) in the late 1970s. Such early RSOs as Bed-and-Breakfast Rocky Mountains, Bed-and-Breakfast Nebraska, Bed-and-Breakfast Philadelphia, and scores more provided the marketing efforts and all-day telephone confirmations in their respective cities, states, or regions that no individual B&B house could afford to supply on its own.

An explosion in the use of B&Bs soon followed. The cost-conscious public, on arrival in a large city, had only to look under "B" in the telephone book to find the area-wide reservations service that could recommend any number of B&Bs and then confirm space at them.

To aid matters more, various telephone companies soon created a "bed-and-breakfast" category in the *Yellow Pages,* enabling travelers to find those few ornery RSO services whose names did not begin with "B": Sweet Dreams and Toast, Urban Ventures, Pinellas County Bed-and-Breakfast, etc.

Suddenly, the public had a surefire means of always uncovering a nearby B&B. But more important, they were able at last to deal only with homes that had been prescreened for suitability by a larger organization.

The single greatest dread of the traveler—arriving at an improper lodging, to be met by an unshaven and bleary-eyed proprietor—was overcome, and Americans by the tens of thousands began flocking to guest-accepting homes confirmed and vouched-for by a regional "reservations service organization."

The Negative Reaction

And then the reaction set in.

First from the hotel industry. Whether America's commercial innkeepers are behind the banning of B&Bs in Carmel and Santa Fe is hard to determine. But there are suspicions of their part in drafting fire regulations that impose unreasonable burdens (in my opinion) on the

B&B homes provide us with a refreshing and cheaper alternative to the stale and increasingly standard hotel.

bed-and-breakfast industry. A recently enacted New York State fire ordinance (admittedly, the nation's most stringent) requires elaborate sprinklers, expensive extra stairs, and special fire doors of any establishment housing more than four paying visitors on a habitual basis. The application of such rules to an easily evacuated, one-story ranch house or simple two-story home seems a bit much.

Other attempts to put B&Bs out of business have focused on residential zoning laws that forbid the taking of "boarders." But most courts have responded that the boarder ban was meant to refer to guests who were full-time residents of the city, not transient visitors, and that other significant differences also made the rules inapplicable.

Such zoning fights—the disputed interpretation of various vague prohibitions against commercial activity—are obviously the result of fears that a steady stream of B&B visitors will cheapen a residential neighborhood, attracting motor vans, backpackers, impecunious wanderers, and the like to an area of quiet homes.

As sensitive as we all might be to such concerns, there seems no evidence at all to support the prediction. B&B houses have no signs outside, nor are they open to walk-in members of the public—as in a hotel—but only to specific individuals who have made reservations in advance. Far from harming a community, experience shows that a thriving bed-and-breakfast industry attracts the best sort of additional tourism: sensitive and reasonably well-financed travelers who prefer the charm of a private home to an impersonal hotel or flashy motel. It brings considerable extra income, even prosperity, to the areas in which those homes are located.

Why You're Not Seeking a B&B Inn

A problem of equal weight has been the adverse reactions of some travelers to the rates charged by B & B "inns," which are frequently higher than in a hotel. Confusing a B & B inn with a B & B house, such disgruntled guests have proceeded to damn the entire movement. It is important that, somehow, both the B & B proprietors and the writers of B & B guidebooks adopt a proper semantic distinction between B & Bs that are inns and those that are homes.

A B & B inn is a multiroom structure wholly devoted to transient visitors. It is often a place of exquisite decor, down comforters, punctilious attentions, and cinnamon croissants (or strawberry-flavored quiche) for breakfast. Its prices are, often justifiably, higher than those of hotels.

By contrast, a B & B home is that of a normal, private family that has simply decided to supplement its income by set-

Confusing a B&B inn with a B&B house, disgruntled guests have proceeded to damn the entire movement.

ting aside one or two spare rooms—rarely more—for occasional paying guests. The family does not derive its entire income from that activity, but simply an extra $3,000 to $6,000 a year—the average earnings cited by most reports on the B & B industry (supplemented by the family's frequent ability to write off a portion of its home expenses or home purchase price on their taxes).

Places that are B & B houses as opposed to B & B inns continue to charge 40% to 50% less than comparable hotels all over the country. Yet because they are confused with B & B inns, they are suspected of gouging. The industry needs different names for different categories.

Becoming a B&B Host

What should someone do who is tempted to enter the bed-and-breakfast field? If you, for instance, should have a spare room or two in your attractive and well-located home, should you simply phone up the nearest "reservations service organization" forthwith (they're listed in the *Yellow Pages* under "Bed and Breakfast Accommodations") and ask them to list you? (The RSO fee is usually 20% to 30% of the sums they generate for you.)

Greater deliberation is called for. If you live in a large city, check first to learn whether a local "urban independent night school" (a Learning Annex, Discovery Center, Open University, or some such) is offering a one-night course in "How to Start a Bed-and-Breakfast Business." There you'll learn of additional pitfalls in addition to prospects.

Or else order a copy of one of the several books on the subject, such as *Open Your Own Bed & Breakfast* by Barbara Notarius and Gail Brewer (New York: John Wiley & Sons; $14.95). Its chapters ("Is It for You?," "Financial Considerations," "Advertising," "Working with a Reservations Service," etc.) deal with just about every question you may have.

Ms. Notarius, herself a successful B & B host, has recently formed a consulting service that operates periodic one-day seminars around the country ($175) for would-be hosts of B & Bs, and also provides personal, one-on-one advice to persons contemplating the more serious step of opening a multiroom B & B inn. Contact **Barbara Notarius, Alexander Hamilton House, 49 Van Wyck Street, Croton-on-Hudson, NY 10520 (phone 914/271-6737).**

Or for a more intensive look at B & B inns, not homes, order *So . . . You Want to Be an Innkeeper* ($14.95 through the mail from **Professional Association of Innkeepers International, P.O. Box 90710, Santa Barbara, CA 93190 (phone 805/569-1853 or fax 805/682-1016)**. The several authors of this book also issue an innkeeping newsletter and operate three-day workshops ($395) twice a year for people aspiring to enter the field. For information on both, write to the address above. Alternative book, alternative seminars: Carl Glassman's "How to Start and Run Your Own B & B" (for persons aspiring to let from 2 to 10 rooms), $14.95 from Stockpole Books, 800/732-3669; Glassman's own seminars and consultancies run $450 for one person, $500 for two, including overnight accommodations (call his "Inn School" in New Hope, PA, at 215/862-2570 or 2520). For slightly more expensive seminars, but scheduled more frequently and in more numerous and scattered locations, contact Oates & Bredfeldt, 802/254-5931, or fax 802/254-3221.

In a B&B home, the family does not derive its entire income from that activity.

A wise man once said that Hell consisted of being condemned to stay, each night into eternity, in a different Holiday Inn. Through the judicious use of B & Bs, that need not be your fate.

They provide us with a refreshing and cheaper alternative to the stale and increasingly standard hotel.

"Swapping Homes" (or Apartments)—And Thus Staying for Free

"You Stay in My House, While I Stay in Yours"

I t's called a "Vacation Exchange," and it's not the same as the "Hospitality Exchange" we discussed earlier in this chapter. On the latter, you stay as a guest in someone's home, while they remain in residence; you sleep in a spare room or on a cot; you meet your hosts, have breakfast with them, often socialize with them. And you are more or less expected (but not required) to provide hospitality in your own home or apartment at some later date, maybe (but not necessarily) to the actual person who hosted you.

By contrast, a "Vacation Exchange" involves a *simultaneous* swap or exchange of apartments or homes; you stay in their home or apartment while they stay in yours, all during the identical period of your respective vacations. You rarely meet the people whose home or apartment you're using, because you've passed them in mid-air, so to speak, when you began your vacation. On that carefully scheduled date, you flew to their home city, while they flew to yours.

The vacation exchange is also a much more frequent travel activity, supporting a number of fairly large exchange organizations. Why? Because, when all is said and done, it's the single most logical, reasonable, sensible, indeed brilliant, method of vacationing in travel today. Instead of leaving your home or apartment empty and unused during the time of your vacation, you derive a benefit from it, you treat it as an asset. You "trade" it temporarily for an overseas home or apartment of equivalent quality, eliminating all costs of lodgings from your vacation budget.

You trade other assets, as well, like your friends. You give to your exchangee the names of friends who might be willing to have them over for a drink, or come to their aid in case of problems. They do the same for you in their city. Often you permit them to use your car while you're away, in exchange for them permitting you to use their car while you stay in their home or apartment. Through an exchange of correspondence, you make the necessary arrangements—sometimes you tell them that the key will be found under the flower pot at the front door—and on the appointed day, you set off to claim your exchange. As mentioned before, they fly to your home in the U.S., while you fly to theirs in Barcelona, the south of France, London, Bangkok, or wherever. Neither of you has a penny of accommodations expenses. But more important, you live like a resident, not a tourist, in the city you've chosen. You enjoy an incomparable experience utterly unavailable to the standard tourist. In fact, you're no longer a tourist at all, but a traveler.

English house on a vacation exchange. *Courtesy Landfair Home Exchange Club.*

I've been on two vacation exchanges myself, have spoken with dozens of people who have also done so, and frankly, I've never heard a critical word about the experience, nor enjoyed anything other than an excellent stay myself. And bear in mind: each house or apartment serves as a "hostage" for the proper maintenance and upkeep of the other; you take awfully good care of the apartment or home in which you're staying, because you're so very anxious that they're exhibiting a similar attitude toward yours.

> **It's the single most logical, reasonable, sensible, indeed brilliant, method of vacationing in travel today.**

Some smart travelers find vacation exchanges on their own; they arrange to have a friend overseas post a notice for them on various bulletin boards, or simply ask them to spread the word. Most do it through a vacation exchange service or club, of which at least a half-dozen are active at any one time.

The vacation exchange clubs charge you a fee for including a notice—a one-paragraph description of your home or apartment, perhaps a photo of it, an indication of when you'd like to take your vacation and thus engage in an exchange—in a directory containing many hundreds of such notices, which is then sent to members around the world. All through the cold winter months,

you sit at home turning the pages of the directory and dreaming about where you'd like to stay in spring, summer, or fall, and when you've spotted a likely candidate, you write to them and propose a vacation exchange. The arrangements are then made through an exchange of correspondence.

The vacation exchange was the brainchild 30 years ago of a New York City high school teacher named Ostroff, who had a large family and therefore a difficult time finding an affordable summer vacation location. It then occurred to him that other high school teachers across the country might be in the same fix, and he sent a round-robin letter to several hundred of them, suggesting that they all swap apartments or homes for the summer. Someone living in Billings, Montana, might live in his apartment in New York, while he and his family lived in their apartment in Billings. Thus was born the first Vacation Exchange Club (bearing that title), which eventually—through two changes in ownership—came to be located in Key West, Florida.

Each house or apartment serves as a "hostage" for the proper upkeep of the other.

Specially for this edition of *The New World of Travel,* I've again phoned the several major vacation exchange clubs to learn their current conditions, prices, and policies.

Vacation Exchange Club (P.O.B. 650, Key West, Florida 33041, 800/638-3841) is the direct successor to the original vacation exchange club; it charges $65 a year for membership, for which you get five catalogs—a main one and four supplements published throughout the year. Specialty: Europe. Average length of each exchange: a month. If you'd like a free "information pac" before committing, simply call the above number and leave your name and address on the firm's answering machine. VEC is a big one, and seems the picture of efficiency in dealing with its members.

Intervac U.S. (P.O.B. 590504, San Francisco, California 94159, 800/756-HOME or 415/435-3497), of which Lori Horne is founder and co-owner, also charges $65 a year ($60 for seniors over 62), plus $13 for postage and handling. She sends out three directories a year, starting with the first, 544-page version on December 15. U.S. listings account for 40% of each directory, followed by homes or apartments in France, Great Britain, Spain, Germany, Sweden, Italy, Netherlands, Denmark, the Czech Republic, Poland, Japan, and Mexico—in that order. And Mrs. Horne is currently soliciting listings for Australia and New Zealand, and hopes to have some in the next book. "My husband and children and I have exchanged 14 times in Europe," she adds, as proof of her experience in doing so.

Trading Homes International (P.O.B. 787, Hermosa Beach, California 90254, 800/877-8723) also asks $65 a year, this time for three books a year of approximately 3,000 listings apiece. Locations covered include South Africa, both Eastern and Western Europe, the Caribbean, the U.S., Canada, Australia, and New Zealand. Owner Judy Saavedra points out that most of her members are retirees who are always exchanging and therefore rarely at home; "they're going all the time." And what does she do for her own vacations? She "exchanges." Trading Homes belongs to the International Home Exchange (as does Landfair, below), from which it obtains at least 2,000 of its potential exchangees.

Worldwide Home Exchange Club (806 Brantford Avenue, Silver Spring, Maryland 20904, 301/680-8950) represents the exchange club of the same name located at 58 Hans Crescent in London, England. Their charge: $29 a year, but they suggest that you pay an additional $7 for airmail, to get an immediate copy of their first directory (which comes out immediately after January 1) and supplementary edition (April), which are printed and sent from London. Fifteen hundred listings are offered, most of homes and apartments for exchange in Britain, with other listings from the U.S., Canada, Japan, Australia, New Zealand, and even a few from Africa and South America.

The Invented City (41 Sutter Street, Suite 1090, San Francisco, CA 94104, phone 800/788-CITY or 415/673-0347, or fax 415/673-6909): A relatively new firm started by 36-year-old Glenn London who, with his M.A. in library science, works in the day as a library researcher. "I felt I could create a more enjoyable, creative directory, using natural language and not a coding system. My listings are so designed that you can decide when and why you wish to visit a particular destination." His charge: $50 a year, for which you appear in one directory, but immediately receive the previous three catalogues upon joining. You also receive the following two directories, for a total of six (each runs 75 to 150 pages). His listings are strongest in Canada and the United States, then Britain, Scandinavia, Switzerland, and Australia.

Landfair Home (54 Landfair Crescent, Scarborough, Ontario, Canada M1J3A7 (phone 416/431-4493) or Landfair Home (6432 Alemendra Street, Fort Pierce, Florida 34951 (407/467-0634): In business for five years now, with a 3,000-member listing of potential exchangees in Australia, Canada, New Zealand, the U.S., Egypt, Zimbabwe, a scattering of homes in Asia, and all the countries of Europe. Their charge is $50 a year for their catalogs, in addition to several free pamphlets of hints about exchanges, including sample letters, regret letters, tips on travel and tipping, advice on who pays for what, and how to prepare for your guests. They also take great pains to include fax numbers to speed up the process of correspondence between members. One official told me about a Canadian/French exchange, on which the French guests accidentally damaged the air conditioner of their hosts, and left a note saying they would pay for a new one. The Canadians never expected to hear more of the matter, and were stunned when they received a check for triple the amount an air conditioner would cost in Canada.

But Is It Safe? Reliable?

How can you know that the home or apartments you'll be receiving will be the equivalent of yours? How can you protect yourself against the urge to exaggerate the accommodation by the foreign residents who will be describing their homes or apartments in the directories of the vacation exchange organizations?

Because those questions have been posed by a great many readers, I put them to Judy Saavedra, president of Trading Homes International (see above). She responded, in effect, as follows:

The people who do receive a misdescribed home of poor quality are those who haven't done their homework. It's important to engage in more than one exchange of correspondence, even phone the person overseas, to confirm the exact nature of their home or apartment, and their own personal background, their occupation, and the like. You request photos; you may even request a video of the home in question, and present them with a video of yours. About half the persons who engage in vacation exchanges have done so before; therefore, ask them for the names, addresses, and numbers of other Americans who have stayed in their homes, so that you can seek an endorsement from them. Ask them, perhaps, to supply you with other references. By putting the proper questions, by learning more about the exchangee than you would discover from the short listing in the directory, you can almost always assure yourself that you are exchanging with a reliable person.

Ms. Saavedra states that she rarely receives complaints from her club members, and that the overwhelming majority of vacation exchanges are conducted to the entire satisfaction of both parties. And meantime, this mode of travel remains, in my firm opinion, the most sensible, logical, and effective means of enjoying a rewarding (and nearly cost-free) vacation.

VI

New and Cheaper Lodgings, for People Weary of Standard Hotels

Removing the "Youth" from "Youth Hostels"

A Revolution Has Altered the Character of These Inexpensive Lodgings, Making Them Available to Mature Adventurers of Every Age

It was a mixed-up scene, to say the least. But strangely affecting. In a corner of the lounge, a middle-aged pianist sat riffling off a Schubert cadenza while a teenage music-lover turned the pages of her sheet music. At a chessboard nearby, two college students stared at their rooks and knights while a white-haired senior offered occasional advice. And at an overstuffed couch under a notice-filled bulletin board, several eager young people sought travel advice from a couple in their forties.

If you were now to learn that this jumbling of the generations—young with old, newly retired with newly wed—was occurring not in a school, but in a youth hostel, you'd probably be startled. Unknown as yet to the vast majority of American travelers, every youth hostel organization in the world (other than in the German state of Bavaria) has eliminated the maximum-age limitation on youth-hostel membership or the right to use youth-hostel facilities. A small but growing population of every age and condition—married and single, elderly, middle-aged, baby boomer, yuppie, and preppie—is today flocking to make use of the cheapest lodgings and most dynamic travel facilities on earth.

What Is a Youth Hostel?

And what are these structures that now accept "young people of all ages"—to use a newly coined slogan of the hostels? They range from ancient castles to modern farmhouses, from Buddhist temples to converted water mills, from rambling Victorian mansions to four-masted sailing ships to glass-walled high-rises in the center of great cities—some 5,000 hostels in all (in 74 different countries), of which 160 are here in the United States. While the beds they offer are often double-decker cots in privacy-lacking dormitories (but segregated by sex, with men in one wing, women in another), their facilities are otherwise comfortable and clean, closely supervised by "hostel parents," social, cheery, priced in pennies—and now multigenerational in clientele, as I was recently able quite personally to confirm.

Whether married or single, elderly, middle-aged, or baby-boomer, yuppie or preppie, you may now make use of the cheapest accommodations on earth.

The scene that began this essay was one I witnessed recently in the public areas of the Washington, D.C., youth hostel short blocks from the White House. I had arrived in Washington on a Friday afternoon, without reservations, never dreaming that every hotel in town would be sold out. They were. Shaken and dismayed, but vaguely aware of the revolution in youth-hostel policies, I rushed from the Capitol Hilton (where I had just been turned down) to the Capitol

Hostel, if it could be called that. And moments later I was ensconced in a quite decent (if somewhat dreary) single room at the grand rate of $29 a night, tax included. I could have stayed in the dorms for only $12 a night.

If the locale had been Europe, Mexico, or the Far East instead of Washington, D.C., I could have enjoyed similar facilities for as little as $7, $8, or $9 a night, sometimes with breakfast included. Only in the United States, and only in the nation's capital at that, do youth-hostel prices rise to the princely levels I encountered that night. Almost everywhere else they amount to a near-negligible expense, permitting seniors to enjoy a major extension of their time spent on travels.

Prior to retirement most of those seniors had money but no time. Now they have time but less money. The ability to use $8-per-person hostels instead of $50-per-person hotels suddenly enables mature citizens—even those on Social Security—to enjoy the same three-month stays abroad that many younger Americans experience on their summer vacations. How many retired Americans could undertake trips of that length if they were compelled to pay normal hotel rates on each and every night?

The "Senior" Revolution

What brought about this revolution? Some hostelers point to the laws against age discrimination enacted in numerous enlightened countries. Some mention the growing realization by youth-hostel organizations of their need for income and patronage in those non-summer months of the year when young people are in school and unable to use hostels. Still others suggest that the lowering of age bars, occurring gradually in different countries, came about when hostel-loving "baby boomers" approached their middle years and insisted on the right to continue using hostel accommodations. "Hosteling gets into your blood and you can't get rid of it," say Hal and Glenda Wennberg of central Maryland, who met at a hostel in 1946 and soon were husband and wife. Though the American youth-hostel organization has always, in theory, been open to people of all ages (unlike its European counterparts), it is only recently that youth hostels have openly advertised the right of seniors to join and participate. In Europe, formal decisions were required, and taken, to accomplish the same goal.

"The reason we use hostels," says an elderly hosteler and former college lecturer from Nebraska, Jane Holden, "is because hosteling is an attitude, not simply a source of cheap accommodations for penniless young people. That attitude never changes. To me, the finest moments of life are in meeting people from different countries and backgrounds, and extending friendship to them. Even if it means trading off a bit of comfort and privacy."

Do mature hostelers find it difficult to mix with members 40 years younger than they? "Not at all," say Edwin and Jeanne Erlanger, hostelers since the mid-1950s. "Once people work together in the kitchen or begin discussing that day's news, the barriers just fade away. Wherever it is—Japan, Austria, Mexico—the generations have far more in common than you'd think." One prominent San Francisco member of Golden Gate Youth Hostels, the sassy, 74-year-old Miriam Blaustein, is also a leading activist in the highly political Gray Panthers. "I am still as youthful mentally as I ever was!" she states. "But I know my limits. I will not exceed them, nor will I impede what the younger people are doing. My work in youth hostels is part of a broader effort against 'ageism.'"

When seniors first began using youth hostels in heavy numbers, some youth-hostel "parents" (managers) persisted in giving preference in reservations to young members; that's now ended, says an official of American Youth Hostels, Inc., and he has never received a single complaint of age discrimination. Other mature guests were a bit nonplussed by the dormitories assigned to them, although many soon found that hostel managements were at pains to provide them with such private rooms as existed. Still another AYH executive points out that the trend in youth-hostel construction around the world is to rooms housing no more than four or five people, and occasionally to the standard twin-bedded or single-room variety.

They range from ancient castles to modern farmhouses, from Buddhist temples to converted water mills, from rambling Victorian mansions to four-masted sailing ships.

An often-heard proposal is formally to eliminate the word "youth" from the organization's title. Though that idea was rejected by the organization's board of directors, individual hostels have taken steps to do just that. In the Washington, D.C., structure, the word "Youth" in a large neon sign has been replaced by the word "International"—Washington International Hostel—and staff members inside patiently explain that the "youth" in the title of their sponsoring organization means "young in spirit" or "young in outlook," and not in chronological terms. As

Youth hostel on the Appalachian Trail. *Courtesy American Youth Hostels, photo by Toby B. Pyle.*

if the dream of Ponce de León were finally at hand, today's mature citizens find "eternal youth" in a youth hostel.

Enter Elderhostel

But now a caution. This newly acquired ability by mature and senior citizens to make use of youth hostels should not be confused with a wholly separate program of study tours called Elderhostel. Limited to people over the age of 60 (but open as well to their spouses of any age), "Elderhostel weeks" are conducted by the Elderhostel organization of Boston, Massachusetts, at more than 1,500 universities and other educational institutions in the U.S. and abroad. Domestically, Elderhostel programs last for one week and cost $320 per person, plus the cost of transportation to the site. Internationally, Elderhostel programs are usually of three weeks' duration—a week apiece in each of three foreign centers—and average $3,000 per person, including air fare. In each case participants stay in unused or temporarily vacated university residence halls or youth hostels, receive all three meals each day, and attend at least four-and-a-half hours a day of classroom instruction.

What sort of instruction? The courses range from "Modern Italian History" to theories of Albert Einstein to "The Architecture of Jerusalem"—to any topic at all, in fact, so long as that subject does not deal with problems of aging or other issues uniquely affecting senior citizens. The goal of Elderhostel is to permit senior citizens to remain vital and alive to current concerns, and the formula has proved immensely popular. Reacting to course announcements in Elderhostel's quarterly free catalog (supplemented by intermittent newsletters), nearly 300,000 people over age 60 will pursue such instruction in 1996. That catalog is today stocked in most public libraries, but can also be obtained by contacting **Elderhostel, 75 Federal St., Boston, MA 02110 (phone 617/426-7788)**.

Meanwhile, to simply stay at youth hostels regardless of your age, get a youth-hostel membership card from **Hosteling International-American Youth Hostels, 733 15th Street NW, Suite 840, Washington, D.C. 20005 (phone 202/783-6171)**, or a local youth hostel council in your own city, if one exists. Enclose $10 if you are 17 or under, $25 if you are between 18 and 54, $15 if you are 55 or older. You'll receive the card, and a manual listing youth-hostel facilities of the United States. For an additional $11.95 (plus $2 for postage and handling), you'll receive a similar but more extensive handbook of youth hostels in Europe and the Mediterranean area, and still another $10.95 (plus another $2 for postage and handling) will bring you the same for Africa, Asia, Australia, and New Zealand. And suddenly a brave new world of remarkably inexpensive lodgings becomes available to you, permitting almost constant travel—month after month—for an outlay that would barely secure two or three nights at the average hotel!

The Rise of the "Private Hostel"

A Hundred Converted Hotels Now Sell Lodgings by the Bed, Not the Room, to Respectable Adults

Like a shadowy presence, without ads or flashy signs, a hundred "private hostels" charging $10 to $17 a night have quietly emerged in America's largest cities. And while their amenities are not of the level of the nation's similarly priced budget motels—Red Roof Inns, Econotels, Motel 6s, and the like—they are not, like the latter, on the outskirts of town, along deadening highways, but in the very center: in the heart of San Francisco or New York, in downtown Los Angeles or near the Chicago Loop, at the harbor of Seattle or a block from the Greyhound Station in Tucson.

They emerged in apparent response to the lodging needs of cost-conscious European and Asian tourists now flooding into the United States. Sensing a profit, or simply wanting to be of aid, an unlikely mix of entrepreneurs and idealists began adopting one of three time-honored approaches toward solving a shortage of transient housing. They bought or leased bankrupt, shabby hotels, and quickly touched them up. They leased a floor or two of a standard modest hotel, and proclaimed the space a "hostel." Or they converted residential or specialized buildings—a winery, a rambling Victorian home—into public-accommodations use. Into the rooms of each such establishment they brought multiple beds (three or four beds per room in most cases, small dormitories of double-decker cots in others), for such is the key to hostel operation, and the secret of their ability to charge less. More beds are packed into a given space than in normal hotels, maintaining income while slashing rates.

Unlike the budget motels, private hostels are found not on the outskirts, along deadening highways, but in the very center.

When you stay at a "private hostel," just as at an official "youth hostel," you pay by the bed, not by the room. You stay, in the usual case, in a room with strangers of all ages (but of the same sex). Although, if you're traveling as a couple or group, you often occupy the room with people chosen only by yourself, that isn't guaranteed, and the opposite situation is often lauded by the visionary founders of some hostels. "We bring the traveler a new sociocultural experience," I was told by one hostel owner. "Sharing a room with tourists of other nations is a means of breaking down barriers."

I first learned of the new "private hostels" in the *Yellow Pages*. Looking for a hotel, I chanced upon a category called "hostels"; and as goosepimples slowly spread upon my arms, I awoke to the fact that the establishments listed were not the standard "youth hostels," but a new breed of budget lodgings. "Then felt I like some watcher of the skies," in Keats's phrase, "when a new planet swims into his ken."

I have now seen a half dozen private hostels and interviewed (by phone) the managers of others, and here is how they differ from the more familiar youth hostels:

Although both the youth hostels and the new private hostels accept people of all ages—the term "youth" in the title of the former is an increasing misnomer and anachronism—the private hostels tend to attract an older average age range and get fewer actual youths. The private hostels also have smaller rooms and fewer large dormitories, and place no more than three or four beds in their private rooms. That contrasts with the "pack-'em-in," dormitory-oriented philosophy of the youth hostels. "Our guests value the camaraderie of our public rooms and lounges," says one private hostel manager, "but they place a greater emphasis on privacy in their sleeping arrangements." Also, since most private hostels are in former hotels, their rooms are usually equipped with private baths—"private," that is, for the three or four people in that room—with fewer of the larger communal facilities found in youth hostels.

And since the age of the average guest in the private hostels is higher, the latter have fewer of the distinctive, youth-oriented operating policies of the youth hostels: fewer curfews and other forms of strict supervision.

The hundred or so private hostels consist of about 55 fully independent properties and two "chains": the **International Travelers Club ("Interclub"), headquartered at the Venice Beach Cotel, 25 Windward Ave., Venice, CA 90291 (phone 310/399-7649)**, and the **American Association of International Hostels (A.A.I.H.), headquartered at the Santa Fe International Hostel, 1412 Cerrillos Rd., Santa Fe, NM 87505 (phone 505/988-1153)**.

A.A.I.H. is a loose marketing organization of 36 independently owned hostels in roughly that many major cities, all using the term "international" in their titles—New Orleans International Hostel, Denver International Hostel, Miami

Beach International Hostel—despite the fact that most guests aren't "international" at all, but simply cost-conscious American travelers. The group is headed by a 20-year veteran of American Youth Hostels, who left that organization after acrimonious policy disputes. His new "international hostels" charge a youth hostel-like average of $10 to $12 per person for their occasional dormitories, up to $17.50 per person per night for their more numerous double, triple, or four-bedded rooms, and perpetuate a great many other youth hostel traditions: guests are "requested" (but not required) to perform a few light chores each day (making their own beds, sweeping up), rooms and floors are segregated by sex, and bus station-type lockers are frequently used for luggage and valuables.

Outstanding hostels in the A.A.I.H. chain: Key West, first and foremost (phone 305/296-5719); Orlando, Denver, Santa Fe, and (especially) Huntington Beach, California, the latter 40 minutes south of Los Angeles. Guests seem to feel less enthusiastic about the branches in downtown Los Angeles, San Francisco, and Portland (Oregon).

The "Ritz-Carltons" of the private hostels are those of the International Travelers Club. Indeed, some of these $15-a-night lodgings are so well endowed that they are classified by their sponsors not as "hostels" at all, but as "cotels"— "community hotels"—in which few rooms contain more than three beds. Yet like the others they normally rent by the bed, not the room, and go for $13 to $15 per person per night.

The unique creation of two young, international businessmen—Urs Jakob and Klaus Stölting—who had tired of traditional commerce, they are staffed by international volunteers, decorated in wild, eclectic fashion (wall murals, fishing nets, giant plants) to create a "sense of place," occupy period buildings in a number of instances, and adhere to highly liberal policies that encourage constant socializing and parties, which makes them—in the words of one guest— "a cross between a YMCA and a Club Med." The "club" currently consists of seven structures in the United States and Canada, and another six in Australia, New Zealand, Switzerland, and Kupang (Timor), Indonesia. Their ideal guest, according to Urs Jakob, is an around-the-world traveler taking six months or so for the trip. A former emphasis on West Coast locations (Los Angeles, San Francisco, Hawaii) has recently been balanced by the decision to open a branch ("the Gershwin") in New York.

The "cotels," with their notice-packed bulletin boards, paperback libraries, and eager amateur managers—each encouraged to let imagination soar—are all radically different in appearance. The International Travelers Club Cotel in Venice Beach, California, is the old (1901) St. Charles Hotel, a national landmark building that once hosted Charlie Chaplin. Musicians in its café were playing lively folk songs in the course of my own visit. The International Travelers Club

More beds are packed into a given space, maintaining income while slashing rates.

Cotel Globe in expensive San Francisco is a mix of hostel rooms (two double-decker beds, $15 per person) and hotel rooms ($29 per person double, $44 single), all with private bath and floors with green shag rugs and artfully done oil trims spattered by a volunteer on skateboard. In the less private International Travelers Club Hostel Waikiki, lobby furniture is from a Japanese sushi bar and ceilings are covered by bamboo shoots and beach mats.

At each of the club's hostels or cotels, and in sharp contrast to the "early-to-bed, early-to-rise" atmosphere of the official youth hostels, curfews are unknown and conversations go on late into the night. "People here are adults," says Jakob, "and expected to behave reasonably. We don't treat them as in an institution." Nor is the performance of house chores expected of guests. Perhaps because of that, a great many guests are in their forties and fifties (though most are 20 to 35), some European, some American, all seeking budget lodgings, but with a social atmosphere. To encourage patronage by "international travelers," some of the private hostels require even their American guests to check in with their passports.

For a list of leading A.A.I.H. or International Travelers Club hostels or cotels, either contact the organizations named above, or look in the *Yellow Pages* under "Hostels," keeping in mind that these "Poor Man's Hiltons" come and go with dizzying rapidity. A recent edition of the Manhattan *Yellow Pages* contained such listings, while the current edition—inexplicably—doesn't, despite the thriving operation of several hostels. Persevere.

The New World of Travel 1997

The lifeblood of the Arthur Frommer travel guides is the correspondence received from readers, commenting on the establishments recommended in the texts and recommending new establishments. Each such letter is carefully studied, and when a particular lead seems promising, it is followed up and personally checked.

It is hoped that *The New World of Travel* will receive similar assistance from its readers. A yearly publication, issued near the start of each year, *The New World of Travel* will constantly grow. And since much of its content relates to organizations that lack the means to market themselves properly, or come to the attention of a travel journalist, your help is invaluable in alerting me to the organizations—hospitality exchanges, alternative resorts, new travel clubs, and the like—that you have discovered.

If you become aware of a new travel organization, program, or development that deserves to be described in our next edition, *The New World of Travel 1997*, won't you please let me know about it? Send your letters to Arthur Frommer, *The New World of Travel*, 1841 Broadway, New York, NY 10023. All letters will be acknowledged, and all are warmly appreciated, in advance, by the author.

In a Housekeeping Van:
The Art of "Gypsying"

On No More Than Their Social Security Income, Some Americans Are Able to Keep Constantly Traveling

To all the standard forms of travel, add a new one: gypsying. It consists of staying constantly on the move—year after year, exploring multiple countries—but living on almost nothing (or, at best, on Social Security income).

And if that seems a pipe dream, adolescent and unreal, hold on, reserve judgment. Unending travel, by normal people, is the passionate theme of what may well become a minor travel classic, published several years back by John Muir, of Santa Fe, and distributed by W. W. Norton.

The book is *Gypsying After 40*. Its author, Robert W. Harris, is a middle-aged Santa Fe architect who discovered 18 years ago that he had unfinished goals, a passion to view the world, a yearning to return to fundamentals, and a deep concern about the pressured, money-focused nature of his life.

So he became a "gypsy."

Though he and his wife had few resources, their savings sufficed to buy a housekeeping van from a used-car dealer in London. In it, they learned that people can greatly control the level of their material needs (and thus their travel costs), reducing those wants in a drastic degree by simply making psychological adjustments. Living in sturdy but simple clothes, preparing their own meals in the van from foodstuffs purchased en route, using the same unpretentious vehicle for both accommodations and transportation, they learned to live as travelers for a fraction of the sum that others spend as tourists.

"Gypsying" consists of staying constantly on the move—year after year, exploring multiple countries—but living on almost nothing (or, at best, on Social Security income).

And were thus able to travel without cease.

Today they are in their 18th year of continual, "long-term" travel, crisscrossing nation after nation, month after month, on costs that average (independent of the earlier purchase price of the van) a remarkable $1,200 a month—the sum that many retired couples enjoy from Social Security alone. And the resulting character of their life, they believe, makes pitiful the structured, earthbound, higher-spending existence of the rest of us.

Apart from continual spiritual experiences that Harris lyrically describes—"When travel took command of my life, extraordinary events shook the core of my being"—he relearned as a "gypsy" to savor the most ordinary values, patterns, and events of life.

"Poetry and beauty became infinitely more important to us than security. . . . The arrival of dawn, the goings-on around us—insects moving,

animals grazing, farmers harvesting—became spectacles. . . . Rich curiosity and heightened awareness increased."

No more for them the tourist throngs and standard attractions: "The strong personal character and dignity of people as they live day-to-day became the focus of our travels. . . . The gypsy life afforded time to cavort with nature, dive into deep wells of reading, warm the fires of friendship, wrestle with meditations."

Most wondrous of all, he discovered, too, that multitudes of others were "gypsying" along the byways of Europe and North Africa, Mexico and the Far West: "Thousands of people make long-term travel their main mode of existence and awake each morning as if it were the shining first day of their lives."

How is it done? How, on a small retirement income, can one travel without let-up? *Gypsying After 40* prescribes a few simple rules:

• **The modest van:** Self-transportation is the key, not a resplendent, gas-guzzling motorhome, but a van converted inexpensively into living space, cheap to run, and so unpretentious as to offer no target to vandals or thieves. (In some cases, a live-in boat does the job.)

• **"Free camping":** You eschew, to the extent possible, the organized, pay-to-enter campgrounds, and simply park the van at night in legally permitted places: village greens, churchyards, even gravesites, public areas for pasturing sheep, on farms (after permission has been obtained), castle grounds, in city parks, at well-secured freight trucking areas in port cities, alongside marinas or historic ruins (where you tip the guards or invite them for a drink in the van).

"If you free-camp," writes Harris, "you do not need to have a specific destination in mind, nor a campground to reach before dark. You amble along, unhurried. . . . You savor each moment."

You also meet a better class of people, he implies, "a woman camping alone at interesting, scenic ruins, busily sketching . . . a large family stopping where they could swim, sun, and fish."

• **Rural settings:** You stay mainly in small towns or in farm locations, where you live for a quarter of the usual price; you dart daily into the big cities from your rural base, and return there at night.

• **Warm-weather countries:** You of course avoid the colder climes. You traverse the sights of northern Europe only in summer, the Mediterranean countries in spring and fall, North Africa (Morocco, especially) or Mexico in winter.

• **You slow down:** You avoid expense by careful deliberation, and by patience in securing the right air or sea fares.

• **And finally:** You avoid hotels, restaurants, and high-season tourist locations like the plague.

There is, of course, far more to gypsying than this; it is set forth in 250 closely reasoned pages, available today in most bookstores.

I met Robert Harris and his wife, Megan, at a television talk show on travel. He is a white-haired, white-bearded, ebullient elf of a man, glowing with life and vigor; she, a still-attractive matron-turned-gypsy, is blessed with a glamour undimmed by life in a van.

And what were they confiding to each other in the moments before the broadcast?

Their desire to return to the road.

> **"Thousands of people make long-term travel their main mode of existence and awake each morning as if it were the shining first day of their lives."**

At Home on the Road: The RV Life

The Range of Motorhome Options Has Greatly Increased Your Ability to Enjoy Meaningful, Low-cost Vacations in the U.S.A.

It's the opposite of chic; somewhat rustic and rough. Yet the fastest-growing means for vacationing in America is the recreational vehicle. And though I'd be drummed from high society for saying so, the people using them are the finest travelers our country has.

You meet them with increasing frequency. They can be your best friends who have just returned from a three-month trip through the national parks—in a shiny new motorhome—and claim it's the best thing they've ever done. They are your neighbors who have bought a trailer they're going to use to "winter" in a luxury RV resort of Florida. They are images of yourself as you daydream about getting away from it all, buying a recreational vehicle, and taking off to see the great outdoors, the sights of the Southwest, the scattered grandchildren across the land.

But how do you get started? Buying a recreational vehicle—an RV—is a major investment that can even go over the six-figure mark. Is it worth the outlay? Will you enjoy the lifestyle of the semi-nomad? Will you get restless and claustrophobic, or will you have the travel experience of a lifetime? A bit of analysis is in order:

The Vehicles Themselves

"RVs"—a generic term for a conveyance that combines transportation with living quarters—come in two varieties. They can be motorized (like motorhomes or van conversions) or towable units (like travel trailers, truck campers, and folding camp trailers).

The motorhomes, most popular among retired Americans, are built on or as part of a self-propelled vehicle chassis, with kitchen, sleeping, bathroom, and dining facilities all easily accessible to the driver's cab from the inside. They range from 18 to 33 feet in length, can sleep from two to eight people, and cost from $22,000 for "compacts" to $48,000 for larger types, with luxury-status models going way up, to $150,000 and more.

Conversions are cheaper (but smaller). These are vans, originally manufactured by an automaker, that have been modified for recreation purposes through the installation of side windows, carpeting, paneling, custom seats and sofas, and assorted accessories. They can sleep from two to four people, and sell for an average of $19,000.

Travel trailers are hard-sided units designed to be towed by an auto, van, or pickup truck, and can be unhitched from the tow vehicle. They sleep four to eight people, and provide such comforts as kitchen, toilet, sleeping, dining, and living facilities, electric and water systems, and modern appliances. Models range from $5,000 to $36,000, depending on size and features.

Truck campers are camping units that are loaded onto the bed or chassis of a pickup truck. Many have kitchen and bathroom facilities. They sleep two to six, and go for $2,000 to $10,000.

Folding camping trailers are units with collapsible sides that fold for lightweight towing by a motorized vehicle. Set up, they provide kitchen, dining, and sleeping facilities for four to eight people, and sell for between $1,500 and $8,000.

> **In an RV, you follow your own totally flexible time schedule, without fixed reservations anywhere, without depending on others (hotels, planes, trains).**

The Advantages

In an RV, you follow your own totally flexible time schedule, without fixed reservations anywhere, without depending on others (hotels, trains, planes). You don't constantly pack and unpack; in fact, you carry no luggage. You cook when you like, eat out only when you wish, say

Stampede rally. *Courtesy Creative World Travel, Inc.*

good-bye to greasy spoons, and usually enjoy home-prepared food.

You can have your pets with you. You can visit friends or relatives anywhere in the country without imposing on them: your RV, parked in their driveway, becomes your own private guest cottage— as well as your summer beach house, your winter chalet.

> **You can visit friends and relatives anywhere in the country without imposing on them: your RV, parked in their driveway, becomes your own private guest cottage.**

You make friends easily upon arriving at a camping ground or RV resort. RV-ers are, in general, enthusiasts who love their lifestyle and like sharing it with new people. They are constantly attending rallies, caravans, campouts, meeting with other RV-ers to share common interests.

"It's difficult to be lonely in a campground," one confirmed RV-er told me. "Our luxury RV resort in Florida ($15 a night) was constantly holding social events. Between dinners and galas, folk dances and exercise classes, meeting new people was not only simple—it was unavoidable."

And RV travel is economical. You can purchase fresh local produce on the road and cook your own meals. Your stay at campgrounds is usually nominal ($5 to $20 a night is typical). And there's no one to tip. A recent study showed that an RV vacation cost about half the expense of a car/hotel vacation, one-third the cost of a bus/ hotel or train/hotel holiday, and one-fourth the cost of an air/hotel vacation.

The Drawbacks

But RV travel is not for everyone—it may not be for you. A Philadelphia couple I know who recently spent four months traveling across country in a motorhome issued the following caveats: "Be sure," they said, "you feel extremely comfortable with whomever you will be traveling with; you're going to spend long periods of time in close quarters. Be sure you're an expert driver and enjoy spending long periods on the road. Above all, don't take this kind of trip unless you're extremely flexible, elastic, and able to cope with new situations, which happen all the time. Mechanical breakdowns are not uncommon and you have to be able to handle them without getting upset."

Renting Before Buying

Like many first-time RV-ers, my informants began by renting a motorhome, got used to driving a large vehicle and used to spending a great deal of driving time together. Now they're so enthusiastic, they're planning to sell their large suburban home, move into a small apartment, buy an RV, and spend at least six months on the road each year. "The excitement and variety of life cannot be compared with any travel experience we've ever had—and we're experienced foreign travelers," they say. "It's a new kind of life, a brand-new world we never saw before."

The Rental Process

The first step is to look in your local telephone directory under the category "Recreation Vehicles—Renting and Leasing." Or you can call one of the two major national companies that have toll-free 800 numbers: **Cruise America (800/327-7778); and America En Route 800/582-8888**). A third major firm, **Altman's Winnebago,** has only a local number (818/ 960-1884), but you can write to them: **Altman's America, 6323 Sepulveda Blvd., Van Nuys, CA 91411,** as well as to **El Monte RV Center,** another interesting firm, at **12061 East Valley Boulevard, El Monte, CA 91732, phone 818/443-6158.** It's also useful to obtain the book called *Who's Who in RV Rentals,* listing the names and rates of more than a hundred other dealers; it's $5 from the **Recreation Vehicle Rental Association, 3251 Old Lee Hwy., Suite 500, Fairfax, VA 22030 (phone 703/591-7130).**

Rental costs vary considerably, depending on type of vehicle, when and for how long you want it, season, and other variables. From one such company, I secured a quote of $39 a day plus 39¢ per mile for a particularly elegant 22-foot camper-trailer sleeping two adults and two children (and there are cheaper versions, and smaller, 13-foot trailers from other firms). One of the "grander" motorhomes—either a 26-foot Alumalite by Holiday Rambler or a 27-foot Southwester by Fleetwood—will average $600 to $700 a week, plus low-cost mileage (19¢ per mile after an initial number of free miles). But that's for a vehicle that can sleep six people and is fully self-contained, with such added features as a microwave oven, roof air conditioning, its own generator and propane tank (so that a hookup is not necessary), power steering, and almost everything else you can name.

It is usually cheaper to rent from a private individual, but then you must be aware of the risk you take if a breakdown should occur; a private owner can usually do little for you, while with a major company, repairs are either handled on the spot or you are given a new vehicle and put back on the road within 24 hours. Rental dealers may also apply the cost

The most important step is advance study and comparison shopping before you rent an RV.

of a rental to a future purchase. They can provide you with broad forms of insurance. Some will arrange tour packages if you're traveling to popular state or national parks or historic landmarks. Others offer orientation sessions and packages that include linens and cookware.

The most important step is advance study and comparison shopping before you rent. Make sure you understand the terms of the agreement, take your vehicle out for a test spin, and reserve as far in advance as possible. Indeed, the "RV life" is becoming so popular that a reservation several months in advance might not be a bad idea.

Cottages, a New Weapon in the Arsenal of Budget Travel

Costing Far Less Than a Villa or Apartment Rental, They Also House You in Areas Unaffected by Mass Tourism

To guesthouses and student dorms, hostels and pensions, to third-class hotels with bathless rooms and private homes with rooms for rent—to all such havens for the budget-minded transatlantic tourist, you can now add a new form of low-cost lodging: the European "cottage." For some of us, these tiny dwellings full of charm can prove the cheapest of all accommodations—and the single best introduction to life in the Old World.

But it's important to know what they are and what they're not.

What Is a Cottage?

First, a European cottage is very different in location and appearance from a vacation home. The latter is generally in jam-packed resort areas, near seashores or mountains, in world-famous locations publicized for years. To rent one, you contact an international real-estate broker—like Blanding's, of Washington, D.C., or Villas International, of New York City—and pore over glossy, four-color photos of designer interiors and pastel throw-cushions. You pay a rather hefty price for your two- to four-week rental—about the same as you'd spend here at home—and fly to the remoter airports, like Nice or Rome, to claim your impressive hideaway.

A cottage, by contrast, is almost never in a resort area—else it would have been grabbed up long ago, restyled and refurbished, and thus transformed into a vacation home. Rather, a European cottage will be found in purely rural locations, near prosaic villages or small towns. Most are in walking distance—true—of pubs, shops, or cafés, but often at least a mile or two away.

They also come from another age, and are the sort of structure rarely built today: of stone, small and boxlike, in period designs with tiny windows, sometimes topped by a thatched roof or ancient tiles.

But they are charming and idyllic, full of repose, a refuge from modern pressures. And however basic they may appear, they are today equipped with the simple essentials: private bath or shower, gas or electric stoves, flip-a-switch heating.

Most important, they're cheap. When occupied by four to six people (in a minimum of two bedrooms, but often with three), they rent for as little as $325 a week in winter, $375 in spring, $450 in summer, even at current exchange rates. Because of that, they're rarely (or only reluctantly) handled by traditional brokers or by the trendy travel agencies that deal in Mediterranean villas and Swiss chalets. But more and more Americans have ferreted them out, and at least a half dozen U.S.-based organizations have emerged in recent years to facilitate the process of booking them.

Organizations and Sources of Information

British Travel Associates, of Elkton, Virginia, is the leading source of British cottage rentals, despite having been in business for only six years. It is a venture launched by the publishers of the prestigious bimonthly *British Travel Report,* who are a bit bewildered—from several indications—by the explosive response to their initial cottage offerings. Currently the fledgling organization represents 35 to 40 British brokers with 5,000 cottages to rent. And these—in locations all over England, Scotland, and Wales—can usually be had for a week, and also for two weeks, but rarely for longer than that because of heavy demand. To beat the rental limitations, some avid Anglophiles move from cottage to cottage, spending a week at each.

These tiny dwellings full of charm can prove the cheapest of all introductions to life in the Old World.

The average cost? Remarkably low. Some lucky renters pay only $325 a week in low season (November through March), $400 a week in mid-season (April, May, September, and October), $450 a week in high season (June through August)—and those are the total rates for four to six people. Although the charges go higher in upgraded categories, the three cheapest categories (A, B, and C) are hugely popular and highly praised by people who have stayed in them.

Consider, for example, the timbered Churn Cottage near Siddington, Gloucestershire, in the bucolic Cotswolds. Set on a 750-acre farm, but close to the city of Cirencester, its facilities include three bedrooms (for five people), large kitchen and dining room, bathroom, color TV, and garage, in a setting for quiet walks along the River Churn and fishing for local trout, with village shops and pub nearby. Though this one is

In the Cotswalds, complete with garden.
Courtesy Heart of England Cottages, Inc.

two categories higher than the A level, it rents for only $420 a week in low season, $550 a week in mid-season, and $700 a week in high season. The last rate works out to barely more than $25 per person per night.

Or try the B-level, thatch-roofed Medieval Cottage in the tiny village of Wrangaton, Devon, 12 miles from the coast at the edge of the Dartmoor National Park, with Torquay and other delightful towns nearby. It offers two bedrooms for four people, a kitchen, lounge, bathroom, color TV, and parking, for approximately $400 a week in low season, $500 per week in mid-season, and $600 a week in high season— $22 per person per day in the last instance.

> **A** European cottage is radically different in location and appearance from a vacation home.

For a catalog that pictures and describes 500 representative examples of the 5,000 cottages available to you, send $4 to **British Travel Associates, P.O. Box 299, Elkton, VA 22827 (phone 703/289-6514, or toll free 800/327-6097 outside Virginia)**, and state your preferences, the dates you need, and the kind of group you are. Within 24 hours BTA will propose a specific cottage rental suiting your needs, and everything proceeds from there.

For comparative purposes, you might also send for the programs of **Heart of England Cottages, P.O. Box 878, Eufaula, AL 36072 (phone 334/687-9800)**, enclosing $3.75 for an assortment of cottage brochures, including some for Ireland as well (the $3.75 will be deducted from the cost of any subsequent bookings, which start at $300 a week); Heart of England's owner, Peter Trodd, recently told me, in his thick British accent: "My wife and I are both Limeys, so we know the country like the back of our hand, and can offer personal advice and guidance." True to his word, his brochures are full of insiders' tips and asides (". . . the area is excellent for conservationists, being the home of the Natterjack Toad").

The *Gîtes* of France

In France, the cottages are 20,000 in number, similarly priced or even lower in cost than the British variety (which is to say, remarkably cheap), and known as *gîtes* (pronounced "zheet"), an antiquated medieval term for "abode" or "lodging." Again, they're found mainly in countryside locations, but nowhere near resorts, among populations whose warmth and generosity toward visitors are the very opposite of some Parisian attitudes. From your *gîte*, by bike or rented car, you'll drive to shop in nearby French villages, explore historic sights, enjoy ravishing landscapes, practice your French, and conserve your cash. *Gîtes* rent for as little as $350 a week (for a minimum of four people, remember); a usual high of $600 to $700 a week, in a long high season of April through

October (though they can run higher in August); and for less than that—say, $300 a week—in March or November. Rentals can be had for a single week, except in July and August, when a two-week stay is required.

Why are the *gîtes* so cheap? Because they're rent-controlled. In the immediate postwar years, when thousands of the French abandoned their ancient residences to move to cities or more modern homes, the French government offered subsidies to preserve and maintain the *gîtes,* on condition that they be offered for vacation rentals at low prices. Today the *gîtes* of France remain a largely governmental institution administered by the 95 *départements* of France, and marketed by the government-sponsored Fédération de Gîtes. With typical French flair, each *gîte* is awarded a symbol of either one, two, or three ears of corn, to rate its comparative quality.

I'm looking at several photographs of *gîtes* as I write these words. One, a charming shuttered cottage with coral-tile roof, as in a van Gogh painting, is 37 miles from the Riviera Coast, in Regusse, the *département* of Var. It's rated three ears of corn, can sleep up to six people, and costs only $450 a week in any month other than July or August (when the charge is $750 a week).

Another, a large and ancient stone-walled structure in St. Germain sur Vienne, in the *département* known as Indre et Loire, eight miles from the renowned Chinon (site of the castle), is also a three-ears-of-corn winner that can house up to five people and yet rents for only $350 a week in April, May, October, and November, $700 a week in June and September, $750 a week in July and August.

The chief U.S.-based source of *gîtes* is **The French Experience, Inc., 370 Lexington Ave., Suite 812, New York, NY 10017 (phone 212/986-1115)**. Write for their catalog, called "France Beyond Clichés," which contains additional information and application forms. And don't confuse the rental of an entire *gîte,* for one to four weeks, with a system for obtaining bed-and-breakfast in private French homes; the latter are called *gîtes de chambres* or *gîtes d'étape,* and I'll have more on those in next year's edition of this book.

In the meantime, picture yourself living like a resident, not a tourist, in France, ensconced in your own private *gîte:* wandering to a French village market, where luscious vegetables and exquisitely presented cuts of meat are arrayed before you; standing with your spatula and a *Larousse Gastronomique* in a French kitchen, attempting to outdo Julia Child; savoring the taste of that fresh Mâcon or Beaujolais as you pour it from a pitcher into a cool stone mug. Ooh-la-la!

Camping in the Caribbean

On Six Major Islands or Locales, Supervised Sites Await Your Tent—for As Little as $3 a Night

If you're like me, then on your first trip to the sultry Caribbean you have at some point asked: "Why am I staying in a hotel? With heat so intense, and nights so balmy, why must I pay a king's ransom for space in a high-rise tower? Why can't I simply sleep on a beach, under canvas, for peanuts?"

Well, glory be, the very same thought has now occurred to a growing legion of open-air entrepreneurs. And today, commercial campsites await your tent in multiple, major Caribbean locations. And I'm referring to organized and supervised sites, attended at night, with showers, toilets, and—often—electricity.

Though some tropical islands forbid camping (Bermuda is one, except for organized Scout groups and the like) and others discourage it (Antigua), while still others permit it but then provide no organized facilities for it (Trinidad/Tobago, Dominican Republic, Grenada), six enlightened locales have made the activity into a major tourist resource:

Puerto Rico

Puerto Rico is one such place, although it burdens the sport with a touch of bureaucracy, a required permit obtained in the manner explained below. Yet fully seven public beaches (*balnearios*) renowned for their swimming now possess supervised campsites, of which the best endowed (electricity, showers) are at Luquillo and Cerro Gordo. Luquillo, with 58 sites renting for $15 per site per night, $19 with roof, is in eastern Puerto Rico (Rte. 3, km marker 35.4), on a full mile of white sand shaded by majestic coconut palms. Cerro Gordo, with 60 tent sites renting for the same, is in northern Puerto Rico (Rte. 690, near Vega Alta), on a beach almost as grand. More spartan sites lacking electricity (you use lanterns) are: Añasco, in western Puerto Rico (Rte. 3, km 77; $12 per campsite, $34 per cabin); Punta Guillarte, in southeastern Puerto Rico (Rte. 3, km 128, near Arroyo; tent sites for $12, cabins for $34); Seven Seas Beach, near the marina area of Fajardo in eastern Puerto Rico (Rte. 987 connects Fajardo to Seven Seas Beach, where tent sites are $12 a night); and finally, the rapidly developing island of Vieques, off the eastern coast of Puerto Rico (where campsites rent for $12 nightly on Sun Bay—"Bahía del Sol"—off Rte. 997, looking out onto the eerie glow of Phosphorous Bay).

Elsewhere in Vieques, at the feminist retreat called New Dawn, mainly for women, tents can be pitched on platform sites (limit of three people per site) for $10 a night, with breakfast and dinner available in the adjoining main house for an extra $16 per person daily. For feminist tenting, write **New Dawn Adventures, P.O. Box 1512, Vieques, PR 00765 (phone 809/741-0495).** For all other Puerto Rican camping locations, write for an application form (resulting in a permit) and reservations to **Departamento de Recreación y Deportes, Compañía de Fomento y Recreativo, Oficina de Reservaciones para Centros Vaccacionales, Apartado 3207, San Juan, PR 00904 (phone 809/722-1771 or 809/721-2800, ext. 341,** and ask to speak with Irma Batista, who speaks English).

British Virgin Islands

The British Virgin Islands are a second renters' heaven. On the islands of Jost van Dyke and Tortola, facilities aren't simply in the form of bare sites for pitching your own tent, but include already erected, two-person tents on elevated wooden platforms, with cot beds, lanterns, linen, and even cooking utensils. Such elaborate canvas lodgings rent to two people for $20 a night ($3 for a third person) at Brewers Bay Campground in Tortola, and for $25 to $35 a night ($5 for a third person) at Tula's N&N Campground on Jost van Dyke. Cost-conscious as I may be, I'd still choose the more expensive Tula's on enchanting Jost van Dyke (whose population is all of 130 people), which provides campers with coal or wood for cooking, two restaurants in the area, a grocery store next door, and several rope hammocks along the beach (a bare campsite at Tula's is $15 for up to three people). The smaller Brewers Bay Campground has fresh-water showers (as does Tula's), a beach bar and tiny restaurant, and a beachfront location about three miles from Road Town, with its 1,000 inhabitants (overly urbanized by my standards). For reservations or information, contact: **Tula's N&N Campground, Little Harbour, Jost van Dyke, British Virgin Islands (phone 809/77-40774 or 809/49-59302, asking for Cynthia Jones); or Brewers Bay**

> **I**n Puerto Rico, seven public beaches renowned for their swimming now possess supervised campsites—of these, Luquillo and Cerro Gordo have the best facilities.

Campground, P.O. Box 185, Road Town, Tortola, British Virgin Islands (phone 809/49-43463 or 809/49-59699). An alternative and perhaps better mailing address for Tula's (your letter will reach them faster) is P.O. Box 8364, St. Thomas, U.S. Virgin Islands 00801.

U.S. Virgin Islands

The U.S. Virgin Islands offer superlative camping on the stunning, white sand beaches of the island of St. John, two-thirds of which is a national park. Cinnamon Bay Campground, operated for the U.S. Park Service by the elegant Rosewood Hotels organization, is the standout. Its bare campsites (for erecting your own tent) are less than a two-minute walk from the sea; are serviced by a cafeteria, convenience store, lavatories, and shower in separate buildings; and rent for only $15 a day for two people throughout the year, $5 per third or fourth person. Park naturalists attached to the camp lead you on all-day hikes or provide snorkeling instruction. Not within my own definition of low-cost camping, but popular, is a separate section of 54 already erected 10-by-14-foot tents on wooden floors, and with cot beds, stove, ice chest, and utensils; the latter rent to two people for $46 a day from September 1 to December 19, $67 a day from December 20 to March 31, and $46 a day from April 1 to August 31, with third and fourth persons paying $8 extra. For bare sites, book directly with the local manager at Cinnamon Bay Campground, P.O. Box 720, Cruz Bay, St. John, U.S. Virgin Islands 00830 (phone 809/776-6330). But for those furnished, luxury tents, contact Rosewood Hotels and Resorts in Dallas, Texas (phone 800/928-8889). Down the coast on the same island, the well-known Maho Bay Camps rents furnished, kitchen-equipped, canvas-sided, hillside cottages for $60 (off-season) or $90 (high season) per cottage per night, but those (in my view) can't qualify for low-cost camping status either. Still, if you're interested, write Maho Bay Camps, 17-A E. 73rd St., New York, NY 10021 (phone 212/472-9453, or toll free 800/392-9004 outside New York State).

Belize

Belize (not an island, but a Central American country in the Caribbean) provides camping on its popular *cayes*—thin, water-surrounded, beach-lined strips of land just off its coast. Three of the closely grouped cayes are called the Bluefield Range, and there, at a working lobster-and-fishing camp known as Ricardo's Beach Huts and Lobster Camp (phone 011-501-2-31609 or 011-501-2-44970, asking to speak with Ricardo or his brother, Roberto), sites can be rented for pitching your tents for about $9 a night. But Ricardo and Roberto would prefer you take their "package" for $150, which gives you round-trip transportation by boat (theirs) from Belize City; three days and two nights in a beach hut on stilts above the sea (which is almost like camping, as the huts are rustic, and without flush toilets or showers); and three good meals daily. The boat leaves from 59 North Front Street, which is opposite the Belize Immigration Department; you can check schedules, make bookings, and get other information from the nearby Mira-Rio Hotel. Important: Ricardo's is closed from July through September. Elsewhere among the cayes, the ultra-budget Caye Caulker has several wooden beachfront "hotels" whose proprietors, I am told by several recent visitors, will permit you to pitch your tent in back for a uniform $5 per person per night. Here, you simply appear on the spot and ask. And off the southern city of Dangriga, Tobacco Caye offers already erected, two-person tents for $12 per person, and three meals a day for a total of $18. What's special about Tobacco Caye is that it sits right on the reef, a boon for divers (you get there by boat from Dangriga).

For non-caye camping in Belize, at the so-called Hopkins Village of the Garifuna

Indians (Afro-Caribbean) in the south of the country, the charge is $5 for pitching your tent, or you can rent space in the bunkhouse for $7. (Facilities here are rather primitive, on the beach near a typical Garifuna village, but safe and rewarding). Call Charles Halsall of Personalized Services for reservations, and while you're at it, ask him about inland camping at Jungle View, in Cayo, near San Ignacio ($10 per campsite for two), or at the Cockscombe Basin Jaguar Preserve and Wildlife Sanctuary (where you pay $8 for accommodations under a roof in the heart of this world-famous reserve).

Jamaica

Jamaica offers supervised camping, with electricity and running water, in all three of its major tourist areas, but for more than most others charge. Near Montego Bay, Damali Beach Village rents sites for $9 per person (not per site) per night, and will also rent you a tent (if you haven't brought your own) for $4 extra per night. A restaurant, bar, and water sports are all nearby. Contact **Damali Beach Village, Whitesand P.O., Montego Bay, Jamaica (phone 809/953-2387)**. At Ocho Rios, Hummingbird Haven charges $9 per person per night for a bare site, but has no tents for rent. It does provide showers, toilets and basins, electric lights for campers, and dogs for security. Take the minibus to get there ($2) and not an expensive taxi ($50). And contact **Hummingbird Haven, P.O. Box 95, Ocho Rios, Jamaica (phone 809/974-5188)**. Near Negril Beach, on those cliffs with steps descending into the sea, Lighthouse Park offers tent spaces for $8 per person per night; and nearby, for a younger crowd, Negril Roots Bamboo on the beach charges only $6 per person, and also rents tents for $2 more. Contact **Lighthouse Park, West End, Negril, Jamaica (phone 809/957-4346)**; or **Negril Roots Bamboo, Negril P.O., Westmoreland, Jamaica (phone 809/957-4479)**. For organized camping in the Blue Mountains of central Jamaica, contact **Jamaica Alternative Tourism, P.O. Box 216, Kingston 7, Jamaica (phone 809/927-2097)**, whose president, the dynamic Peter Bentley, is a source for all manner of Jamaica adventure tours.

Since campsites are also used by the local population, they afford you a rare and rewarding chance to meet the Caribbean people on an equal footing, not tourist-to-bellman or tourist-to-chambermaid. And they place you in the open air, among settings of awesome natural beauty.

> **S**ince campsites are also used by the local population, they afford you a rare and rewarding chance to meet the Caribbean people on an equal footing.

The Village Apartment, Your Base for an "Untour"

A Former University
Professor Sends
Thousands Each Year
to Experience the
Typical Life of
Hamlets Bypassed
by Commerce and
Tourism

Housed in a hotel, taking meals in a restaurant, all in the commercial center of a large city, how could one hope to experience the culture and lifestyle of a foreign people?

That was the basic flaw in traditional tourism, as it appeared to a university professor named Harold Taussig, who lived in a suburb of Philadelphia.

So in 1976 he took the step of forming a travel company named Idyll Ltd. to provide "untours" for "untourists." These consist of three-week stays in housekeeping apartments located in rural villages of Austria, Switzerland, Germany, France, and Italy.

Now you probably haven't heard of Idyll, or untours, or untourists, because Professor Taussig doesn't advertise and never has, but relies solely on "word-of-mouth" for his bookings. Nor does he market his untours through travel agents. In that way, he saves a 10% commission and keeps prices low.

But from a total of six clients in 1976, his untours were sold to more than 2,900 customers in 1995, virtually all from personal recommendations. Current bookings indicate an even larger, geometric increase in 1996, despite the current weakness of the U.S. dollar in Europe.

What's Different About Untours?

How do "untours" differ from the villa rentals of international real-estate brokers? The latter assign you to trendy vacation homes in popular seaside or mountain resorts, intended for and inundated by tourists.

Untours, by contrast, takes you to towns that tourists have never heard of, to such unlikely locations as Meiringen, Switzerland (pop. 4,000), or to the dozing, dreaming St. Goar, Germany (pop. 2,000).

There you live—usually—in a two-family house, enjoying separate quarters and entrances, but close to foreign, small-town neighbors, downstairs. You shop at the local butcher or grocer, wander to the tiny post office and chat with its one-person staff, share the daily cycles and rhythms of village life.

To an extent currently unknown in the United States, Taussig says, village life remains vibrant and viable in Europe. Governments there subsidize their agriculture and agricultural communities to a far greater degree than here, and villagers need not commute to jobs in larger towns or otherwise forsake their village roots. Accordingly, he claims, the untourist is able to experience the highlights of a rural culture that has hardly changed in hundreds of years.

Untours' catalog. *Courtesy Idyll, Ltd.*

Among the villages of Europe, he chooses the untouristy for his untourists, rejecting such well-known, postcard-pretty hamlets as Gstaad or Oberammergau, Zermatt or Velden. "Have you ever wondered," he writes in a 60-page newsletter sent to past and potential untourists, "what these alleged paradises were like before everybody else discovered them?"

They were like Breconshire, he says, the former Welsh location for his untours in Britain; there an Idyll representative, cooking an evening meal of roast lamb for her American guests, sends "her little girl running down the hedgerow to a neighbor's garden to borrow some mint for the sauce. . . . She has mint in her own garden but it's not

Untours takes you to towns that tourists have never heard of.

exactly the right sort for mint sauce, and she particularly likes the mint picked just minutes before she uses it."

In preparation for their stays at these idyllic Edens, untourists receive a heavy packet of typewritten booklets providing them with hints and rules of conduct, hand-drawn diagrams ("unmaps") of their airport arrivals and village locations, inked overlays enabling them to decipher European railroad timetables, handy foreign phrases, suggestions for walks and hikes outside each particular village, and other carefully tested tidbits of information, written as if in a letter to a friend.

On an "untour," you shop at the local butcher or grocer, wander to the tiny post office and chat with its one-person staff, share the daily cycles and rhythms of village life.

Upon arrival, they are met by members of Idyll's staff, who escort them to the village destination, get them settled, and remain accessible throughout the summer in a nearby town for problem-solving and advice.

As if in a co-op, all staff of Idyll Ltd. participate with Taussig in all major decisions, and set the profit markup on Idyll's prices at just the level needed to provide each of them with a living wage. Such is Taussig's vision of a "just world," according to him. That policy, and the zero cost of advertising, probably account for Idyll's low prices, which are remarkable indeed in this expensive travel year.

The Destinations

Idyll's 1996 untours to Germany (three weeks in length, running from early May through October) include round-trip air fare on Lufthansa between New York and Frankfurt, an unlimited-mileage German railpass for each person, help on arrival and an orientation briefing, a half-day sightseeing excursion, and the fully equipped apartment, and cost as little as $1,419

for each of four people traveling together, $1,535 for each of three, $1,626 for each of two.

Idyll's 1996 untours to Switzerland, its most popular program, are also for three weeks, departing on Swissair from New York or Boston at various intervals from early May to late October. They include round-trip air, transfers, excursions, assistance, a "Swiss Pass" for unlimited transportation (bus or train) throughout Switzerland, and the apartment for 21 nights, and cost as little as $1,598 for each of four people traveling together, $1,644 for each of three, $1,820 for each of two.

Idyll's 1996 untours to Austria are on Swissair to Salzburg (via Zurich) from early May to mid-October, and last three weeks; they include transatlantic air, transfers, car or train with unlimited mileage throughout, and the apartment. Rates are $1,413 for each of four people traveling together, $1,498 for each of three, $1,619 for each of two. Add-ons are available from other Lufthansa departure cities in the U.S.

In recent years, untours has supplemented its village programs with some city stays (Brussels and Amsterdam among them), but has kept the spirit of being a temporary resident of Europe by using apartment accommodations throughout. Its greatest success among the city vacations has been a "Hapsburg Untour" consisting of a week apiece (again, in self-catering apartments) in Prague, Budapest, and Vienna. Features include air travel from New York or Boston into Prague and returning from Vienna; first-class rail from Prague to Budapest; Danube hydrofoil; transportation passes for each city; luggage transfers, orientation, and staff support. The package, while costing more than the other untour programs, is well under hotel programs: four people traveling together each pay $2,108, three people each pay $2,275, and two pay $2,371. In addition, because of the special popularity of Prague, Idyll offers a two-week untour in that city alone, offering round-trip air travel from New York or Boston, full staff support, and a city transportation pass. Two persons sharing an apartment each pay $1,423 for the package.

For brochures, schedules, ratesheets, and bulky newsletters, contact **Idyll Ltd., P.O. Box 405, Media, PA 19065 (phone 610/565-5242 or fax 610/565-5142).** You'll find rates and dates for the numerous programs in France and Italy that we haven't the space to describe in this edition. You'll be impressed, I think, by what you read.

The New World of Travel 1997

The lifeblood of the Arthur Frommer travel guides is the correspondence received from readers, commenting on the establishments recommended in the texts and recommending new establishments. Each such letter is carefully studied, and when a particular lead seems promising, it is followed up and personally checked.

It is hoped that *The New World of Travel* will receive similar assistance from its readers. A yearly publication, issued near the start of each year, *The New World of Travel* will constantly grow. And since much of its content relates to organizations that lack the means to market themselves properly, or come to the attention of a travel journalist, your help is invaluable in alerting me to the organizations—hospitality exchanges, alternative resorts, new travel clubs, and the like—that you have discovered.

If you become aware of a new travel organization, program, or development that deserves to be described in our next edition, *The New World of Travel 1997*, won't you please let me know about it? Send your letters to Arthur Frommer, *The New World of Travel*, 1841 Broadway, New York, NY 10023. All letters will be acknowledged, and all are warmly appreciated, in advance, by the author.

"Formula 1," Star of Budget Travel to Europe

A Mammoth European Hotel Chain Has Just Created the Cheapest Modern Lodgings on Earth

If they were built in America, to the same plans and using the same factory-like methods of construction, they would rent for an astonishing $18 a night per room. As it is, under the costlier conditions of Western Europe (higher land costs, more rigid construction codes), the same rooms in brand-new buildings rent, nevertheless, for only $26 a night—and that's again per *room*, not per person. Employing the most remarkable new techniques in hotel building and room design, a European hotel chain has just created the cheapest modern lodgings on earth.

They're called Formula 1 hotels (or, in the French, Formule 1), and there are already 450 of them, in France, Belgium, the U.K., and Germany, with 500 more planned for construction in a dozen other European countries in the decade ahead. Owned by the Accor group of

Paris—operators of Sofitels, Novotels, and Ibis and Urbis hotels, which together constitute the world's largest chain of wholly owned hotels—Formula 1 is surely the single most important development in low-cost tourism in years.

The "formula" is not for everyone. Just 8 feet wide and 12 feet long, Accor's rooms are among the smallest anywhere, yet they are meant to house up to three people (the third sleeps in a bunk bed elevated on a loft-like platform above the double bed). Elsewhere in the room, a triangular sink with hot and cold running water is ingeniously placed in one corner, taking up hardly any room, while a triangular writing desk/makeup counter is in another corner, set flush into the adjoining walls. A television set with built-in alarm clock is suspended high on a wall, angled toward the main bed. Clothing is hung from a rack placed underneath the loft bed, the latter reached by a ladder. And a tiny stool for sitting at the desk/makeup table is pushed underneath that fixture when not in use, enabling guests to walk around the bed. The bed itself takes up almost all space in the room.

Only eight weeks are needed to build a 100-room Formula 1 hotel, using prefabricated units that are trucked from a central factory to the site. And yet the result is a strong, valid building, with interior corridors, a tiny lobby, and an equally small coffee shop with bar and stools, enabling guests to enjoy a self-served continental breakfast. For years, hotel people have talked about "manufacturing" prefabricated hotels in this manner. The French, with their customary verve and flair for futuristic designs, have now done it. Bear in mind that Formula 1s are not at all like the "hotel-coffins" announced several years ago by the Japanese—stacked containers, each large enough to accommodate one supine body—but are composed of stand-up, walk-around rooms, however tiny they may be. Rooms even have a window—one apiece.

While the hotels are open year around, they are staffed only from 6:30 to 10am and from 5 to 10pm, presumably permitting their one-shift personnel to take on other jobs in between. Outside of staffed hours, an automatic, on-site reservations machine makes rooms available to persons seeking them. The latter simply stick their credit cards into a slot, are assigned a room, and are then simultaneously billed for the night on their credit-card account. The doors to their rooms are also opened by the credit card, but only for the amount of time that they are booked. Security is total.

If there is any controversial aspect to the Formula 1 concept—and any main reason why they are so much cheaper than our own Motel 6s, Sleep Inns, Red Roof Inns, and other American budget motels—it is that their rooms are without private bath, although with sinks and hot and cold running water. The showers and toilets are "down the hall"—one such shower-and-toilet room for every four guest bedrooms. The deliberate decision to omit private facilities caused some observers to predict, mistakenly as it turns out, that Formula 1 would not prove popular with the public. In fact, they are nearly always filled. What overcame the earlier, expected reaction, in my view, is the following:

First, a ratio of only four rooms to every shower and toilet is much better than is found in the average European pension or guesthouse. The lines or waits to use such facilities are almost never experienced in a Formula 1 hotel.

Second, an automated chemical method of cleaning such facilities after each use—opening and closing the door after use locks the room for a time and starts up machines that chemically clean the shower, toilet, and floor area—makes each such room far more sanitary than is usually the case, say Formula 1 officials. The room is then reopened through the insertion of the next guest's credit card. Although German law requires that private facilities be attached to

> **O**nly eight weeks are needed to build a Formula 1 hotel, using prefabricated units that are trucked from a central factory to the site.

each guest room in the Formula 1 hotels planned for Germany, the contrary policy of Formula 1 will remain unchanged for France, the Benelux nations, England, Italy, and Spain, officials insist. In this fashion, they hope to maintain Formula 1 room rates at less than half the prevailing level of other budget facilities, and at half the level that might have been required if Formula 1 hotels had been built with one bathroom to each guest room.

Is there a "Formula 1" in the future for North America?

Where are they presently found? Of the 450-odd Formula 1s presently open, nearly 400 are in France—at least one apiece in or just outside each of the 200 largest towns of that country.

A dozen or so are on the outskirts of Paris, or otherwise near the French capital. Closest to town are Formula 1s in Aulnay-sous-Bois, Cergy St.-Christophe, Cergy Pontoise St.-Martin, Conflaus St.-Honorine, and Rungis-Orly.

A bit farther out are brand-new Formula 1s in Sarcelles, Savigny-Epinay, St.-Denis, and Maurepas. Visitors to Paris can save a bundle by staying in a Formula 1 on the outskirts, and then taking the bus or subway each day to the center.

Twenty Formula 1s are currently open in Germany, a dozen in Belgium, four in Great Britain (with many more to come). Apart from the Formula 1s planned for Western Europe, units are currently contemplated for Czechoslovakia, Hungary, and Poland, spurred by the surging tourism to Central and Eastern Europe.

Is there a "Formula 1" in the future for North America? It is perhaps significant that the Accor group, parents of Formula 1, recently acquired the Motel 6 chain of the United States. Since the average Motel 6 is like a palace compared with a Formula 1, it would seem to me that space exists for a new category of super-budget hotel undercutting what we have earlier regarded as rock-bottom in prices and amenities. But though I've asked them all, not one Formula 1 official will specify U.S. plans for either Formula 1 or Motel 6.

Until they do, it at least behooves every budget-minded, Europe-bound traveler to acquire a current list of every Formula 1, their addresses, and their phone numbers. For a directory (with details) of the 400-odd Formula 1s in France, write **Renseignements, Chaine des Hotels Formule 1, Immeuble Le Descartes, 29 Promenade Michel Simon, 93166 Noisy-le-Grand Cedex, France.**

Signage at the Formula 1 hotels.
Courtesy ACCOR.

For a list of the 20-or-so Formula 1s in Germany, contact **Formule 1 Hotelbetriebs GMBH, 5–9 Frankenthalerstrasse, 8000 Munchen 90, Germany (phone 089/680-91-300 or fax 089/680- 91-610)**. For the dozen Formula 1s in Belgium, write **NV Formule 1 Hotels Belgium SA, Olmenstraat, B-1831 Diegem, Belgium, or phone (32) 2-720-20-82 or fax (32) 2-725-87-88.** For the few Formula 1s in Great Britain (Doncaster, Hull, Peterborough, and Teesside), write **Information, Ref. PS1, F1 (UK) Limited, 177 Hammersmith Road, London W6 7JJ, U.K.** For the three Formula 1s in the Netherlands (Amsterdam, Groningen, and Heerlen-Zuid), write to the Formula 1 office in Belgium, above. And for the single Formula 1 in Switzerland (Lausanne), write to the Formula 1 office in France, above.

Learn to Bargain in the Marketplace of Hotels

By Ridding Yourself of Pompous Dignity, You Can Save Thousands in the Years Ahead

If the class—ahem!—will come to order, we shall discuss the single most important skill in all the world of travel: how to "bargain down" the price of hotel rooms. That talent can save you thousands in the years ahead.

Start from the premise that nothing in this life is more "perishable" than a hotel room. If such a room should go unrented on a particular night, its value for that night can never again be recouped by the owner of that hotel.

Accordingly, it behooves that owner to rent the room for almost any price rather than leave it unoccupied. Why? Because the cost of placing a guest in the room, as opposed to keeping it empty, is measured in terms of a dollar or two: a change of towels and sheets, a bit of electricity, a cake of soap. A reduced (but still a reasonable) amount of room income is therefore better than no income at all.

Such reasoning has led smart hoteliers the world over to authorize their front-desk clerks to respond favorably to requests for discounts, if that should be what's needed to fill rooms on a slow night. And every nationality of traveler the world over is aware of their willingness to do so, and therefore bargains—except the American.

Bargaining with Dignity

Why not Americans? Because to most of us the very act of bargaining is vulgar and degrading.

No one else regards it as such. If you will stand in the lobby of a large Venetian hotel on a November afternoon, when 60% of the rooms in Venice are empty, chances are that you'll soon spot a well-dressed English tourist or an affluent German tourist or a French one approaching the desk and politely stating: "I am looking for a room that costs no more than 60,000 lire" (about $40).

This tourist knows full well that there is no such thing here as a room for 60,000 lire. He is bargaining. He is saying, in effect: "If you will rent me a room for 60,000 lire, I will stay in your hotel. Otherwise, I will stroll down the street and seek another hotel."

In other words, to bargain over hotel rates does not require that you comport yourself like a hysterical fishwife or a tobacco auctioneer. It can be done—as in the above example—with dignity, by indirection.

Often it requires only that you use a "code word" to convey to the desk clerk that you are "shopping." How many times have you heard a traveler inquire as to whether the hotel grants a "corporate rate" or a "commercial rate"—thus bargaining, and usually successfully, for a reduced rate?

What's to prevent you from doing the same? Why can't you name the corporation or firm for which you work and then speculate: "I'm sure we must have a special rate at this hotel." If the hotel is empty and you appear disposed to leave

the hotel unless a discount is granted, will anyone challenge the statement? Does anyone really care whether your company has made such arrangements? Or are they anxious to fill their hotel?

Or else you name your occupation and ask for a reduction based on that. You ask for a "teacher's rate" or for a "student's rate." You request a "civil servant's rate" or a "minister's rate" (that always works). You might as well ask for a "stenographer's rate" or for a "dentist's rate." What matters is that you are subtly (and politely) communicating the message that you will stay at the hotel only if they grant you a discount.

When I was a travel agent, I used to phone from the airport, announce that I was seeking a room, but only if I could have a "travel agent's rate." And in that fashion I was usually able to cut my hotel costs in half.

It just so happened that I was telling the truth—I *was* a travel agent. Yet in 20 years of using the tactic, not once was I ever asked to prove it. For, in reality, the hotels didn't care. If the night was a slow one and they needed the business, they were quite happy to accept

To bargain over hotel rates does not require that you act like a hysterical fishwife or a tobacco auctioneer.

any assertion of status as an excuse for cutting the rate and keeping the guest.

Recently I phoned two professors at the prestigious Cornell University School of Hotel Administration to confirm these hotel policies, and although both pleaded to remain nameless, they instantly did.

What Not to Do

Why, then, I asked, do some hotel guests encounter rejections of their requests for reductions?

It is primarily because, they replied, most people phone nationwide toll-free "800" numbers to seek reservations and rates. The minions who man the phones at central reservations headquarters of the large hotel chains have no authority to cut rates. Rather, one should place the call directly to the hotel and speak to someone more entrepreneurially inclined. If those local, and directly interested, people are made to know that you will stay at the hotel only if a lower rate is found, they'll often find that rate.

All hotels quote from "the top down," added one professor. "When you tell them the rate is unsatisfactory, they'll quite frequently find a lower one."

The second frequent mistake, say my informants, is to make the request—tired and burdened with luggage—in the lobby of the hotel. Once at the front desk, you are presumed by most hotel personnel to be in no position to walk out if discounts aren't given. A better course, they say, is to phone from the airport or train terminal, and announce from there that you are seeking a room that costs "no more than $—." Such a call is obviously from a "shopper," and the desk clerk will take pains to do what's necessary to make the sale—provided, of course, that the night is a slow one.

Best of all is to write ahead. In scheduling a vacation trip to Barbados or Jamaica in the dead month of June, for instance, you advise the hotel: "I am planning a stay, but only if I can secure a room for no more than $40 a night." "It so happens we have such a room" will come the instant reply.

"Ask and it shall be given," says the Bible.

The final error, say my academic friends, is to bargain at the wrong time of year. Obviously, bargaining will not work during peak hotel seasons, when hotels are confident they will fill up. But all hotels have slow weeks or months, or slow "down cycles" during a week. Hotels in business centers like New York, Chicago, or Philadelphia are packed to capacity Monday through Thursday, then empty and hurting Friday through Sunday. The traveler who pays full rate—who fails to bargain—on weekend nights is a chump. That traveler is simply subsidizing the weekend stays of package tourists enjoying rooms at half the rate.

Never make your reservation through the toll-free 800 numbers; rather, call directly to the hotel and speak to someone more entrepreneurially inclined.

Conversely, in resort locations like Atlantic City or Las Vegas, hotels are full on Friday and Saturday nights but often quiet at other times. If you're a Monday arrival at Harrah's or the Golden Nugget, bargain!

In a country that currently deifies the "free market" and worships the likes of Adam Smith and Milton Friedman, isn't it surprising that we as individuals should be reluctant to bargain over the price of a hotel room? Who decrees that hotel rates are fixed in stone? Who denies us the right as free consumers to flex our economic muscle?

Travelers of all nations, unite! You have nothing to lose but your pomposity! You have savings to win!

VII

"Cooperative Camping," the Smartest New Idea in Travel

Sharing the Tasks and the Costs in a 14-Seat Van

It Is a Sensible Travel Method for People Reluctant to Transport Camping Equipment and Vehicle to Areas Overseas or Far Away

"When I use a word, it means just what I choose it to mean—neither more nor less." Those were the sentiments of Humpty Dumpty in Lewis Carroll's *Through the Looking Glass.* They could have applied to the antics of travel brochure writers in describing the activity of cooperative camping. By refusing to use the term—substituting instead a dozen or so contrived titles that only they understand—the pamphlet authors have so confused matters as to conceal this marvelous travel mode from 80% of the people who could have benefitted from it.

Cooperative camping (the name they won't use) is a cheap and sensible travel method for people who haven't the energy, funds, or commitment to buy and then transport their own camping equipment and/or camping vehicle to regions overseas or far away. The operators of cooperative camping tours print literature in which they describe dozens of potential itineraries throughout the United States, Mexico, and Europe. They schedule departures for each itinerary, take bookings from widely scattered individuals, and ultimately assemble a group of about 14 for each departure.

When the group of 14 reaches the jumping-off point (London, Mexico City, Los Angeles, or New York), they board a 14-person van furnished by the operator and driven by a professional guide— the only paid employee on the trip. The vehicle is already supplied with up to eight state-of-the-art tents, elaborate camping utensils, and (sometimes) sleeping bags—although most companies require that you provide the latter. Except for that last item, passengers avoid all the expense and burden of outfitting themselves for camping.

On the first day of the trip, participants vote to establish a "food kitty," fixing the sum they will collectively spend each day for campfire meals. Members of the group, in rotation, shop for groceries along the way, and then rotate the cooking and cleaning chores. They each pitch their own tent each night and pack it away in the morning. The driver drives. Since the group carries its own accommodations (the tents) and needn't adhere to hotel reservations, they are able either to follow the preplanned itinerary or make broad deviations from it. They are also able to travel through areas where standard hotels aren't found.

The entire trip is unstructured and fun, close to nature and informal, adventurous, instructive—and cheap. The average cooperative camping tour costs around $35 a day, plus air fare, and plus about $4 per person per day in contributions to the food kitty.

The Major Companies

So why haven't you heard of it? Blame the following: TrekAmerica, of Blairstown, New Jersey, is the largest U.S. operator of cooperative camping tours, but ought to be spanked for semantic inexactness. A "trek" isn't what they do; in holiday travel, a "trek" is an organized walk along the lower slopes of the Himalayas, Andes, or Swiss Alps, in which porters or pack animals carry your gear. Such adventure travel companies as Himalayan Travel, Mountain Travel, and Journeys operate treks. Cooperative camping tours of the sort organized by TrekAmerica are often to distinctly unadventurous places—Yellowstone, Salt Lake City, Yosemite—but are accomplished through the delightful, semi-adventurous mode of camping.

The vehicle is already supplied with up to eight state-of-the-art tents and elaborate camping gear.

Despite my quibbles, the company is a superb source of cooperative camping: 32 itineraries through North America, from two to nine weeks in length, with up to two dozen yearly departures per itinerary, at daily costs of $40 to $50 plus air fare, and plus a food kitty of about $30 a week. But passengers are limited to the age group of 18 to 38. For their colorful catalogs, contact **TrekAmerica, P.O. Box 470 Blairstown, NJ 07825 (phone 800/221-0596 or 908/ 362-9198).**

AmeriCan Adventures, Inc. (the name resulting from a recent merger with a Canadian organization), of Culver City, California, is TrekAmerica's major competitor, but with two substantial differences: it actually encourages older travelers (into their sixties) to join its largely youthful clientele, and actually places the words "camping holidays" in small letters on the front cover of its catalog. Progress! Again, it offers a broad array of cooperative camping itineraries through all major sections of the U.S., and to Canada, Alaska, and Mexico as well. The latter trip south of the border, for 26 days, is especially interesting. A large percentage of passengers are English-speaking foreigners, and that, too, lends interest. Prices start at $38 a day but can go as high as $60, plus a food kitty contribution of $6 a day. Manager John Yance told me of passengers who traveled with AmeriCan as long ago as 15 years and are still having reunions. "They are still keeping up with each other's life stories." Contact: **AmeriCan Adventures, Inc., 6762A Centinela Avenue, Culver City, CA 90230 (phone 800/864-0335 or 310/390-7495)** for this highly recommended organization.

Roadrunner International Treks of Culver City, California, is closely associated with AmeriCan, and operates a similar cooperative program, but substituting overnight stays in hostels for tents, at an average daily cost of $45 to $57 per person, plus a food kitty of $42 per person per week. Itineraries are throughout the United States for one to four weeks; a great many passengers are British (with mature persons into their sixties encouraged to join; and transportation is by 13-seater Clubwagon van, thus invalidating their use of the word "trek." A highly informative catalog is yours for the asking. Contact: **Roadrunner, c/o AmeriCan, 6762A Centinela Avenue, Culver City, CA 90230, but this time phone 800/873-5872.**

Himalayan Travel of Stanford, Connecticut, is a prominent operator of mountain trekking tours (see our trekking chapter), but also offers cooperative camping programs through South America and southern Africa. Trips are in a 14-passenger van, and cost as little as $40 a day for five weeks, plus air fare. Contact: **Himalayan Travel, Inc., 112 Prospect Street, Greenwich, CT 06901 (phone 203/359-3711, or toll free 800/225-2380 outside Connecticut),** from which four-color brochures are available.

From Georgia to Great Britain

A regional tour operator, Wilderness Southeast, of Savannah, Georgia, runs "cooperative camping" tours (they supply the vehicle, tents, and cooking gear; participants pitch the tents and rotate the cooking) to wilderness areas in the Florida Everglades and Okefenokee Swamp, the coastal "barrier" islands of Georgia and South Carolina, the Great Smoky Mountains of North Carolina, and frequently as well to Belize and Costa Rica. Tours are 4 days to 10 days in length; are led by dedicated naturalists; appeal to all age groups, and indeed are sold to people 20 through 70 years of age; and average $80 to $100 a day, all inclusive, plus transportation to the starting point. Though those are high prices for cooperative camping, they are apparently justified by the rather short length of most tours. Already 22 years old, yet little known outside Savannah, the nonprofit organization publishes a compelling, well-organized catalog of trips, and richly deserves attention from all parts of America. Contact **Wilderness Southeast, 711 Sandtown Rd., Savannah, GA 31410 (phone 912/897-5108).**

In Britain, an organization called Travelbug of London operates a remarkably inexpensive 12-day camping/hosteling trip through the length and breadth of England, Scotland, and Wales, for approximately $479 per person (that's $40 a day), plus air fare to London. Travelbug provides a van and driver, tents, folding camp beds and blankets, all cooking and eating utensils, and operates the tour from April through October. Suitable for people of all ages, it is surely the cheapest approach to Britain presently being offered by anyone. The well-designed itinerary takes in Bath and the Wye Valley, Wales and the Lake District, Edinburgh and York, Warwick, Stratford, and Blenheim, among other locations.

Elsewhere in this 5th edition of *The New World of Travel,* in the chapter called "Ten Varied Travel Organizations That Bring You Better, Cheaper Travel," I've described the well-operated and long-established San Francisco company The Green Tortoise, which operates "the foam-rubber bus" (people of all ages ride in it). Although you sleep in the bus, and not in a tent, on those trips, the activity is otherwise akin to "cooperative camping" and should be considered as an alternative to the trips described in this "cooperative camping" chapter.

A Last Example

Cooperative camping is also the solution to a shortage of tourist housing in Alaska. Already notoriously short of peak-season accommodations, the 49th state is best visited in any event on excursions into its parks and uninhabited wilderness, where few or no lodgings exist. The company that enables you to do so: CampAlaska Tours, for tourists of all ages.

You supply the sleeping bag, they provide all else: 14-passenger vehicle with driver, state-of-the-art tents, other camping gear and cooking equipment (in the classic fashion of "cooperative camping" tours). Tours average $85 a day (plus a food kitty contribution of $8 a day), last 7 to 28 days (but average 10), depart from early June to mid-September, and transport no more than 12 individuals booking each departure (of which more than 100 such departures are available). They leave mainly from Anchorage, and include all overland and ferry transportation, entrance to national parks and campgrounds, services of CampAlaska's guide, and use of their camping equipment. You visit

Participants vote to establish a "food kitty," fixing the sum they will spend each day for campfire meals.

the continent's most spectacular natural wonders, breathe exhilarating air, go fishing, climbing, trekking, and rafting.

For irresistible literature, contact: **CampAlaska Tours, P.O. Box 872247, Wasilla, AK 99687 (phone 800/376-9438 or 907/376-9438).**

"Overlanding," the Last Great Travel Adventure

In Self-Sufficient "Expedition Trucks," Modern-Day Tourists Travel for 7 to 42 Weeks Across Asia, Africa, or South America

When Marco Polo traveled in the 13th century from Venice to the Chinese court of Kublai Khan, he became the first person to use "overlanding" as a method of tourism. He made scarcely any use of sea routes or even river transport, went for great distances where there were no roads, and slept every night in cloth tents, not inns.

That's "overlanding." And amazingly enough, today thousands of tourists are using much the same methods, as offered by several overland tour companies of Britain, to accomplish journeys almost as long (7 to 42 weeks), just as exotic (trans-Asia, trans-Africa), and nearly as full of insight, learning, and satisfaction.

Overlanding is the closest modern approach to the experience of the great explorers. Although it uses several familiar practices of "cooperative camping" (people become participants in the mechanics of their own trip, sharing the cooking and pitching the tents), it differs in radical respects from the far tamer activities of the cooperative camping tour operators. The latter take you to commercial campsites near large cities or well-visited attractions, and travel from place to place on modern highways, or at least paved ones.

The overlanding companies go on dirt roads, or backroads, or where there are no roads at all, in underdeveloped areas of untouched fascination, the largely uncharted. Their journeys are through the rawest countryside, not near cities, in circumstances that afford the closest contact with rural people of Asia, Africa, and South America, their three principal destinations.

Overlanders offer travel adventure and unpredictability (though almost complete safety). On such a trip, you encounter, let's say, a washed-out bridge and must shift routes. You find that sand dunes have shifted and obliterated tracks through the Sahara, and again you improvise. In Zaire, you take out batteries from your own vehicle to start the stilled motor of a ferry that must take you across a raging stream. In Cameroon, you discover that the border to Nigeria has been closed for political reasons, and again you and your group make decisions about where to go next.

Riding High Above the Ground

The key to overlanding is the "expedition truck," usually an open-sided, 20-passenger, British-made Bedford with extremely high ground clearance. This permits the vehicle to drive along a riverbed if the roads have been washed out, to come on and off primitive ferries, to negotiate a boulder-strewn path.

The vehicle has so much storage capacity as to be virtually self-sufficient. It carries 200 gallons of fuel (for a 2,000-mile range), 100 gallons of drinking water, oil enough for 12,000 miles, gas stoves, and a huge supply of food. Do these provisions seem excessive? Well, one particularly important route for overlanders, bringing them to the very heart of the Dark Continent, is from Tamanrasset, Algeria, to Gao, Mali. The distance is 1,000 miles on a soft sand track—up to 10 days of driving—unaided by a single filling

Their journeys are through the rawest countryside, in close contact with rural people.

station, a single store, or a single house, with no wood for a fire and no food nearby. Overlanders value the capacity of their Bedford truck.

The development of such vehicles some 30 years ago gave overlanding its start, on a route much favored by the British and Australian adventurers who make up half the audience for it: from London to central India. For nearly 20 years, until conditions in Iran and Afghanistan became unstable, over-landing companies in Britain sent out many dozens of departures each year on a three-month journey somewhat similar to that of Marco Polo: from Europe to and through Turkey into Persia (Iran) and through what is now Afghanistan to India.

The overlanding companies continue to operate that three-month route to this day (for $3,540), though they skirt through only the barest part of Iran (completely away from Teheran) and substitute the Baluchistan Desert of southern Pakistan for the former route through Afghanistan. Even so, most American participants ask to overfly Iran (and do so), leaving the group in Turkey and then awaiting arrival of the truck in Pakistan. Unfortunately, too, the new Pakistan-for-Afghanistan routing has eliminated much of the former dramatic encounter with tribespeople and colorful cultures along the way.

Therefore, in recent years, trans-Africa and trans-South America trips have overtaken the trans-Asian jaunts in popularity. People sign up many months ahead for the 15-week trip from

London to Dover and Europe, and then through North and Central Africa to Nairobi in East Africa. Or they opt for a longer, 19-week journey that includes West Africa as well.

More recently, a number of one-month to six-month trips through South America—seeking out the unusual and the out-of-the-way—have begun to enjoy heavy bookings. And overland operators have now begun to operate shorter, two-week, three-week, and four-week varieties as well, of which a series of 16-day safaris through Kenya and Tanzania are by far the most popular. These cost as little as $1,600, including round-trip air fare from London, less than half of what you'd pay for the usual two-week safari booked from an American firm.

> **The key to overlanding is the "expedition truck," with so much storage capacity as to be virtually self-sufficient.**

Companies and Costs

Astonishingly, most long-term (one month and more) overlanding tours cost only $40 to $50 per person per day, including meals, but plus air fare to the jumping-off point (which is London in most instances). Participants come equipped with only their clothing and a sleeping bag; the overlanding company provides everything else: vehicle, fuel, food, tents, cooking equipment, a driver/leader. One such firm—Guerba Expeditions, represented in the U.S. by Adventure Center, see below—provides three paid personnel per truck (a driver/leader, assistant, and a cook), yet charges only $2 to $3 a day more than the others. While all members of a Guerba expedition continue to participate in chores and cooking, they do so to a slightly lesser extent than is usual.

Guerba, from its base in London (write to, or stop in at, Trailfinders Limited, at 42 Earls Court Road, London W8 6EJ, phone 0171-938-3939, for Guerba's literature or to book a Guerba departure), takes participants aged 18 through 65 on all their overland itineraries. Another major company, Encounter Overland, of London (267 Old Brompton Road, London SW5 9JA, phone 071-370-6845, fax 071-244-9737), limits its passengers to those aged 18 through 40. A third, Dragoman (94 Camp Green, Debenham, Stowmarket, Suffolk, phone 0728-861133), has no problem with clients aged 18 to 55 or 60, depending on the trip. Though nearly a dozen other companies in Britain offer overlanding tours of differing durations and destinations, and their number is joined by one or two companies in Holland, I am reliably told that Guerba (with 20 expedition trucks), Encounter Overland (with 40 such vehicles), and Dragoman (with more), account for more than 70% of the market. Of each 20 people who board one of their trucks for this supreme adventure, four or five are generally British, four or five Australian, three from the U.S., three Canadian, two from New Zealand, and two or so are English-speaking northern Europeans.

All three companies are represented in the United States by Adventure Center of northern California, which makes their yearly catalogs available free of charge, and then accepts bookings on their overland programs. And all three publications are so colorful, well written, and compelling as to awaken the Marco Polo in each of us. Contact **Adventure Center, 1311 63rd St., Suite 200, Emeryville, CA 94608 (phone toll free 800/227-8747, or to 510/654-1879). You can also fax your inquiry to 510/654-4200.**

VIII

New Modes of Travel

Trekking As a Cheap and Fulfilling Mode of Travel

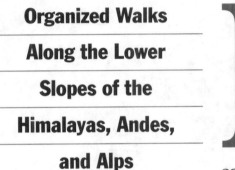

Organized Walks Along the Lower Slopes of the Himalayas, Andes, and Alps

Like the character from Molière who suddenly discovers that he's been speaking "prose" all his life, a growing number of Americans have learned that "trekking" is the unfamiliar word for their favorite vacation activity. Though only the barest handful of travel agents understand the term—and some misuse it horribly—international trekking has become a substantial travel activity for at least 20,000 Americans each year, and is currently marketed by upward of five major nationwide organizations.

In oversimplified terms, trekking is walking—the healthiest sport on earth—but walking of a special nature, elevated to a high art and mental adventure.

Unlike the hiking and backpacking pursued by individuals, trekking is an intricate, organized, group activity in which porters or pack animals carry your camping gear, cooking utensils, and food from one overnight campsite to another. Relieved of that weight, you're able to go where roads and paths aren't, through the most exotic of nations, over breathtaking terrain, but without performing feats of endurance or possessing mountaineering skills. Persons in their middle age are a familiar sight on treks, as are families and even seniors into their seventies.

That's not to say that minimal vigor isn't required—it is. Yet hundreds of perfectly ordinary, normally sedentary (even chubby) Americans are today found in such unlikely locations as the historic, 18,000-foot-high base camp in Nepal used by intrepid climbers for the assault on Mount Everest. They get there by trekking—organized walking—without setting a single metal wedge into stone or tugging a single rope.

And they achieve that forever-memorable trip for total land costs of less than $80 a day (plus air fare to and from Nepal, in this instance); trekking is one of the cheapest of travel modes, considering the distance you've covered and the highly personal nature of your travel arrangements (groups are never more than 15 people in number). No money goes toward hotels or restaurants, because no such places exist in the areas for trekking. Apart from the one-time purchase of tents and gear by the trekking company, labor alone—the chief guide, the cook, the Nepali or Peruvian porters, let's say—are the only major expense of the venture.

Trekking Destinations

I used the example of Nepal and Peru advisedly. For reasons not entirely clear to me, almost all international treks are operated to mountain areas of the world: the Himalayas, the Andes, the Swiss Alps in particular. (While you don't go atop them, you walk along their easy lower slopes, usually at elevations of 8,000 to 10,000 feet.) Though it is theoretically possible to trek through lowland valleys supplied with roads, it is apparently felt inappropriate and uninspiring to do so.

The mountain kingdom of Nepal, at the northern border of India, is the chief trekking destination, accounting for nearly 40% of all treks. The associated Indian states of Kashmir, Sikkim, and Ladakh, and portions of Bhutan, Pakistan, and Tibet, draw another 10% of all trekkers. Together these areas flank the full length of the most remarkable geographical feature on earth—the 1,500-mile-long chain of the Himalayas, the world's tallest mountains.

Trekking is walking of a special nature, elevated to a high art and mental adventure.

It was Nepal, almost entirely covered by mountains, that set off the trend to trekking. A country with scarcely any roads at all, isolated from the outside world until the 1950s, its widely scattered mountainside villages harbor 35 different ethnic groups, whose ways of life have been scarcely touched by outside influences.

The people of Nepal have a particular tradition of hospitality to strangers. As you trek the trails from village to village along the south slope of the Himalayas, you are invited to tea in small council chambers, sometimes to stay the night in the homes of villagers or in monasteries.

With unlimited access to the world's greatest mountains, in this peaceful Shangri-La whose half-Hindu, half-Buddhist population coexists without conflict, your own near-spiritual reactions are almost too intimate to describe. You awake at 6:30am, when a cup of steaming tea or coffee is thrust through the flaps of your tent by a member of the cooking staff. Accompanied by experienced Sherpa guides, you take to the trails, trekking 7 to 10 miles a day at your own pace. The trip starts and ends in the otherworldly capital of Kathmandu, reached by air via New Delhi or Bangkok.

The Peruvian Andes, and that section of it known as the Cordillera Blanca, is next in popularity, accounting for perhaps 30% of all treks. From Lima you fly to Cuzco and there, your gear stowed atop a mountain burro, you embark on a 5-day, 35-mile walk along the ancient Inca Trail to the lost city of Machú Picchú, passing awesome Incan ruins unseen by conventional tourists. Again from Lima, you go by car to Huaraz to embark on an 8-day trek through the heart of Peru's highest mountain area. For an enhanced 14-day (Inca Empire) trip of this nature, as packaged by some of the trekking companies, you pay $1,080 (plus air fare to Peru)—an average of $77 a day for your all-inclusive needs in Peru.

Relieved of your backpacks, you're able to go where roads and paths aren't, but without performing feats of endurance or possessing mountaineering skills.

In the Swiss Alps (a 10% share of the trekking industry), hut-to-hut trekking replaces the traditional variety, with vans bringing your food, clothing, and bedding to austere and unattended mountain lodges scattered among the mountain trails, a day's march from each other. The classic trip is of the Mont Blanc massif, on a trail dominated by the tallest of Europe's mountain peaks. Trips cost as little as $995 for 15 days (plus air fare to Switzerland), including lodging, meals, and the services of a support vehicle that moves camp each day.

The Major Trekking Specialists

Himalayan Travel, Inc., of Stamford, Connecticut, proudly occupies the low end of the trekking industry in price: its consistently low rates for land arrangements ($90 a day, all inclusive) are matched by similar marvels in air fares, bringing you round trip between New York and Kathmandu for $1,600, plus $32 tax (compared with the $1,800 from East Coast cities and $1,700 from West Coast cities charged by most other companies). How that fare is achieved is shrouded in secrecy and the subject of controversy. Its specialty, naturally, is Nepal (40 different treks there, 200 yearly departures), but all other mountain areas are also offered; and through its representation of a leading British trekking company, Sherpa, an extensive program of low-cost treks in the Swiss Alps, the Pyrénées, the Tyrol, and Turkey is also available. Ask for the Sherpa catalog when requesting other literature from **Himalayan Travel, Inc., 112 Prospect Street, Stamford CT 06901 (phone 203/359-3711 or 800/368-2749 outside Connecticut).**

Wilderness Travel, of Berkeley, California, is the price competitor to Himalayan Travel, offering similar treks (including those to Nepal and the Alps), but with almost as much emphasis on the mountain areas of Europe and South America, to which more than a quarter of its passengers go. Both the founders of Wilderness Travel have spent considerable time in Peru and the Patagonian region of Argentina and Chile; fittingly, the company's 24-day Patagonia Expedition is a highlight of all trekking

Trekkers and friends. *Courtesy Overseas Adventure Travel.*

programs. Impressive, too, are the expertise and experience of Wilderness's tour leaders, many with Peace Corps backgrounds or graduate degrees. (In a recent communication to me, they've noted that their clientele has gotten older over the years, and that, consequently, they've improved the amenities of their treks.) For interesting literature, contact **Wilderness Travel, 801 Allston Way, Berkeley, CA 94710 (phone 415/548-0420 or toll free 800/247-6700 outside California).**

Mountain Travel-Sobek of El Cerrito, California, is the largest and oldest of the companies, operating an extraordinary variety of treks on at least five continents. Called "deluxe" by its competitors, its rates—in my reading of them—are only slightly above the industry level: an average of $90 a day in Nepal, from $90 to $150 a day in other mountain regions (plus air fare, of course). Those other areas include Russia, India, Peru, Papua New Guinea, Patagonia, Turkey, and Tibet. Like all trekking companies, Mountain Travel provides the tents, foam sleeping pads, and cooking gear; you provide the sleeping bag. For free, four-color literature, contact **Mountain Travel-Sobek, 6420 Fairmount Ave., El Cerrito, CA 94530 (phone toll free 800/227-2384 or 510/527-8105)**, but for the unabridged, 84-page Mountain Travel catalog, add $2 (which includes postage and handling).

Journeys, of Ann Arbor, Michigan, stresses the cross-cultural aspects of a trek to a far greater extent than the adventure-oriented others. It makes an intense effort to bring about meetings between trekkers and the hill people of each area. Even prior to departure, it involves its trekkers in cultural training for the trip, then delivers daily briefings en route and along the trail by speakers ranging from Buddhist monks and naturalists to ordinary villagers (through interpreters). Specialists to Asia, especially Nepal and Ladakh, since 1978, and highly regarded even by its competitors, Journeys also offers some departures to Latin America, Japan, and Africa, and charges the "going rate" of about $100 a day plus air fare. Contact **Journeys, 4011 Jackson Rd., Ann Arbor, MI 48103 (phone 313/665-4407 or toll free 800/255-8735 outside Michigan)**, for a well-written, well-illustrated catalog.

Above the Clouds Trekking, of Worcester, Massachusetts, is still another small company whose strong suit is Nepal (and the Andes), with Europe (the Cotswolds, the Dordogne, Ireland) a strong second. "Everest from the East," using the less-traveled route there, is among its innovative, $100-a-day offerings in Nepal; the "Mountains, Monasteries, and Markets" trek is its most popular tour. Like Journeys, the company stresses cross-cultural lessons, and designs its treks to maximize contacts with local residents. For brochures, contact **Above the Clouds Trekking, P.O. Box 398, Worcester, MA 01602 (phone 508/799-4499 or toll free 800/233-4499).**

Worldwide Adventures, of Toronto, is the leading Canadian trekking company, attracting more and more participants from the U.S. Treks average $100 a day (U.S.), and go to: Nepal, Ladakh, Bhutan, Tibet, the Andes, and Switzerland, and sometimes include bicycling on a part of the itinerary. You'll be impressed, I think, by its innovative approach set forth in a 32-page catalog, obtained from: **Worldwide Adventures, 36 Finch Avenue West, North York, Ontario MZN 2G9 (phone 416/221-3000 or 800/387-1483).**

And for a trekking company owned and operated by Nepalese themselves (perhaps the most socially responsible way to trek), you'll want to consider booking with Amadablam Adventures of Kathmandu. Under such tantalizing titles as "In Search of the Yak," "Glaciers and Monasteries" and "Explore the Forbidden Kingdom" (a trek to Mustang, a region closed to trekkers until 1992), they specialize in ferreting out the lesser-known and uncrowded routes. Prices in

Nepal average $70 per person per day, with the price dropping to a remarkable $55 per person per day for their 29-day "Classic Nepal" trek (prices for Tibet and India range from $92 a day to $148 a day, depending on the destination).

For more information and a brochure, contact their U.S. representative, **Adventure Center,** **1311 63rd Street, Suite 200, Emeryville, CA 94608 (phone 510/654-1879 or 800/227-8747).**

Trekking! Is this not the ultimate trip, the answer to the vapid vacation, the plastic "package," the madding throng? "When you have to walk six days to a village," a trekker once told me, "you can be pretty sure it is unspoiled by tourism."

A Search for Reliable Sources
of Bicycle Tours

**A Dozen Companies
That Take You Biking
to All Parts of
the World**

ranklin Roosevelt did it in his youth, gliding for weeks along the country roads of Switzerland and Germany in the course of an enchanted summer.

John F. Kennedy, Jr., did it several years ago, on vacation from prep school. And so have many more from other wealthy, or at least moderately well-off, families.

On the lanes and roads of rural France, on the always-level pavements of cycle-loving Holland, over the softly rolling hills of Vermont, in Oregon, and even in Hawaii, increasing numbers of Americans—of ever-increasing age—are flocking to the group bicycle tour.

But why is the activity so expensive—often $200 and more a day? Why are bicycle tours more costly, on occasion, than tours by escorted motorcoach? After all, it is you and your two legs that provide the transportation, eliminating a costly vehicle.

Or is that the case?

What most of us fail to consider, in scanning the bicycle brochures, is that a vehicle almost always does accompany the group, to carry luggage. Unless you've opted for the most rugged form of tour, carrying nothing but your cycling costume, a van or truck and a paid driver follow the bicycling tour at a discreet distance.

Because that group is usually limited to 20 or so people the cost of the vehicle and driver is also divided among fewer people than on a 45-seat motorcoach trip. And because the mode of travel appeals to a more limited audience, all other costs—marketing of the tour, scouting the itinerary, escorting the group—are also proportionately higher per person.

Thus bicycle tours, except in rare instances (see below), will continue to cost a hefty sum—but one that's justified by advantages aplenty: the best sort of exercise in the open air, the closeness to nature and contact with rural people, the scenery, and the relief from urban pressures.

But there are pitfalls. They mainly stem from the ease with which underfinanced or inexperienced people can schedule a bicycle tour. Because so many shaky operators flood the mails each year with ill-conceived programs destined to cause trouble, I've sought to ferret out the firms that have made a substantial, long-term commitment to this travel sport. The list is by no means complete; if you know of others, please write to me at the address given in the Preface.

> Their sometimes hefty price is justified by advantages aplenty: the best sort of exercise in the open air, the closeness to nature and contact with rural people, a relief from urban pressures.

Unless otherwise stated, all tours accept members of any age, provide a supply van, and will rent you a bike (for an extra charge) if you haven't brought your own.

Twelve Bicycle Tour Specialists

Vermont Bicycle Touring, of Bristol, Vermont: The pioneer in country inn cycling, 24 years old, it operates primarily in the unspoiled state of Vermont, with its well-maintained and relatively traffic-free roads. Overseas (and, despite its name, Vermont Bicycle Touring also operates cycling tours in Europe and New Zealand, sometimes through a subsidiary called Travent International), lodgings are in multi-starred hotels of a very high quality level, and therefore cost as much as $350 a day, which is to me unthinkable for a bicycle tour. For the better-priced domestic tours, a mouth-watering, four-color, 45-page catalog can be had by contacting **Vermont Bicycle Touring, P.O. Box 711, Bristol, VT 05443 (phone 802/453-4811**). There you'll also learn about an experimental new summer trip to England ($1,599 plus air fare, for 14 days), 10- to 12-day trips to Holland and France for $1,200 plus air fare, and two winter programs to Hawaii and New Zealand. Vermont, however, remains the chief emphasis.

Brooks Country Cycling Tours, of New York City, is another long-established (17 years) and rather budget-minded operator of bicycle tours in the eastern United States, Louisiana, and Europe. They claim that through low overhead, word-of-mouth marketing and low advertising expenditures, they undercut the others and thus charge an average of only $136 a day for their domestic tours (Martha's Vineyard, Nantucket, Newport, the horse-and-wine country of Virginia), and only $180 a day (plus air fare) for their many overseas destinations (including a cycling trip through Holland on which your baggage is carried by barge, where you also stay overnight). Manager Arlene Brooks told me of an encounter with the client of another bicycling company she met in Provence who was paying $1,000 more than she would have paid for a Brooks Country Cycling tour of the same area (the other tour featured a nightly cocktail party). Contact

Biking through the chateau country.
Courtesy Butterfield & Robinson.

Brooks Country Cycling Tours, 140 West 83rd Street, New York, NY 10024 (phone 212/874-5151).

Euro-Bike Tours, of DeKalb, Illinois: Well-priced tours of Europe (by the pricey standards of bike touring, about $235 a day, plus air fare), most of two weeks' duration. Interesting itineraries (the Dordogne of France, the islands of Scandinavia, Hungary, and Austria, the "Romantic Road" of Germany) operate May through early October, on which you receive room, breakfast, and 30% of your dinners, and stay in high-quality, but non-first-class hotels. This appears to be an especially good choice for singles, as 50% of their clientele is of that status. Contact **Euro-Bike Tours, P.O. Box 990, DeKalb, IL 60115 (phone 800/321-6060 or 815/758-8851).**

International Bicycle Tours of Essex, Connecticut, specializes in tours for cyclers over 50; the company lays heavy stress on the gentle pace of their tours. Says manager Frank Behrendt: "Our trips are more leisurely, not races or marathons. We make many stops and take it slow so that people can enjoy the scenery. Two weeks ago, we had an 88-year-old man on one of our tours." Traveling primarily to Holland (whose flat terrain is ideal for the older cycler), Austria and Denmark, IBT's trips use high-quality hotels, supply breakfast and several dinners, and cost $1,320 per person for one-week tours, $1,780 for the two-week variety (plus air fare)—the latter working out to about $127 a day, a value. Contact **International Bicycle Tours, 7 Champlin Square, P.O. Box 754, Essex, CT 06426 (phone 203/767-7005)**, and also inquire about their domestic tours (to Mount Dora in Florida, Cape Cod, Pennsylvania Dutch Country).

Butterfield & Robinson, of Toronto: A highly elegant (and quite expensive, in my view) company active as well in the United States. Its major bike program is to Europe (France, Italy, England, especially); uses high-quality villas, castles, country homes, and châteaux; includes two meals a day (with minor exceptions) at top restaurants; throws in "wine tastings"; and averages $375 (some tours more, some less) per person per day, not including air fare to Europe. For a 100-page catalog, like a costly picture book, contact **Butterfield & Robinson, 70 Bond St., Suite 300, Toronto, ON, M5B 1X3 Canada (phone 416/864-1354, or toll free 800/268-8415 in Canada, 800/387-1147 outside Canada).**

Gerhard's Bicycle Odysseys, of Portland, Oregon: From May through September, two-week tours to Germany, Austria, France, and Norway, at an average of $225 a day, plus air fare. All are personally led by German-born Gerhard Meng, now in his 22nd year of bicycle-tour operation. Fine country hotels are used; cyclists receive daily breakfast and almost all dinners; New Zealand in February and March, Denmark in summer, have recently been added to the roster of itineraries. Contact **Gerhard's Bicycle Odysseys, P.O. Box 757, Portland, OR 97207 (phone 503/223-2402).**

Backroads Bicycle Touring, of Berkeley, California. Operating more than a thousand trips a year, they've recently become the largest of the bicycle tour companies, and their trips span the globe: the U.S., all of Europe, China, Thailand, Bali, New Zealand, Mexico and Costa Rica, Chile, and Argentina, as well as France, England, Thailand, and Ireland—all well described in a slick, 103-page free catalog. Groups are of all ages; if seniors find some itineraries too taxing, they can ride in the support van (the aptly named "sag wagon") for part of each day. Tours include three meals daily, plus accommodations in fine inns, and average $220 a day, though some are camping itineraries costing $110 a day (on the latter, Backroads claims to cook remarkable meals in their "kitchen on wheels"). Contact **Backroads Bicycle Touring, 1516 5th St., Berkeley, CA 94710-1740 (phone 415/527-1555 or toll free 800/533-2573 outside California)**. This is a top firm, now in its second decade and growing fast.

A bicycle-tour operator of particular renown uses high-quality villas, castles, country homes, and châteaux.

Paradise Pedallers, of Charlotte, North Carolina: Two-week and three-week tours of New Zealand, December through March, at $190 a day (plus round-trip air fare) for inns or motels and two meals a day; and yet a support van accompanies the group, in addition to two experienced guides pedaling alongside. Contact **Paradise Pedallers, 1 West Jordan Street, Brevard, NC 28712 (phone 704/884-7475)**, and inquire especially about their one-week tours of Florida, North and South Carolina, Georgia, and Bermuda.

Forum Travel International, of Pleasant Hill, California: In business for 31 years, it claims to be one of the oldest and largest of America's bicycle operators. It achieves that status, in part, by offering—in addition to the standard forms of group bicycle touring—a non-group method of cycling in some of the countries it tours. How does that work? Every morning, you're given a highly detailed map to your next destination, are told when dinner will be served, and then have the entire day to peddle as fast or slowly as you may wish, stopping to sightsee or slumber at the side of the road. When you eventually arrive at your hotel, your luggage awaits, having been delivered there by a van that morning. In this manner, the bicycling tour operator does not need two escorts per group (one to accompany the group, one to drive the van), but only one—the van driver. Non-group tours of this sort average only $120 a day per person (plus air fare) for two meals and fine lodgings, and are offered in France, Bavaria, Switzerland, Austria, Hungary, Ireland, Scotland, Portugal, and Tuscany; tours to other countries are done in the standard group fashion and cost more. Contact **Forum Travel International, 91 Gregory Lane, Suite 21, Pleasant Hill, CA 94523 (phone 510/671-2900)**.

Bicycle Africa, of Bellevue, Washington: For a very special type of traveler, full of adventure and insight, this is a program of two- and four-week bicycle tours to either Uganda, Tanzania, Tunisia, Zimbabwe, Mali, Burkina Faso, Togo, or Benin, operated throughout the year. Because no traveling van is used, and accommodations are spartan, costs average only $35 to $50 day, including everything except air fare to Africa (which runs around $1,000 round-trip to West Africa, $1,500 to southern Africa). "We journey through cultures, history, landscapes, cuisines, and lifestyles, close enough to touch them," says a spokesperson; "we enjoy this fascinating and diverse continent on a personal level not usually attainable by tourists." And, says a recent participant, "the trip, a month long, is worth four years of college anthropology courses; it was the greatest experience of my life." For detailed information and brochures, contact **Bicycle Africa, International Bicycle Fund, 4887 Columbia Dr., South Seattle, WA 98108-1919 (phone 206/628-9314)**.

The Sierra Club, of San Francisco: Operated by the fierce and powerful environmentalist organization, 500,000 members strong, this is my own personal favorite of all the programs, a nationwide array of one-week to 10-day tours within the United States, on which often no "sag wagon" is provided and leaders are unpaid volunteers. Because of that, costs average only $55 a day, including all lodgings and meals. You provide your own bike and are responsible for its upkeep. Programs run from late spring to early autumn; sample tours are "Biking through Civil War History" (7 days for $480), "The Frank Lloyd Wright Wisconsin Tour" (7 days for $400), "Cycling Prince Edward Island and the Magdalens" (8 days for $490), "Bicycling the Big Island, Hawaii" (7 days for $395), "Mountain Biking New York's Adirondack Forest" (7 days for $440), "Mountain Biking the Alaskan Wilderness" (14 days for $1,295)—you get the picture. Tours are always planned to allow maximum independence to participants; you are required to reach the destination each evening, but are otherwise free to wander and detour as you like. Pace is vigorous but not agonizing; changes of clothes are carried in panniers attached to hubcaps or in handlebar bags; groups are limited to 15 people. For detailed listings, contact the **Sierra Club, 730 Polk St., San Francisco, CA 94109 (phone 415/923-5630)**, and send $2 for the yearly, January/February edition of *Sierra,* which contains a directory of all bike tours scheduled for the year.

Hosteling International-American Youth Hostels, of Washington, D.C.: The price champion of all the bicycle operators, for people of all ages, its trips average $40 to $50 a day in the U.S., $55 to $75 a day in Europe, including all three meals (cooperatively prepared by the group) daily, but plus air fare to the jumping-off point in the U.S. (air fare to Europe is included in the cost). That's because spartan hostels are used for lodgings, and no van accompanies the group; rather, you balance a knapsack over the rear wheel. Contact **Hosteling International—American Youth Hostels, 733 15th Street NW, Suite 840, Washington, D.C. 20005 (phone 202/783-6161)**.

Good News for Devotees of the Meandering Cruise by Freighter

After Declining to a Dangerous Level of Capacity, the Passenger-Carrying Freighter Is on the Rise Again

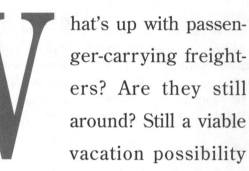

What's up with passenger-carrying freighters? Are they still around? Still a viable vacation possibility for retired Americans with lots of time?

Had those questions been put as recently as 10 years ago, the answer to them might have been a shaky "No." Capping a decade-long decline, the number of such ships sailing from U.S. ports fell to a paltry 45 or so in 1986. The departure from the field of two major cargo lines, Moore McCormack and Delta; the replacement of several older passenger-freighters with newer, all-freight vessels; a spasmodic reluctance by younger cargo executives to bother with passengers—all threatened to end the activity.

Since freighters are limited to a passenger complement of only 12 persons (otherwise they'd be required by law to carry an expensive doctor), the recent decline reduced the U.S. openings to fewer than 400 berths a month.

Gradually, you heard less—saw fewer ads and newsletter mentions—about those long, leisurely sails to Durban and Dar es Salaam, to Mombasa and Yokohama. Diehards fretted and festered on waiting lists for a year and more; others, more desperate, flew to Hamburg, or Gdynia, Poland, to board the few Europe-originating passenger freighters.

Yet suddenly—in 1987—the picture changed. As with a pendulum, a Hegelian counterreaction, 1987 saw a sharp, upward swing to more than 60 passenger freighters. And from 1988 to 1995, still more. A recent, radical mechanization of ship functions has reduced the need for crew, freeing additional cabin space for passengers. A cyclical glut in cargo capacity has forced lines to search for new revenue sources, which can only come from passengers.

Thus the German-owned Columbus Line (phone 212/432-1700) has reentered the field with eight new passenger freighters sailing from both coasts to Australia and New Zealand; the British-owned Pace Line plies the same route with several passenger-adapted ships added in 1995.

The Cast Line now carries passengers on a number of vessels from Montréal to Antwerp. Mineral Shipping has assigned additional ships to the classic task of "tramp steaming"—wandering the seas like a driven Ahab, dashing here and there as radio messages direct, changing course in mid-Atlantic to pick up containers from South America, diverting them to the west coast of Africa, and providing 12 lucky passengers with the cruise of their lives.

(By freighter tradition, passengers pay for a fixed number of days; if the trip comes in early, they receive a refund; if it takes longer—as it often does—they receive the extra days free.)

Come 1996, and we shall also see the return of more "cargo liners"—freighters deliberately built to carry 90 and more passengers. The Norwegian-owned Navaran Line has already supplied us with one such vessel (the M/V Americana, higher in category and price than the average freighter) sailing from the East Coast to South America on a near-regular schedule, and you can reach them at **111 Pavonia Avenue, Jersey City, NJ 07310 (phone 800/ 451-1639 or 201/798-5656)**; more of these enhanced-cargo/passenger ships are expected to reach the market shortly.

Waiting lists are thus back to a normal six weeks to four and five months. Last-minute berths are increasingly available. Freighter fans are once again full of expectations and plans.

Why such eagerness? Because the activity is incomparable.

You visit exotic, untouristed ports. Time stretches before you, unlimited, unpressured. You dine with ship's officers, have the run of the ship, attend periodic barbecues on deck and biweekly parties, dart into the galley to fix your own sandwich or pour a beer, as the mood hits. You delight in the intimacy of a lengthy, shared, unstructured experience, gathering at night around the VCR and its extensive library of tapes that all the ships now carry.

> **You visit exotic, untouristed ports. Time stretches before you, unlimited, unpressured. You have the run of the ship, dine with the ship's officers. You delight in the intimacy of a lengthy, shared experience.**

You incur half the cost of the average passenger liner. While benchmark rates are an average of $90 a day, some budget-style ships charge as little as $75 or $80 a day, some overseas-originating freighters as little as $65 a day.

What is asked of you is flexibility (you rarely know exact sailing dates until a week or so ahead) and time (voyages last for 30 days, 45 days, even 70 and 90 days).

Passenger-carrying freighter. *Courtesy Ford's Freighter Guides.*

number of freighter companies into the passenger business. She has since been succeeded by veteran freighter specialist Mary Mostue, whom I find fully as knowledgeable and personable.

Ms. Mostue derides the widely held notion that freighter capacity is incapable of meeting the demand. "There is always space around if you don't care where you go," she says. "We can move a person in two weeks. Only when you insist on, say, New Zealand, or hot-weather ports in winter, must you wait three or four months for a ship."

To prove the point, Mostue's 26-times-a-year "Freighter Space Advisory," a smartly edited six-page newsletter, devotes itself to photos and descriptions of ships leaving in the next month or two from both U.S. and foreign ports.

The recent show-stopper: a periodic departure from Charleston, sailing to New Orleans, then to Houston, then through the Panama Canal to Sydney, Melbourne, and Brisbane (Australia), from there to three ports in New Zealand, back to the Panama Canal, and finishing in Philadelphia—a full 70 days at sea. Off-season cost (March through September) is $5,190 per person, whether single or double, amounting to $74 a day; in high season (October through May), $8,100 single, $7,300 per person in a double.

Contact **Freighter World Cruises, Inc., 180 S. Lake Ave., Suite 335, Pasadena, CA 91101 (phone 818/449-3106)**, and send $33 for a one-year subscription to the "Freighter Space Advisory"; the same firm then makes the reservations and handles all details.

TravLtips of Flushing, New York, is the other combination freighter–travel agency/newsletter company, except that its publication, a bimonthly,

Because of that, passengers are invariably in their 60s and early 70s and retired (unless they're professors on sabbatical or writers seeking seclusion—several authors are known to sail on three or four freighter cruises each year). Interestingly, most freighter lines have recently raised their maximum age limits from 69 to 79 (and occasionally higher)—a tribute to the increasing vigor of today's senior citizens.

What is asked of you is flexibility (you rarely know exact sailing dates until a week or so ahead) and time (voyages last for 30 days, 45 days, even 70 and 90 days).

The largest of the passenger/freight companies is the Lykes Line, with upward of 28 ships in service; Columbus Lines is the next most numerous, with 10 ships. Polish Ocean Lines is among the cheapest ($70 to $85 a day), occasionally sailing from Port Newark.

Sources of Freighter Information

Freighter World Cruises, Inc., of Pasadena, California, was the base of the late Mary LeBlanc, an industry pioneer who personally propelled a is a slick and elaborate 32-page magazine (*TravLtips*), devoted not only to "freightering" (through first-person accounts by subscribers of their own recent trips), but to exotic or long-term sailings by ordinary passenger ships—the kind that would appeal to the heavily traveled, sophisticated devotees of freighters.

Currently edited and administered by the 40-year-old son of its founder, the late Ed Kirk, the publication/organization is staffed by several experienced reservationists and other cruise experts.

Send $15 for a one-year subscription (and membership), or $25 for two years to **TravLtips, 163-07 Depot Rd. (P.O. Box 580-188), Flushing, NY 11358 (phone 718/ 939-2400 or toll free 800/872-8584 outside New York State).** From the same address, and without yet committing to membership, you can also request a free pamphlet of frequently asked questions about passenger-freighters ("Can I bring a pet?," "Can I work my way across?," "Is it cheaper than a plane?"—the answer to that last question being no).

Unlike the first two organizations, the 35-year-old Freighter Travel Club, of Roy, Washington, makes no reservations, sells no trips or tickets, and simply confines itself to publication of a monthly eight-page newsletter, with charming and helpful contents. Send $18 (for a one-year subscription), or $32 for two years, to **Freighter Travel Club of America, 3524 Harts Lake Rd., Roy, WA 98580,** addressing any specific inquiries to its veteran editor, a walking encyclopedia of freighter lore, Leland J. Pledger.

The larger companies are supplemented by a handful of smaller, travel agency specialists in freighters—often a single person—of which **Van Dyck's Cruises and Tours, 1301 66th Street North, St. Petersburg, FL 33710 (phone 813/381-5151 or 800/282-5151),** has been in business for more than 25 years; Jan Van Dyck is the owner. Consider, too, a firm called **Sea the Difference, 420 Fifth Avenue, New York, NY 10018, (phone 800/ 666-9333 or 212/354-4409),** top U.S. representative for one of the biggest of the European freighter operators—Mediterranean Shipping. They are 50 ships strong, of which 30 are currently carrying passengers on 11 different itineraries to the Mediterranean, Africa, Europe, and the Indian Ocean. The latter's most popular sailings are those that go trans-Atlantic from the U.S. east coast to northern Europe in the summer months.

The Trend to the Tiny Ship

Increasing Numbers of Vacationers Are Opting for Intimate Vessels Able to Take Them to Secluded Places

On the quays leading to a store-lined main street, a scraggly group of hawkers fidgets nervously as they await the imminent on-slaught of 1,400 visitors. At curbside stands bearing English-language signs, they will have short minutes to dispose of their cheap straw hats, their gaudy T-shirts.

As the tenders deposit a regiment of humanity from the giant vessel anchored offshore, noise and confusion erupt. A military band blares away. The first arrivals go dashing to a celebrated perfume shop, while others rush to ranks of foul-smelling tour buses or to stand in line for casino admission.

And that is the scene encountered as many as seven times in a single week by Americans sailing through the Caribbean on certain massive cruise ships. Others, repelled by the urban qualities they traveled so many miles to avoid, are opting for a wholly different seagoing experience, on a "tiny" ship—one that accommodates 60 to 150 passengers and goes to quiet ports or secluded beaches.

In a backlash from current cruise-ship trends (one line is contemplating construction of a 5,000-passenger behemoth), a market is growing for yacht-like vessels with shallow drafts enabling them to go directly onto palm-lined shores or to small marinas in cozy bays.

Their customers often are an affluent but unpretentious lot who relax on board in shorts and sandals, follow no schedules at all, and attend no ship "events"—there aren't any.

Ashore, they dine quietly in the fresh-fish restaurant of a backwater town, or lie reading a paperback novel in a rope hammock, hearing nothing but sea gulls and waves.

Among the "tiny" ships that bring you that form of paradise are:

Windjammer Cruises

Like that cabin boy in *Two Years Before the Mast,* you'll stumble in dazed excitement onto the teakwood decks of an actual ocean schooner with sails—as sleek as a greyhound, but with the tiny, cot-equipped cabins you'd expect on so narrow a vessel.

You have the run of the entire ship: bowsprit, rigging, even crow's nest and at the wheel—and are actually encouraged to help the professional crew with steering the ship. Each day you anchor off a quiet beach or tiny port, to which your lunch is brought by kitchen crew wading through the surf. You live throughout in shorts and sandals, in sheer relaxation or happy camaraderie with like-minded, unpretentious, adventure-seeking people from all over the world who have heard of these renowned ships. They range in size from the "giant" S/V *Fantome* (126 passengers) and S/V *Polynesia* (128 passengers) down to the S/V *Flying Cloud* (80 passengers) and M/S *Yankee Clipper* (66

A market is growing for yachtlike vessels with shallow drafts enabling them to go directly onto palm-lined shores or to small marinas in cozy bays.

passengers, a former scientific survey ship equipped with two large sails). You sail through the Grenadines, the exotic Leeward Islands of the Caribbean, the British Virgin Islands, and to other highlights of the West Indies. And you pay only $525 to $925 for a six-day cruise in most cabins, plus air fare from the U.S. ($299 from the East Coast, $499 from the West Coast). For

The S/V *Fantome* in full sail. *Courtesy Windjammer Barefoot Cruises, Ltd.*

details, contact **Windjammer Barefoot Cruises, P.O. Box 120, Miami Beach, FL 33119 (phone toll free 800/327-2601 for reservations or information, 800/327-2600 for brochures)**, and ask them also about their monthly singles' cruises with guaranteed ratios of 50/50 for men and women.

American-Canadian Caribbean Line

Budget-priced cruises of Central and South America in winter, the inland waterways of Rhode Island, Montréal, Québec, the Great Lakes, and "Intercoastal" in summer, on yachtlike ships carrying as few as 78 passengers apiece. Rates range from a low $99 to $185 per person per day, not including air fare to embarkation cities. On each ship used in the winter season, "bow ramps" allow passengers to walk, not climb, from the ship to the most isolated and inviting beaches. For literature, contact **American-Canadian Caribbean Line, Inc., P.O. Box 368, Warren, RI 02885 (phone 401/247-0955, or toll free 800/ 556-7450 outside Rhode Island)**.

You have the run of the entire ship: bowsprit, rigging, even crow's nest and at the wheel.

Clipper Cruise Line

Elegant luxury yachts carrying only 100 and 138 passengers apiece, the *Yorktown Clipper* and the *Nantucket Clipper* confine themselves to the most secluded and lightly trafficked waterways, using rubber Zodiac landing craft to access the wildest of beaches and romantic hidden coves. In winter, they sail the Virgin Islands, the Grenadines, the Windward and Leeward Islands, the Lesser Antilles, and the Orinoco River. In spring, they go to Costa Rica, Mexico, the Pacific Northwest, the intercoastal waterways. In summer, they return to spring destinations but sail them in the reverse order (and include Alaska). Naturalists and several other varieties of scientists are on board to deliver lectures. For all their exquisite attentions and amenities, prices are not extreme: $220 to $300 per person per day for most cabins, but plus a specially reduced air fare to embarkation points. For literature, contact **Clipper Cruise Line, Windsor Building, 7711 Bonhomme Ave., St. Louis, MO 63105 (phone 314/727-2929 or toll free 800/325-0010 outside Missouri)**.

Windstar Sail Cruises

The newest (1987), longest (440 feet), tallest (masts 20 stories tall), and maybe largest of the world's sailing ships is the *Wind Star,* berthed at the island of Barbados, from which it makes weekly one-week cruises to such magical spots as Mustique, Bequia, Tobago Cay, Palm Island, St. Lucia, and other unlikely ports of call (for the standard ships). It places its passengers in cabins 185 square feet in size, and plies them with every luxury (like impulsively buying 300 pounds of lobster at a native market for consumption at a beach barbecue that day). The total passenger complement is 148, on ships whose sails are directed by computer; the mood is casual elegance, the charge about $300 per person per day—which is not as high as you'd expect for an experience as exclusive as this. A sister ship, the *Wind Song,* sails year-round from Tahiti, while still a third vessel of identical size and design, the *Wind Spirit,* sails along the French and Italian Rivieras in summer, the islands of St. Thomas, St. Barts, St. Maarten, and Virgin Gorda in winter, all for approximately the same rates (which do not, however, include air fare to and from embarkation points). For details, contact **Windstar Sail Cruises, Ltd., 300 Elliot Ave. West, Seattle, WA 98119 (phone 206/ 281-3535 or toll free 800/258-7245 for information, 800/626-9900 for brochures)**.

I have not mentioned the *Sea Goddess* ships of the Cunard Lines because their rates are truly high, and out of reach for the great majority of our readers; nor have I included several vessels whose 400-passenger size disqualifies them from inclusion in this discussion.

Sailing the Tall Ships

Low-Cost Schooner Cruises for Non-Standard Sailors

What do you do if you're lured by the sea but you can't stand the increasing sameness, the crushing uniformity, of the world's large cruise ships?

It's a growing problem. As cruising becomes big business, conducted by billion-dollar corporations, ships are becoming alike in their atmosphere, amenities, and programs. All feel compelled to offer mindless, Las Vegas–style revues at night, Bingo in the afternoon, mass aerobics and jogging tracks, crowded shore excursions, and big movie theaters. Though each will claim to have distinct characteristics—"Italian-style cruising," computer classes, lectures by ecologists—in my opinion there's not a dime's worth of difference among most of them.

Unless you're talking of the "Tall Ships." In schooners carrying 30 to 90 passengers, under canvas sails billowing in the wind, a small but select number of American vacationers are enjoying the classic thrills of the sea as it used to be, in the days before "The Love Boat" converted a rather elitist intellectual activity into a robotlike, mass-volume routine. Those lucky few are also paying half the cost of a standard cruise, about $110 a day.

But the schooners aren't for everyone. Cabins are tiny, beds are often bunks, meals family-style and without choice, planned activities few, and nightlife nil. Instead of pursuing an active schedule, passengers simply stretch out on deck to peruse a paperback, go snorkeling when the mood hits, stroll deep in thought along the undeveloped beaches that shelter the ship by day. Does that sound bad? It's exactly the reason why many Americans wouldn't dream of cruising except in a "Tall Ship."

The wind-driven vessels (they all have supplementary motors) making regular weekly cruises throughout the year, and accepting bookings from the public at large, are—as best I can determine—17 in number: 5 operated by Windjammer Barefoot Cruises, Inc., and 12 offered by a total of five other firms. Windjammer created this travel mode back in 1947, and is said by some to have grown a bit jaded, though others still sing its praises. The remaining firms have all emerged in the past decade to do battle with Windjammer, and perhaps try harder.

Here is what cruising was like before "The Love Boat" converted a rather elitist intellectual activity into a standard holiday of rote-like scheduled events.

Except for Blackbeard's Cruises and Bounty Voyages (see below), all the lines operate their one-week trips on a rather truncated basis: their ships usually stay in the port of embarkation for an initial night, and then spend five remaining nights at sea—not really a full week. Some ships do, other ships don't, provide private facilities; read the brochures carefully. But all supply a wonderful closeness to the sea and nature, a devil-may-care informality, a loosening of habits and inhibitions—and isn't that what a vacation is for?

Windjammer Barefoot Cruises, Inc., P.O. Box 120, Miami Beach, FL 33119 (phone toll free 800/327-2601, 800/432-3364 in Florida), has—as earlier noted—a multiple fleet (five schooners) and the largest ships (carrying 66 to 126 passengers apiece, double the capacity of the other lines), but those attributes of size aren't regarded as advantages by everyone; some prefer the greater intimacy, camaraderie, and informality of the other lines. One of its fleet, the *Mandalay,* undertakes successive 13-day cruises of the Caribbean (West Indies and Grenadines) for prices ranging from $1,550 to $1,800 per person for most cabins, while the others house you for one night in port and then for five at sea (British Virgin Islands, West Indies, and Grenadines) for $825 to $1,025 per person; persons staying on board for 12 consecutive nights get (a) a $25 discount, and (b) free lodgings on board on the intermediate Saturday and Sunday when the ship is in port. Since the ships vary their itineraries each week, never repeating an island in succession, numerous passengers opt for the two-week pattern, and spend their two intermediate nights exploring the port of embarkation on foot, returning each night to the ship for meals and bed. Islands from which Windjammer sails throughout the year include Antigua, Tortola, St. Maarten, Trinidad, and Grenada. Islands visited: dozens. And inexpensive air fares are made available by the line to each departure point.

Blackbeard's Cruises, P.O. Box 661091, Miami FL 33266 (phone 305/888-1226 or toll free 800/327-9600 outside Florida), operates three 65-foot sloops, housing 22 passengers and six crew members apiece, that make seven-day/six-night cruises from Miami to the Bahamas, primarily for diving. Boats leave Miami on Saturday afternoons throughout the year, return the following Friday morning, charge $649 per person for the entire week, take you for three to four dives a day off the boat, then spend the nights in calm anchorages on the placid "lee" side of Bimini, Freeport, or the Berry Islands. Can you go if you're not a diver? Absolutely, says the small firm (in business for 16 years), provided you're not expecting a "shuffleboard [activity-filled] cruise." Rather, the nondiver will pass the time "snorkeling off the beach, shell-hunting on deserted islands . . . staying up late for conversation under the stars . . . or simply sleeping in."

Yankee Schooner Cruises, P.O. Box 696, Camden, ME 04843 (phone 207/ 236-4449 or toll free 800/255-4449 outside Maine), sails the chilly waters of Maine in summer and early fall (late May through late September), then repeats its pattern of continuous one-week cruises in the U.S. and British Virgin Islands from early December to mid-April. This is a one-ship firm, but what a ship: the 137-foot schooner *Roseway,* built in 1925 of sturdy oak,

with varnished mahogany walls throughout and other elegant fittings for its complement of 36 passengers. You board on Sunday afternoon, then sail with the tide on Monday, returning to port (Camden in Maine, St. Thomas in the U.S. Virgin Islands) by midday Saturday. Prices vary, but average (except for a surcharged race week) $95 a day in

> **C**abins are tiny, beds are often bunks, meals family-style and without choice, planned activities few, and nightlife nil.

Maine, $105 to $140 a day in the Virgin Islands. This time, scuba-diving is not at all stressed (although available), but snorkeling is, along with swimming, beach lolling, windsurfing, beachcombing, and reading.

Dirigo Cruises, 39 Waterside Lane, Clinton, CT 06413 (phone 203/669-7068), takes reservations for the 140-foot, traditionally rigged (as in the 1860s) schooner *Soren Larson,* and the 85-year-old *Sylvina W. Beal,* of which the former sails the South Pacific, while the latter goes to the Caribbean in winter, the U.S. East Coast in summer. Prices on both average $100 to $110 per person per day. Passengers are encouraged to assist the crew, but spend most of their time swimming, snorkeling, or navigating the two small sailboats carried aboard.

Tall Ship Adventures, Inc., 1389 South Havana Street, Aurora, CO 80012 (phone toll free 800/662-0090), operates the most elegant of the authentic sailing ships—the 36-passenger *Sir Francis Drake*—with private "heads" and showers for every cabin, full-size double beds in some, and elaborate meals. Its one-week rates are thus a bit elevated, but still well below those of standard cruise ships: $995 per person in a cabin with upper and lower beds, $1,195 with side-by-side beds; children under 12 sharing a cabin with their parents receive a 50% discount. For this, you cruise in winter (summer rates are $100 less per person) through both the

A "Star Clipper." *Courtesy Star Clippers.*

U.S. and British Virgin Islands, visiting St. Thomas, St. John, Jost van Dyke, Peter Island, Dead Man's Chest, Cooper's Island, Tortola, and Virgin Gorda. And at night you enjoy what most schooners deliberately omit from their facilities: a lounge with stereo, video, and TV.

Worldwide Adventures, 36 Finch Avenue West, Toronto M2N2G9, Ontario, Canada (phone 416/221-3000 or 800/387-1483), is the agent for another popular "tall ship" alongside and over the Great Barrier Reef of Australia, and involves its passengers in snorkeling and guided reef walks. With 30 passengers, a crew of six, and a 120-foot vessel with three masts, the *Coral Trekker* departs Australia's Queensland Coast weekly throughout the year, and charges a uniform $895 per person per week in a double, not including air fare to and from Australia.

Traverse Tall Ship Company, 133390 S.W. Bayshore Drive, Traverse City, MI (phone 619/941-2000 or 800/968-8800), operates six-day cruises of the waters of the Great Lakes, aboard the traditional Schooner *Manitou,* from Northport, Michigan, in July and August ($799 for the week) and three-day cruises for between $325 and $375 per person in June and September.

And finally, **Star Clippers, 4101 Salzado Avenue, Coral Gables, FL 33146 (phone 800/442-0551),** operates large and brand-new "tall ships" (360 feet long, 180 passengers, 72 in crew) in the Caribbean and Mediterranean, luxuriously outfitted, but at rates higher than those we've been considering. Nevertheless, there are some dates when rates for some cabins drop to $138 per person per day, and you might want to write for a catalog.

Merely to scan the illustrated pages of each company's brochure is to thrill to an eternal urge. "Oh, I must go down to the seas again," wrote poet laureate John Masefield, "To the lonely sea and the sky/And all I ask is a Tall Ship/And a star to steer her by."

Country Walking Tours Are Another Major New Discovery

Walking Inn to Inn, While a Van Carries Gear Ahead

Are you a "Closet" Walker? While others jog on their vacations, or go bicycling or white-water rafting, do you simply sneak off to walk, in utter bliss, for miles and miles?

If so, you're one of a growing number of Americans who go away to walk—even to places thousands of miles from home. They believe, along with the American Heart Association, that brisk walking is the most healthful holiday sport, as aerobic as running (and far easier on the joints), and the best possible way to approach the life and people of an unfamiliar destination. The popularity of walking has resulted in the emergence of a surprising number of walking-tour operators covering every part of the globe.

With some operators, you walk inn to inn while a van carries your gear ahead or brings you lunch. With others,

Walking tours are as aerobic as running (and far easier on the joints), and the best possible way to approach the life and people of an unfamiliar destination.

you remain three or four days at a time in one base—a country hotel or a cluster of B&Bs—and walk from there. While England is clearly the most popular destination for walking vacations, few of the world's flatlands are spared attention by walking-tour operators. I've surveyed eight major ones:

Knapsack Tours, 5961 Zinn Dr., Oakland, CA 94611 (phone 510/339-0160), despite its name, says that backpacks are never needed on its four tours each year, to Switzerland (in mid-June for two weeks at $1,785, three weeks at $2,685, not including air fare); to Yosemite (first half of August, for $795 a week), to the Canadian Rockies (mid-September, 12 days for $1,385); to the Golden Gate Headlands/ San Francisco area (mid-August, five days, costing $365; can be added to the Yosemite trip); and to Olympic Park, Washington (five days in early September, $485). Vans carry luggage; daily hikes are four to six hours long and prices are kept down by the use of modest lodgings appropriate (in my opinion) to the unpretentious nature of the activity. Moreover, singles share rooms with hikers of the same sex, eliminating any single supplement.

Samvinn Travel, 12 Austurstraeti (P.O. Box 910), Reykjavik 121, Iceland (phone 354/1-69-1010), operates both 11-day walking tours (usually $1,295) and 5-day walking tours (for $625) of largely uninhabited areas of Iceland, with accommodations in schools and huts scattered among eerie lava fields and craters. On most tours, a bus takes participants from base to base for daily hikes. Dates are late June through August; add air fare to Iceland. Write for a compelling catalog.

Wilderness Southeast, 711 Sandtown Road, Savannah, GA 31410-5108, discussed in our chapter on cooperative camping, also goes walking through some of the roughest terrain in Costa Rica, for 10 days at a time, and $1,500 in charges (including everything except air fare to that nation). You pass gurgling and rumbling active volcanoes, jungle waterfalls and natural swimming pools, and rainforests, accompanied by skilled naturalists. But as strenuous as it is, you stay each night in comfortable lodges. By contrast, a 10-day "Jungle Backpack" tour for $1,080 per person including all three meals daily, takes you camping in two-person tents—and you carry your own gear. Back in Georgia, a four-day hike around the state's largest barrier island (Cumberland) costs $310 for everything, and is so relatively tame that families are invited.

SBS Walk'n the West, 376C Rockrimmon Boulevard, Colorado Springs, CO 80919 (phone 719/531-9577) deals in "soft adventures," hikes without camping for "active folks over fifty" (with younger ones invited, too). A small, family-run business, it operates once-a-month hikes, March through December, each of a week's duration, through nature sites of Colorado, Utah, Arizona, Washington, and California, including the red sandstone arches of Canyonlands National Park, the rainforest and mountains of Olympic National Park, and the wildflower-laden trails leading to Pike's Peak. Each trip is led by owners Sue and Bob Shott, who guarantee a ratio of one hike leader to each six persons (for groups larger than 12, they add their son and daughter-in-law to staff). Rates, including one hotel for the entire week, all meals, and transportation from the hotel to the kick-off point, are $985 per person, double occupancy.

British Coastal Trails ("BCT"), Scenic Walking Tours, 1001 "B" Avenue, Suite 302, Coronado, CA 92118 (phone 619/ 437-1211) is much pricier, but places you into manor houses, unique country inns, and even on a comfortable sleeping barge that trails you as you walk. Though they offer walking tours to France, Italy, Switzerland, and the American West, their specialty is Britain, and treks include "The Coast to Coast Walk" from Whitby on the North Sea, through British national parks and the Lake District to St. Bees Head on the Irish Sea; "Ancient Land of Dorset" (the pre-history of Britain: Bronze age burial mounds, fossils, and the 13th-century Salisbury Cathedral); "Scottish Borders and Northumberland" (12th-century abbeys and stone villages). Trips are characterized as either "leisurely" (6 to 8 miles a day) or "long distance" (12 to 15 miles a day), and cost $1,795 for eight days, $1,985 for twelve days, $2,695 for 16 days, but with stiff single supplements for hikers traveling alone.

As for other walking tours of Britain, a group known as the Rambler's Association, at 4 Wandsworth Rd., London, publishes a magazine called *The Rambler,* which describes walk opportunities and lists organized tours throughout the country.

But some avid walkers are upset about the commercialization of strolling through Britain, believing the activity should always be do-it-yourself in style, *sans* tour operators. Such is the belief of Richard Hayward, of Seattle, Washington, who teaches classes in the area about the joys of unorganized walking tours.

The whole point of walking, in Hayward's view, is to meet people of the host country. It is especially easy, he says, to meet Britons, "for whom walking is a national pastime. They care about the countryside, and if they meet you in that setting, their old-world reserve melts away and you are one of them. Organized walking tours can be a waste of time and energy because you don't meet the people as readily."

Hayward has compiled a list of books that supply itineraries for independent walking tours of England and Wales. For a copy, send $3 and a stamped, self-addressed envelope to **Richard Hayward, British Footpaths, 914 Mason St., Bellingham, WA 98225.**

While others sit stolidly in a bus, the smart traveler walks.

And finally, all three of the largest bicycling tour operators have now added hiking trips to their repertoire. **Backroads, 1516 Fifth Street, Suite L312, Berkeley, CA 94710-9861 (phone 510/527-1555 or 800/462-2848)**, takes you walking throughout the U.S. and to 15 other countries, on tours that range from the rock-bottom walk-and-then-camp variety to those using elegant inns for hikers' overnights. And thus, the identical hike through Baja California, for six days, can cost $735 per camper or $1,298 per sybarite. Similarly, six days of wandering through Nova Scotia fishing villages, and along its rugged coastline, can cost $698 to campers and $1,275 to those using inns. The luxury-loving **Butterfield & Robinson, 70 Bond Street, Toronto, Ontario, Canada M5BIX3 (phone 416/864-1354 or 800/678-1147)** does the same in Europe's most chic areas, but only uses top-quality lodgings and charges its traditionally

British Coastal Trails. *Courtesy BCT Scenic Walking.*

high prices ($3,095 per person for eight days strolling the vineyards and hilltowns of Tuscany, is typical). And finally, **Hiking Holidays, Monkton Road, P.O. Box 711, Bristol VT 05443 (phone 802/453-4811)**, a division of Vermont Bicycle Touring, operates more modestly in its own home base of Vermont, in the Shenandoah and Blue Ridge Mountains, near the Bay of Fundy in Canada, and occasionally in Britain, France, and Ireland. U.S trips run $549 or $649 for five days; $1,699 to $1,799 for a full week in Europe.

While others sit stolidly in a bus, gaining pounds by the mile, the smart traveler walks, and gains health, in addition to contact with people, nature, life.

IX

Enlarging Your Mind Through Study Vacations

A Yank at Oxford—or Cambridge (Summer-Style)

Short Summer Study Courses at the Great British Universities Offer an Unusual Supplement to the Standard English Holiday

hey are known as "quads" because they spread between the enclosing wings of a quadrangular building, and they are magical beyond compare—otherworldly and still, their silence challenged only by the chirpings of a thrush, yet the very air within seems to pulse with the joy of human achievement, 800 years of learning. They are the "quads" of the colleges at Oxford and Cambridge, some so old that one built in the 1300s is still known as New College.

Who among us hasn't dreamed of studying there? How many of the most eminent Americans still harbor a secret disappointment over having failed to win a Rhodes Scholarship or some other form of admission to the ancient universities of Britain?

Well, life in this instance affords a second chance (for a week to a month, at least). From late June through early September, most of the major British universities—Oxford and Cambridge among them—offer study courses of one, two, three, four, and six weeks' duration, to overseas visitors of any age, with adults quite definitely preferred. While a summer week or more in the quiet, near-deserted quads isn't quite the opportunity you may have craved in younger days, it provides a memorable communion with these awesome institutions, and a learning experience that has edified and enchanted many discerning visitors before you.

By the end of spring, the undergrads of Oxford and Cambridge, in their abbreviated black cloaks flung over tweedy suits and dresses (you won't be wearing one), have all departed for the beaches and hills; but instruction in summer is by the unvarnished "real thing": eminent dons (teaching masters) who pursue a clipped and no-nonsense approach to learning that contrasts quite refreshingly with some American pedagogy. The mind responds—stretching to accommodate difficult concepts and queries, directly and sometimes brutally put. At night you join your instructors in the always-active pubs of the university towns, enjoying conversation as heady as a glass of good brandy. Though individual tutorials aren't provided to summer students, opportunities abound to continue classroom discussion in less formal settings.

In all other respects the experience is reasonably akin to that of British university life. You live in the temporarily vacated quarters of an Oxford or Cambridge student. You dine at the long, wooden refectory tables of an Oxford or Cambridge dining hall—though "High Table," the elevated realm from which faculty members take their wine-accompanied meals, is normally vacant at these times. You roam the stacks of the historic Bodleian Library of Oxford, browse among ancient tomes in the hush of Cambridge's Pepysian Library, lie on the sunlight-flecked grass as you cope with the heavy reading load that most courses entail.

Curricula

What courses do you pursue? While Shakespeare and other giants of English literature dominate the lists—and attract the greater number of international students—most remaining studies deal with contemporary aspects of British life and institutions: "Political Thought in England," "The English Educational System," "The United Kingdom Economy," "History of English Painting," among a wide selection of others.

The top summer programs are those offered by departments of the two great universities that concern themselves with extension or continuing education. Cambridge's "official" program, the International Summer School, offers the broadest choice of courses and, unlike Oxford, makes no great point of imposing deadlines for application. It operates a first "term" of four weeks in July, a second "term" of two weeks in early August, permits you to take either or both, and charges upward of £1,395 ($2,092) for the first term of four weeks (i.e., about $523 a week), £850 for the second term of two weeks (about $637 per week). Charges include all tuition, a single room

While a summer week or more in the quiet, near-deserted quads isn't quite the opportunity you craved in younger days, it provides a memorable communion with these awesome institutions.

in a university residence, the services of a "scout" to clean your room (but not otherwise to wait upon you), and two meals a day (breakfast and dinner) in a soaring Gothic hall of ancient stone. For catalog and application forms, contact **University of Cambridge International Programmes, Board of Continuing Education, Madingley Hall, Cambridge CB3 8AQ (phone (0954)210636 or fax (0954) 210677)**, and specify your preference among the International Summer School, Literature Summer School, and Art History Summer School, attended in total by more than 1,500 people each year.

Oxford's "official" summer course offers two broad programs. The first, "The University of Oxford Summer Programme in English Literature," consists of two three-week sessions of subjects ranging from Shakespeare to Modern

Instruction in summer is by the unvarnished "real thing": eminent dons (teaching masters) who pursue a clipped and no-nonsense approach to learning.

Literary Theory (you can take either, or else both for a total of six weeks), from early July to mid-August. Here, the approach is profound and serious: participants are expected to attend 45 hours of lectures and 48 hours of individual tutorials (and

also to prepare a paper) over the six-week period, and courses are designed only for those comfortable with university-level studies (which usually means senior undergrads, post-grads, teachers and other professionals, gifted alumni with English "majors"). Students live in ancient Exeter College (founded in 1314), receive three meals a day, and pay £1,185 (about $1,785) for the three weeks (about $597 a week, which strikes me as most reasonable), only £2,255 for the entire six weeks (about $563 a week).

The second Oxford program is more for relaxation-craving vacationers (but of a somewhat brainy level). It consists of one-week seminars in the "Oxford Experience," often related to the history of Oxford (1995's curriculum included "Treasures of Oxford," "Inspired at Oxford: Creative Writing," "British Garden History"). Cost for the week is a reasonable £490 ($735) for lodgings in Christ Church College, all meals and tuition.

For literature or applications, write to: **Mrs. Janet Briggs, University of Oxford Department for Continuing Education, 1 Wellington Square, Oxford OX1 2JA,** or send

a fax to Mrs. Briggs at 44-865-270314. Alternatively, you can request the applications forms from **U.S. Student Programs Division, Institute of International Education, 809 United Nations Plaza, New York, NY 10017 (212/883-8200).**

If the "official" programs are full, or if you have only two weeks available for study, you can opt for a number of "unofficial" courses organized by various Oxford and Cambridge dons on a purely private, entrepreneurial basis; the latter simply rent the use of classrooms and lodgings, and announce their own programs, some for durations of as little as two weeks. Typical are the courses offered at Oxford in "Modern British History and Politics" by the so-called Institute for British and Irish Studies; these are given in July and early August, for either two, three, four, or five weeks, intensively from 9am to 6pm, for a cost to you of about $800 a week, including tuition, lodging, all three meals daily, and weekly theater tickets and excursions. Contact the Institute c/o its U.S. representative, **Dr. E. C. Johnson, IBIS, Camford House, Almont, CO 81210 (phone 303/248-0477, or toll free 800/327-4247 outside Colorado),** or call the institute directly in England (phone 0865/270980). Dr. Johnson and the institute (both highly regarded by me) also offer summer programs for adults in history, literature, and international law at Trinity College, Dublin, and University College, London.

No one suggests that courses such as these should be the sole activity of a British vacation; they can be combined, instead, with the most standard sightseeing and recreation. But what an opportunity awaits! The smart traveler seizes the chance, if the chance exists, to experience these hallowed institutions of learning in the manner they deserve: not as casual tourists, but as students, in the endless quest for light.

Low-Cost Language Schools Abroad

The Careful Use of Travel to Acquire Fluency in a Foreign Tongue

"Of course you don't get our business! Of course we don't send you our orders! You don't speak our language!"

Such words of reproach from a normally courteous European surprised even the speaker, stirred some long-smouldering resentment, led to further indictment.

"It isn't that we're asking you to engage in technical discussions with us. But at a simple dinner party you can't carry on the most routine conversation with the lady on your left. You Americans take the cake!"

Why, among all the achievers of the world, do the overwhelming number of Americans fail to possess a second language? Or a third?

Sheer indolence is a first explanation. Torpor. Thoughtless indifference, largely stemming from unpleasant, subconscious memories of uninspiring language courses at ol' State U. Mistaken smugness ("they all speak English"). And failure to make the proper use of travel opportunities. Since languages can be acquired with surprising ease in situations where you are "immersed" in them, the mere decision to travel solo, unaccompanied by English-speaking spouse or companion, can yield the most remarkable results. When that vacation trip is further pursued at a European language school, in an off-season period when the tourists have fled and all you hear is one foreign language, at breakfast and in classes, on television and at the movies, in restaurants and bars, one language unendingly—the results are astonishing indeed. You speak!

The mere decision to travel solo, unaccompanied by English-speaking spouse or companion, can yield the most remarkable results.

This fall and winter a great many bright Americans will enhance their cultural perspectives, careers, and lives by pursuing short language courses overseas, partially funded by European governments. They will achieve fluency, or near-fluency, in one of four major European tongues—French, Spanish, German, or Italian—at schools whose traditions, settings, and low costs provide the greatest of travel pleasures in addition to instruction.

Most of the schools share common features, of which the most important is the timing of one-month classes to begin near the first of each month; schedule your applications and arrivals accordingly. Most will provide you with lodgings in the homes of private families, where you'll again be immersed in the local language. State-operated schools are usually considerably cheaper than private ones, without a loss of quality or intensity. Schools in secondary cities will send you to cheaper accommodations than those in famous ones: thus the families with whom you'll stay in Perugia will charge a third of what you'll pay in Florence.

You choose from the following:

For French

Ancestor to all the great European language schools, founded in 1883 to advance French culture and the French language to all the world, is the powerful Alliance Française. Directly funded (in part) by the French Foreign Ministry, it operates low-cost French-language schools in more than 130 nations, but its soul remains in a great gray building on Paris's Left Bank, at boulevard Raspail 101, steps away from the trendy cafés, art galleries, and way-out boutiques of the busier boulevard St. Germain.

In the large stone courtyard of the giant school, teeming with Egyptian caftans, African turbans, Canadian blue jeans, the atmosphere may be international but only one language is spoken: French. And French is spoken at every moment and exclusively throughout the day, in the very first class you attend, in the on-premises cafeteria where you take your meals, at theatrical performances and lectures in the school's auditorium. You are in class at least three and a half hours a day, then in earphone-equipped language laboratories for supplemental practice, then at near-mandatory social events—yet you pay only 1,200 francs ($240) a month, quite obviously subsidized, for all tuition, and house yourself in any of dozens of inexpensive Left Bank hotels clustered in this section of the Latin Quarter; there, too, you hear and speak French exclusively.

Alliance Française classes must be taken for a minimum of four weeks, starting at the beginning of each month, and application should be made at least a month in advance. For further information and forms, write: **Alliance Française de Paris, boulevard Raspail 101, 75270 Paris CEDEX 06, France.**

For Italian

Choosing from a score of major, Italy-based Italian-language schools, the clear consensus of the experts (I've spoken with three) favors the state-operated University for Foreigners of Perugia (Università Italiana per Stranieri) and the Cultural Center for Foreigners of Florence (Centro Culturale per Stranieri). Both are in that broad region of Italy (Tuscany and Umbria) where the purest form of Italian is said to be spoken.

At Perugia, an Intensive Preparatory Course (five and a half hours of classroom instruction a day, of which hours are devoted to conversation and language laboratories) is priced at only 510,000 lire ($340) for a month—$85 a week. A normal beginner's course (four hours a day), for either one, two, or three months, costs only 238,000 lire ($140) per month. Compare those rates with what you'd pay to a private language school at home!

Nonintensive courses start every two weeks, and may be taken for as little as a month. Students attend classes in a vast, baroque-style palazzo, stay with Italian families in private homes ($110 a month), and take their meals ($1.50 apiece) in one of two University of Perugia canteens. Weekends, they journey for culture and conversation to nearby Assisi, Orvieto, Spoleto.

At the more leisurely Florence school, where classroom time occupies only two and a half hours a day, but is supplemented with homework and language labs, courses run for 10 weeks, start at regular quarterly intervals, and cost 445,000 lire ($300) for the entire term, independent of room-and-board costs. If you're fixed on Florence but can't stay 10 weeks, or can't get into the official school, try the one-month, four-hour-a-day sessions of the prestigious but private (and costlier) Dante Alighieri Society ($275 a month, not including room and board).

Write for information and/or application forms to: **Università Italiana per Stranieri, Palazzo Gallenga, piazza Fortebraccio, 4, 06100 Perugia, Italy; Centro Culturale per Stranieri, Università degli Studi, via Vittorio Emanuele 64, 50134 Florence, Italy; or Società Dante Alighieri, via Gino Capponi 4, 50121 Florence, Italy.**

And for a list of additional language schools in other Italian cities, contact the **Italian Cultural Institute, 686 Park Ave., New York, NY 10021 (phone 212/879-4242),** or one of their branch offices: in **Washington, D.C., at 1717 Massachusetts Avenue, Washington, D.C. 20036 (phone 202/ 387-5161); or in Los Angeles at 12400 Wilshire Blvd., Suite 310, Los Angeles, CA 90025 (phone 213/207-4737).** Alternatively, contact **Louise Harber, Foreign Language Programs, P.O. Box 5409, Grand Central Station, New York, NY 10163 (phone 212/662-1090),** who represents several such schools in Italy, and can also arrange for you to study Italian in the actual home of an Italian language teacher, living there as well.

For German

The influential world role of German commerce and culture (1 out of every 10 books on earth is published in German) lends continuing importance to German-language study. Germany's own government provides heavily subsidized instruction via its Goethe Institutes, of which more than 100 are found in 60 countries, and 16 are maintained in Germany itself. The latter are marvelously diverse, in both large cities (Munich, Berlin), university towns (Göttingen, Mannheim), and idyllic countryside locations (Prien and Murnau in rural Bavaria).

If you've the time for an eight-week course, you can make your own selection of a Goethe Institute (and city) from the 16 available. Busier people able to devote only four weeks to it are confined to three locations: Rothenburg-ob-der-Tauber (that perfectly preserved medieval village on the "Romantic Road" near Nuremberg, from June through January). Prien (an hour from Munich, December through March only), and Boppard (in the Valley of the Lorelei, along the Rhine, from February through May).

In each you are given 24 hours a week of classroom instruction, supplemented by at least 10 hours a week of private study, and additional

Courtyard of the Colegio d'Espagna. *Courtesy Colegio de Espana.*

sessions of conversation with German residents dragooned in for the purpose. Each institute makes all the arrangements for your room and board with a private family, and charges a total for the entire month—tuition, materials, room, and board—of 1,190 marks (approximately $900).

For further information and application forms, contact **Goethe House, 666 Third Ave., New York, NY 10028 (phone 212/972-3960)**. The U.S.-based branch will then forward your completed form to the Goethe Institute you've selected.

For Spanish

Salamanca is the place. Emphatically. Without a second thought. It is the heart of Old Castile, where Spanish is noble and pure, untainted by the Gallego accents of the northwest, the Catalán of the east, the assorted dialects of the south.

The brightest of travelers achieve fluency, or near-fluency, in one of the four major European languages at schools whose glorious traditions, settings, and remarkably low costs provide the greatest of travel pleasures in addition to instruction.

Its monumental University of Salamanca (dating from 1226) is one of the world's oldest. Together with similar medieval academies in Padua and Bologna, it developed an early tradition for attracting international students, and that reputation—even stronger today—has a wholesome impact on language studies there. Because students are from dozens of countries scattered from Japan to Yemen, the only common language among them is Spanish. You either speak it or suffer muteness.

Though Salamanca is only two and a half hours from Madrid, it is no Madrid in cost: $18 a day is more than enough for room and all three meals at scores of guest-accepting private homes. And tuition at the private language schools is as low as the University of Salamanca's, enabling you to study one-on-one with your teacher, or in small groups of seven or eight, for as little as you'd pay elsewhere in a class of 20. I like, for that reason, an intensely personal school called Salminter (Escuela Salmantina de Estudios Internacionales), which charges only $350 per month for four hours of instruction, five days a week.

Dominant among the other all-year-round private schools is the Colegio de España, whose intensive four-week course starting at the beginning of every month (four hours daily, in classes limited to 15 students) costs a remarkable 39,000 pesetas ($340) a month, to which you add about $90 a week for room and board. Weekends, its students travel by short bus rides to Ávila, Segovia, and Valladolid, though the older adults among them (like me on previous trips) scarcely budge from a sidewalk café seat on the historic Plaza Mayor—barred to traffic, and like a baroque drawing room, except out-of-doors. Churches and museums with the next-equivalent of Goyas, Velázquezes, and El Grecos are short steps away.

When people ask why I don't prefer the more accessible Spanish-language schools of Mexico to those of Spain, I answer diplomatically that Mexico is Mexico, but Spain is . . . well, Spain.

For applications or further information on the Salminter school, write or phone **Salminter, calle Toro 34–36, 2nd floor, 37002 Salamanca, Spain (phone 923/ 211-808).** For the larger Colegio, contact **Colegio de España, calle Compañía 65, 37008 Salamanca, Spain (phone 023/ 214-788).** For enrollment in Spanish-language courses at the equally reputable Colegio Miguel de Unamuno in Salamanca, contact the **Language Studies Enrollment Center, P.O. Box 5095, Anaheim, CA 92814 (phone 714/527-2918).**

If, on the other hand, you would prefer to pursue your language studies in Madrid, you would do well to contact the five-year-old **Domine Escuela de Español, calle José Abascal 44, 1 dcha., 28003 Madrid, Spain (phone 01/ 442-83-33 or 01/442-83-55),** highly recommended to me by several recent visitors there, but costlier than the Salamanca schools.

The Love Boat and the Learn Boat

Expedition Cruising Brings Education to the High Seas

You step aboard to the strains of Vivaldi and search in vain for a single casino. At night you amuse yourself not in a seagoing cabaret, but in that long-forgotten art of serious conversation with fellow passengers, over a brandy in a relaxing lounge. If a film is shown, it's of exotic tribespeople in an actual setting or of hump-backed whales off the Patagonian fjords.

And when you retire to cabin or bunk, you're first handed a half-hour's reading for the day ahead.

You've heard of the "Love Boat." Now meet the "Learn Boat." Though it may seem like a contradiction in terms, the combination of cruising and education is creating a potent new vacation lure for thousands of intellectually curious Americans.

Every week nearly a dozen small ships—and their number seems to be growing—depart from Mediterranean, Central and South American, and South Pacific ports on so-called expedition cruises staffed by naturalists, anthropologists, and cultural historians.

The major programs are four in number:

Swan Hellenic Cruises

Cheapest of the lot—a remarkable value—are two-week cruises of the eastern Mediterranean aboard the 300-passenger M.T.S. *Orpheus,* operated continuously from April to early December each year by the distinguished Swan Hellenic organization of the venerable P & O Lines of Britain.

Here you look in depth at the origins of the Greco-Christian-Judaic civilization, accompanied at all times by a minimum of five—often as many as six—British university lecturers, museum people, clergy, and authors. The dean of Merton College, Oxford, frequently lectures on board and ashore. So do several professors of ancient history at Cambridge, the archeology editor of *The Illustrated London News,* a former dean of Salisbury Cathedral, a director of the Imperial War Museum.

"I so treasured our afternoon at Ephesus," wrote one passenger, "because as we sat in the theater, the guest lecturer read to us from Acts 19 and instantly brought alive the story of the silversmiths who demonstrated against St. Paul in defense of their livelihood—the making of idols to the goddess Diana."

For such a profound combination of cultural discovery and water-borne pleasures, 17 days in length, you pay a total of $4,900 (in the bulk of cabins), which includes round-trip air fare between several U.S. East Coast cities and London ($200 more from the West Coast), and round-trip air between London and either Athens, Thessaloniki, or Venice, from which the ship departs. You're put up for two nights at a first-class hotel in London (one night before the cruise, one night after), and then cruise for a full 14 nights to the "isles of Greece," the coasts of Turkey, Croatia, Bulgaria. The trip is so very all-inclusive—such a splendid example of the refreshing British insistence on moderate travel costs—that even the daily shore excursions (with their eminent lecturers) are thrown in at no extra charge.

They depart from Mediterranean, South American, and South Pacific ports, staffed by naturalists, anthropologists, and cultural historians.

Swan Hellenic Cruises are represented in the U.S. by **Esplanade Tours, 581 Boylston St., Boston, MA 02116 (phone 617/266-7465, or toll free 800/426-5492 outside Massachusetts).** Contact them for a fascinating catalog.

Society Expeditions

Now you're on voyages of daring (but deluxe) exploration and discovery, into the most mysterious and remote regions of the earth: the islands of Borneo, Indonesia, and the South Pacific, the Arctic, the Russian Far East, and Papua New Guinea.

On a Society Expedition, the bent is distinctly naturalistic or anthropological, far less historical or archaeological than the themes of Swan Hellenic. You visit untouristed shores, not ports, making landfall on motorized rubber landing boats called "Zodiacs."

Thus conveyed, you go to otherwise inaccessible villages or riverbanks, where at night the beat of a shaman's drum raises appeals to ancestral spirits. You walk among upright penguins gathered by the hundreds on a shore of the Falklands. You meet and interact with native Eskimos. To avoid "polluting" their natural or cultural life, your visits are scheduled for widely scattered dates.

The trips are realized aboard the luxuriously fitted, 140-passenger *World Discoverer,* a large vessel, but with the shallow draft, specially ice-hardened hull, and bow-thrusters required for expedition cruising.

Each voyage is accompanied by a team of naturalists, marine biologists, and (sometimes) anthropologists. You sail with the likes of Dr. Johan Reinhard, noted anthropologist; Peter Harrison, who has won international acclaim with his books on sea birds; or Frank Todd, former senior research fellow at Hubbs Sea World Research Institute.

> **Each Society Expeditions voyage is accompanied by a team of naturalists, marine biologists, and (sometimes) anthropologists.**

The World Discoverer circumnavigates the globe, on different itineraries, throughout the year. Passengers, essentially, book segments of the voyage—usually from two to several weeks—and are flown to and from ports at both ends of the segment. Costs average $350 a day for the bulk of cabins and trips.

For a set of mouthwatering, award-winning, large, glossy brochures, contact **Society Expeditions, 2001 Western Avenue, Suite 300, Seattle, WA 98121 (phone 206/728-9400, or toll free 800/548-8669 outside Washington)**.

World Explorer Cruises

This next one's another pipsqueak of a company, as such fleets go, with only one ship, the S.S. *Universe*. But it provides a serious learning experience, in addition to considerable value: two-week cruises of Alaskan waters each summer (May to mid-September) for the same price that many others charge for a one-week cruise (about $2,495 per person for most inside cabins). How is it done? By eliminating glitzy, Las Vegas–style revues; by serving three normal meals daily, and a couple of snacks, in place of the six Lucullan orgies of eating featured on other lines; by catering to serious, unpretentious people more interested in the daily lectures by eminent naturalists the S.S. *Universe* carries aboard than in expensive cocktail lounges and seagoing casinos. In short: your type of ship. Contact **World Explorer Cruises, 555 Montgomery St., San Francisco, CA 94111 (phone 415/391-9262, or toll free 800/854-3835)**.

Sven-Olof Lindblad's Special Expeditions

This final firm operates the smallest of expedition ships, some carrying as few as 36 passengers, in addition to such "larger" vessels as the 250-passenger *Adriana* (cruising the coast of West Africa). An example of the smaller variety, and its major pride, is the new *Caledonian Star*, sailing the Red Sea and the Indian Ocean on trips of 12 to 19 days apiece, for prices averaging $4,000 to $5,000 per person, not including air fare. On the larger (164 passengers) and even newer (October 1990) *Frontier Spirit,* whose captain (Heinz Aye) has been called "the Captain Cook of the 20th century," passengers will sail the waters, and visit the shores, of Antarctica in winter, the South Pacific and Great Barrier Reef in spring, and the Northwest Passage in summer, at rates of $300 to $400 per person per day. The average trips are two or three weeks in length.

Other year-round programs of Special Expeditions: To West Africa and New Guinea; to Indonesian waters, embarking from Djakarta on a 36-passenger luxury catamaran yacht (world-renowned divers and naturalists accompany you); to Baja California for diving; and to the Galápagos Islands (a specialty). Seasonal programs: along Russia's Volga River, and to the North Cape of Norway. For brochures, contact **Special Expeditions, Inc., 720 Fifth Avenue, New York, NY 10019 (phone 212/765-7740 or 800/762-0003)**.

Biological Journeys

A last set of "learn boats" known as Biological Journeys is considerably cheaper than most others (around $285 per person per day), despite the fact that they limit the size of their ships to

Whale watching in the Sea of Cortez.
Courtesy Biological Journeys.

30 passengers. They go whale watching along the shores of Baja, California from January through March; are then off to the Galápagos Islands in April; to the High Arctic in July, always pursuing the most profound scientific studies. For informative literature, always printed on recycled paper, write or call **Biological Journeys, 1696 Ocean Drive, McKinleyville, CA 95521 (phone 707/839-0178 or 800/ 548-7555)**. A sister company, Dolphin Charters, operates scholarly cruises for 7 to 10 days apiece in the waters of British Columbia and Alaska, always accompanied by trained naturalists; same average daily charges. Most passengers also stay for a few days in the local villages where cruises depart, to soak up a bit of cold-weather culture. This time, write or phone **Dolphin Charters, 1007 Leneve Place, El Cerrito, CA 94530 (510/527-9622)**.

So what will it be, the "Love Boat" or the "Learn Boat," the libido or learning? Some say that expedition cruising allows the best of both.

The Arts-and-Crafts Vacation:
A Sign of Our Times

**Back to Basics,
on a Vacation Devoted
to Acquiring a
Manual Skill**

They resemble resorts, with their outdoor pools and tennis courts, their wooden lodge buildings and country barns, their guests in skimpy sports clothes.

But there all likeness ends. Within the barns are lathes and looms, potters' wheels and blacksmith's forge, all heavily in use throughout the day by guests in throes of creation. At a growing number of residential countryside crafts centers, more and more Americans are devoting their vacations to the mastery of a folk manufacture—the ability, say, to make a ladderback chair or an earthenware vase, a hand-bound book or a rough wool cloak.

For them, the activity is a rewarding expression of art, a satisfying connection with the past, a deeply pleasurable return to human basics (in a time of high technology), and therefore the best possible use of leisure time.

Six awesomely scenic locations are especially active in the world of arts-and-crafts vacations:

Penland School, of Penland, North Carolina, an hour's drive from Asheville, is the big one, a sprawling complex of 50 buildings on 450 acres of Blue Ridge Mountain land. A pioneer in creating new American forms of craft art, it urges its guests to let their imaginations soar, tolerates outlandish experiments, even uses a bevy of Macintosh computers to enhance students' "vision" (by devising new geometrical forms). "We blur the overlapping lines between fine and applied arts," says the school's director. The new approach is then applied to all the standard materials—wood, clay, fibers, glass, iron, metals, and paper—and results each week in countless varieties of stunning products emerging from classes taught by eminent figures. Sessions run from mid-March to mid-November; are two, two and a half, and eight weeks in duration; are open to students of all levels of skill; and average $250 a week, plus room-and-board fees of $200 (dorms) to $300 (double with private bath) per person per week. For more information or reservations, contact **Penland School, Penland, NC 28765 (phone 704/ 765-2359)**.

Anderson Ranch Arts Center, at Snowmass Village, Colorado, is a somewhat costlier alternative of equal fame; it's found in the Rockies, 10 miles west of Aspen, 200 miles from Denver, at an elevation of 8,200 feet. Many of the nation's most renowned craftspeople—prize winners, manufacturers of crafts, academics in the field—come here each summer (late May to early September) to teach one- and two-week classes in woodworking and furniture design, ceramics, bronze casting, and bookmaking

(just those four crafts, and no others), in addition to courses in photography, sculpture, and painting. Some have such outstanding reputations that they attract other professionals, who make up a third of some classes otherwise composed of sheer novices—the advantages for these beginners are obvious. Interdisciplinary studies combining people

Within the barns are lathes and looms, potters' wheels and blacksmith's forge, all heavily in use by guests in throes of creation.

from different fields are especially interesting at this high-quality gathering of leaders in crafts instruction, all in a setting of old ranch buildings refurbished to provide considerable comfort in both lodgings and labs. Tuition, including lab fees, is usually $325 to $400 for one week, $425 to $795 for two weeks, to which you add room-and-board costs of $270 to $390 a week, depending on room category. For further

Haystack Mountain School of Crafts.
Courtesy Haystack Mountain School of Crafts, photo by Joseph Molitor.

information, contact **Anderson Ranch Arts Center, P.O. Box 5598, Snowmass Village, CO 81615 (phone 303/923-3181)**.

Arrowmont School of Arts and Crafts, in Gatlinburg, Tennessee, a mile down a scenic road from a main entrance to Great Smoky Mountains National Park, is another nationally known visual arts complex, particularly noted for its instruction in odd new techniques: patination of metal, anodizing of aluminum, granulation of sterling silver, combining "media" on cloth; it is also, according to one faculty member, "the wood-turning capital of America" (and teaches the standard crafts as well). One- and two-week sessions are offered in March, June, July, and August, to persons of varying skills, including those of no previous crafts experience at all. Some students, energized by creative excitement, work up to 15 hours a day in well-equipped workshops or in the 4,000-tome library of arts and crafts. On average, figure on costs of $315 to $425 a week for everything. For further information, contact **Arrowmont School of Arts and Crafts, P.O. Box 567, Gatlinburg, TN 37738 (phone 615/436-5860)**.

> **"We blur the overlapping lines between fine and applied arts,"** says a director of the summertime center.

Augusta Heritage Arts Workshops, at Davis & Elkins College in Elkins, West Virginia, at the edge of the Monongahela National Forest, differs sharply from the others in its emphasis on traditional crafts—not innovative ones—designed to preserve and transmit a proud Appalachian heritage of designs. Accordingly, classes are in such homespun subjects as stonemasonry, quiltmaking, knifemaking, black-smithing, basketry, folk carving and whittling, bobbin lacemaking, spinning, and log construction. Nevertheless, director Doug Hill contends that some classes here—"contemporary quilt design," "create your own weaving"—are moving old-style crafts into the future. There are five separate summer weeks, early July to mid-August (you can sign up for one or more weeks); tuition averages a low $265 a week; and room and board adds only $200 a week more and is provided in college residence halls and dining rooms. Contact **Augusta Heritage Arts Workshops, c/o Davis & Elkins College, 100 Campus Drive, Elkins, WV 26241 (phone 304/636-1900, ext. 209)**.

John C. Campbell Folk School, in Brasstown, North Carolina, a 365-acre campus nestled between the Smokies and the Blue Ridge Mountains, is still another of those primarily regional schools that seek to instruct in traditional, southern Appalachian crafts, and not in the unrestrained modern approach to the decorative arts. Most courses are confined to such old-world pursuits as spinning, knitting, quilting, woodcarving, pottery, blacksmithing, enameling, chair-bottoming, and the like, all heavily functional—the abstract is generally eschewed. Still, the spirit here is dynamic and joyous, and courses (one and two weeks in length) are offered year around (except for occasional holiday weeks), at times when other schools are closed. Most students pay around $425 a week for everything (room, board, tuition, lab fees), but that charge can rise by another $100 for certain wood-turning and metal-finishing courses. For more information, contact the **John C. Campbell Folk School, Brasstown, NC 28902 (phone 704/837-2775 or toll free 800/FOLKSCH)**.

Haystack Mountain School of Crafts, in Deer Isle, Maine, is the only northeastern location among the major crafts centers, overlooking the Atlantic Ocean from a spectacular wooded slope. A much-discussed architectural achievement, it consists of two dozen shingled structures—some lodgings, some workshops—with high-pitched roofs, all connected by wooden walkways elevated from the ground. Here, from mid-June through mid-September only, roughly 80 students at a time, of all ages and degrees of skill, including beginners, come together in successive one-, two-, and three-week sessions to study crafts of clay, fibers, glass, metals, and wood, in studios that never close—they remain open for inspiration around the clock. High standards, intense activity; charges total (for room, board, shop fees, and tuition) $700 for two weeks, $1,000 for three weeks, in bunkhouse accommodations. For more information, contact **Haystack Mountain School of Crafts, P.O. Box 518, Deer Isle, ME 04627 (phone 207/348-2306)**.

For summertime crafts courses in Britain and Mexico, contact the **National Registration Center for Study Abroad, P.O. Box 1393, Milwaukee, WI 53201 (phone 414/278-0631)**, requesting their free catalogs entitled "Britain Art and Craft Programs" and "Craft Workshops in Mexico." And for tours of the studios of noted craftspeople all over the world, contact **Craft World Tours, Inc., 6776 Warboys Rd., Byron, NY 14422 (phone 716/548-2667)**.

Vacationing for Health, at a Medically Supervised Resort

It's Smart to Vacation at a Reducing Center

Our Own Durham, North Carolina—"Fat City"—Has Become Dieting Capital of the World

We felt a bit sheepish as we entered the steakhouse, carrying our tiny scales and concealed measuring cups. But we needn't have worried. Here in Durham, North Carolina, dieting capital of the world, people are used to the sight of overweight visitors on a "dining out experience." Every week of the year, hundreds of reducers from across the country are in attendance at four different nutrition/exercise schools in this key southern hub, with its equable climate and accessible location.

Some come because they are seriously obese and with associated illnesses; others, simply to devote their vacation time to the loss of 10 or 15 pounds of excess weight. And why not? What better use of leisure than to improve one's health?

At the Mecca of Fat

I arrived in winter, flying from the February storms and sub-zero chills of the Northeast into the brisk but springlike weather of the Raleigh/ Durham Airport, which is fast becoming a major destination for more and more airlines (American, USAir, others).

By the time I left six days later, I had lost seven pounds. But more important, I had gained lessons of nutrition that dozens of earlier diet books and articles had always failed to drive home. Durham's success, in my view, results from the unique quality of a residential dieting experience, in which one is wrenched from normal routines, isolated from family pressures, and forced to reflect without distraction upon a lifetime of thoughtless and destructive eating habits.

What better use of leisure time than to improve one's health?

While most short-term "fat farms" and fad diets have an overwhelming record of recidivism—people quickly regain the weight they've lost—some of Durham's establishments claim a 70% record of "wins": patients, upon returning home, either maintain their weight loss or continue to drop additional pounds.

That's probably because most of the Durham centers preach the use of a balanced assortment of popular foods, close in taste and appearance to the average American diet, but prepared without harmful fats and saturated oils, and served in moderate—but filling—portions. Though most Durham programs restrict their patients to a daily intake of only 800 calories over the two- to four-week duration of their stays (a quantity of food that, to my surprise, proved entirely adequate and caused no great discomfort), their aim is to prepare the student for resumption of a far more normal, but properly chosen, 1,200- to 1,500-calorie diet upon returning home.

The lesson is taught in a hard, daily round of classroom lectures, seminars, laboratory workshops, and one-on-one consultations.

My own "rehabilitation" occurred at what may well be the largest of the Durham schools, Duke University's Diet and Fitness Center ("DFC"), where my fellow students, among others, ranged from a seriously overweight minister of the Gospel, to a portly legal aid lawyer, to an only slightly pudgy drama teacher from a midwestern high school. Despite the wide diversity of weights and backgrounds, there emerged a touching camaraderie among us, sensitive and supportive. Though we joked about food, we knew the depth of commitment on each one's part to break harmful eating habits.

At night we drove with one another to various Durham movies so that we could fill the hours between dinner and bed, but unaided there by a single kernel of popcorn, let alone the buttered kind. One afternoon and evening we ourselves planned and prepared a festive, calorie-conscious banquet. Accompanied by a nutritionist, we shopped at a supermarket, bought only the healthiest of ingredients, cooked the meal in one of Duke's well-equipped kitchens, and then consumed it—blackened redfish, baked potato, a Caesar salad without a single yolk, an exquisite Key lime parfait of skim milk, egg whites, and sugarless pudding—at candlelit tables.

Daytimes, we flocked to the gym for low-impact aerobics, later in the day to a heated pool for water aerobics. We walked and cycled, played hilarious games of volleyball, memorized calorie-counts in our moments of rest. One memorable night we had our restaurant experience and learned how to cope with the realities outside our diet center. But mostly we went to class after class, consultation after consultation, with nutritionists, behavioral psychologists, fitness experts, and even physicians.

Four Centers

All this costs considerably less than a trendy spa (the cheaper ones are usually $1,600 a week) or a Pritikin Longevity Center (the two most prominent charge $4,300 per person double for a two-week program, $7,250, per person double, for a month). At Duke's DFC, the fees run $1,199 per person for a four-week stay, $575 for additional weeks, and cover everything except lodging: meals, exercise, complex medical and psychological evaluations, swimming and gym work, classroom lectures, and workshops. Most participants then stay in a $45- to $55-a-night, one-bedroom apartment in Duke Towers (a comfortable, modern, but low-rise hotel) across the road, or in a number of cheaper (as little as $450 a month) nearby motels (and one large B&B house) recommended by the DFC. For brochures, contact **Duke University Diet and Fitness Center, 804 W. Trinity Ave., Durham, NC 27701 (phone 919/ 684-6331 or 800/362-8446, extension 1).**

Space doesn't permit a lengthy discussion of Durham's several other diet centers. Structure House follows much the same approach as at the DFC, but with a far greater emphasis on behavioral and psychological counseling, and is nearly the same size. It maintains its own lodgings on its own impressive grounds and rarely permits its patients to live "off campus." Guests may stay from one to eight weeks, and total charges, including meals and lodging, average $1,300 a week for the first four weeks. Contact **Structure House, 3017 Pickett Rd., Durham, NC 27705 (phone 919/688-7379 or toll free 800/553-0052).**

Duke's Center for Living emphasizes cardiovascular fitness, gained through diet and exercise, with weight loss simply an added dividend. It is visited, in roughly equal portions, either for preventive purposes or following an actual heart attack. And it requires a three-week stay. Three-week charges for meals, exercises, medical tests, and supervision amount to approximately $3,750; but participants provide their own lodging, which most do by staying either at the Duke Motor Lodge, the Durham Sheraton, the Fairfield Inn, the Campus Oaks Apartments, or other such lodgings. Contact the **Duke Center for Living, Duke University Medical Center, P.O. Box 3022, Durham, NC 27710 (phone 800/235- 3853 or 919 660-6600).**

"Rice House" (formally known as the "Heart Disease Reversal Clinic and Rice Diet Program"), in a modest white frame residence, prescribes a far more radical regimen than the other three (initially, simply rice and fruit), provides little behavioral counseling or fitness exercises, and is primarily for seriously ill or seriously obese persons who need to lose weight fast and massively. Although administrators of several other diet centers disagree with its approach, they

Durham's success results from the unique quality of a residential dieting experience, in which one is wrenched from normal routines, isolated from family pressures, and forced to reflect without distraction upon a lifetime of destructive eating habits.

always speak of it with respect; but a stay there is to be prescribed only by your physician.

Rice House is administered from **1821 Green Street, Durham, NC 27705 (phone 919/286-2243)**, where patients undergo an exhaustive, initial checkup ($750). After that, they pay about $2,616 per month for continual medical evaluations, lab tests, and those three— spartan—daily meals at the modest Rice House. The program is apparently based on the belief that modifications to the normal American diet— the goal of the other centers—are not sufficient, but rather a wholly new and healthier diet (low salt, low protein) must be substituted.

As for me, I'll stick with the more moderate adjustments to the typical American diet prescribed by DFC; they seem capable of being sustained after you have returned home from Durham—and isn't that the point?

Bear in mind that some dieters simply check into a low-cost motel in Durham for a week or two, without entering a center, and take their meals at the several Durham restaurants that now cater to them and cook in fat-free, low-calorie style. Other such lodgings have instituted a program of on-site low-calorie meals, and added the services of a doctor who calls at the hotel.

On the Trail of Eternal Youth, at a European Spa

Can 200 Million Europeans Be Wrong? Or Is There Validity to the Treatments at European Health Resorts?

As I lowered my limbs into that unheated tub of carbonated water, piped in from peat bogs of the Belgian Ardennes, I felt slightly chilly, faintly embarrassed, and more than a bit dubious about the whole thing.

Yet in 20 minutes my arms and legs were as heavy as lead, my head dropped to my chest, and I could barely stagger to a nearby cot before falling asleep. Hours later I awoke vigorous and refreshed.

I was at a "baths establishment" in the Belgian city of Spa, taking a cure of the sort pursued each year by hundreds of thousands of Europeans.

Courtesy Great Spas of the World.

American doctors think "water cures" are unscientific garbage. European doctors think American doctors, on this point, are boobs.

For centuries, physicians overseas have been sending their patients to spas chosen as carefully as specific medicines for particular ailments—this spa for arthritis, that spa for asthma, still another for neuritis or gallstones or worse. And today so many thousands of Americans are following their lead that a small but thriving segment of the travel industry—close to a dozen U.S. tour operators—has emerged to package the transatlantic health vacation as its sole activity.

Beauty vs. Health

Why the trend to foreign spas? Let me suggest a reason or two.

Compared with a European spa, the average American spa is like an elementary school next to Harvard, like a pickup softball team next to the New York Mets. Such dazzling resorts as The Golden Door, La Costa, The Palms, and Rancho La Puerta are almost wholly concerned with diet, exercise, and massage. Their aim is cosmetic; their methods are hardly the stuff of medical journals.

European spas pursue therapy, the prevention of illness. They operate under strict medical supervision and are recognized by national health plans, which reimburse their costs (if a doctor has prescribed the treatment) to residents of all European Community countries. They screen patients and turn away those for whom their particular treatments are inappropriate. In short, they practice a form of "alternative medicine," stressing natural, health-giving substances in the earth, waters, and minerals around us, or biological substances taken from our fellow animals.

Though none of this has impressed the American medical profession, neither did acupuncture years ago, or the Lamaze method for natural childbirth, or numerous other overseas-originating practices until they were forced upon our M.D.s by popular insistence. That thousands of distinguished European doctors opt for spa therapy is unsettling at the very least, and indicates the wisdom of keeping an open mind.

American doctors think "water cures" are unscientific garbage. European doctors think American doctors, on this point, are boobs.

Certainly no such doubts are harbored by the tour operator specialists in the health-and-fitness field. "Have you ever noticed," says Gerie Tully of Santé International, "that many Europeans are far less prone to winter colds and other common ailments than we are here? They visit a spa once a year, for two weeks or so, and renew themselves for the next 12 months." "While the statistics are difficult to verify," says Willy Maurer of Distinguished Spa Resorts, "there is simply no denying the effectiveness of spa therapy. Too many centuries have proven it, too many case studies, too many strong reactions. And remember: this is the chosen course of highly intelligent people, in mature, sophisticated nations."

For centuries, physicians overseas have been sending their patients to spas chosen as carefully as specific medicines for particular ailments— this spa for arthritis, that spa for asthma, still another for neuritis or gallstones or worse.

Though overseas spas are frequently identified with mineral waters and hot mud—"thermal cures," "balneotherapy," "taking the waters"— their concerns extend to three other significant treatments: live-cell injections (heavily done in Switzerland), Procaine-based cures (Romania), and anti-psoriasis regimens (Israel, in resorts along the Dead Sea). For each there's a tour operator (or several), and each has a "package" for every purse.

Live-Cell Therapy

Not the dream of Faust, or eternal youth, but at least a slowing of the aging process is the aim of this radical treatment created by the legendary Paul Niehans in the early 1930s, at his Clinic La Prairie near Montreux. Niehans, who remained active until the age of 89, administered the therapy to thousands of rather affluent persons (including Pope Pius XII, Winston Churchill, and Joan Crawford), and his clinic has since given it to a total of 50,000 seekers from around the world. Fetal cells from an unborn lamb are injected into the muscles; because the embryo has not yet developed the properties that would normally cause it to be rejected by other human tissues, it remains in the body, causing other cells to stay active and dynamic (so goes the theory).

As you'd expect, the treatment is fiendishly expensive in the main Swiss clinics: as much as $7,500 plus air fare at the ultra-deluxe Biotonus Bon Port Clinic (classic Niehans injections) overlooking Lake Geneva; $8,000 to $8,500 for six nights at Clinic Lemana ("cell-vital" injections) near Montreux; $9,000 a week at Clinique La Prairie; but only $5,800 for five nights at the Cellmed Center in the luxurious Le Mirador Hotel in Vevey.

Cheaper versions exist outside of Switzerland. In London, the much-publicized "youth doctor," Peter Stephans, injects a serum of cells and placenta, at fees, including examination and post-injection care, of about $2,200 (but without room and board, for which patients make independent arrangements). In Andorra, at the Hotel Roc Blanc, cell regeneration therapy (same as Niehans' treatment, but with freeze-dried cells substituted for live ones) costs $2300 a week for treatments, physician's fees, all meals, and accommodations. And in Paris, the president of the International Association of Physicians for Age Retardation, the English-speaking Dr. André Rouveix, charges approximately $1,350 (without room and board) for his own approaches to cell therapy (which include placenta "implants") at his heavily visited Clinique Nicolo.

For one-week packages using the services of the above three physicians, or for a stay at the Transvital Centers in Switzerland, contact **Santé International, 211 East 43rd Street, Suite 1404, New York, NY 10017 (phone 212/599-0382 or 800/SPA-TIME)**; its president, Gerie Tully, a former patient of Dr. Stephans and recipient of such therapy, is a stunning blonde looking 15 years younger than her true age. For one-week packages to La Prairie, or the Hotel Roc Blanc, contact **Spa Finders, 91 Fifth Avenue, Suite 301, New York, NY 10003 (phone 212/ 924-6800 or 800/255-7727)**.

Procaine-Based Therapies

One of the rare chemicals used at European spas, Procaine is a derivative of Novocaine, widely reputed to dilate the blood vessels and thereby bring greater oxygen to tissues and cells from increased blood circulation. Mixed with other substances into a serum known as Gerovital H3 and Aslavital (both denied admission into the U.S. by the F.D.A.), it is administered to many thousands of elderly Europeans each year as a treatment for diseases and declines of the aged. But though the substance is found in every spa (and in unauthorized forms, highly controversial and of disputed effectiveness, in European pharmacies), the cognoscenti get their Procaine in Bucharest at the clinics and resorts founded by the late Prof. Dr. Ana Aslan, who created Gerovital and Aslavital in the mid-1950s, and remained active until her mid-80s.

The key Procaine clinics are at the modern Vital Hotel Heilbrunn in Salzkammergut, the Biotonus Bon Port Clinic on the shores of Lake Geneva in Montreux, the Hotel Roc Blanc in Andorra (also a center for cell therapy), and Grand Hotel Sauerhof in Baden. Tour operators are, once again, Spa Finders and Santé International (names and addresses listed above), charging from $2,300 a week at the Hotel Roc Blanc and up to $7,500 for 10 days at the Biotonus Bon Port Clinic. All prices include full board, lab tests, and daily treatments, in handsome settings, all state-of-the-art.

For comparison, and much lower prices (an average of $550 to $630 a week in high season, less $20 to $50 between mid-September and April), you might also request the Romanian brochures of **Health Tours International, Inc, 25 West 43rd Street, Suite 805, New York, N.Y. 10036 (phone 212/997-8510).**

Anti-Psoriasis Treatments

Called "climatotherapy"—climate therapy—it consists of only sea and sun. But it's pursued in the briny sea and ultraviolet sun found only at the lowest point on earth, along the shores of the Dead Sea in Israel, 1,300 feet below sea level. There, in waters with the world's highest concentration of salts, whose constant evaporation produces a mist that prevents sunburning rays from reaching the earth, victims of skin-blemishing psoriasis lie safely under the burning sun and bathe for half an hour daily in the jelly-like sea.

What results is like a biblical miracle: remission of psoriasis for substantial periods in a remarkable percentage of cases. The subject of weighty medical studies for more than 20 years, the benefits of these Israeli spas are today confirmed by exact clinical data of which other therapies can only dream; many physicians are no longer skeptical—and one weeps for psoriasis sufferers who are unaware of the healing Dead Sea.

Along the Dead Sea, the specialist spas for psoriasis are the Moriah Gardens (not to be confused with the Moriah Dead Sea Spa), the entirely separate Moriah Plaza Dead Sea Hotel, and Ein Bokek. The major U.S. tour operator for them is **Spa Finders,** (see above) rapidly acquiring a near-monopoly in this area. And the rates are unusually moderate by spa standards: an average of $1,600 to $2,200 per person for an all-inclusive, two-week package (lodging, meals, treatments), but with air fare extra. Summer is the best time for treatment.

Water Cures

And finally you have the classic treatments—"carbogaseous baths," "fango mud," "vapor inhalations," underwater massage, saunas, "Kneipp foot baths," "thalassotherapy," "algae baths," and repeated draughts of mineral water—as practiced with exquisite deliberation (different treatments, different spas, for different ailments) at quite literally hundreds of spas in Italy, Austria, Slovenia, France, Belgium, Germany, and Switzerland. While your average celebrated U.S. spa charges $1,800 a week and up (to as much as $3,000 a week at The Golden Door) for its "beauty care" and "weight loss," a European spa can be had for as little as $600 a week in the Slovenian locations, for an average of $1,200 a week (depending on spa) in Italy (where Abano, Montecatini, and Ischia are the key names), and for $1,250 and up per winter week in Switzerland. The properties and programs are all lavishly described in glossy catalogs mailed free by Santé International and Distinguished Spa Resorts from the addresses set forth for them above.

The Ultimate Question

Is there anything to it? I tend to think there is; but whether or not, it is surely the worst smugness, a form of jingoism, to dismiss the claims of European spas out-of-hand and without investigation, as so many do.

Shakespeare warned that "there are more things in heaven and earth, Horatio, than are dreamt of in your philosophy." Perhaps there is more to medicine than the chemical-based prescriptions of U.S. doctors.

Vacationing at a Holistic Health Resort

A New Variety of Spa, Not for Weight Reduction, Not for Stress Reduction, but for "Wellness"

"Machines receive preventive maintenance; why not people? Why should we wait until illness strikes us down before we attend to our health?"

With those words, a wise old doctor once explained to me why he had turned at the end of his career to the practice of "holistic" medicine. An eminently sensible approach to life, with which almost no one can disagree, holistic methods of strengthening the body to fend off future illness have attracted the attention of millions of Americans, and created a thriving vacation industry of "holistic health farms" and "holistic health resorts."

None of these institutions, to my knowledge, disavows traditional approaches to medicine. "Holistic physicians" will readily prescribe an antibiotic for infection, or even perform surgery if it is needed.

But the same physicians believe in supplementing the standard therapies with alternative ones: better nutrition, exercise, stress reduction, and relaxation. People, they claim, should actively pursue "wellness" before they become sick, a process—essentially—of self-education and modifying lifestyles. The decision to vacation at a "wellness spa"—holistic centers where guests receive "preventive health workups" and seek to adapt to a healthier mode—is an obvious first step.

> **It seems a sensible approach to life, with which almost no one can disagree.**

Heartwood Institute

On 200 acres in the mountains of northern California, five hours by car north of San Francisco, this is the classic "holistic retreat," and astonishingly cheap: it charges $455 a week in single rooms, $385 per person in doubles, $315 on a campsite, including three vegetarian meals a day and use of sauna, hot tub, and pool. Accommodations are mainly bunkhouses with small, simple rooms, not far from a "community center" and restaurant in a picturesque log lodge with outside dining deck. When guests arrive to pursue a one-week or two-week "wellness retreat," trained counselors aid them to choose from a variety of therapies in massage and bodywork, nutrition and exercise, at nominal extra costs. The institute's credo? That illness results from imbalances in the body's normal state; that balance can be restored, as it often is in Asian medicine, by alternative therapies such as acupuncture or Ayurveda, lifestyle changes, modified nutrition, herbal preparations, homeopathy, still other treatments. Throughout the year, more intensive workshops are then scheduled at Heartwood in the full range of therapies under study by holistic practitioners: massage and yoga, "bodywork" and hypnotherapy, "energy balancing" and hydrotherapy—all, of course, for tuition charges (though fairly reasonable ones) not imposed upon people participating in a simple retreat. For information, contact **Heartwood Institute, 220 Harmony Lane, Garberville, CA 95542 (phone 707/923-5004)**.

Rates at other "holistic resorts" vary widely from those of Heartwood, and from each other.

Northern Pines Health Resort

For instance, in the lake district of southern Maine near Portland, about two and a half hours by car from Boston, Northern Pines Health Resort charges $495 to $675 per person for a full week, for which it places you in lakefront log cabins or rustic country cottages on 80 acres of pine forests and rolling hills. Although some guests here simply lie in a hammock and read for that week, most pursue an active daily schedule of exercises, hikes, canoeing, sailing, swimming, and classes in aerobics, yoga, nutrition, stress management, weight control, shoulder massage, and "morning stretch." Meals, served in a large, lakeside lodge, are vegetarian; and rates throughout the year, including all three such meals, classes, hot tub, sauna, and use of boating equipment, are $744 to $796 per person per week in a lakeside cabin, $827 in a better hillside or "yurt" lodging, $993 in a cedar or pine cottage. For information, contact **Northern Pines Health Resort, Rte. 85 (R.R. 1, Box 279), Raymond, ME 04071 (phone 207/655-7624)**.

Murrieta Hot Springs Resort

Ninety minutes south of Los Angeles, on 47 acres of rolling hills dotted with palm trees, this is a rather upscale version of the more typical health farm, with Spanish-style buildings, tiled walks, and elaborately manicured grounds. Yet rates are rather reasonable by health-spa standards: $795 per person per week in a double room ($945 single), including all three vegetarian meals daily, spa mineral baths with "energizing bodywrap," exercise program, mud bath, and full use of all hot-springs pools and saunas. Accommodations are in cozy cottages or terraced lodgings. Throughout the day, courses in stress management, exercise, diet, bodywork, "awareness," and health information are presented to guests free of charge. For information, contact **Murrieta Hot Springs Resort, 28779 Via Las Flores, Murrieta, CA 92362 (phone 714/677- 9661 or toll free 800/322-4542 outside California).**

Harbin Hot Springs

On 1,100 wooded acres in a valley of northern California, two and a half hours by car from San Francisco, Harbin Hot Springs is a simpler (rooms without private bath), and far less expensive West Coast alternative to Murrieta; guests enjoy the very same species of natural, warm mineral-water pools (one of 112° Fahrenheit, open all night and all year), but stay in dormitories, unpretentious private lodgings, or even on campsites. In addition to soaking (without speaking, a requirement) in the celebrated hot springs, hiking, sunbathing, and enjoying—according to one staff member—a "meditative atmosphere," guests sign up for one of numerous courses in exotic massage—Swedish, shiatsu, acupressure, watsu (water shiatsu)—at rates as low as $15 per bout of instruction. Room rates per person are $105 a week on campsites, $154 a week in dorms, $336 a week in rooms ($105 for the second person), to which you add $20 a day for two vegetarian meals. For information, contact **Harbin Hot Springs, P.O. Box 82, Middletown, CA 95461 (phone 707/987-2477 or 707/987-0379).**

Royal Court Hotel and Natural Health Resort

And finally, on a hillside high overlooking Montego Bay, Jamaica, the Royal Court Hotel is an unusually pleasant, sunny, and blissfully quiet health resort of about 20 rooms, all of which I've inspected. Its owners, Dr. and Mrs. Anthony and Dorothy Vendryes, are both dedicated to the holistic health approach, although Dr. Vendryes **Holistic physicians believe that people should actively pursue "wellness" before they become sick, a process—essentially— of self-education and modifying lifestyles.** also practices traditional medicine at a nearby hospital. Meals are low-fat vegetarian; exercise equipment is abundant; activities include daily yoga and other exercises, as well as trips to the beach, hikes, and health workshops. Best way to book is through the hotel's U.S.

"Aquacizes" in a mineral pool.
Courtesy Harbin Hot Springs.

representative, **New World Holidays, Inc., P.O. Box 20071, Cherokee Station, New York, NY 10028 (phone 212/628-0451)**, whose Royal Court packages run $779 for a week in off-season (late April through mid-September), otherwise $879 to $1,049, for seven nights' accommodations, all meals, classes, and massage.

For reasons of space, I have obviously compressed the theories of "holistic health" into almost absurdly simple form. For a more complete exposition, request a program guide of the Heartwood Institute described above, enclosing $2 to cover costs.

The New World of Travel 1997

The lifeblood of the Arthur Frommer travel guides is the correspondence received from readers, commenting on the establishments recommended in the texts and recommending new establishments. Each such letter is carefully studied, and when a particular lead seems promising, it is followed up and personally checked.

It is hoped that *The New World of Travel* will receive similar assistance from its readers. A yearly publication, issued near the start of each year, *The New World of Travel* will constantly grow. And since much of its content relates to organizations that lack the means to market themselves properly, or come to the attention of a travel journalist, your help is invaluable in alerting me to the organizations—hospitality exchanges, alternative resorts, new travel clubs, and the like—that you have discovered.

If you become aware of a new travel organization, program, or development that deserves to be described in our next edition, *The New World of Travel 1997*, won't you please let me know about it? Send your letters to Arthur Frommer, *The New World of Travel*, 1841 Broadway, New York, NY 10023. All letters will be acknowledged, and all are warmly appreciated, in advance, by the author.

Vacations at Pritikin Centers Are High Priced but Healthy

Bland Meals and Mild Exercise at Miami Beach and Santa Monica

The good news is that the approach seems to work, restoring your health, increasing your longevity.

The bad news is that it's rather expensive: an average of $4,300 for two weeks, $7,250 for a month, even when two people are taking the "cure" together.

Yet Americans continue to throng the Pritikin diet centers, devoting their two- to four-week vacations to a disciplined regimen of bland meals and mild exercise. And a major expansion of the Pritikin facilities—as planned by the 38-year-old son of the company's founder, the late Nathan Pritikin—will soon bring Pritikin-style vacations or treatments into the geographical reach of more and more people.

Residential Pritikin centers are currently in operation in Santa Monica, California, and Miami Beach, Florida. Each advances the message first proclaimed by Pritikin in 1974: that most of the major degenerative diseases of our time—heart disease, diabetes, atherosclerosis—are largely caused by excessively high blood-fat levels, and that their prevention and cure could be brought about by reducing those levels through diet and exercise.

Sounds commonplace now, doesn't it? But it was revolutionary then. Heart-disease patients were being routinely treated by drugs and surgery, told to avoid exercise, and then sent back to eating the standard American diet of meat, eggs, and dairy products.

> **E**ach of the centers advances the claim that most degenerative diseases are caused by excessively high blood-fat levels.

Instead, Pritikin advocated a diet that consisted of only 10% fat and only 15% protein, but a full 75% of complex carbohydrates, the last mainly from fruits, vegetables, and whole grains. He counseled an avoidance of all extra fats and oils (other than those naturally in grains and lean meats), all simple sugars (honey and molasses as well as sugar), all salt, coffee, and tea, and all foods rich in cholesterol (eggs, shellfish, animal organs and skin).

And each Pritikin patient or vacationer, regardless of age, was to engage in daily exercise, mainly walking.

On such a program, he maintained, the middle age of life could be stretched to cover the years between 40 and 80, rather than those from 40 to 60. Old age would begin at 80, not at 55 or 60.

Pritikin staff will cite all sorts of statistics—I won't repeat them here—to bolster their claims that the treatment has had remarkable results for the 50,000-odd people who have thus far passed through the two residential centers. What is unarguable is that strong word-of-mouth comment has kept both facilities busy and well occupied, despite the founder's death from leukemia in 1985.

Programs, Costs, and Meals

Each center offers programs for 13 and 26 days. The shorter course is for those overweight or interested in preventing future illness or reducing stress, or who have hypertension or mild diabetes (currently treated by oral medication). The second program, while available to anyone, is primarily designed for those suffering from the more serious health problems of heart disease, insulin-demanding diabetes, obesity, gout, and claudication.

No matter which program you select, you're busy from early morning till early evening, taking pre-breakfast walks along the beach or on country lanes, exercising three times a day, attending cooking classes, lectures, or supermarket expeditions.

A cooking class at Pritikin. *Courtesy Pritikin Longevity Center.*

The New World of Travel 1997

The lifeblood of the Arthur Frommer travel guides is the correspondence received from readers, commenting on the establishments recommended in the texts and recommending new establishments. Each such letter is carefully studied, and when a particular lead seems promising, it is followed up and personally checked.

It is hoped that *The New World of Travel* will receive similar assistance from its readers. A yearly publication, issued near the start of each year, *The New World of Travel* will constantly grow. And since much of its content relates to organizations that lack the means to market themselves properly, or come to the attention of a travel journalist, your help is invaluable in alerting me to the organizations—hospitality exchanges, alternative resorts, new travel clubs, and the like—that you have discovered.

If you become aware of a new travel organization, program, or development that deserves to be described in our next edition, *The New World of Travel 1997,* won't you please let me know about it? Send your letters to Arthur Frommer, *The New World of Travel,* 1841 Broadway, New York, NY 10023. All letters will be acknowledged, and all are warmly appreciated, in advance, by the author.

Personalized medical supervision is a major feature of the program. Depending on their health needs, guests are assigned to a specialist in either cardiology or internal medicine (Pritikin physicians are all Pritikin enthusiasts and live the programs themselves).

As for the meals, they are—reportedly—much better than in the early years of Pritikin. Although no extra fat is added to foods, and no salt, sugar, or caffeine is permitted, chefs still manage to turn out tasty fare. Meals are largely vegetarian, but with some fish or chicken served several times a week. You eat five times a day, so you never get hungry. Snacks might consist of vegetables and soup, Pritikin "chips" and salsa, fresh fruits. Dishes include "enchilada pie," potato pancakes, Moroccan orange-and-carrot salad, sweet-and-sour cabbage, ratatouille, paella, vegetable pot pie, and yogurt-marinated chicken.

Desserts might be carrot cake or strawberries Romanoff.

For all this, you pay a substantial price if you are traveling alone, but considerably less on a per-person basis if you are with a spouse or companion. For a 13-day session, including medical costs, the fees average $6,000 or so for one person, but only $8,600, at most, for two. For a 26-day session, fees are as much as $9,900 for one person, but only $14,500 for two. Major medical plans may cover that portion of the cost that is attributed to medical attention. And some guests have been known to treat the entire expense as tax deductible, provided they have been directed to take the program by their doctor (consult your tax adviser about IRS regulations).

Is it necessary for the Pritikin experience to be so very expensive? Physicians with whom I've spoken think it well worth the price and not out of line with costs in the more exclusive spas (not to mention alternative costs of surgery, hospitalization, time lost from work).

The other, lower-cost alternative is a planned new chain of health-and-fitness clubs for people over 40, embodying the Pritikin principles. Three are currently in operation in Los Angeles and Houston, with several

> **The meals are reportedly much better than in the early years of Pritikin; they are largely vegetarian but with some fish or chicken served several times a week.**

> **Each Pritikin patient or vacationer is busy from morning till early evening, taking pre-breakfast walks, exercising three times a day, attending cooking classes and lectures.**

more due to open soon. These, in essence, are "outpatient" facilities, with Pritikin-style restaurants on the premises and a 30-hour program of instruction presented three nights a week for four weeks, all at the moderate charge of $300 to $400.

Vacationing at the Residential Facilities

Meanwhile the better course—if you can afford it—is to spend a two-week or four-week vacation at an actual Pritikin residential facility. The **Pritikin Longevity Center, 1910 Ocean Front Walk, Santa Monica, CA 90405 (phone toll free 800/421-9911, 800/ 421-0981 in California)**, is the largest (150 guests) and the mother center (some would call it the "mother church"). It enjoys a superb beachfront location facing 10 miles of boardwalk, on which, conceivably, you might walk from Malibu to Palos Verdes.

The somewhat similar **Pritikin Longevity Center, 5875 Collins Ave., Miami Beach, FL 33140 (phone 305/866-2237 or toll free 800/327-4914 outside Florida)**, is housed in a small resort hotel on an ocean beach that is swimmable year round. A recent expansion of facilities permits the center to accommodate up to 95 guests at a time. There's a large beachfront pool, and an oceanfront gym.

At both centers, weekday visitors are welcome to take a free tour. At Miami Beach, says the general director, you may even be invited to take a meal with guests.

Vacationing with the Seventh-Day Adventists

A Less Costly Form of Pritikin-Like Treatments for Mature Americans

You are 55 and you feel yourself—faintly but perceptibly—slowing down. You are overweight and high in cholesterol. You are anxious and stressed. You have heard of the Pritikin Centers, where health can supposedly be restored, but you can't afford the tab (as much as $7,500 for a month).

So what do you do?

You call the Seventh-Day Adventists (and I am perfectly serious). For prices averaging $3,000 a month they offer residential health retreats all across the U.S.A., where diet, exercise, and atmosphere are akin to those maintained in the costly health resorts, but at less than half the price.

The Adventists have long been known for their interest in health and nutrition, and for their consequent longevity. Studies in California have revealed a much lower incidence of heart attacks and strokes among them, as compared with other population groups in the state. Early in the century an Adventist named Kellogg began producing strange but effective breakfast foods called "wheat flakes" and "corn flakes," while his brother in the same town founded the famous Battle Creek (Michigan) Sanitorium. Today Adventists operate large and prestigious hospitals—notably, Loma Linda in California and Castle Medical Center in Hawaii—from which smaller, no-frills, nonprofit, inexpensive health retreats have been spun off.

Diet and Exercise, Not Religion

At each such center the policy is determinedly vegetarian. Adventists are normally advised (but not required) to consume a purely "vegan" diet of fruits, vegetables, legumes, and for those able to handle them, modest amounts of such high-fat foods as nuts, avocados, and olives. Scarcely any "free fats"—i.e., those not found in whole foods—are used.

Which means no butter or marmalade on rolls, no oils in salad dressings, and foods sautéed in water rather than oil (the Adventists and the Pritikin people are in agreement on the virtual elimination of "free fats"). Complex carbohydrates are the basis of their diet (again in agreement with Pritikin; Pritikin, however, does allow small amounts of poultry, fish, and dairy products).

For all its spartan features, Adventist food can be surprisingly tasty. At my own recent lunch in the Adventist-run Living Springs of Putnam Valley, New York, I took repeated helpings from a buffet of salad, steamed vegetables, and cashew chow mein.

Careful attention to diet is combined, at the centers, with exercise in the open air, sunbathing, a mammoth intake of water (six to eight glasses a day), hydrotherapy treatments

Lifestyle medicine at an Adventist resort. *Courtesy Uchee Pines Institute.*

(saunas, alternate hot and cold showers), and temperance: the total avoidance of coffee, alcohol, tobacco, and irritating spices.

Those strictures are translated into programs that begin early in the morning with brisk outdoor walking, followed by a hearty breakfast, daily lectures by physicians, hydrotherapy, classes on remedies utilizing water, vegetarian cooking classes, more walking, a large meal at lunch, educational seminars, more walking or exercising, a light evening meal, then perhaps a slide show on some aspect of health.

What does not take place is religious proselytizing. "People of all persuasions and no persuasion come here," says Leatha Mellow of the center known as the Weimar Institute, in California. "We've had Catholic priests, Jews, Christians, and atheists. We do maintain a spiritual emphasis, but it is nondenominational and nonsectarian."

In health matters, by contrast, the centers are fierce advocates. Like Pritikin, they believe a proper diet can avoid the major degenerative diseases of our time—heart disease, diabetes, atherosclerosis—and pursue their cures intensively in two- to four-week programs at the various locations.

The Seven Major Centers

Living Springs Lifestyle Center, 136 Bryant Pond Rd., Putnam Valley, NY 10579 (phone 914/526-2800 or toll free 800/729-9355): In the foothills of the Berkshire Mountains, about an hour's drive from New York City, it is a large but homey building overlooking an 18-acre pond with swans. Guests occupy attractive private rooms, all with private bath, for which they pay weekly year-round rates of $799 per person in a double room, $1,295 single, including all three meals daily and all treatments.

Hartland Wellness Center, P.O. Box 1, Rapidan, VA 22733 (phone 703/672-3100 or 800/763-9355). It's among the best of the Adventist health retreats, on a 760-acre country estate at the foot of the Blue Ridge Mountains,

two hours from Washington, D.C., with especially modern treatment facilities; there's wide-ranging instruction in stress management, vegetarian cooking, and more; hydrotherapy and massage; individual counselling with physician, nurse, exercise counsellor, and therapist. Administrator Will Evert calls Hartland "a place to address serious health concerns or simply to have a healthy holiday." All accommodations are in private rooms with private bath, for which the charge is $1,500 for 10 days, $2,500 for 18 days, a value. Participants are 18 to 90 in age, and experience natural treatments without chemicals or drugs. A head nurse at the center once told me: "We believe services like these should be made available to everyone, and not just those with a lot of money. Some people call and say, 'I'll pay any price.' Others still say, 'I can't afford it.'"

What does not take place is religious proselytizing.

Wildwood Lifestyle Center and Hospital, Wildwood, GA 30757 (phone 706/820-1493 or toll free 800/634-9355): A modern facility on 500 acres of trails and hills, at an elevation of 700 feet, between Mount Raccoon and Mount Lookout. Rooms are attractive, and each has its own sunny patio. On a 24-day program, rates are $3,495 in a semiprivate room, $4,095 for a private room with bath, $3,927 for a private room with shared bath. On the 17-day program, rates in a semiprivate room are only $2,895; a private room with bath is $3,320.

Uchee Pines Lifestyle Center, 30 Uchee Pines Road #75, Seale, AL 36875 (phone 205/855-4764): In a climate that is generally warm the year round (though rainy in winter), this is a country house set in 250 wooded acres, with lovely gardens and trails. An 18-day program is offered, at charges of $2,595 for the first "patient," $2,395 for a patient/companion. Occasionally guests will be accepted for shorter programs, and fees will then be prorated.

Poland Spring Health Institute, RFD 1, Box 4300, Summit Spring Road, Poland Spring, ME 04274 (phone 207/998-2894):

Smallest of the retreats (10 guests only), but with a broad variety of activities, including cross-country skiing in winter. It is an old New England farmhouse with attached barn housing the guests and various hydrotherapy facilities. Down the road is a clinic with medical offices. Rates are $745 per person per week for semiprivate rooms, $950 a week for private rooms; but most rooms share a bath. The average stay is two weeks. And, oh yes, this is the same Poland Spring of the world-famous mineral waters; the institute has its own well, and guests therefore drink the same water as in the bottled product.

Says one Adventist nurse: "We believe services like these should be made available to everyone, and not just those with a lot of money."

Weimar Institute, P.O. Box 486, Weimar, CA 95736 (phone 916/637-4111 or toll free 800/525-9191): It enjoys the most idyllic of Adventist retreat locations—on some 450 acres in the foothills of the Sierras, about 50 miles northeast of Sacramento, off Interstate 80—but is atypically expensive: $4,475 for the first "patient" on a 19-day program, $3,575 for that patient's companion. Guests do a great deal of walking through hundreds of acres of hiking trails, and occupy rooms that are all supplied with private bath. "The nutrition and exercise plan," the Institute proudly states, "is medically supervised, with remarkable results in diabetes, heart disease, arthritis, allergies, excess weight, and stress."

Black Hills Health and Education Center, P.O. Box 19, Hermosa, SD 57744 (phone 605/255-4101 or 605/255-4687): In the Black Hills of South Dakota, in a scenic valley surrounded by rimrock cliffs, this is a "change-your-lifestyle" retreat whose diet is free from refined products and cholesterol, low in fat and salt. Daily exercise is stressed, including visits to a large, natural indoor pool fed by hot springs; physical examinations and numerous blood-chemistry tests are administered by a medical doctor. The emphasis is on a 20-day program costing $2,395 for a single room (including meals and all else), $1,600 per person double, only $1,400 per person if you park your own motorhome on one of the center's camping sites.

(Note that the well-known Total Health Foundation in Yakima, Washington—formerly a Seventh-Day Adventist retreat—no longer seems to be operating, at least not in its previous location.)

Write for literature, then call. Staff members at all seven centers are, in my experience, gentle, caring people.

Vacationing, for a Change, at a Whole-Grain Resort

At Macrobiotic Centers Clustered on Both Coasts, the Cuisine Is As Soothing As the Setting

Just as you occasionally need a vacation (which is presumably why you are reading this book), so does your stomach occasionally need a vacation. Both can achieve that restful interlude at a macrobiotic center, of which our nation has a dozen. Without necessarily subscribing to the tenets of macrobiotics—a diet of cooked whole grains and vegetables—you can turn for a time to a gentler form of life, lacking in stress, free of fats, and full of companionship among the most amiable people.

Many thousands of Americans make an exclusive use of the macrobiotic cuisine, which they often first encounter and learn to prepare at residential centers clustered on the two coasts.

Contrary to a popular misconception, macrobiotics has no necessary connection to Zen, Zen Buddhism, or even Buddhism, although a great many of the last persuasion adhere to the theory. It is a purely secular approach to nutrition based on the teachings of the late George Ohsawa, born in Japan, who believed in essence that people should live in harmony with what he perceived as natural cycles and elements of the physical universe. Thus they should eat only those foods that had grown for centuries in the places where those people lived. They should, in the United States, emphasize grains, the staff of life, supplemented by vegetables, beans, vegetarian soups—on occasion a bit of fish.

Just as you occasionally need a vacation, so does your stomach occasionally need a vacation.

Translating those ingredients into tasty meals takes skill. Accordingly, all macrobiotic centers include cooking courses in their schedules, taught to all guests. Yet even in the hands of a gourmet cook, the subtly flavored macrobiotic dishes are bland compared with the steak and potatoes of the average American diet, and thus offer a radical change of pace—a soothing one—to the average American.

You pursue that relaxing course in centers operated by disciples of Ohsawa, of whom Japanese-born Michio Kushi on the East Coast and Herman Aihara on the West Coast are certainly the most prominent. Out of a dozen possible choices, you may want to request schedules and literature from:

The Two Main Centers

Vega Study Center, of Oroville, California: Ninety minutes north of Sacramento, in an old and sleepy town of Victorian homes and later shops and stores of the 1920s, is this large, residential, teaching base of Herman and Cornellia Aihara. Their courses (including "hands-on" cooking classes) run for one to two weeks throughout the year, and cost $620 for one week, $1,240 for two weeks, with full board. Guests live in shared rooms with pine beds and wonderfully firm futon mattresses; wake at 7am for meditation, Eastern-style exercises, and tea; attend lectures delivered by the charming Aihara himself; and eat classic macrobiotic meals often prepared by Cornellia. Two new members of the staff—David Briscoe (author of *A Personal Peace*), and his wife Cindy assist with both teaching and cooking. Contact **Vega Study Center, 1511 Robinson St., Oroville, CA 95965 (phone 916/ 533-7702)**, for an interesting catalog.

The Kushi Foundation, in the Berkshires of western Massachusetts: Placid and still, on 600 mountain acres, its main building is an old mansion with spiraling wooden staircases and stone fireplaces for cool evenings. It is an appropriate setting for the calm and gentle lectures of Michio Kushi and his wife, Aveline. Seven-day residential seminars on emotional harmony and healthy

Vega Study Center. *Courtesy Vega Study Center.*

food preparation cost approximately $985 for a shared room and all meals. A unique opportunity to study with the "master" (although sometimes he's not in attendance; check first). Write or phone the **Kushi Foundation, Berkshire Center Program, P.O. Box 7, Becket, MA 01223 (phone 413/623-5741)**.

The Summer Camps

And then there are the macrobiotic summer camps, for a cheap, refreshing, and restorative holiday in the open air. Try the 200-guest International Macrobiotic Institute Summer Camp, usually from late July to late August, in a comfortable hotel in the Swiss Alps, near Kiental (approximately $615 per person for the week)— contact its U.S. agent: the **International Macrobiotic Institute, RD 3, P.O. Box 692, Mile Hill Road, Valatie, NY 12184 (phone 518/392-6776)**; or the Macrobiotic Summer Conference, in August at Bryant College in Smithfield, Rhode Island ($625 to $800 per person for the week, depending on the accommodations)—contact the **Kushi Foundation, Macrobiotic Summer Conference, P.O. Box 7, Becket, MA 01223 (phone 413/623-5741)**. The Swiss gathering (administered by the Kiental Institute) supplements the cooking demonstrations and instruction with shiatsu massage, hiking, swimming under a nearby waterfall or in a heated pool, and visits to an authentic "sweat lodge" on the premises.

The Bryant College conference consists of more than 100 courses by at least 50 teachers in such subjects as "Diet and Disease," "Cooking Macro," and such. In spring and fall, "Macrobiotic Weekend Intensives" take place around the country at charges of $300 per person for three days of instruction, accommodations, and healthy eating. Contact: **Harriet's Kitchen, 1136 Oaks Boulevard, Winter Park, Florida,** for current dates and locations. And for other macrobiotic holiday options, send $2.95 for the latest issue of "Macrochef" (a 76-page tabloid) to **Macrochef, 243 Dickinson Street, Philadelphia, PA 19147 (215/551-1430)**.

> **M**acrobiotics is the theory that people should live in harmony with the natural cycles and elements of the physical universe.

I have, in my description of macrobiotics at the beginning of this chapter, compressed a complex subject into a simplistic and inadequate paragraph. I have failed, in particular, to explore the emphasis of the theory on the need to properly balance the expansive (*yin*) and contractive (*yang*) varieties of food, and their counterparts in other areas, or the claims that a macrobiotic way of life can prevent or cure serious illness.

All this you'll hear—and more—in one of the most restful interludes of your life, as you grant time off to your overworked and suffering stomach.

America's Cheapest High-Quality Spas

Vacations for Health and Reducing, at Less than $1,100 a Week

Why pay $3,000 a week when all you receive at lunch are a carrot-raisin salad and a tiny baked apple? When the "program" consists of your own physical exertions in jogging, bending, stretching, and leaping? When "optional entertainment" consists of a five-mile hike along mountain trails that are free of charge to all?

Too many Americans have been discouraged from booking a spa vacation by the frightening rates of the famous resorts—the only ones of which you hear. At the elegant Golden Door and Canyon Ranch, at Maine Chance and Doral's Saturnia, prices do indeed often start at $2,000 to $3,000 for a week and quickly climb from there. Even at the several well-known "budget" versions of the glitzy names (Rancho La Puerta,

Heartwood), weekly rates average $1,400 to $1,700, to which a hefty air fare need be added.

Unadvertised, and largely unknown outside their immediate areas, are at least 30 locally marketed spas in every region of the nation that, in my opinion, will provide you with the very same reductions of weight and stress, the very same toning of muscles and spirit, for under $1,100 a week, and often for considerably less than that.

They deserve to be better known. For as modest as they may look, these spas provide the very same well-planned meals totaling 900 to 1,200 calories per day, the same highly active regimen of group aerobics and individual workouts, the same walks in the open country air, the same instruction in proper nutrition and behavior modification.

The best establishments I've found are listed below. Unless otherwise noted, the rates cited are for a full seven-day stay in establishments with active programs of exercise and instruction, and serving nothing other than low-calorie meals.

Tennessee Fitness Center, near Waynesboro, Tennessee, is surely the cheapest of all, and yet one of the best. The site: an attractive, hilly, woodsy setting in western Tennessee, 95 miles southwest of Nashville, where it runs you ragged with morning-till-night exercise sessions, water "aerobics" in the pool, and fast-striding hikes designed for a rather youthful clientele, though offered to persons of all ages. And it serves precisely the same sort of calorie-controlled meals for which other ritzier spas charge $1,700 and $2,500 a week. But the Tennessee Fitness Center charges only $449 per person for a week in a quad room (including all meals and exercise classes), $499 per person in a double, $699 single—and the two-story, chalet-like lodgings are tastefully decorated, comfortable, and scrupulously clean. I've heard raves for the Tennessee Fitness Center from people whose judgment I trust. Contact: **Tennessee Fitness Center, Rte three, Box 411, Waynesboro, TN 38485 (phone 615/722-5589 or 800/235-8365)**.

Runner-up in terms of cost: The National Institute of Fitness in Utah (southwest corner of the state, some 120 miles north of Las Vegas), a collection of geodesic domes on the desert floor of red sandstone canyons. Also remarkably cheap ($894 per person per week for double room and all meals, less for multiple beds or multiweek stays), yet remarkably well-equipped and with a serious approach to nutrition that for many results in permanent weight loss. "For the price we charge," says the institute's owner, "we are the number one fitness resort of the world." Amazingly enough, I have heard similar raves from several people who paid recent visits. Guests work out on the most modern sports equipment, swim in a large heated indoor pool, engage in numerous

> **They provide the very same well-planned meals totaling 900 to 1,200 calories per day, the same hyperactive regimen, the same workouts, walks, and instruction.**

At the New Age Health Spa. *Courtesy New Age Health Spa.*

exercise classes daily, eat meals designed to cut fat and cholesterol, and often experience dramatic reductions in blood pressure and clothing sizes. Contact: **National Institute of Fitness, 202 N. Snow Canyon Road, P.O. Box 938, Ivins, UT 84738 (phone 801/628-4338).**

Jimmy LeSage's New Life Spa, in Killington, Vermont, three hours by car from Boston, five hours from New York City, charges $990 per person double in spring, $1,090 in summer, and $100 more for a single room. It has somewhat the reputation of a marine boot camp, with its seemingly endless regimen that begins at 7:30am, and includes such frolics as a five- to seven-mile morning hike, aerobics and "aquarobics," lower-body workouts, upper-body workouts, and afternoon mountain walks (straight up and down), all coming blessedly to an end at 5pm with a final 45 minutes of easy-motion yoga. Calorie intake is limited to 1,000 per day; it is claimed that guests lose seven to eight pounds a week for men and four to five pounds for women. This resort has been highly regarded for 16 years, and is the place to which Mel Zuckerman, founder of Canyon Ranch, comes to spend his own summer vacation. The setting is breathtaking, in the mountains of a popular winter ski area that is used for spa purposes only from May through October. For additional information, contact **Jimmy LeSage's Fitness Vacations, P.O. Box 395, Killington, VT 05751 (phone 802/228-4676 for information, 800/228-4676 for reservations).**

For all who have stood dumbfounded and aghast at the sky-high rates of the nationally known "fat farms," here is good news.

The New Age Health Spa, of Neversink, New York (in the Catskill Mountains), two and a half hours by car from New York City, charges summer rates of $884 to $1,117 per person double (depending on room size), $1,292 to $1,493 single; $767 to $977 per person triple; fall and winter rates decline by as much as $100 per person. Though innovative and open-minded, it is no more "New Age" than many other classic spas I've visited, and it is scarcely different from other, far more expensive resorts. The facilities are extensive (indoor pool, well-equipped exercise rooms, saunas, etc.), meals are high quality but meant to ensure weight loss, rooms are rustic and plain but entirely pleasant, management is passionate (not to say fanatical) about current-day theories of good nutrition (low fat, low sodium, low calorie) and exercise, and the setting—on a hillside overlooking a vast expanse of other rolling green hills—is as awesome as you'd wish. For further details, contact the **New Age Health Spa, Neversink, NY 12765 (phone 914/985-7601 or toll free 800/NU-AGE-4-U).**

The Shangri-La Health Resort, in Bonita Springs, Florida, roughly halfway between Fort Meyers and Naples on the state's west coast, has rates of $945 per person double in winter, $995 single (and offers impressive off-season discounts of up to $300, from mid-April through October). This retreat is quite unlike the others previously mentioned in its emphasis on "natural health" methods that stress the consumption of raw foods (vegetables, fruits, nuts), sometimes eaten "monotrophically" (one food at a time per meal). Aside from four cooked dinners a week (like a rice casserole, a buckwheat kasha, a lentil chop suey), all other meals are raw, from the freshest of organically grown legumes and such. A fanatically loyal repeat clientele of raw-food vegetarians account for most of the occupancy in this 14-acre expanse of multiple buildings, jogging paths, game courts, heated pool, and more. For literature, contact the **Shangri-La Health Resort, P.O. Box 2328, Bonita Springs, FL 33959 (phone 813/992-3811).**

The Palms at Palm Springs, in Palm Springs, California, a two-hour drive from Los Angeles, has rates of $750 per person double (plus 14% service charge) with shared bath, $785 with private bath, from $1,295 single, all during the high winter season. As glamorous as you might wish, located in an area of elegant resorts, the Palms offers you a choice of 14 optional fitness classes a day in addition to meals limited to a spartan but well-balanced 750 calories per day, which virtually guarantees a daily weight loss of nearly a pound. Though it only barely fits within our budget standards, the Palms' desert mountainscape and good-quality lodgings make it a value. For details, contact **The Palms at Palm Springs, 572 N. Indian Ave., Palm Springs, CA 92262 (phone 619/325-1111).**

The Lake Austin Resort, about 30 miles from Austin, Texas, charges $1,120 per person double for a week in their lakeside cottages, $175 more for a single room. At this complex of rustic-style buildings in the rolling hill country of Texas, men generally consume 1,200 calories daily, women get 900 calories, derived from low-fat foods made tasty by dousing them with the salsa stacked on every table, or by nibbling ever-present jalapeño peppers with your unsugared bran cereal—true southwestern touches. A jam-packed exercise schedule is accompanied by classes in behavior modification (including a visit to a supermarket for unlearning bad habits in selecting food). An enthusiastic staff of fitness experts works alongside guests in 45-minute sessions of aerobics and toning in pools and gyms. In late November and all of December (until Christmas) you'll often find reduced prices at this leading health center. For complete details, contact the **Lake Austin Resort, 1705 Quinlan Rd., Austin, TX 78732 (phone 512/266-2444 or toll free 800/847-5637).**

The Carmel Country Spa, in Carmel Valley, California, inland from Carmel and Monterey, charges $833 per person double, $1,183 single. In addition to prescribing a spartan 700- to 800-calorie-a-day regimen, this establishment pursues such a no-nonsense approach to exercise that it makes each such session near mandatory: "You will return to the pool at 2pm for Aquathinics," "You will begin Hatha Yoga at 3:30pm," "You will break for a cup of hot potassium broth at 10:30am," etc., states the rather threatening schedule. Spirits are lifted by the spa's breathtaking Shangri-La–like setting and year-round temperatures in the mid-70s, all in a mountain-flanked valley of northern California, a 40-minute hike from the beach-lined Pacific coast. Rooms are well furnished and located in small hillside cottages reached by picturesque paths. Additional luxuries include an Olympic-size pool, hot tubs, a staff of professional masseuses. For further information, contact the **Carmel Country Spa, 10 Country Club Way, Carmel Valley, CA 93924 (phone 408/ 659-3486 or 800/KOUNTRY).**

Deerfield Manor, in East Stroudsburg, Pennsylvania, two hours from New York City, has rates of $699 to $799 per person double, $200 more for single rooms, and a $100-per-week supplement to all rates for July and August stays. This is a large and sprawling country home on 12 acres of Pocono forest that offers comfortable air-conditioned rooms with private bath, several lounges, a heated outdoor pool and separate gym, carefully prepared meals limited to 750 to 900 calories daily, a small but caring staff of physical therapists, and a full-scale program of aerobics and body workouts, extensive hiking, swimming exercises, and yoga and relaxation techniques. Book and music libraries supplement a video collection for quiet evenings leading to an early bedtime. Mainly for women, but occasionally booked by men and couples, Deerfield Manor is open from late April to mid-November only. For details, write or call **Deerfield Manor, 650 Resica Falls Road, East Stroudsburg, PA 18301 (phone 717/ 223-0160 or toll free 800/852-4494).**

The Oaks at Ojai is 50 miles east of Santa Barbara, California. A usual average of $900 to $1,015 per week per person in double rooms, a stiff $1,295 in singles, slightly more for double-occupancy cottages away from the main lodge, all plus a 12% service charge, make this a high-end budget selection. Impressive in both its fervor and facilities, the rustic (beamed ceilings, stone fireplaces) but elegant Oaks is a fitting country-inn addition to the art colony town of Ojai, offering a remarkable program of nearly

20 daily exercise classes and lectures. Meals are frequently gourmet in quality, but made without salt, white sugar, or white flour and containing a total of only 1,000 calories daily. Equipment and exercise areas are of top quality, as is the large staff that attends to a varied clientele of both sexes and all ages. For more information, contact **The Oaks at Ojai, 122 E. Ojai Ave., Ojai, CA 93023 (phone 805/646-5573)**.

Next time you go on vacation, consider trying a cheap or moderately priced spa. Isn't the active pursuit of health a better use of leisure time than simply loafing for a week or two?

The New World of Travel 1997

The lifeblood of the Arthur Frommer travel guides is the correspondence received from readers, commenting on the establishments recommended in the texts and recommending new establishments. Each such letter is carefully studied, and when a particular lead seems promising, it is followed up and personally checked.

It is hoped that *The New World of Travel* will receive similar assistance from its readers. A yearly publication, issued near the start of each year, *The New World of Travel* will constantly grow. And since much of its content relates to organizations that lack the means to market themselves properly, or come to the attention of a travel journalist, your help is invaluable in alerting me to the organizations—hospitality exchanges, alternative resorts, new travel clubs, and the like—that you have discovered.

If you become aware of a new travel organization, program, or development that deserves to be described in our next edition, *The New World of Travel 1997*, won't you please let me know about it? Send your letters to Arthur Frommer, *The New World of Travel*, 1841 Broadway, New York, NY 10023. All letters will be acknowledged, and all are warmly appreciated, in advance, by the author.

The Cheap New Spas of Mexico and the Caribbean

Six Resorts for Less than $650 a Week

o your pulses twitch when you read the rates of U.S. health resorts? Does vision blur, and pounding set in, at the sight of a $2,000-per-week, per-person, price tag for aerobics-and-avocado?

As in so many other instances in travel, a trip beyond our borders can sometimes achieve the very same vacation experience for far less money. Though low-cost spas do exist at home (and are increasingly available), I've been struck by the growing popularity of six dirt-cheap health resorts and spa-type hotels in Mexico and the Caribbean. And while the added air fare may consume part of the savings, isn't the foreign setting a plus?

Courtesy Rio Caliente Spa and
Mineral Hot Springs.

Consider the following:

Rio Caliente, Mexico: In the valley of a remote pine forest about an hour by taxi from the airport of Guadalajara, Rio Caliente is Mexico's holistic-health-inclined, yoga-oriented, New Age–style spa and mineral hot springs. Guests—who represent a broad range of ages, backgrounds, and interests—"take the waters" in one of four heavily salted (of lithium and selenium) and mineral-rich pools or in a natural steam room;

As in so many other instances in travel, a trip beyond our borders can achieve substantial savings.

alternate between meditation, yoga, tai-chi, aquatic and non-impact aerobics, hiking, or horseback riding; and consume a slimming, vegetarian diet low in sodium and fat. Various forms of massage, and the services of an M.D./ acupuncturist, are available on the grounds. Bear in mind that the social program and setting are not for swingers or other standard resort types; that children are not admitted; and that a pervasive, stressless, hush prevails over the 30 acres of stunning terrain, in a constantly moderate climate. For all this, you pay only $70 or so dollars a day for room and all three meals, and a remarkable $20 for each one-hour massage, $8 for detoxifying mudwraps. Request bookings or brochures from **Spa Vacations Ltd., P.O. Box 897, Millbrae, CA 94030 (phone 800/ 200-2927)**.

Ixtapan, Mexico: The closest Mexican equivalent to our own luxury spas, the large (250 suites) and well-equipped Ixtapan Resort Hotel and Spa emphasizes its thermal pools and Roman baths, but also takes pains to limit its spa guests to 900 calories a day of well-prepared diet meals. On the all-inclusive, Sunday-to-Sunday spa program costing only $885 per person double occupancy,

RIO CALIENTE

and $995 single, guests take a daily morning walk followed by aquatic exercise, steam bath and daily massage, facial, and gymnastics. Then, three times a week, and also included in the price, they receive mudwraps and loofa baths, hair treatment, manicures, and pedicures, staying all the while in attractive junior suites that would cost far more in the U.S. Don't confuse this location with Ixtapa on the Pacific coast; this is near Ixtapan de la Sal, south of Mexico City, and also near the silver-producing city of Taxco. For brochures or bookings, contact **E & M Associates, 211 E. 43rd St., New York, NY 10017 (phone 212/599-8280 or toll free 800/223-9832).**

La Casa de Vida, Rio Grande, Puerto Rico: A small, holistic health farm in the foothills of the El Yunque rain forest, the Instituto is open year round for both day visitors and overnight guests, but is most interesting for its series of five-day workshops scattered throughout the year. These cost an all-inclusive total of $495 per person, and deal with varying topics of mind/health relationships, as presented (usually) by psychoanalyst Dr. Jane Goldberg of New York and Boston. Participants engage in aquatic exercises and mountain trekking, eat the freshest of vegetarian meals, and have plenty of free time—after their classroom sessions—for ocean swimming. For a simple and unstructured stay outside the workshop periods, the rate can decline to $65 per person per night, double occupancy. More complete information on both options is available by writing or phoning **La Casa de Vida, either at its New York office (41 East 20th Street phone 673-2272) or in Puerto Rico (809/887-4359).**

Baños de Coamo, Puerto Rico: This one is only for taking a classic "water cure." Built around a forcefully gushing, thermal hot springs, the modest country inn with 48 air-conditioned but rather plain rooms is nevertheless an officially designated *parador* of the Puerto Rican government. Its rates are marvelously low—$54 for one person, $64 for two, not including meals—but virtually all you do for health is bathe in the therapeutic hot waters that Ponce de León also experienced in his quest for the Fountain of Youth nearly 500 years ago (Franklin D. Roosevelt was a more recent visitor). Two swimming pools (one with the thermal waters), a tennis court, and a restaurant complete the amenities; but only a half hour away by car is Ponce, second-largest city of Puerto Rico, with its famed Ponce Museum of Art, newly restored Perla Theatre, and other attractions. Contact **Baños de Coamo, Road 546, Coamo, PR 00640 (phone 809/825-2186).**

Avandaro Golf and Spa Resort: In the Sierra Madre mountains, near the Colonial town of Valle de Bravo, it takes a rather relaxed approach to health, favoring rest over exercise (though there's plenty of the latter, together with tennis courts, pool, golf), massage over treadmills. And there are Jacuzzis everywhere, saunas

At one location, you bathe in the same hot-water spring that Ponce de León tested for his "Fountain of Youth."

and steam rooms, high-pressure massage showers, and high-quality accommodations that feature working fireplaces in each room. The "Dream Week" plan, including suite accommodations, all meals, unlimited tennis and golf, guided hikes, and more, costs only $149 a day per person in a double room, $193 single. Contact the resort's U.S. representative, **Sante International, 211 East 43rd Street, Suite 1404, New York, NY 10017 (phone 212/599-0382 or 800/SPA-TIME).**

Villa Bejar, Mexico: On the shores of Lake Tequesquitengo, rather quiet and serene during the week, lively and active with the start-up of a floating discotheque on weekends; it is a superb spa and a fine value, with extensive and up-to-the-minute, computerized exercise machines. Bejar pledges that every guest will receive a medical checkup, six body massages, one deep cleansing facial and two "hydrating" facials, a reflexology treatment, mud or seaweed wrap, and of course unlimited visits to the resort's spa, which comes with Evian showers, hydro-pool, saunas, Jacuzzis, and assorted other treatments. All for only $120 a day, including full board as well. Again, bookings can be made through Sante International, at its address or phone number listed immediately above.

XI

New Destinations for Better and Cheaper Trips

Thailand, a Travel "Must" in Every Season

. . . and the Important

Activities Include

a Trip to the

Hill Tribes

When they heard I was planning a summer trip to Thailand, my friends were aghast. "It's the monsoon season!" they cried. "You'll float away! No one goes there in summer."

No one except hundreds of thousands of Europeans, Japanese, Australians, Singaporeans, and other Asians, all having a perfectly wonderful time. Such is the nonsense about climate—"England is unbearable in January," "Rio is freezing in July"—that discourages so many Americans from traveling to destinations during their most desirable, off-season months.

While June through August is indeed the time of tropical downpour ("monsoon") in Southeast Asia, most of the rains are concentrated cloudbursts of, at most, an hour's duration, occurring late in the day or even at night. By timing your touring, and taking shelter for a short while when necessary, you enjoy a normal stay in what is perhaps the most dynamic touristic situation on earth.

Thailand (the former Siam of *The King and I* fame) is booming. With nearly five million visitors in 1994, and more than that in 1995, it has joined the ranks of the mega-destinations.

Part of the reason is price. Except at the grand hotels, tourists can eat for $1 simply by patronizing the tiny local restaurants that number in the thousands in Bangkok alone.

Then, by carefully selecting a guesthouse in any Thai town, rooms are secured for as little as $4 a night—and that's for two people. "$5-a-day" living is alive and well in Thailand!

The economy is also booming, at a rate of increase that topped 5%, and figures to do almost as well in 1996. With its relatively stable political conditions (won at the cost of a government dominated by the military) and huge, cheap labor force, the nation is attracting new factories and investments diverted in part from Hong Kong and, more recently, China. Cranes and construction are everywhere, as manufacturers rush to erect assembly lines for their labor-intensive activities.

"$5-a-day" living is alive and well in Thailand!

The result is a near-constant condition of traffic gridlock in Bangkok, the most monumental crush of autos, buses, trucks, and motorcycles of any city. Unless you time your movements with surgical precision to avoid the heaviest flow, you find yourself spending an hour or two in a taxi or *tuk-tuk* (tiny three-wheeled vehicles rented for a pittance) to reach even nearby points. There is no subway.

So tourists take to the river—the muddy and broad Chao Phraya—which courses in a loop through the center of Bangkok, servicing its key attractions. From any number of hotels, you wander on foot to crude riverside landings where public express boats (fares: 15¢ to 35¢) or specially hired under $1 "needle boats" take you on a fast and wind-blown ride past exotic markets and slum dwellings to the magnificent Buddhist temples and complexes of such temples on or near the river's edge. Bangkok's Grand Palace is the most magnificent of these, a glittering fairyland of multiroofed, fire-spewing structures and conical monuments covered with glass and mosaics in the most brilliant tones of yellow and red. The nearby Wat (temple) Phra Kaeo, housing the sacred Emerald Buddha, and the adjacent (to the Grand Palace) Wat Po, with its 140-foot-long Reclining Buddha, are nearly as impressive, as is the more ancient Wat Arun (Temple of the Dawn) on the other side of the river.

All these stellar sights of Bangkok, as well as its several floating markets and crocodile farm, are easily and cheaply viewed by boat and on foot, without the need to enter a single taxi, tuk-tuk, or bus.

Other Bangkok residents beat the traffic jams by casually hopping aboard the rear seat of one of the thousands of motorcycles that also fill the thoroughfares and easily weave into and out of the traffic. Spotting a well-dressed woman who you could swear was the wife or girlfriend of the man driving the motorcycle, you are then amazed to see her alight at a street corner, hand a small coin to the driver (for the ride), and coolly stroll away.

While traffic problems can be wearying, all is redeemed by the sunny dispositions, the warm and generous natures, of the Thai people, a joy to meet. Buddhists to an overwhelming extent (90% to 95% of the population), their religion is one of the world's most tolerant and open-minded, not to say permissive. As always in travel, it is vital to steep yourself in the culture (including the religion) of the nation before arriving there; and for Thailand, such books as *Living Buddhism* by Andrew Powell (New York: Harmony Books, 1989) are invaluable.

Even without attempting a book-length study, every traveler can at least peruse the brief discussions of Buddhism in such widely available sources as the *Encyclopaedia Britannica*. Reading there of the young Indian prince (Siddartha

Gautama) who left his family's palace in the mid-500s B.C. to pursue first enlightenment, and then nirvana, the tourist's eye is trained to see (and understand) the tens of thousands of images of the Buddha in Thailand—here a Buddha meditating, there a Buddha reclining on his side before death. The unique Theravada form of Buddhism that prevails in Thailand sees Buddha as a supremely wise philosopher, not as a divine being. The Thais appear to downplay all other aspects of the supernatural to a greater extent than do most other people, despite the frequent presence of tiny "spirit houses" that serve almost as a joyful tribute to nature in the front yards of houses and buildings all over Thailand.

To reach the essence of Thai culture, the single indispensable day-trip from Bangkok is to the Buddhist ruins of Ayutthaya, the ancient capital of Thailand that was demolished by Burmese invaders in the 18th century. Going one way by riverboat, the other way by bus (one and a half hours), you view a broad variety of country and small-town sights, which reach their apotheosis in the magnificently preserved and/or restored temples, palaces, fortresses, and gates of the once-great city.

From Bangkok, most European tourists head next to the nearby beaches of Pattaya City or the more remote seaside pleasures of the island of Phuket, to the south. Americans, in general, do not follow their lead (or find it sensible to have flown several thousands of miles just to lie on a beach). Those who do, prefer the more tasteful resort settings of Phuket to the increasingly crowded, often-shabby aspects of Pattaya; the latter area also houses a considerable spillover from the amazingly prolific nighttime bar scene (with famous "bar girls") of Bangkok.

Rather, most U.S. visitors immediately fly on from Bangkok to the city of Chiang Mai in the north, primarily for the direct factory-outlet shopping—better than Bangkok's—in the area around that town of 200,000 residents (no longer the sleepy place portrayed in the guidebooks). On a one-day "industrial tour" of Chiang Mai's outskirts, made either by tour bus or in a cheap tuk-tuk that you have rented yourself, you go to a succession of paper-umbrella factories (featuring hand-painted parasols), leather-goods factories, teakwood-furniture factories, silver works, jewelry firms, ceramics factories, jade carvers, lacquer manufacturers, and—most important of all—to the mills that weave renowned Thai silks (of intense, radiant hues) and then work

Thailand is an Emerging World nation valuable for the insights it provides into pressing issues of our time.

them into suits, dresses, blouses, sarongs and bathrobes, scarves, and neckties. Buying directly from the manufacturer, one seems to do better than at the famed Night Market of Chiang Mai or in the shopping centers of Bangkok, and certainly better than in the pricey Jim Thompson's, the best-known silk outlet of Bangkok, which is thronged at all hours with affluent tourists.

From Chiang Mai, a three-hour ride by bus or car takes you farther north to the town of Chiang Rai in the area of the "Golden Triangle," where Thailand abuts Burma and Laos. In Chiang Rai, a visit to a travel agency will result the very next day in a one-night or two-night trek to the isolated hill tribes living on mountain peaks overlooking the border. It's a singular, mind-boggling experience, and one that's described directly below.

Thailand is an Emerging World nation valuable for the insights it provides into pressing issues of our time (population growth, famine and poverty, drug cultivation, exploitation of cheap labor and women, authoritarian governments). But it is also a developing nation, in which a growing middle class coexists with a much larger population of very low income or impoverished people, and where legislators debate whether to enact Thailand's first "social security" system (which they were doing at the time of my visit).

For its Asian culture and economic development, for low costs and charming people, Thailand is currently a "hot" destination that should be on anyone's travel list. And there's still another aspect of Thailand that almost alone is worth the trip:

A Visit to the Hill Tribes

In the mountains of northern Thailand, above the teakwood forests and rice fields of the Mae Kok Delta, a broad range of Western tourists—from youthful backpackers to middle-aged professionals—are currently enjoying what may be the world's last real opportunity to share the life of an isolated and primitive people, scarcely removed from the world of a thousand years ago. If you are to join them, you must do so quickly, because the very contact between the modern visitors and their innocent hosts is gradually erasing the differences between them.

Though pockets of primitive people survive throughout the world—in Papua New Guinea, for one, or in the Amazon or deepest Mongolia—none can be seen with the ease or lack of substantial expense that attends a trek to the hill tribes of Southeast Asia. And none, to my knowledge, permits visitors to sleep overnight in their villages as the hill tribes do—and as I did.

In contrast to the lengthy preparations for a trek through the Himalayas or Andes, an impulse decision—made in your comfortable Bangkok hotel room—transforms you into a Thailand trekker within 24 hours. You need no special equipment other than jeans, sturdy walking shoes, and a T-shirt, and you can book onto a hill-tribe trek lasting only one, two, or three days, although the very limited one-day variety is scarcely advisable.

The trek begins with a one-hour flight from Bangkok to Chiang Mai in the north of Thailand. The nation's second-largest city, but with only 200,000 residents, Chiang Mai is a once-sleepy, temple-bestrewn cultural center now transformed by tourism into a teeming bazaar of shops and small factories (on the outskirts) of arts and crafts.

It is in Chiang Mai, from any of a score of travel agencies, that arrangements can be made for a hill tribe trek. I made mine with Fairyland Tours, which assigned a former hill-tribe member—Asoepa (pronounced "Ah-soo") Saenya—as the trekking guide; he was an inspired choice. Depending on the number of people in your party, the journey is priced at $40 to $100 per person for a two-day/one-night version, all included. Never buy the trek from the costly tour desk in your hotel.

Even cheaper arrangements can be had from the travel agencies in the actual jumping-off point for the trek, which is the smaller town of Chiang Rai, three hours by car or public bus (85 baht, $3.40) from Chiang Mai. The winding, hilly ride from Chiang Mai to Chiang Rai takes you to the northernmost part of Thailand near the borders of Burma and Laos, adjoining the infamous "Golden Triangle" area, where much of the world's opium is said to be grown (its production is banned in Thailand). As you bounce along for most of the morning, the view outside is of endless rice fields flooded a foot thick. Barefoot peasants in conical bamboo hats—an affecting scene, unchanged for centuries—stand jack-knifed over the water as they press each shoot of rice into the muddy earth.

Once in Chiang Rai, at a crude, wooden landing on the Mae Kok River, you transfer to a narrow motorized "needle boat" for a further ride of one and a half hours into the jungle area leading to the hill tribes. Your possessions have been reduced to a single khaki rucksack carrying a change of underwear and socks and a canteen of distilled water, but now you have been joined by porters carrying bags of vegetables and chicken and additional water for your meals in the mountains.

By now you have left civilization altogether. There are no nearby roads, not even the rural village scenes that dot the route between Chiang Mai and Chiang Rai. You begin to perceive ponderous shapes lumbering through the thick reeds at the river's edge: elephants. And then, at a muddy riverbank, you disembark onto a path leading to a cluster of thatched huts. Here members of a partially abandoned hill tribe, the Karens, live suspended, as it were, halfway between the near-isolation of the peak dwellers and the more modern life of Chiang Rai.

A young Karen *mahout* (elephant driver) helps you into a basket-like platform atop a wrinkled elephant, and forthwith you embark on another $2^1/_2$-hour leg of your trip to the hill tribes: a swaying, bucking, somewhat precarious journey as the giant beast steps carefully along muddy jungle paths leading upward, always upward. This time you are passing terraced rice paddies that actual hill-tribe people have carved from the mountain slopes and then cultivated with water borne there in bamboo pipes. Each morning from their mountain homes the tribespeople descend several thousands of feet to eke out a marginal existence from the poor mountain lands on which their rice and vegetables are grown.

Mercifully, the elephant ride ends, only to be followed by a $2^1/_2$-hour climb on foot up mountain paths that zigzag through even thicker jungle vegetation. We are now above the clouds. Though the climb is arduous and sweaty, it requires no mountaineering skills and can be accomplished with periodic rest stops by mid-lifers like myself.

And then, in open sunlight, the jungle growth ends and you step into a scene of prehistory.

In front of you is a mountaintop village of 30 or so huts made solely of thatch and reeds and bamboo mats affixed with wooden pegs to crude posts, all beige and gray. It is a sight of the sort that Gauguin saw, or that Margaret Mead studied. Without a single device or machine, without running water or even lanterns, without vehicles or signs, without literacy or news— humankind in a state of nature.

Ranged in a central clearing, without advance notice of your arrival, are women of the hill tribes in their normal dress, but so colorful as to dazzle the senses. Around their heads are elaborate beaded caps with high protruding maneplates of beaten silver behind their knotted hair. From ear to ear hang multihued, multistrand necklaces that loop beneath their chins. Some of the glitter comes from ancient Tibetan coins sewn to the caps. The nomadic hill tribes are a people of vaguely Tibetan origin who have progressively moved south to Burma and Thailand in numbers of several hundred thousand, but scattered among temporary villages averaging no more than 100 or 150 people apiece. They are animists, believing in earth spirits, and recognize no modern nation.

Though pockets of primitive people survive throughout the world, none can be visited as easily as the hill tribes of Southeast Asia.

As dusk falls and workers return from the fields, we tourists wander the village in complete freedom, gazing at the pre-evening activities, while the hill people gaze back at us in friendly, innocent curiosity. Half-clad children scamper about among the cows, chickens, dogs, and pigs that mix in playful confusion with the human beings of whose life they are a part. As in the Middle Ages, the animals eat and sleep in or near the same structures that house their masters.

It is evening. The women—but not the men— light clay pipes of tobacco. The men squat upon their haunches and heatedly discuss village policies. To an extent unknown in the modern world, conversation is their chief distraction.

Later, in the hut of the chief on a mat of woven rush, we eat the dinner that our trek guide has prepared. On another section of the mat, and in an adjoining room, the chief and his family and friends eat their more heavily spiced meal of rice and vegetables. We glance at our hosts, who grin back sheepishly at us.

There is no verbal contact between us; their language isn't even Thai. But a different form of communication passes between us. We are observing their society, their living quarters, their evening meal.

The chief's wife hands us lighted tapers to illuminate the hut in which we are to sleep. As we bed down for the night on hard raised pallets of bamboo, other people of the village stroll inside to gaze innocently at us, our clothes, our equipment. Later, we awake feeling a bit astonished that we have spent not simply a daytime interlude but overnight with a primitive people—and we sense how increasingly natural it is for us to be among them.

Each one of us, as the visit lengthens, grows more absorbed in thought. We are assessing the difference between civilization and a life in nature; we are weighing both the pains and rewards of a bygone life, when matters were simpler.

We spend a final hour or so simply strolling among the villagers, watching as they pound their corn, attend to their children, feed their animals. As we take our leave, we buy several trinkets from the colorfully clad women. They, in dignified response, give each of us a free necklace of beads, from which a small gourd hangs.

Afterward: a three-hour walk down another part of the mountain, through jungle-like vegetation, passing radiant waterfalls; a ride by van on rutted paths to the main road outside Chiang Rai; a bus for three hours to Chiang Mai and a modern hotel where musicians play Cole Porter melodies from the stage of a slick coffeeshop.

And that—as it now seems hard to believe—was a travel experience I had at a day's remove from the bustling city life of Bangkok in the company of other worldly tourists from developed nations. Who knows how long the same will remain available, and with its present rewards?

The Undiscovered Caribbean

Thirty-three Barely Visited Islands Afford a Unique Vacation to the Discriminating Traveler

For Americans of taste and intelligence, much of the Caribbean has been ruined. On island after island, the building of multiple high-rise hotels, squeezed side by side onto a single beach area (I'm thinking, for instance, of Aruba), has wrought terrible damage to the fragile atmosphere of these once-innocent spots.

On some islands, casino activity now dominates all other attractions. Slick shopping malls, like the ones we have at home, are replacing the smaller commerce of before. Hawkers roam the beach, pestering you to buy. The motors of waterski boats shatter the calm.

But just when everything seemed gloomiest, along comes an important guidebook to provide us with relief. It's called *Undiscovered Islands of the Caribbean*—the author is California travel agent Burl

Willes—and it was recently published by John Muir of Santa Fe and distributed to bookstores by W. W. Norton of New York ($14.95).

In it you'll learn of those peaceful locales where people can still string a hammock to a pair of palms and recline therein with a paperback novel for the entire day, always without another soul in sight and with no sound other than the lapping of waves. Where they can walk barefoot down the near-deserted streets of a town and then through swinging doors into a wooden bar, where they are greeted with smiles by the denizens within. Where tiny restaurants prepare the fish that they have caught that morning and serve it with slices of lemon on a wooden plank.

> **Here are peaceful locales without another soul in sight, and no sound other than the lapping of the waves, where people string their hammocks to a pair of palms and read Proust or Joseph Campbell.**

"Undiscovered islands"? Willes isn't referring, of course, to the totally unknown—uninhabited—islands; those aren't of use to anyone. Rather, his definition is of islands without high-rise or substantial (100-room) hotels, that are endowed instead with a scattered handful of tiny lodgings, guesthouses, or private homes accepting guests. In his book he describes 33 such places, out of a potential total of 100 islands meeting his criteria for gentle, natural vacations. The remainder will presumably be treated in a subsequent, expanded edition of the current guidebook.

Where are these magical isles? Five, he says, are cayes of the stable Central American nation of Belize, none with a grand hotel, but all with the modest two-story variety. Five are charming islets of the Grenadines (Carriacou, Petit Martinique, Union Island, Mayreau, and Canouan), three are off the large French island of Guadeloupe (Marie-Galante, Terre de Haut, Terre de Bas), four are off the coasts of Venezuela (Isla de Coche, Isla de Cubagua) and Puerto Rico (Vieques, Culebra), and seven are dots of land in the Turks and Caicos (Pine Cay, North Caicos, Middle Caicos, South Caicos, Salt Cay Island, Grand Turk Island, and Providenciales).

Three are in the Leeward Islands (Saba, Barbuda, Montserrat), three are in the Bahamas (Green Turtle Cay, Long Island, the Exumas), and two are off Mexico's Yucatán peninsula (Isla Mujeres, Isla Holbox). Only in his naming of bustling, burgeoning Isla Mujeres do I take issue with Willes. And his inclusion of Puerto Rico's Vieques—where numerous developers have big plans—is perhaps arguable as well.

To Willes's credit, he does not include or describe those virtually private islands, like Mustique, where wealthy individuals have built homes that they then rent on occasion to the public. Rather, his recommendations are of breathtaking bargains, which often charge as little as $20 to $50 for a double room, and only rarely go higher than that. That's because the little-known lodgings on the "undiscovered" islands are small 10-room hotels or guesthouses converted, in most cases, from former residences and operated in simple style.

Take, for example, Posada Vista Mar on Vieques, where, according to Willes, "an unbelievably thoughtful Vieques woman named Olga rents out a half dozen small, clean but spartan rooms behind her screened-in restaurant. The sound of crickets and the island's famous tree frogs creates a vibrant chorus at night, and the bleating of Olga's goats combines with the crowing of roosters in the early morn. When it was time for us to catch a ferry to Fajardo, Olga woke us up before dawn, served us 'coffee on the house,' and said goodbye with a kiss. Rates are $25 per night, including tax."

Are these, however, desperation prices for unsuitable lodgings, offered by a desperately poor people? I put these questions to Burl Willes in a recent telephone interview:

"I don't consider them poor," he responded; "they are happy people, with a pride in their island community that is often lost in larger cities or countries. Perhaps they are poor by our standards, but on small islands the people share, they don't starve, and they're delighted to pick up this small extra income for rooms that are simple but clean and dignified."

"On these islands," he continued, "you travel as a visitor, not a tourist. The people are easier to meet, and are grateful for your visit."

"How difficult is it to reach the tiny islands?" I asked. "A fifteen-minute plane ride, perhaps a one-hour ferry ride, at most, from the larger island to which they're adjacent. That's all that is required, yet so few of us take that extra step."

Now more of us will, thanks to *Undiscovered Islands of the Caribbean*. And be assured that most of Burl Willes's recommendations are of higher-quality lodgings than Olga's, though no less gracious, no less refined.

Here tiny restaurants prepare the fish that they have caught that morning and serve it with slices of lemon on a wooden plank.

A Mixed Bag of Pleasures
on the Island of Bali

Though No Longer

Without Problems, It

Is Culturally Enriching

and Dirt Cheap

The term "tropical paradise" was once synonymous with the Indonesian island of Bali. It no longer is. Bali's capital city of Denpasar is overcrowded and a bit honky-tonk, and its much-depicted beaches are today lined with hotels, discos, beach vendors, and masseurs who often plead and shout at you to use their embarrassingly cheap services.

But if Bali is no longer floral headdresses and grass skirts, it is nonetheless an exciting and culturally enriching destination, and one of the cheapest on earth. What's important is that you know where, and where not, to go.

Of the three main beach areas, one—the elegant Nusa Dua—is scarcely Balinese at all, unless you count the artificial Bali-style façades pasted onto its five-star resorts. This is where pampered tourists go, to a wide shopping boulevard with immaculate boutiques and an attractive beach that could be anywhere in the world.

The beach area of Sanur is only slightly better, though a deluxe Bali Hyatt and equally deluxe Sanur Beach Hotel are jarring notes on a scene that begins to partake of what you expected to find in Bali. At least here you can enjoy the famed low prices of Bali: $30 to $35 for a double with bath and two breakfasts at such comfortable lodgings as the Queen Bali Hotel, a block from the beach; $30 to $45 per double in modern bungalows surrounded by graceful gardens and Balinese stone temple motifs at the Bali Sanur Bungalows; only $2 for a steak dinner at the Mango Restaurant, and only $3.50 per person for a stunning Indonesian *rijstaffel* of varied dishes—grilled chicken on bamboo sticks, with peanut sauce, shrimp curry, and a dozen other courses on tiny plates. Even the high-quality Bali Beach Hotel here charges only $20 for its multicourse Beach Buffet dinner and dance performance under the stars, all to the strains of gamelan music and softly clashing cymbals. The downscale Kuta Beach area is Bali's most popular, with its smooth white sand that stretches for miles and is dotted with palms. But this is the haunt of Australian young people—including a few rowdy surfers, not exactly intellectual types. Still, their presence here, and the weak purchasing power of the Australian dollar, support a broad industry of budget-priced facilities.

Even "upscale" hotels in the Kuta Beach area—like the new Sahid Bali Seaside Cottages—charge an average of only $60 a night for a double room. In the town of Kuta itself, amid busy streets of stores, clubs, and restaurants, less expensive cottages/rooms/pensions—basic but clean—cost $20 for an air-conditioned double with private bath and hot water; $15 per double with fan only, bath and hot water; $12 with fan and bath but no hot water; and an amazing $6 for two people without private bath. And breakfast is included!

Kuta's room bargains are matched by those of its restaurants and shopping. In my own favorite restaurant, patronized by that small sliver of book-reading tourists (it's called Made's Warung, and you eat on a tiled balcony under a bamboo roof), fruit salad with black rice is the equivalent of 65¢, and nasi campur (white rice mixed with up to seven kinds of meat, with coconut sauce and peanuts) is well under $1. This you wash down with draughts of a potent rice drink known as an "Arak Attack," at 45¢ a cup.

And in the shops of Kuta, prices are far lower than in many other Balinese locales: under $15 for snakeskin shoes and sandals custom-made in the color of your choice, under $25 for leather suitcases, $10 for stylish batik sundresses, about $12 for elaborate sterling-silver bracelets.

In Kuta, you begin to glimpse the all-pervasive role of the Hindu religion in Bali, so different from the prevailing Islamic culture in the rest of Indonesia. Brightly colored offerings of flowers, food, and incense, placed on coconut palms as an offering to dead relatives and the gods, are so thickly placed that you must literally maneuver your way around them when walking down the street, even Kuta's main shopping strip. You would not see these in such profusion in Nusa Dua or Sanur.

What's important is that you know where, and where not, to go.

Some tourists choose Kuta as their base, for its low costs and ample nightlife, but then flee from the beaches (not the best aspects of Bali) for daily excursions into the more important inland and mountain areas, all less touched by tourism, more thoroughly Balinese. Transportation is so cheap in Bali that some even skip the more basic forms of getting about—so-called *bimos* (public pickup trucks) costing under $1 to any point in Bali, motorcycles for $5 a day, rental cars for $15—and hire a van-with-driver for the day and early evening, for only $40. By comparison shopping to find a driver capable of providing the cultural/historic context of what you are viewing, you are able to properly visit the chief attractions of Bali.

These are, first, its major hillside and lakeside temples in constant, daily use by the Balinese (conduct yourself with proper respect inside); then, the healing rituals, crematory funerals, and remarkable fire-dance ceremonies held daily in several key villages. Then, too, several villages each specialize in a single craft—stonecarving in Batbulan, silver working in Celuk, woodcarving in Mas—and a skilled driver-guide can direct you to them. Finally, lively "night markets" (kerosene-lit stalls and carts), not at all oriented toward tourists, flourish in Denpasar and at least a dozen other towns.

My own driver-guide, in one day, took us (among other places) to little-known hot springs scattered about the island, then to drink coconut wine cross-legged on a mat with elders of his village, then to four different night markets barely touched by the outside world.

Rather than base myself in Kuta, however, I'd opt for the best of all worlds by skipping the beaches altogether and heading directly to the mountain town of Ubud, which approximates and sometimes surpasses what travelers dream of finding in Bali. Here, nestled in brilliant-green mountains and rice terraces, a community world renowned for its paintings carries on a daily round of art and ritual, more visibly than in any other part of Bali, while accommodating tourists at the same time. The tourists are also different here; quiet and respectful, sometimes wearing the traditional sarong, they go strolling a short distance outside town and soon pass farms and then participants in religious processions. Village women lead the march, their heads stacked high with brightly colored, pink-and-green temple offerings. At night, the same tourists sit on platform balconies built into the hills and listen to gamelans and the sound of the Campuan River.

The lodgings of Ubud are outstanding. My idea of paradise is a cluster of bungalows with patios and thatched roofs called the Tjetjak Inn, all built alongside a hill above the river, and all with sweeping views. You awake here to the sounds of the river and its traffic, and glimpse workers gathering thatch across the river. You sunbathe on nearby boulders and swim in the river, and the price of all this is $16 per cabin, including a hearty breakfast for two, eaten on the porch. Less scenic (but still adequate) rooms in private homes rent for under $10 per double, with bath and breakfast, but without hot water or flush toilets. And in the center of Ubud, wonderfully picturesque and historic, is a former palace complex, Puri Saren Agung, charging $32 per double room, including breakfast.

Shops in Ubud sell carved and painted wooden art (masks and mobiles of painted fish or birds) for $8.50 to $11, carved and painted frames with floral motifs for $4.50 to $20, silver jewelry for $1 to $25, and of course a massive array of paintings—the town's specialty—for widely varying prices, but cheap.

Although you can take a thrice-daily $2 shuttle bus from Ubud to the beach area of Kuta, a great many visitors in Ubud travel on to the far less crowded beach at Candidasa, in eastern Bali, another approximation of a "tropical paradise." Here, residents and especially fishermen outnumber the tourists, and you see a steady stream of Balinese walking back and forth to the beach with various varieties of work on their heads. Temples decorated with streamers and food offerings adorn the scene; the mood is quiet but somehow celebrational. Rates for simple but clean rooms in Candidasa range from $9 (no hot water) to $22 (air-conditioned, hot water), and there are far more basic quarters for under $5 per double. For another $5 you can rent a motorbike, and for still another $15, hire a guide who comes with his or her own motorbike. And thus equipped, you chug from Candidasa to the former Balinese capital of Singaraja (stopping to buy bananas for the onslaught of friendly monkeys that await you on the ride), to the enchanting Lake Batur, the northern beach of Lovina, and numerous traditional villages where bones of the dead are prominently on display.

As you can see, the Hindu culture of Bali, and its superb natural sights, are all accessible, and accessible cheaply, to the tourist who avoids the heavily touristed beach areas to the south. It all depends on knowing where to go.

Garuda Indonesian Airlines flies to Bali from Los Angeles for as little as $1,155 round-trip. So does Continental Airways (via Guam), Qantas (via Australia), and Malaysian Airlines (via Kuala Lumpur).

The New World of Travel 1997

The life blood of the Arthur Frommer travel guides is the correspondence received from readers, commenting on the establishments recommended in the texts and recommending new establishments. Each such letter is carefully studied, and when a particular lead seems promising, it is followed up and personally checked.

It is hoped *The New World of Travel* will receive similar assistance from its readers. A yearly publication, issued near the start of each year, *The New World of Travel* will constantly grow. And since much of its contents relates to organizations that lack the means to market themselves properly, or come to the attention of a travel journalist, your help is invaluable in alerting me to the organizations—hospitality exchanges, alternative resorts, new travel clubs, and the like—that you have discovered.

If you become aware of a new travel organization, program, or development that deserves to be described in our next edition, *The New World of Travel 1997,* won't you please let me know about it? Send your letters to Arthur Frommer, *The New World of Travel,* 1841 Broadway, New York, NY 10023. All letters will be acknowledged, and all are warmly appreciated in advance, by the author.

Five Small Towns Prove That Historic Preservation Brings Touristic Wealth

Though Hardly Household Names, They Enjoy a Steady Flow of Visitors

Madison, Indiana; Guthrie, Oklahoma; Rugby, Tennessee; Stevensville, Maryland; and Las Vegas, New Mexico (not Nevada, but New Mexico)—these aren't exactly household words. Each is a tiny village, or at best a small town of fewer than 14,000 souls. And none is near a great natural wonder or other touristic sight. Yet each enjoys a thriving tourist trade that fills its hotels, restaurants, and shops on weekends in winter, and throughout the week at other times. And why?

Because each has preserved its past. Each has had the presence of mind to banish development to the outskirts of town, to prohibit the high-rise and the shopping mall near the center, to preserve and maintain historic structures as precious jewels. Therein lies a lesson for scores of other American communities with similar potential.

The tourism enjoyed by these small towns is based on an aspect of human nature: the satisfaction people derive from communing with the past. People travel in part for that reason. They gain solace, strength, or inspiration from a contact with structures of earlier times, feel part of humankind, less alienated and apart; they seek roots. Though historic preservation is not undertaken for touristic reasons—but rather to preserve the continuum of culture, the basis of civilization—it throws off important dividends to the industry of tourism.

And therefore when people feel uncertain about whether to prevent the real-estate developers from placing parking garages or gas stations in their historic downtown districts, they might want to ponder the achievements of five small towns that have followed the course of preservation—unyielding hostility to the forces of commercial greed.

Madison, Indiana

In a valley of the Ohio River, and alongside that river, Madison's downtown stretches for dozens of blocks without a single high-rise, a scene of gentle beauty. Here is found every major example of 19th-century architectural style: Gothic, Georgian, Regency, classic revival, Federal, Americanized Italian villa, and—of course—Victorian, all fiercely protected against demolition and replacement.

Has commerce suffered from these limits placed upon the developers? Exactly the opposite has occurred, say numerous spokespeople; Madison is a vital, bustling, modern city whose normal commerce is simply enhanced by tourism to its downtown area, whose entire expanse has now been placed on the National Register of Historic Places. For accommodations, try the Broadway Historic Hotel (operating since 1859), the Victoria Inn, Cliff House, or one of the numerous historic bed-and-breakfast homes. To reach Madison, simply drive for less than two hours from either Louisville, Kentucky, or Cincinnati, Ohio.

Stevensville, Maryland

On Kent Island, in Chesapeake Bay, within commuting distance of Baltimore, Washington, D.C., and Annapolis, Stevensville is the smallest of the recent success stories, but thriving and growing not only in a commercial sense, but in its opportunities for residential living in town houses and apartments. And yet the developer of this once-typical turn-of-the-century Eastern Shore town has been scrupulous in maintaining the Victorian character of the town's period structures, unaltered by a single new façade, a single neon sign. Those buildings were saved when the simultaneous construction (in the 1950s) of the Chesapeake Bay Bridge and busy Maryland Rte. 50 drew traffic away from

Each has had the presence of mind to banish development to the outskirts of town. of town.

the rail and port facilities located near the enchanting Victorian town. While other areas of Kent Island erupted into shopping malls and the like, Stevensville slumbered until taken in hand by a businessman with a sense of taste. Even his new office building there is only two stories high and in traditional style. If you do decide to visit, you'll want to stay at the nearby Kent Manor Inn, built in 1820, which has 25 super-comfortable rooms. From the eastern end of the Chesapeake Bay Bridge, turn down Maryland Rte. 18 to reach Stevensville.

Guthrie, Oklahoma

Nearly 100 years ago the great Oklahoma land rush brought thousands in a single week to create the town of Guthrie in Victorian style and splendor. The first capital of Oklahoma, by 1910 Guthrie had over 50 miles of sidewalk lined by handsome buildings of every sort, but then declined with startling suddenness when the capital moved 28 miles south to Oklahoma City. As other Oklahoma cities "boomed"—replacing their historic centers with ugly high-rise offices—Guthrie remained unaltered, and today enjoys the largest commercial historic district in the National Register of Historic Places: 100 Victorian business buildings, 2,300 certifiably Victorian homes, an amazing treasure unmarred by modern towers. Looking for the "Old West"? You'll find it in Guthrie. And a lively array of rodeos and ranch shows, resident theaters and museums, keep things lively beyond the lure of architecture.

> **Though historic preservation is undertaken to preserve the continuum of culture, the basis for civilization, it throws off important dividends.**

Las Vegas, New Mexico

Long overshadowed by its namesake in Nevada, Las Vegas was once the supply city for a vital fort guarding the Santa Fe Trail, and then a key stop on the Atchison, Topeka and the Santa Fe railroad. By 1882 it was nearly the size of Albuquerque and Denver, but then ceased growing as additional rail lines bypassed its own. Today, with 900 buildings on the National Register, its decades-long economic torpor is viewed as a blessing, and tourism is increasingly pushed as a major activity. Though heavily visited, it is not nearly as "touristy" as Santa Fe, and its several historic districts—with their many stone residences and stone commercial buildings—provide a fascinating glimpse into American history. For lodgings, try for a room at the imposing La Castaneda Hotel, built by Fred Harvey in 1898.

Rugby, Tennessee

An "intentional community" founded in the 1880s by English author Thomas Hughes *(Tom Brown's Schooldays)*, who envisioned it as a rural cooperative, yet with high-peaked Victorian buildings and ornamental gardens. Though the gentlemen farmers he attracted there never really succeeded in an economic sense (some dressed for tea at 4pm), the village survived and today zealously maintains and preserves its 17 original structures (which include a church, schoolhouse, public library, and bookshop, all built in the 1880s). Thousands of visitors stop by each month, at this location in the Cumberland Plateau of eastern Tennessee, some staying at B&Bs maintained in historic homes. Rugby can be visited from March 1 to December 15.

Costa Rica, for a Different Sort of Tropical Vacation

On the T-Shirts of the Teenagers Here, the Words "Costa Rica Air Force" Are Emblazoned near the Neck; Filling the Space Below Is a Huge Dove

They abolished the army here more than 40 years ago, and have lived in perfect peace and tranquillity ever since. They enjoy the highest per-capita income in Central America, a fully functioning democracy, the presence of North American retirees totaling 35,000 people, and a president who won the Nobel Peace Prize for his plan to end the fighting in nearby Nicaragua and El Salvador.

But the beaches are 80 miles from the capital city, and the seaside hotels are small lodgings that haven't yet attracted masses of foreign visitors. While that's a disturbing fact for traditional tourists, it's a positive plus for special ones. Costa Rica is the destination par excellence for people seeking the pleasures of the tropics without the pressures of crowds and casinos. It affords you a chance to experience Central America without danger, to explore and discuss the politics of the region with open-minded, uncoerced residents, to combine rest for the body with stimulation for the mind, pleasure with learning.

The country is peaceful and stable, its cities calm and well ordered.

But what exactly do you, as a tourist, do there? Because the capital city of San José is in a central valley, 80 miles from the sea on either side, your initial activities are different from those you scheduled for more standard tropical destinations located on a coast, near beaches. Here, before attending to countryside pleasures, you first experience the distinctly urban life of a great Central American center, conversing with its highly opinionated, politically alert people, visiting attractions of cultural interest, taking Spanish lessons, attending highly charged lectures (in English) on social and regional concerns.

The Life of San José

The opening step is a remarkably cheap and effective, three-day "crash course" in the Spanish language at the Instituto Universal de Idiomas in the heart of downtown San José, Costa Rica's capital. For six hours a day on each of three days (Tuesday, Wednesday, and Thursday) each week, their university-level instructors will provide you with a basic underpinning in that useful subject for a total charge of only $120, and a $45 registration and book fee. Reserve your place by contacting the **Instituto Universal de Idiomas, 751-2150 Moravia, San José, Costa Rica (phone 011-506-223-9662).**

More serious travelers will opt for a one-month course in Spanish (three hours a day for five days a week, for four weeks) at the same instituto, costing an equally remarkable total of only $390, including materials and registration. To ensure your immersion in the subject, the instituto will then arrange your room and board with one of 20 Costa Rican families in the area, for $100 a week, including two meals daily and laundry service. Classroom instruction is with a usual total of three or four other students, a maximum of six. Private lessons, either supplementing the group instruction or substituting for it, are $9 an hour, which contrasts radically with what you'd pay for Spanish instruction here at home. (Two-week and three-week courses without homestays are available for $250 and $320, respectively.)

A shorter, but perhaps more elaborate, introduction to the language and culture of Central America, in a country club–like setting within the elegant residential neighborhood of Los Yoses (20 minutes by bus from downtown San José), is provided by the Forester Institute; its classrooms enjoy an awesome view of the surrounding mountains, and the chirping of birds.

At Forester, you choose from either two-week, three-week, or four-week classes (maximum of eight

A sunny classroom at the Forester Institute. *Courtesy Forester Instituto Internacional.*

students per class) in either "Language" or "Language and Culture." The former involves four hours a day of instruction; the latter supplements classroom instruction with daily excursions, cultural activities, and conferences (on both political and cultural themes). On both programs, students are placed with carefully selected but non-English-speaking Costa Rican families where they receive a private room, breakfasts, dinners, and laundry service.

Charge for Forester's language program, including the homestay, is $675 for two weeks, $855 for three weeks, $1,020 for four weeks. The more extensive language-and-culture program (including the homestay) runs $815 for two weeks, $1,065 for three weeks, $1,300 for four weeks. Contact Forester's U.S. representative: **Charlene Biddulph, 249 S. U.S. Hwy. 101, Suite 226, Solana Beach, CA 92075 (phone 619/943-0204).**

Two final examples of Costa Rica's programs for total immersion in the Spanish language start, first, with David Kaufman's Centro Linguistico CONVERSA, in a large and rambling farmhouse atop a hill about five miles from the center of San José. There, you'll be brought each morning by Jeep from your lodgings with a Spanish-speaking private family in the nearby town of Santa Ana, and given five and a half hours of daily classroom instruction in addition to other practice sessions exclusively in Spanish. After four weeks, you speak! Total cost of the four-week course, taught every month but December, and including all lodging, meals, tuition, everything: $1,850 for one person, $3,500 per couple. Contact **Centro Linguistico CONVERSA, Apartado no. 17, 1007 Centro Colón, San José, Costa Rica (phone 011-506-221-7649).** The Centro's U.S. representative is Dr. Brian Adams, phone 800/292-9872, who will be happy to provide you with additional information. That toll-free number is his wife's travel agency; leave your name and number, and Dr. Adams or Pat Adams (his wife) will phone back.

Or try the month-long "total immersion" regimen of the ICAI organization (described more fully below) for $1,298. That includes room and board with a private family, tuition, classroom materials, excursions, cultural and sightseeing activities, and instruction in classes limited to six students. For information, contact the organization's U.S. office: **ICAI School of Languages, P.O. Box 5095, Anaheim, CA 92814 (phone 714/527-2918).**

Realities of Central America

With or without a knowledge of Spanish, you can attend courses presented in English on the present-day realities of Central American societies at the Central American Institute for International Affairs ("ICAI") in San José, founded in part by the Organization of American States. ICAI offers numerous short-term (three weeks to one month) programs co-sponsored by about a dozen U.S. universities, to which outsiders are admitted, but only if they have some college training or other background in the social sciences. Lecturers are leading scholars or political figures of Central America; classes are supplemented by field trips, such as to a Nicaraguan refugee camp in Costa Rica's Limón Province; and students are housed (room and two meals a day) with Costa Rican families. Though prices vary, figure about $1,005 for a three-week course of instruction, including room and two meals a day. For information, contact **Roberto de la Ossa, Director, ICAI, Apartado Postal 3316, San José, Costa Rica (phone 011-506-2 33-85-71).**

More casual learning, and again usually in English: at the Monday evening lectures of the Quaker-run **Friends Peace Center** in San José, or at their periodic, frequent workshops, many of which are conducted in English (phone first—011-506-2 33-61-68—to determine if they are). And you can browse through numerous hard-to-find newspapers and magazines dealing with Central American issues at the center's extensive library. Its address, in the strange directional terms of San José, but comprehensible to any taxi driver, is: "c 15 a 6, no. 13–36." Taxis to most points in San José are rarely more than $2 in cost.

If you would simply like the experience of living with a Costa Rican family on your visit to San José, contact **Señora Soledad Zamora (phone 011-506-2 24-79-37**), who serves as a one-woman booking agency for nearly 80 such families in and around the city (and mainly in the suburb of San Pedro, 15 minutes out). For a $15 fee, Señora Soledad will place you with a family that charges $10 to $15 a day, full board. Since she does not speak English, ask to speak with her daughter, Silvia, or with one of the American students usually living at Señora Soledad's home, if you yourself do not speak Spanish. Staying with a host family, you soon will.

Costs and Cultural Opportunities

For the standard tourist to Costa Rica desiring standard accommodations, the choices are broad and at wonderfully low rates. They range from such standouts as the deluxe Corobici Hotel (as little as $120 for a double room) to the tourist/first-class Gran Hotel Costa Rica ($71 per double) and Ambassador Hotel

Here are the pleasures of the tropics without the pressures of crowds and casinos.

($50 for a double), to the charming Hotel Don Carlos ($56 per double) to the more basic Costa Rica Inn ($29.95 per double) to the Toruma Youth Hostel ($4.90 per person per night). Restaurants offer meals with music at such outstanding values as El Balcon de Europa (Costa Rican dishes from $4 to $6) and Miró's Bistro (a giant platter of rice with shrimp for $4.95). Nightlife is centered at El Pueblo, a sparkling-white village of Spanish colonial architecture whose varied components—discos, bars, restaurants with guitar players and accordions—could not be exhausted in a week of going out

each night. At the complex's La Cocina de Leña restaurant, where musicians wander in to play, a mammoth plate called "gallo pinto" (mixed rice and beans, meat, eggs, and sour cream) sells for the Costa Rican equivalent of $4.20.

Suitably housed and fed in the year-round, spring-like climate of San José, you then attend symphonic or dance performances (tickets for under $10) at the famed National Theater; visit the art exhibits and presentations at the Costa Rica–North American Cultural Center; wander among the modern art, primarily by Central American artists, at the Galería J. Garcia Monge or in the galleries of the Central Bank on the Cultural Plaza; view pre-Columbian art at the National Museum of Costa Rica.

But mainly you meet the politically alert, fiercely independent people of Costa Rica, and hear their varied reactions to conditions in Central America and policies of other nations toward Central America. And then, if you wish, you can head to the beaches, surrounded by jungle-like national parks.

Into the Country

When you then strike out into the hinterland, your vacation is again utterly different from what you've experienced in more standard resorts, in high-rise hotels. It is not only different, it is more human, more removed from urban atmospheres, better.

Because the Costa Ricans are fiercely determined to protect their beach areas from the excesses of a Miami or Acapulco, they have limited seaside hotels to the height of a palm tree, and placed many of them back from the sea, on hillsides or enveloped by trees. About the closest equivalent to a standard resort area is that sector (actually a province) of Costa Rica's Pacific coast called Guanacaste, where the several small one- and two-story hotels on four particular beaches—Tamarindo, Ocotal, Condovac, and Flamingo—are the chief draws, but charge no more than $40 to $60 for a single room, $60 to

$85 for a double, even in high season. Those rates contrast sharply with the levels of other tropical countries available to North Americans.

Amazingly, you can fly from San José to Guanacaste for only $16 each way, or go by bus for infinitely less, or drive there from San José in four hours on the Pan American Highway.

Rather than stay at the resorts of Guanacaste, however, I'd pursue the more exotic pleasures of the nation's national parks and nature reserves, teeming with wildlife and wonders. They are the true, standout attractions of Costa Rica.

Manuel Antonio National Park

Reached by air from San José for only $18 each way, this 1,700-acre preserve on the Pacific Ocean is a series of crescent-shaped, white-sand beaches surrounded by lush tropical jungle and verdant volcanic cliffs; mention its name to a "Tico" (a Costa Rican) and you'll provoke exclamatory superlatives, sighs, and dreamy smiles. It is one of the few places on earth where you can luxuriate on a beach and experience jungle (including white-faced monkeys) at the same time. You walk to the beaches along well-marked jungle paths, enjoy breathtaking views of azure seas and sharp cliffs from atop lookout areas on Cathedral Point (a bit more difficult to reach), view wildlife in a hundred forms, then frolic in the warm surf with Tico families, who later tap and sway to salsa music—and prepare enormous lunches for their beachside stays.

Although campers can remain overnight in the park, at designated sites (receiving fresh water, bathroom facilities, and picnic tables, for $1), the hotels are outside its grounds, but immediately alongside or less than two miles away. The top lodgings are the Spanish-colonial duplex villas of La Mariposa, built into the otherwise untouched, lush countryside, with one of the world's most spectacular ocean views and Costa Rica's highest rates: $95 per person per night, including breakfast and dinner served in an elegant pavilion amid jungle flowers and palms.

You dine to the strains of classical music, enjoying such treats as stuffed quail baked in red wine or heart-of-palm brioche. For reservations (which you will need here), phone toll free 800/223-6510 in the U.S., or directly to La Mariposa in Costa Rica at 011-506-2 77-03-55.

Lesser priced, but perfectly adequate and just as exotic: the small Hotel Divisamar, directly across the road from La Mariposa ($49 double, without meals), and the nearby Hotel Karahe ($51 double), the latter with a moderately priced restaurant. Rock-bottom in cost, but proper: the Costa Linda Youth Hostel, accepting people of all ages, for $6 per bed per night.

Monteverde Cloud Forest Reserve

By express bus from San José ($3.80), or by rental car, a great many visitors schedule time for still another major attraction: the mystical, cloud-enshrouded, 25,000-acre reserve of Monteverde in the Tilaran Mountains, 6,000 feet above the sea. Protected and maintained by a world-renowned, Quaker-founded science institute, it harbors hundreds of varieties of mammals and birds (including the mythical Quetzal and the elusive golden toad; you'll almost certainly spot the former), lush jungle with 80 miles of wood- or rock-carpeted trails, waterfalls, orchids, and a dense shroud of white cloud—you feel somewhere between land and sky. For $64 per person, including all three meals, you can stay in the lodge/farm known as the Hotel Montana (call 011-506-2 61-18-46 in San José for reservations) or for $35, including meals, in the Belmar Hotel or Pension Quetzal, or for $23, including all three meals, in the Flora Mar, or for $4 a night, without meals, in the dormlike "field station" of the Tropical Science Center ("T.S.C.," headquartered at Apartado 8-3870, San José 1000, Costa Rica, phone 011-506-2 22-62-41; phone them in advance for a bunk). And at the club known as the Golden Toad in the nearby town of Santa Elena, Latin and rock music are played most nights.

The Jungle Train

Still other visitors take the six- to eight-hour trip on the slow "Jungle Train" from San José to Limón, where they proceed by bus for another hour to the 1,500 acres of coral reef that make up Cahuita National Park of Costa Rica. After that day-long ride through tropical vegetation and coffee plantations along mountains and in green valleys, so close to village life as to enable eye contact with Ticos going about their daily business, they repair for rest to the pleasant Hotel Cahuita ($25 per very basic double room), with garden, pool, and patio restaurant. In the park, snorkeling equipment is rented for $6.50 to explore the exquisite coral reef.

Some of these sights, and still others, can be managed on shorter day-trips from San José (where a dozen travel agencies will make the arrangements), but staying overnight or for several nights at small lodgings affords you a different and better contact with the primeval life of tropical jungles, mountains, and sea—the kind of experience that used to be the accustomed lot of travelers before high-rise hotels standardized the world.

For assistance in visiting these and other attractions of Costa Rica, I like the services of OTEC, a well-staffed, non-profit organization of student travel that specializes in trips and discounts for the young, but actually handles the needs of all ages and of nonstudents. They're found on the second floor of the Victoria Building in San José ("a 3, c 3/5"; phone 011-506-2 22-08-66), where they answer questions and offer to make you one of their traveling groups, which brings you a radical saving from the price levels of other commercial tour operators. Contact them ahead of time if you're planning a special interest or group tour of Costa Rica, by writing: **OTEC, P.O. Box 323, San José 1002, Costa Rica.**

For additional information on this inexpensive and inspiring nation, contact the Miami office of the **Costa Rica Tourist Board** (phone 305/358-2150, or toll free 800/327-7033 outside Florida). The national carrier, LACSA, and Eastern Airlines, service San José directly from several U.S. cities, and numerous other airlines go there via their own national gateways.

An Introduction to Belize

Shunned by Many Because of Its Location in Central America, It Is Peaceful, Stable, Filled with Activities—And Cheap

Weather-beaten wooden homes and streets made of white sand. "Hotels" with 10 rooms and "restaurants" with five tables. Barefoot informality and yarn-spinning residents with all the time in the world. Electricity that doesn't always work, schedules that aren't always met.

If you're yearning for the Caribbean as it once was, you'll find it in the Caribbean's newest nation, which formerly was British Honduras. Two hours by air from Miami, and yet touristically underdeveloped, it awaits you on the edge of Central America—some would say "on the edge of the world"—just below the Yucatán peninsula of Mexico, between Guatemala and Honduras.

It is remarkably peaceful, stable, democratic. Though its tiny population (175,000 people in an area the size of Massachusetts) is split among a dozen ethnic groups—Mayan Indians, Chinese, "Anglos," Créoles, Hindus, mestizos, Hispanics, even a recent community of horse-and-buggy Mennonites—they live in perfect harmony, enjoy a British-style parliamentary government, intermarry, and serve as a lesson for all of us. What's more, their official language is English!

As for its touristic attractions, Belize possesses the second-longest (after Australia) barrier reef on earth, a teeming coral formation of sea life, shapes, and colors that draws scuba divers and sailors from around the world. Along the reef are then dozens of "cayes" (pronounced "keys")—narrow, beach-lined islands of remarkable beauty, dotted with small hotels (often 10 rooms apiece) of modest, friendly pretensions.

You have two vacation choices on a trip to Belize—you can sun, swim, sail, or scuba-dive on and off the cayes, or you can explore the inner mainland in pursuit of Mayan ruins and culture, wildlife, and other natural history.

On the mainland, only one major city is found, of no great visitor interest. This is Belize City, with only 60,000 people, but site of an international airport well serviced by a number of carriers (I'll list them later). From here, you take smaller planes to the cayes.

Inland of Belize City is of greater appeal: 65% of the country's land area is uninhabited jungle—supporting jaguars, no less—and scattered about are relics, temples, even cities, of the once-mammoth Mayan civilization that flourished from the 3rd to the 10th century in what is now Belize.

You have two vacation choices, therefore, on a trip to Belize, and many tourists combine them both. You can sun, swim, sail, or scuba dive on and off the cayes. Or you can explore the inner mainland, pursuing bents of archaeology, wildlife and other natural history, Mayan ruins and culture, and all forms of jungle adventure travel.

The Mainland

The region on the mainland best suited to accommodate tourists is the Cayo District (two hours by car from Belize City), which has several exotic but comfortable lodges, and is accessible to the formidable Mayan ceremonial site of Xunantunich and the impressive natural wonders of Mountain Pine Ridge. Alternatively, you go south down the coast to Dangriga, viewing the world's only jaguar preserve and the life of Garifuna Indians, who allow visitors (if they're so inclined) to participate in their rituals. Because life hereabouts is rustic, with treacherous roads and nonexistent (usually) signposts, you accomplish all this not by rental car, but on organized small-group tours operated weekly and well by several Belizean tour operators. In my opinion, it's best to pursue the mainland portion of your trip first (say, for four days) and follow up with R&R on those sunny, pleasant cayes for two or three concluding days of your trip.

Upon the mainland, so rich is the Mayan heritage of Belize, so diverse its wildlife and flora, that the resulting travel choices are fairly dizzying.

If you can somehow manage the time, sign on for Lascelle Tillett's eight-day/seven-night "In Search of the Ancient Maya" (as little as $743 per person, when at least four persons are in the group, for touring, lodging, and two meals a day on most days); contact **S & L Travel Services, P.O. Box 700, Belize City, Belize, Central America (phone 501-2-77593)**, which takes you to a dozen ancient ceremonial centers, Mayan trading sites, excavated village ruins dating as far back as 2,500 B.C. Your stops include Altun Ha (the country's most extensively excavated Mayan pyramids, mounds, ball courts, burial chambers, reservoirs) and Xunantunich (tallest man-made structure in Belize, with elaborate stucco friezes); and then your tour darts over the Guatemalan border to view the grandeur of famous Tikal (a Mayan royal city flourishing from 600 B.C. to A.D. 950, when it was mysteriously abandoned). On the way, while still in Belize, you visit the current "digs" at Caracol, which university archeologists believe will ultimately unearth a pre–Classic Age Mayan city three times as large as Tikal and every bit as grand. A truncated version of the same tour (four days, three nights) costs only $268 per person when four persons are gathered for it.

Or if you're inclined to less vigorous touring, but in the same prime location (the well-located Cayo District), you can contact the English couple who own the palm-thatched safari lodge called **Chaa Creek Cottages, P. O. Box 53, San Ignacio, Cayo, Belize (phone 601/ 92-2037)**, from which every standard tour is offered. Charges here are $62.50 per person per night, double occupancy. Or you can stay at the newer, basic but charming, **Windy Hill Cottages (phone 92-2017)**, where double rooms rent for a total of $70 a night (i.e., $35 per person). Finally, if you're not up to a jungle camp at all, you can simply base yourself (for $45 double) in the hillside **San Ignacio Hotel, P.O. Box 33, San Ignacio, Cayo District, Belize (phone 92-2034)**, booking one-day tours, or hiking on your own, from there.

Whatever your hotel choice, you must be sure to include a visit to the mile-long Panti Trail, in the same area and of considerable historic and perhaps scientific interest. It's lined with the remarkably diverse plants, bushes, and trees supplying herbal substances used as medicines by the ancient Mayans, all according to formulas handed down from generation to generation and today known to a 97-year-old Mayan/Belizean priest/doctor (read: medicine man) named Eligio Panti. For 10 years now, scientists headed by Dr. Rosita Arvigo have been "debriefing" Don Eligio of his secrets, attracting attention from learned groups ranging from the New York Botanical Garden to the National Cancer Society. They also conduct guided tours of the trail (daily except Monday, $12), commenting on the strongly apparent medicinal properties of the growths (a tree bark that cures dysentery, a leaf that stops bleeding).

And don't laugh: fully 25% of the world's commercial medicines are derived from plant-based chemicals found in tropical regions (according to Dr. Arvigo).

The Panti Trail begins at Dr. Arvigo's home, "IX Chel" (named for the Mayan goddess of medicine), just beyond San Ignacio off the Western Hwy. The great Mayan ceremonial site of Xunantunich is not far away. To contact Dr. Arvigo for a guided group tour of the Panti Trail ($30 per group), write: **Dr. Rosita Arvigo, General Delivery, San Ignacio Post Office, Cayo District, Belize, or leave a message at 92-2188.**

The Cayes

After an active and sometimes tiring exploration into the interior, a great many visitors turn to those restful strips of water-surrounded land along the barrier reef.

Ambergris Caye is the most highly developed of these narrow lines in the sea, and that mark of distinction will come as a surprise when you first arrive by small plane at the sleepy frontier town of San Pedro, "capital" of Ambergris Caye. It consists of exactly three white-sand-covered "avenues," the unpretentiously named Front, Middle, and Back Streets. On Front (also known as Beach) Street, within the five intersecting blocks of the city center, are small hotels and cabañas (40 of them), interspersed with the basketball court, police station, town hall, school, and local discothèque (Big Daddy's).

On Front Street, the Holiday Hotel ($85 per double room in high season), features the colorful tales and excellent cuisine of the charismatic Celi McCorkle, whom many call the "mother of tourism" in Belize. Farther along, the Coral Beach is a favorite of divers and operated by the "father of diving," Allan Forman, who offers low rates ($50 for the average double room) and generous, family-style meals. You can stay at the Sun Breeze Beach Resort ($90 for a double room, and home of the island's windsurfing school), at Ramon's Reef (in charming, waterside cabañas priced at $110 a day, double), or on the edge of town in the Paradise Hotel much favored by Francis Ford Coppola ($95, double).

It is also possible, either by simply applying door-to-door, or by using the advance services of S & L Travel Services in Belize City (address and phone number above) to obtain $40-a-night rooms at such family-run lodgings as the San Pedrano and its several affiliates run by four brothers and sisters.

From all these havens, the barrier reef is less than a mile out into the sea, supplying not simply the site for snorkeling and dives, but a wonderfully protected area for invigorating sailing and windsurfing; "there's always a breeze in Belize," goes a local saying.

For on-the-spot information and assistance in San Pedro, contact Pany Arceo; he's a dynamic fisherman-turned-guide who offers insight, instruction, and excursions in bonefishing, snorkeling, diving, and bird-watching at considerably lower cost, and with far greater knowledge, than others I've met. Or seek out his sister, Shelley Prevett, who operates the moderately priced and popular restaurant, The Hut ($10 for turtle curry). She provides hard-to-get information (babysitters, air charters, local black-coral-jewelry makers), and will also prepare your own fish catch at half the normal menu price.

Caye Caulker is like a stage setting for a W. Somerset Maugham play, and hotel rooms are widely available for $15 to $30 a night.

The lower-priced, budget alternative to Ambergris Caye—if you can imagine such a thing— is **Caye Caulker,** a few miles farther south in the sea. With only two streets along the beach, it's like a stage setting for a W. Somerset Maugham play, and hotel rooms are widely available for $15 to $30 a night, while several inexpensive "restaurants" are in people's homes. At the popular Tropical Paradise hotel, $30 will get you your own cabaña by the sea. Caye Caulker, though, can be reached only by boat from Belize City (on several services operated daily except Sunday), while Ambergris Caye is more easily serviced by air.

Other cayes (often with only a single hotel apiece) are more difficult of access, and thereby more exclusive: Caye Chapel (the 32-room Pyramid Resort), St. George's Caye (St. George's Lodge), South Water Caye (Blue Marlin Lodge), Glover's Reef (Manta Reef Resort), and Caye Bokel (the fishing-oriented Turneffe Island Lodge, $165 a day per person for room and all three meals, unlimited use of fishing boats, gas for the boats, and guides, all for the purpose of seeking six-pound bonefish, the chief activity), among them. An exception to the pricey tone of the less accessible cayes is Bluefield Range Cayes (a group of three), where beach huts on working lobster and fishing camps rent for under $25 a night. Ricardo's Beach Huts, also offering tent sites for $2.50 per person per night, is one such place.

Some Added Points

As we go to press with this 1996 edition of *The New World of Travel,* a new resort area of Belize—in the tiny fishing village of Placencia, on a charming peninsula in the south of the country—is coming up fast in popularity, for its fishing, diving, and general ambience. It may currently be the country's fastest-growing area for tourists, and already offers several small hotels and lodges with accommodations for $20 a night, plus several rooms in private homes for as little as $4 a night. I'll report further on Placencia in the 1997 edition, but I urge you to inquire about facilities from the information sources listed below.

The chief recreational activity of Belize? Diving. The chief drawback? Car-rental rates—as much as $80 a day. The high season in Belize? November through April, when travelers planning to use standard rooms should not arrive without reservations.

Resources for Touring

Always bear in mind that the relative newness of tourism in Belize adds to its appeal, but also has its drawbacks. Tourists are often surprised to find no air conditioning in many hotels (unnecessary, say the Belizeans, because of their cooling trade winds). And visitors should also be prepared for occasional electricity shortages and lack of hot water, particularly inland. Bring a spirit of adventure—and an open mind.

Your best contact for preparing a trip to Belize is **Tropical Travel Representatives, 5 Grogan's Park Drive, The Woodlands, Texas 77380 (a suburb of Houston), (phone 713/ 367-3386, 713/298-2238 or toll free 800/ 451-8017 outside Texas)**. A combined travel agency and tour operator, its founders, Tommy and Jerisue Thomson, are so enchanted with the country that they exchanged wedding vows on its white sands 11 years ago. Their former newsletter, *Belize Travel News,* ultimately became the highly successful *Belize Currents* magazine, widely distributed by the Embassy of Belize and the Caribbean Tourist Association and available to their clients. (Tropical Travel handles nothing other than Belize, and in my experience is thoroughly reliable.) Other Belize-specializing U.S. travel agents include the high-volume **Ocean Connections (phone 713/996-7800 or toll free 800/331-2458 outside Houston), and Triton Tours (phone 504/464-7964 or toll free 800/426-0226 outside Louisiana).**

Other excellent Belize information resource and travel coordinators are Lascelle Tillett, Sarita Tillett, and Minelia Pou of **S & L Travel Services** in Belize City (**91 North Front Street, P.O. Box 700, Belize City, Belize, phone 501/2-77593 or fax 501/2-77594**). All three have a wealth of information and welcome inquiries that state budget limitations and personal interests. For ultra-cost-conscious travelers whom the U.S. agents cannot accommodate, S & L's services will be well worth the time of a letter or the cost of an overseas telephone call.

Good background reading for Belize is the book *Jaguar* by Alan Rabinowitz (published by Arbor House).

Two airlines service Belize from the States, usually for a round-trip "add-on" fare from Miami of $295, a bit more from New Orleans and Houston. **Taca Airlines (phone 800/ 831-6422)**, operates daily service at that rate from Miami, four times a week from New Orleans and Houston.

Continental Airlines (phone toll free 800/ 231-0856) also flies to Belize, and charges a dramatically low $289 round-trip from Houston, $493 from Newark.

This winter in the Caribbean, you have a choice.

You can crowd into a high-rise hotel and fight for a place at a noisy pool.

Or you can go to Belize.

Guess which I'd choose.

Hot Turkey

Tourism There Is Booming As the World Awakens to Its Attractions and Low Rates

No destination on earth has created more tourist excitement this year than Turkey. As if Aladdin had suddenly rubbed his lamp to give the Islamic world its first big travel hit, Turkey is today awash with visitors throughout the year, bestrewn with new hotels in construction, covered with touring motorcoaches.

Why did it happen so late? What delayed the advent of Turkey's massive tourist popularity? Though many will cite the remarkable cheapness of a Turkish vacation—decent hotels for $30 a night; colorful meals of lamb shish kebab, eggplant, and juicy tomatoes for $5 and $6; in-city transportation via group taxi (dolmus) for 30¢—Turkey has always been that cheap, even cheaper a decade ago.

The explanation seems to stem from political changes that bode well for the long-term health of tourism in Turkey. Stable, democratic, civilian government seems to have been achieved after a period of intermittent military rule. No longer do fanatical religious parties control the Ministry of Tourism, from which they frequently sought to block incoming tourism and the liberalizing influences it brought. Most important, Turkey is currently attempting to enter the Common Market (the European Community) and is supporting the application with widespread advertising and exhibitions that stress its openness to commerce and visitors.

Turkey is a pleasant way-station to the Muslim world, a partially Westernized country that nevertheless grounds its culture and religion on the Koran, a safe and familiar base for commencing your study of Middle Eastern institutions. Though there are mosques everywhere, and veiled women, there's none of the tension felt in similar countries, and people are friendly to foreigners. Signs are in Roman letters, not Arabic script; hotels serve cocktails and wine; the female tourist is tolerated at restaurants and cafés, even alone; and women of the West are able to move about without harassment or scorn, at least in the larger cities and at beachfront resorts.

For tourists, as I've already noted, the country is remarkably cheap, the cheapest of any European nation. With Spain increasingly costly, and Greece getting there, the budget conscious traveler is especially attracted today to Turkey.

Exploring Istanbul

You start, of course, in Istanbul, the former Constantinople. Once the capital of Christianity, then of the great Ottoman Empire, its downtown is a startling forest of needle-like spires sticking into the sky from the minarets of more mosques than you are ever again likely to see in one location.

The key attractions are rather conveniently grouped on a peninsula of sea-surrounded land known generally as Sultanahmet. Here is the rich Topkapi Palace, where a series of often decadent, occasionally impressive, sultans, pashas, and caliphs once disported themselves in sensual style, both at water pipes (still seen at cafés in Istanbul) and with harem dancers; the exhibits inside are disappointing, but the harem exquisite. More impressive, just outside the palace walls, are the Museum of Oriental Art (with Hittite ruins), the Archeological Museum, and the Museum of Tiles.

No longer do fanatical religious parties control the Ministry of Tourism.

From there you easily stroll to the massive Blue Mosque, removing your shoes to enter inside; and then, across the way, to Aghia Sophia, once the largest domed church in all of Christendom, now a mosque but still bearing Byzantine mosaics of biblical scenes.

From the grand mosques, a street called Divan Yolu leads to the Grand Bazaar (Kapali Carsi), perhaps the largest covered bazaar in the world. As you near the vast emporium, numerous "kebab" restaurants tempt you with savory scents and displays of grilled lamb or chicken kebab or sausage kebab, accompanied by that supreme achievement of Turkish farmers: succulent fresh tomatoes, the highlight of a meal that rarely exceeds $4 in cost. As you then pass into the four-block-wide labyrinth of shops that make up the bazaar, you catch your breath at the bargains that smart shopping can secure: excellent leather wallets for under $10, pantaloon-like "harem pants" for only $6, full-length leather coats that can be negotiated down to $200, pages from medieval illuminated Islamic manuscripts—a superb gift—for $10.

The bulk of visitors, after touring Istanbul, head to inexpensive beach resorts on Turkey's Mediterranean coast, but I'd suggest the coast just outside the port city of Izmir ($75 by air from Istanbul); there you can combine sea-bathing with a one-hour trip by *dolmus* or taxi to the unforgettable Roman ruins at Ephesus, where Paul preached. After all, you didn't fly 4,500 miles from the U.S. just to lie on a beach.

Cappadocia

An even better course is to follow up Istanbul with eerie Cappadocia, the highlight of all Turkish visits, in my view, and a great wonder of the world. It is the province of volcanic rock in central Turkey to which tens of thousands of Christians fled in the 7th century from Muslim persecution. And there they proceeded to build and inhabit underground cities—whole cities—carved from the volcanic stone.

Although a military airport at Kayseri, in Cappadocia, receives civilian flights from Istanbul twice a week ($75 for the trip), the timing of that facility permits its use only in one direction—one way, in other words. The other leg is best accomplished by flying from Istanbul to Ankara ($75) and boarding a bus from there for a five-hour ride to Nevsehir, largest city in the region. Motorcoaches leave Nevsehir every two hours and charge only $4.50 for the five-hour journey.

Women of the West are able to move about without harassment or scorn, at least in the larger cities and at beachfront resorts.

Does all this seem overly fatiguing? Not once you have seen Cappadocia. The trip begins in ordinary style, but gradually, in the triangle of land formed by the towns of Nevsehir, Avanos, and Urgup, you encounter a weird alternation of terrain in shapes you have never before seen: cream-colored hills of solid rock undulating like folds of satin, alongside high, conical mounds formed from the eroded volcanic ash of eruptions occurring a millennium ago. Suddenly, within these strange, cone-shaped forms, you take in hundreds upon hundreds of large, oblong, man-made holes cut into the face of each monolith.

It was through these openings that fleeing Christians built whole cities in the rock: churches adorned with fresco paintings, refectories, dormitories, workrooms—all ingeniously carved, and then hidden from view by giant boulders over each entrance. Gazing at them, wrote a young American tourist, Tracie Holder, in a recent letter to me, "I had feelings of wonderment—wonder that these early inhabitants could have thought to hew entire cities from solid rock. To me, Cappadocia attests not simply to the determination of a particular people at a particular time, but to the timeless human spirit which creates civilizations in the face of adversity."

Most visitors to Cappadocia stay in the pleasant town of Urgup, in one of a cluster of small hotels ranging from the comfortable, swimming-pool-equipped Kaya Otel ($69 per double room, including breakfast for two), Boydas Motel ($60 double), and Turban Motel ($60 double, yet also with swimming pool), to the simple but adequate Cinar Otel ($25 per double room) and other more basic lodgings renting for as little as $15 and $10 per double room. Others prefer to stay closer to the Open Air Museum at the village of Goreme (really, a wide spot in the road), at the three-story, red-stucco Pala Otel, paying $25 double.

For meals, I like the Restaurant Allah Allah in the Cappadocian city of Avanos, on the Red River, where my party of four once paid a total of $20 for appetizers, melon, dolmades (stuffed grape leaves), shish kebab of lamb and chicken, Russian salad, wine, and strong Turkish coffee (sweet, in thimble-like cups).

Turkey is an important country of 60 million people, almost the size of France or Germany. And as you may have guessed, it's also a sybaritic experience at the lowest of costs. Get there before it's too late.

A Trip to the Home of the Gods

The Peloponnese. In a lifetime of travel to Greece, spent exclusively in Athens and the Attic peninsula, or in the many islands of that sun-blessed nation, I had never once traveled to the historic peninsular landmass to the southwest of the capital.

What a mistake! Drawn there by a recent "learning vacation" at St. John's College in Santa Fe—a several-day seminar devoted to Thucydides' classic, *The Peloponnesian War*—I journeyed to the awesome altars, temples, and stadia that still dot the area from which the Spartans and Corinthians launched their yearly attacks upon the city-state of Athens. It made most of my other recent holiday trips seem insignificant by comparison.

The Greek islands are pretty, but their pleasures are fairly slight ones: shopping, café life, views. The Peloponnese alters your consciousness. No matter how many times you have read of the ancient

Greek civilization, the "glory that once was Greece," it is a wholly different matter to visit the actual remains of a culture that reached heights of art, architecture, philosophy, and drama that have never since been equalled.

Two-or-so driving hours out of Athens, over the Corinth canal, you reach the ancient outdoor theater of Epidaurus (500 B.C.), carved out of the side of a mountain to seat upwards of 14,000 people. You stand on the stone stage, speaking in conversational tones, and your words are heard by your travel companion seated in the theater's top row. And yet that triumph of ancient science is only an inconsequential "appetizer" to what lies ahead.

From your first overnight base in Napflion, a pretty seaport of medieval vintage, you drive next day in four hours to Olimpia, expecting to see only a few remnants of the field where athletes from the ancient Grecian world gathered every few years to hurl javelins, or wrestle, run, and box, for the sake of sport. What awaits you is a vast open area of columns, promenades, courses, and walls marking the foundations of the temples, treasure houses, running tracks, gymnasia, and "bleachers" the ancients maintained here for the sake of the games—spectacles surpassing the scope of many far more recent "Olympics." In a remarkable museum adjoining those fields of sport are the actual marble friezes that adorned the portico of Olympia's Temple of Zeus. Its central figure is the sun god, Apollo, sculpted by an unknown genius; the visage he created appears on today's Greek currency, and makes the most common drachma note into a thing of haunting beauty.

From an overnight in Olympia, another four hours by car bring you to venerable mountain villages, their elders dozing in the shade, and past other high-altitude sights on the way to ancient Delphi. En route, you detour to a mountain peak at Vassae, on which stands a 2,500-year-old Temple of Apollo, protected today from environmental damage by a vast, circus-like tent erected around it by cautious monument

officials of Greece. Your lunchtime stop, like so many others on the trip, is at a shabby, rustic tavern where pots stand bubbling and steaming on a wood-burning kitchen stove. Because foreign-language menus are nowhere to be found, you are invited to enter the room, lift the lids, gaze at their contents, and then select your choice by simply pointing. Returning to the table, one of those ubiquitous Greek salads is already alongside your plate—tomatoes, feta cheese, onion rings, olives, doused in white olive oil—together with a fresh loaf of bread and pitcher of cheap local wine, chilled and refreshing. Average cost, including one hot plate apiece: less than 1,000 Greek drachmas (about $5) per person.

My own mistaken image of Delphi, prior to seeing it, was of a single stone altar in a verdant meadow, at which a lone, deranged oracle delivered her momentous pronouncements of future events. Envision, instead, the craggy slopes of a mountain ("Parnassus") thousands of feet high, covered with hundreds of yards of the foundation stones of former temples, altars, treasure houses, promenades, statues, arcaded display areas, arches, porticos, and an immense oval theatre. These are the dazzling remains of Delphi, home of the ancient Greek religion. They are the Vatican, Westminster Abbey, the temple walls of Jerusalem, the central Stone at Mecca all rolled into one—a once-mighty spiritual complex now bereft of followers, seen only by tourists sobered by the sight.

From Delphi, another four-or-so hours by car (which includes a short ferry ride from Patras to the mainland) returns you to Athens. And there, no matter how frequent your former visits, you hike one more time to the Parthenon on the Acropolis high overlooking the city. Gutted in a 17th-century bombardment by Venetian gunners, this supreme world treasure is at last undergoing repairs and restoration; massive funds to do so have been contributed by the European Community. In a few years, the Parthenon will no longer be a ruin, but again a proud architectural masterpiece, intact; even in its partially destroyed state it is among the most riveting of all sights, and most tourists follow up their daytime visits with the after-dark "Sound and Light" view of the Acropolis, seen from the nearby small hill of the Pnyx. Some lucky travelers have a moonlight view of the Parthenon from their hotel window, as I recently did.

Tourism to Greece has been badly hurt by the fighting in nearby Yugoslavia, which has frightened off many Europeans from attempting a train ride there, passing through Yugoslavia. The result is that many facilities are underused, and the American tourist arriving by plane or by sea from Italy (Brindisi is the port) is especially favored. Even before the Yugoslavian tragedy, Greece was (with Turkey) the least expensive area of Western Europe. In Athens, at an exchange rate of at least 230 drachmas to the U.S. dollar, good multi-course meals can be had for $8, tourist-class rooms for $40, a taxi ride for $2.

Those financial boons make a trip there especially pleasant, and the planning is aided by an efficient U.S. firm that serves as a central reservations bureau for all 6,300 Greek hotels on the mainland, in the Peloponnese, and on the islands. Phone the **Greek Hotel & Cruise Reservation Center at 800/736-5717** before leaving the U.S., or phone its office in Athens—32/55547—after arriving.

Greece places your own life, and the history of all civilizations, into perspective. Even now, many days later, I am under its spell, and feel the better for it—more humble, more tolerant, less concerned with petty spites and wholly transient matters.

An Ode to Eastern Long Island

Cherished by New Yorkers As Among the Finest Vacation Areas on Earth, It Is —Inexplicably— Unknown to the Rest of the Country

Whenever I am asked to name the area of my favorite beach vacations, I always disappoint people by responding: eastern Long Island. As a travel lunatic who has been to hundreds of seashores all over the world, I am supposed to come up with places queer or exotic, like Pattaya Beach in Thailand or Rostock on the Baltic Sea.

Yet eastern Long Island it is. By a long shot. Beyond dispute. Stubbornly. Till the day I die.

And it dismays me to realize that while other New Yorkers will understand my choice, almost no one else will. Outside the Empire State,

Americans are abysmally unaware of one of the most glorious holiday regions on earth.

The narrow strip of land called Long Island is a largely rural, 130-mile-long extension of a portion of New York City. Along its southern shore on the Atlantic Ocean, about an hour by train from the city, there begins one of the world's longest continuous beaches, extending to the east for more than 60 miles.

It's a remarkable beach, of soft white sand, 50 and more yards wide, flanked by high protecting dunes, and lashed by strong waves topped with foam, invigorating to ride or confront.

So vast is the long, long beach of eastern Long Island that even the multitudes of summer visitors are lost upon it. I once took a French friend to a stretch of sand outside the town of Quogue, and his mouth dropped open. It was the first time in his life that he had encountered a beach that was not literally covered with bodies, each allotted his or her own two-foot-wide pallet, as at Nice, Cannes, or St-Tropez. Here, 30 yards or so separated most sunbathers.

At intervals along the shore, a few miles inland from the beach, are picture-book villages revered by most New Yorkers but unknown to others, and strangely absent from novels or films: Westhampton, Speonk and Quogue, Water Mill, Bridgehampton and Amagansett, Montauk and Sag Harbor (the last facing away from the Atlantic), plus a dozen noteworthy others. F. Scott Fitzgerald placed his *Great Gatsby* on Long Island, but not along the sea, and I suspect that the hundreds of prominent writers and artists who currently inhabit the shores of eastern Long Island are anxious to guard their havens from greater renown.

Summer homes in these parts are fiendishly expensive to rent, but hotels and other lodgings are normally priced, no worse than in other vacation areas, and the budget-minded visitor can find low-cost B&Bs and moderately priced motels. From those they can then descend upon the beaches—all open to the public—or rent fishing boats for adventurous excursions onto the sea. At Montauk especially, but at other ports as well, a series of marinas harbor charter boats of every style and size.

An hour by train from New York City, there begins one of the world's longest continuous beaches, a marvel of fine white sand.

What gives eastern Long Island its special flavor is a unique blend of worldly sophistication and country appearance. This, after all, is where New Yorkers vacation. Famous-name shops of Fifth Avenue alternate with homespun general stores. A small filling station will display a large stack of the *New York Times* for Sunday readers;

OKEANOS *"The Sea Father"*

OKEANOS OCEAN RESEARCH FOUNDATION, INC.
Post Office BOX 776, HAMPTON BAYS, NY 11946
telephone (516) 728-4522   fax (516) 728-4584
* marine education * sea mammal and turtle research * stranding/rescue program * whale watch cruises
a non profit research and educational organization

Symbol of Long Island's Okeanos Ocean Research Foundation. *Courtesy Okeanos Ocean Research Foundation, drawing by Michael Sansone.*

The New World of Travel 1997

The lifeblood of the Arthur Frommer travel guides is the correspondence received from readers, commenting on the establishments recommended in the texts and recommending new establishments. Each such letter is carefully studied, and when a particular lead seems promising, it is followed up and personally checked.

It is hoped that *The New World of Travel* will receive similar assistance from its readers. A yearly publication, issued near the start of each year, *The New World of Travel* will constantly grow. And since much of its content relates to organizations that lack the means to market themselves properly, or come to the attention of a travel journalist, your help is invaluable in alerting me to the organizations—hospitality exchanges, alternative resorts, new travel clubs, and the like—that you have discovered.

If you become aware of a new travel organization, program, or development that deserves to be described in our next edition, *The New World of Travel 1997,* won't you please let me know about it? Send your letters to Arthur Frommer, *The New World of Travel,* 1841 Broadway, New York, NY 10023. All letters will be acknowledged, and all are warmly appreciated, in advance, by the author.

Vanity Fair is on the shelves of 7-Elevens. On the main street of Sag Harbor, a movie theater shows only the most avant-garde of foreign films, while at the entrance to Easthampton, the John Drew Theater previews the most experimental of plays.

The Ozarks it's not.

And yet on the roads leading to the several towns are countless country-style vegetable-and-fruit stands of nearby farms. As one of the great produce-growing areas of America, both the eastern and central parts of Long Island yield tons of sweet corn, juicy tomatoes, sugary strawberries and peaches, excellent potatoes and onions, plus every other legume. And vacationers often make a daily visit to the stands to ensure that their table will bear only the freshest of foods. Some even go so

For a visiting Frenchman, it was the first time in his life he had walked on a beach not covered with bodies.

far as to pick the fruits and vegetables themselves, in the fields directly behind the stands.

You eat here magnificently, of Long Island cherrystone clams and steamers, of scallops and swordfish, of Long Island duckling and home-grown asparagus. At one enormous restaurant called Gosman's Dock, cantilevered over a part of the port of Montauk, and partly outdoors, hundreds of diners feast on superb fresh lobster prepared in every way, and then they puzzle aloud—as I often have—as to why Gosman's lobsters are so very much better than any they've had elsewhere. My French friend, observing the summer gaiety of the wooden dining deck of Gosman's, remarked quite rapturously that it reminded him of a scene by Cézanne. He was similarly impressed by the meals—and especially the wines—of the dining room of the American Hotel in Sag Harbor, surely one of the nation's finest.

Wine, locally produced, is the latest attraction of eastern Long Island, although most of it is from vineyards and wineries of the so-called North Fork of Long Island's eastern end, away from the trendy towns of the South Fork on the Atlantic. Near Jamesport, Mattituck, and Cutchogue on that North Fork, such increasingly distinguished vintners as Pindar, Palmer, and Hargrave run free public tours and tastings of their cellars, and distribute a great deal of their product to the restaurants nearby.

Apart from wining, dining, bathing, sailing, fishing, hiking, playing, and movie/theater-going, what else do you do in eastern Long Island? You visit dozens of historic landmarks, some dating from colonial and revolutionary times, and take in the important and engrossing whaling museums found in several towns. You book yourself on a day-long whale-watching cruise from Montauk (operated by the **Okeanos Ocean Research Foundation** in Hampton

Bays, phone 516/728-4522), or go to yard sales found everywhere, or to summer festivals found weekly, or to famous shops in every town. You participate in every form of recreation and relaxation, browse through frequently encountered bookstores, attend the numerous summer lectures. And when your needs are occasionally urban, you board the Long Island Rail Road for an easy 2- or $2^1/_2$-hour ride into midtown Manhattan.

Don't get me wrong, I love an occasional stay in Acapulco or Aruba, a few days of bathing at Rimini, an autumnal sojourn on the Costa del Sol of Spain. But where can you have all the pleasures of a renowned beach, and at the same time enjoy phones that work, water that's drinkable, and morning delivery of a meaty English-language newspaper? Eastern Long Island, that's where.

For directories of accommodations and restaurants, attractions, events, and activities, contact the **Long Island Convention & Visitors Bureau, Eisenhower Park, 1899 Hempstead Turnpike, East Meadow, NY 11554-1042.**

A Pilgrimage to Arcosanti

Like an Immortal Among the Living, He Is Perhaps the Leading Architect of Our Time. Colleges Would Kill to Have Him on Their Staffs. Others Would Pay Fortunes to Have Him Design Their Skyscrapers, Homes, and Hotels.

Yet he sits in shorts and undershirt in the Arizona desert, 65 miles north of Phoenix, enduring ridicule, stretching funds, but building, always building, his dream city, Arcosanti. To tour through Arizona and not to visit the urban vision of 74-year-old Paolo Soleri is to miss a view of the future as seen by a possible Leonardo da Vinci, at least a sublime Don Quixote, of our century.

The quest for Arcosanti starts in the setting that Soleri detests. From the sprawling tract homes of Phoenix's hushed and endless suburbs (a two-dimensional city in a three-dimensional world, Soleri would say), you at last pass in your rental car into awesome desert mountains, their lower slopes lined with tall saguaro cactus, like toy soldiers guarding the approach to Soleri's domain.

An hour and a quarter's drive brings you to the tiny, uplands community of Cordes Junction (occasional cowboy-types in dusty pickup vans), where you turn onto a bumpy dirt road and follow signs for several miles into the horizon-wide emptiness of the construction site, on a mesa overlooking a dry riverbed valley and facing cliff.

At a visitors' center splashed with sunlight from great round windows, you pay $4 for an hourly tour, and join a daily average total of perhaps 50 Americans, rarely more, who make their arduous way to this site of titanic conflict with prevailing urban concepts. That paltry income helps fund the construction, as does a few hundred dollars of weekly profit from the appearance of periodic Elderhostel groups who live in the few completed apartments, attend daily lectures, and then mold and fire their own tiles to adorn the concrete walls of high-tech arches scattered about. Near the end of their week, they meet Soleri. He descends a rough-hewn ladder from a balcony-studio, and for one or two hours stolen from work, gently and patiently, with good humor and respect for the elders' views, he fields questions and doubts about the monumental project.

To complete Arcosanti would require upward of half a billion dollars and perhaps 20 more years; it is now 3% done, largely from the labor of volunteer college students who flocked here in the 1970s to pour concrete and shape stone. It is obvious from the current lessened pace of construction that today's young people, intent upon their entrance into the corporate culture, are not providing Arcosanti with the support that a more idealistic earlier generation did.

So how, apart from visitors' fees, does Soleri continue to construct Arcosanti? Largely from the sale of windbells. Fiercely refusing to deal with mortgage brokers and venture capitalists, innately unable to beg and solicit at cocktail-party fundraisers, thoroughly unsuited for foundation grants and rich widow's handouts, he devotes off hours to designing these ravishing works in bronze and ceramics, and raises, through their sale, most of the income needed to keep Arcosanti alive. "If 30 years ago, someone had told me that windbells would build Arcosanti, I'd have thought him mad," he smiles.

The trip begins in the setting that Soleri detests: Phoenix, Arizona.

The object of these expenditures is a complex series of interconnected structures—almost like a single building, one part of which will be 25 stories high—designed to house 6,000 persons and to supply them, in the same building, with their workplace, entertainment, culture, and support systems.

It is a city so densely populated and compact as to use only the barest fraction of the land on which it sits—in Arcosanti's case, 14 acres out of 860 surrounding and unused acres. It thus preserves nature instead of paving it over. Its inhabitants are city people and rural folk at one and the same time. From their city, they have only to step outside into vast, adjoining countryside.

Though it houses people to the highest population density on earth, it provides family units with as much as 2,000 square feet of apartment space apiece—far more than most Americans enjoy. That feat is achieved by "miniaturizing" other traditional structures of today's cities, and particularly by eliminating the automobile, with its space-devouring streets, freeways, intersections, garages and parking spaces, curbs and lots. In Arcosanti, one simply walks from one end of the city to the other in ten minutes.

Soleri's city of tomorrow, on a barren desert floor.

The city of Soleri's dream is intensely energy-efficient. It is flanked with vast sloping greenhouses that create a "chimney" effect, wafting sunwarmed air to the adjoining megabuilding, to create both heating and air conditioning, as the seasons require.

It is complex to an extent unimaginable until seen, even in the model you will peruse on the top floor of the visitors' center. In this respect, according to Soleri, it is an upward step in human evolution, leading to higher and more developed forms of social interaction—and perhaps to higher consciousness.

It is an "arcology," in Soleri's phrase, a blending of the best in architecture and ecology. And it is one of several score of single-structure "arcologies" he has designed, whose sketches and detailed drawings appear in his remarkable *The City in the Image of Man* (Cambridge, Mass.: MIT Press, 1969), unfortunately now out of print. There you find the plans for "Novanoah" (a floating, ocean-based city for 400,000 people), "Arcodiga" (a city atop a dam, whose 280,000 residents enjoy unlimited cheap energy and unparalleled water sports and recreation), "Stonebow" (constructed like a giant bridge over a canyon or ravine, for 200,000 persons), "Asteromo" (a city in space, designed like a giant lightbulb to house 70,000), and "Infrababel" (for 100,000, partially underground).

He labors in a spare workroom, enduring ridicule, stretching funds, but building, always building, his dream city, Arcosanti.

Does all this set your teeth on edge? If so, says Soleri, consider the alternative: the sprawling, low-density, energy-inefficient cities of one-family homes in the sunbelt of America.

They spread like permanently enlarging inkblots over once-verdant fields and gardens, devouring ever-greater portions of our remaining countryside. Their geographical expanse is so immense—so dispersed, of such low density—as to separate humanity from its institutions. Every simple function of life—attending a film, shopping, visiting friends—becomes a major undertaking. In them, residents spend interminable, inane hours in highway lines, anxiously tuned to traffic reporters, enduring gridlock and jams, boredom and fatigue. Isolated by distance from their fellow human beings, people are prisoners in their homes, condemned to sit in darkened living rooms staring at TV.

They are retrograde cities, backward and simple, cultural wastelands. Their sheer sterility, in its impact upon the young, cannot help but create a generation to dread.

And so Soleri builds. To demonstrate, to prove. Though his writings are profuse and in every library, he feels compelled to physically create the new metropolis. Without funds or proper assistance, without junior architects to draft the detailed work, without help in a hundred areas, he labors on, doggedly, without complaint.

And Arcosanti grows, but at an infuriatingly slow pace, in a race against the mortal condition of Soleri's own life.

How can you and I help Paolo Soleri? First, we can visit Arcosanti, in the manner just described. The address is: I-17 at **Cordes Junction, Mayer, AZ 86333 (phone 602/632-7135)**.

Second, we can devote our vacations to his five-week "workshops" on the site. There, after a week of instruction primarily in concrete-pouring (the basic material of the city), participants work for four weeks in the actual construction of a tiny unit in the jigsaw-puzzle-like structure of Arcosanti. Cost for the entire five weeks is a remarkable $560—precisely $16 a day—including accommodations, instruction and supervision, and all three meals daily. Workshop schedules are prepared in late fall, and you can write for application forms to: **Registrar, The Cosanti Foundation, 6433 Doubletree Road, Scottsdale, AZ 85253 (or phone 602/948-6145)**.

Finally, we can all help search for a benefactor. Among your acquaintances is there a millionaire seeking immortality as the patron or patroness to a great man? Just a few of those millions could bring in a professional construction company that could speed the development of Arcosanti and draw in further capital.

In an America sprouting with trivial theme parks, deathly parking garages, and redundant shopping centers, aren't there funds for a city that might advance humankind?

A Memoir of Bruges

A Natural Phenomenon Caused It to Miss the Industrial Revolution. If Only More Ancient Cities Had Suffered Such Misfortune!

When we first wander through it, astonished and silent, we try to rein in our excitement. After all, on our trips throughout Europe before visiting Bruges, we have seen other perfectly preserved medieval communities: Carcassonne, Siena, Avila, Rothenburg.

But those were mere villages, small secondary towns. Bruges is a medieval *city* perfectly preserved, a giant, sprawling, ancient metropolis once of world significance, and yet today almost unaltered in its former splendor, its awesome beauty and size.

Suddenly those people of the Middle Ages cease, in our minds, to appear a quaint and backward species. All at once we realize, if we hadn't before, that people have nearly always had aspirations and achievements equivalent to ours. And if we were born, as I was, an American, optimistic and arrogant, rarely looking back, believing in the constant upward progress of human civilization, we feel shaken by Bruges; we learn decisively that humankind has both advanced and declined, that aspects of the past were perhaps superior to the present, that an age nearly 700 years ago, and later reviled as "dark," enjoyed artistic, commercial, and physical prowess of a sort that many later eras and nations have still to attain.

Arrested in time, a Pompeii or a Brigadoon.

Bruges is a city arrested in time. A Pompeii or a Brigadoon. An urban portrait caught as if by stop-frame photography, of a community that died while it was still young. The most heavily visited touristic site in all of Belgium, it is the victim of one of the strangest natural events of history—the "silting of the Zwin"—which snuffed out its commercial life in the late Middle Ages, caused it to miss the Industrial Revolution, and thus paradoxically saved its unique medieval legacy from the wreckers' ball. If only more ancient cities had suffered such misfortune!

Bruges, in medieval times, was the greatest trading center in northern Europe, a multinational marketplace for importing and exporting, storing, and displaying cloths and spices, herrings and wine, every variety of goods. Along its canals and in central squares dozens of wealthy foreign merchants maintained exotic commercial palaces, virtual embassies of their countries in which they lavishly entertained and dealt with the thousands of traders who flocked to a city renowned for its glitter and importance.

The focus of all this movement, the vital access road, was the Zwin, a waterway that connected Bruges to the North Sea. In the mid-1300s, at the height of Bruges' renown, and for reasons still not fully understood, the Zwin began to fill with sand, denying passage to deep-draft ships. By the 1400s it was clogged and impassable.

And Bruges died. Literally died. With the ending of ship traffic, commercial activity virtually ceased, and large portions of the population—some estimate as many as half—left to seek employment in Antwerp and other cities, abandoning their stunning homes, their commercial palaces, their magnificent squares. For 500 years, through the late 19th century, Bruges dozed and declined until a Belgian writer, Georges Rodenbach, inadvertently broadcast its charms to the world in a novel called *Bruges La Morte* (Dead Bruges) and set off a wave of tourism. Soon thereafter, wise minds forbade any further tampering with the facades of Bruges, and the city embarked on its second career, this time as a monumental European tourist destination. I have often felt that if the international airport of Belgium were located outside Bruges, rather than Brussels, overseas tourism to Belgium would triple.

Bruges today is a city of dreams, where every walk brings reveries, every stroll results in unexpected discoveries of beauty. You walk behind a gate, and there is a ravishing courtyard, the kind you'd imagine from the last scene of *Cyrano de Bergerac,* or one you'd find in a monastery cloister, peaceful and green. You walk down a lane and there is a canal and regal swans upon it. You gaze up at buildings and there are exquisite carved-stone emblems of the guilds or functions they once served. Everywhere are canals (in this "Venice of the North") and small arched bridges, cobblestoned streets, ranks of aged medieval structures covered by vines, interspersed with trees—for there are large, flowering trees everywhere—guardians of peaceful repose and quiet, except of course in the majestic main squares where towering belfries, cathedrals, market halls—themselves supreme works of art—draw sightseers to gaze upon them.

And the homes! They all have pointed roofs and are of brick, but brick used for an aesthetic purpose, set in patterns that draw the eye to a focal point, or create designs of beauty and purpose in even modest dwellings, bricks set in curved archway fashion, or bricks set aslant, or bricks that criss-cross upon themselves to make the architect's statement. Just as Italy in the Middle Ages excelled in marble, and France in stone, so medieval Bruges was the creator of brickwork never again equalled in its variety and charm. Compare even the modest commercial structures of Bruges with the mindless and squat, vapid rectangles that constitute the retail architecture of most cities in North America.

How to describe, in my limited remaining space, the facilities and attractions of Bruges? You stay in hotels of architectural distinction, not a single one of modern construction (even the Holiday Inn occupies a period building). You eat in Belgium's finest restaurants. As you pass from meal to meal, in even the modest establishments, you thrill to plates of tissue-thin and palely pink smoked salmon sprinkled with strawberry-flavored vinegar and spiced with red and yellow peppercorns. You precede the meat course with a bowl of tender tiny scallops boiled in a fish-stock soup; you suck the delectable stuffing from a tray of steamed "langoustines" (small crabs) in melted butter-garlic. You exult, at the entrance to even a three-star restaurant, to find yourself treated as a human being whose patronage is welcomed (in sharp contrast to the treatment in great restaurants of other European lands).

You visit and view masterworks of art so numerous and sublime as to rival collections in cities three times the size: Jan van Eyck's *Madonna with Canon Van der Paele* in the Hall of the 15th-Century Flemish Primitives at the Groeninge Museum: Hans Memling's *Mystic Marriage of St. Catherine* in the 12th-century Hospital of St. John, Memling's *Shrine to St. Ursula* in the same enthralling structure. In the 13th-century Church

A city of dreams, where every walk brings reveries, every stroll results in unexpected discoveries of beauty.

of Our Lady you find the only statue by Michelangelo—*Madonna and Child*—to have permanently departed from Italian soil.

You wander a Beguinage where elderly women lived in the 13th century; you shop at tiny lace stores; you are awed by the Palace of Gruuthuse, by the Town Hall (oldest in Belgium—1376) resembling a Gothic wedding cake of pointed spires and elaborate statuary. At the Basilica of the Holy Blood you gaze at the stained cloth said to be from the cloak of Jesus and brought to Bruges in 1150 by a leader of the Second Crusade. In between, you sail the canals dotted with swans, as themes from Mozart filter through your mind and send you into dreams.

Have I exaggerated the charms of Bruges? Ask anyone who has been there. It is a stellar sight of Europe, yet bypassed by the bulk of American tourists in their headlong rush to better-known attractions.

XII

New Ways to Visit Old Destinations

The Other London

By Scorning to Fall into a Tourist Mentality, Visitors Can Greatly Enrich Their Stays in Britain's Capital

t's pleasant, of course, to view the Changing of the Guard, the Beefeaters at the Tower, the face of Big Ben. But is it worth a trip to London—worth the expense, worth the effort—to do just that and nothing more?

I don't think so. Without exposure to the current life of London—the lectures, seminars, and socials, the conferences and classes, where residents mix and mingle—a trip confined to the tourist sights of Britain's capital seems a feeble diversion, a bowl of soup without salt.

How do you, the tourist, meet the people and taste the life of this great English-speaking city?

A first step is the purchase of one of three weekly magazine calendars: *What's On* (£1, $1.60), *Time Out* (£1.50, $2.40), and *City Limits*

(£1.20) ($1.92), sold at all London newsstands. Comprehensive to an extent that's never remotely achieved in their U.S. counterparts, each reviews not only the scheduled concerts, plays, and films of the city, but also dozens of other communal gatherings: meetings of clubs and associations open to all, evening lectures and speeches all across the city, galas and parties, serious dialogues and workshops with political, social, or interpersonal themes. If nothing else, the British are joiners, sensitive to causes, and their confabs listed in the three London weeklies are open to people of all backgrounds, and almost always for free.

Without exposure to the life enjoyed by residents, a trip confined to the tourist sights of London is a feeble diversion.

The tourist who treads off the beaten path—to the weekly debates of the Shavian Society, the numerous public lectures of the Social Democrats, the Thursday poetry readings of the Keats Foundation—becomes a traveler, not a tourist, and enjoys the opportunity to experience other outlooks, a distinctive national culture, an encounter with foreign residents.

Public Affairs at the University of London

But as broad as their coverage is, the London weeklies are relatively mainstream in their approach. Moving to more exotic realms, or to more specialized concerns, requires a trip to the bulletin boards of the central campus of the University of London. Take the Tube (the Underground, or subway) to the Russell Square stop and ask for instructions to nearby Gower Street (site of the university's North Cloister Building, Darwin Theatre, and Birkbeck College) and Malet Street (housing Senate House). At the North Cloister Building, a monitor flashes news of unusually erudite but utterly free lectures of the day, all open to the public at large. At the Darwin Theatre, free lunchtime lectures on Tuesday and Thursday from 1 to 2pm run the gamut of disciplines from physics to fine arts (phone 387-7050, ext. 2043, for advance information). And at Birkbeck College, large posters announce one-time colloquiums and lectures by titled speakers or eminent dons (teaching masters) on "Proust's Recherché," "The Greenhouse Effect," "Problems of the Inner City," both in midafternoon and early evening, open to all, student and nonstudent alike, and free when last I looked.

At Senate House, in addition to finding the ubiquitous bulletin boards with their posters of daily free events, you can pick up a map and catalog of all the schools' faculties and departments, enabling you to pinpoint even the most ultraspecialized lectures. At the School of Oriental and African Studies, you may discover: "Today—Tea and Biscuits at 4:45pm, then lecture ('Indigenous Agricultural Revolutions') at 5pm, free." At the Center of Near and Middle Eastern Studies: Tuesday at 5:30pm, "Tribe and State in Libya," free; Thursday at 6pm, "Ancient Arab Politics," free. Attending are London's brainiest folk, all amenable to continued conversation after the lecture.

Unfortunately, there is no one central source for all the university's free daily lectures; you simply have to wander from building to building to track down the offerings.

Adult Education Institutes

For discussions of a less exalted nature, among ordinary residents of London of all ages, the places to visit are the 20-some-odd adult education institutes (nighttime instruction, mainly) found in all sections of the city. Though the curricula here are of semester-long duration, each school is festooned with posters of both daily and weekly events: tea dances, let's say, on Monday afternoon; Saturday classes on paper-making and other crafts; one-time lectures (open to all) in Chinese culture—those were some recent selections I found at the Camden Institute on Longford Street, NW1 (phone 388-7106). Other centrally located adult education institutes are: the

Central Institute, Stukeley Street, Drury Lane, WC2 (phone 242-9872); the Westminster Institute, Hallfield School, Inverness Terrace, W2 (phone 286-1900); the Mary Ward Institute, Great Ormond Street (phone 831-7711); and the Islington Arts Centre, Shepperton Road, N1 (phone 226-6001), offering seasonal workshops in music, art, and dance, at which outsiders can "drop in" (audit) for a single session at a cost of £2.25 ($4.05).

The "Green" Life of London

And how about spending a weekend in one of the green areas of London, assisting residents to restore and protect the natural environment? Every Saturday and/or Sunday of the year, the British Trust for Conservation Volunteers (c/o The London Ecology Centre, 80 York Way, N1; phone 278-4293) operates a wide range of "day projects" for British people from every walk of life: hedgelaying in North London, tree planting in the East End, creating wildlife areas on formerly developed sites. Minibuses leave at 9:30am from various pickup points and drive participants to the project areas, where tools and instruction are provided. And are tourists invited to join the hardy, affable British volunteers? Yes! says a BTCV official in a recent letter to me. "No need to be a London resident. Anyone can turn up for these tasks; they are free, and all that's needed is a packed lunch. We supply soft drinks, biscuits, and (grotty) coffee."

Weekend-long "residential" projects (you stay Friday and Saturday nights in the countryside outside London, in Kent, Sussex, Surrey, or Essex) are also run by BTCV throughout the year, attracting volunteers of every age and condition, usually dynamic, outgoing Britons. Participants bring old clothes and a sleeping bag, stay in dwellings ranging from youth hostels to village halls, and receive food, transportation, and accommodation for the grand total of £3 ($5.40) per day. "Everything is very informal," adds the BTCV spokesperson, "and it isn't necessary to have experience in the field of conservation."

Here, on your overseas trip, is a meaningful travel experience. Isn't it better than shuttling about in a glass-enclosed tour bus with other Americans and paying an overpriced $150 per night in a crowded hotel?

St. James's

And then you have the multiple activities of London's strangest theological center. Though it's a 300-year-old church, with a pastor as devout as any, St. James's of London bears no resemblance to your ordinary house of worship.

It swings. It trembles. With yoga classes, New Age lectures, seminars on personal relationships, flamenco guitar concerts. And it invites casual visitors, including tourists simply passing through, to join its constant daily doings, in a location only three short blocks from Piccadilly Circus.

No better way exists to escape the often-artificial confines of the tourist and move instead into a real-life setting of dynamic Londoners. Every day of the week, St. James's offers either lectures, one-night classes, crafts markets, meetings of the William Blake Society (the famed English poet and visionary painter was baptized here), workshops (in ecumenical theological literature ranging from the Bhagavad Gita to the Hebrew Talmud), lunchtime recitals, evening concerts (of atonal strains), one-day instruction ("Awakening the Heart through Painting," "Introduction to Meditation"), and other communal events too numerous to list. Far from confining its schedule to church members, it openly solicits visitors of all religious persuasions to join the British at this "international centre for healing, and reconciliation . . . a place for prayer and celebration . . . a forum for the arts."

If nothing else, the British are joiners, and their meetings listed in the three London weeklies are open to all and almost always free of charge.

St. James's of London bears no resemblance to your ordinary house of worship.

Failing, and slated to become a museum (the building is by Sir Christopher Wren), St. James's was revived in 1980 by its then-new rector, the Rev. Donald Reeves, whose Christian teachings encompass political concerns of international security ("The Roots of Violence," a recent lecture) and daring theological speculations ("ideas which provide creative and spiritual alternatives to currently accepted Western thought"). You have only to enter this Anglican/Episcopalian center and its charming interior coffeeshop (Wren's), and scan a daunting array of notices and posters, to be swept up into an active stratum of London life that virtually guarantees you will get to interact with the people. St. James's is at 197 Piccadilly (phone 734-4511), near both the Piccadilly Circus and Green Park subway stops.

Political London

Visitors wishing to participate in the frequent periodic meetings and vigils of the **Campaign for Nuclear Disarmament,** 22 Underwood St. (phone 250-4010), are best advised to pick up a copy of the monthly magazine *Sanity* at newsstands or direct from the organization; it lists each such event, both current and several weeks in advance. Elsewhere in London, the **Conservative Party Bookshop,** 32 Smith Square, near Westminster (phone 222-2004); the **Labour Party Bookshop,** 150 Walworth Rd., near the Elephant & Castle Tube stop (phone 703-0833); and the **Social Democratic Party Bookshop,** 4 Cowley St., near the Westminster Tube stop (phone 622-3811)—all frequently display notices of periodic political seminars open to all and scheduled on a near-weekly basis.

New Age London

The city's major bulletin board for lectures, one-day classes, and workshops in psychic phenomena, from Tarot to acupuncture, from rebirthing to regression, is at the sprawling multiroom shop called **Mysteries,** at 9 Monmouth St. (phone 240-3688). Equipped with its news of weekend festivities, LRT (loving relationships) lectures, and the like, you'll quickly connect with others. Elsewhere in London, holistic health and Eastern approaches to well-being are the theme of the large **East-West Centre,** minutes from the Old Street Tube stop (use Exit 6). In the lobby of its Community Health Foundation are leaflets and postings of activities, including numerous events (like a Friday dinner-and-lecture series) particularly appropriate for short-term tourists in London.

Ecological London

The **London Ecology Centre,** 80 York Way (phone 379-4324), is an impressive hub of activity and second headquarters for more than 70 ecological organizations that hold near-daily get-togethers open to all in the meeting space above the main floor containing a café, giftshop, and bookstore. A visit will give you an overview of Britain's activity in environmental protection. You'll be able to converse with London's ecologists, who seem calm and confident despite their obvious concern over the continual political battles they must wage. To find out more about the meetings of the new "Green Party," call the main office at 673-0045.

Library London

And finally, keep in mind that, just as in U.S. cities, the libraries of London are posting places for community activities and neighborhood lectures, classes, and workshops. Walking into the Westminster Public Library recently, I learned of and then attended that night a free lecture by the headmaster of an Oxford college on "Dynamics of Darwinian Evolution." I will remember that evening, and the ensuing conversations with dynamic Londoners, long after the Changing of the Guard fades from memory.

In London the Real Action Is "On the Fringe"

Britain's "Off-Off-Broadway" Theaters—Often Difficult to Find—Provide Dramatic Excitement, Unsettling Ideas, and Low Ticket Prices

My friend Bill, from Atlanta, Georgia, is a thoughtful man who reads good books and subscribes to brainy periodicals. But when he travels to London, he turns off his mind.

"I hear you can now get tickets to *Starlight Express*," he said, referring to the roller-skate operetta. "And Mary knows a broker who has seats for *Cats*."

Are mindless musicals the only theater reward of a trip to London—or to New York, for that matter? For millions of Americans, the opportunity to enlarge their horizons at night, to escape the ordinary and encounter new ideas, is almost always squandered on their trips to a theater capital by just such a limited choice. And the reason, in part, is a woeful failure on the part of major newspapers in those cities to alert the visitor to the full range of theater opportunities.

In London, the shows patronized by tourists are nearly always those of the West End, in and around Leicester and Trafalgar Squares. In Manhattan, the same are confined to the side streets of Times Square, the so-called Broadway theaters.

Most of these standard productions, in the opinion of a growing number, have been paltry and unworthy ventures, distinctly inferior to the current level of films, either plotless collections of song *(Black and Blue)*, superficial farce *(Run for Your Wife)*, or tired perennials *(The Mousetrap)*. Of the plays on Broadway at any given moment, nowadays only one or two are of real importance (recently, and just barely, *The Grapes of Wrath*), while in London's West End the number rises to perhaps two or three (for instance, *Orpheus Descending* with Vanessa Redgrave, *Richard III* with Derek Jacobi).

For pith and substance, the informed theater-goer turns to the several score "Fringe" productions of London.

For pith, for substance, for excitement on the stage, the informed theater-goer turns to the several score "Fringe theaters" of London. Yet to the tourist reading the London dailies, these are like quasars of a black hole. Although an occasional London newspaper will briefly list half a dozen of the major Fringe productions, none pays them more than the scantiest attention.

What causes a London theater to be regarded as "on the Fringe"?

Unlike the Off-Broadway theaters (fewer than 499 seats) or Off-Off-Broadway theaters (fewer than 100 seats) of New York City, the Fringe theaters of London are distinguished from those of the West End by their location—which is usually outside the central Piccadilly Circus–Leicester Square–Trafalgar Square area. Yet from many hotels, they are no farther by subway than are the better-known playhouses, a matter of half an hour at most. They also charge far less for their seats: an average of £10 ($16) at most, including an occasional compulsory membership fee, as contrasted with a current average of £20 ($30) for most orchestra seats in the West End.

Last week, in the 60 or so theaters of the Fringe (some large, some small), theater-goers could see such plays as those by Sartre and Sophocles, by Ibsen, Chekhov, and Strindberg, by Arthur Miller and Bertolt Brecht. They could watch a theatrical exposé of women's prisons in Britain, performed by ex-inmates; attend a revival of *The Royal Hunt of the Sun* by Peter Shaffer (who wrote *Amadeus*); see socially provocative works by modern playwrights like *The Lover* by Harold Pinter, or politically provocative works like *A Common Woman* by the Italian anarchist Dario Fo. They could thrill to Shakespeare's *Timon of Athens* performed by an all-female cast, or encounter dozens of other dramatic thunderbolts engaging the mind.

To obtain reservations for the Fringe, one simply phones the theater in question or, better yet, goes to a single, central Fringe theater box office in the lobby of the mainstream Duke of York Theatre on St. Martin's Lane, WC2 (phone 0171/379-6002).

What's especially delightful about the Fringe theaters is that most are like community centers, offering not simply a performance, but often a restaurant on premises (for pre- or post-performance dining), scheduled workshops, lectures and seminars during the day, art or photo exhibits, an occasional bookshop, even babysitting "night care" rooms for the infants of theater-going parents. In other words, they are full-scale British institutions which also make it possible for tourists to mingle with a dynamic set of English people and occasionally to meet them—something harder to do in the commercial, tourist- jammed settings of the West End theaters.

Among the more prominent of the Fringe theaters, of near-consistent excellence, are these:

Riverside Studios, Crisp Road (off Queen Caroline Street), Hammersmith, W6 (phone 0181/741-2255), houses, in addition to its stage, a continuing art exhibition, a restaurant-café, and an excellent theater bookshop, plus ongoing courses and lectures.

Royal Court Theatre Upstairs, Sloane Square, SW1W (phone 0171/730-2554). Artistic, experimental, distinguished.

Drill Hall Arts Center, 16 Chenies St., WC1 (phone 0171/637-8270), is a block from the University of London, and is well known for its vegetarian restaurant, The Greenhouse, and its evening babysitting services. Three on-site rehearsal studios are used for classes ranging from aerobic exercises to a study of feminist writers.

Almeida Theatre, Almeida Street, Islington, N1 (phone 0171/359-4404), frequently features international theater as performed by visiting troupes from abroad.

Lyric Studio, King Street, in Hammersmith, W6 (phone 0181/741-8701), attracts well-known performers, and frequently previews shows before their move to the West End. For example, *House of Bernarda Alba* by Garcia Lorca, starring Glenda Jackson, tried out here (at low ticket prices) before it moved to a more prestigious stage.

King's Head Theatre Club, 115 Upper St., N1 (phone 0171/226-1916), is housed in the space above a popular pub, and offers meals before the show.

Wimbledon Studio Theatre, 103 The Broadway, SW19 (phone 0181/542-6141), showing (frequently) classic plays from a large repertoire.

The Courtyard, 10 York Way, N1 (phone 0171/833-0870), presents works of new British playwrights.

And in New York . . .

In New York, information on alternative theater is a bit more readily accessible than in London—but only slightly so: a fairly comprehensive listing of the 40 or more Off-Broadway plays and musicals currently running ($30 for the average ticket, as compared

But to the tourist reading the London dailies, "Fringe theaters" are like quasars of a black hole.

with the $45 and more charged for Broadway shows) appears daily in the *New York Times,* but not always in the other papers.

As for the 50 or so Off-Off-Broadway productions in small 100-seat houses ($12 to $15 per ticket), these appear in full only in the Sunday edition of the *New York Times,* and rarely in the other papers. Rather than look for those fleeting mentions, avid theater buffs pursue Off-Off-Broadway by purchasing the weekly *Village Voice* or *West Side Spirit,* and obtain a less comprehensive review of Off-Off-Broadway in *The New Yorker* and *New York* magazines.

As a New Yorker myself, and a frequent theater-goer, I rarely attend the Broadway shows; I find them too often obvious and contrived, designed for the tired suburbanite, the harried tourist, a form of "aspirin for the middle class," in the words of a wag. For me, the unique impact of theater—a special artistic and cultural experience, unlike that of a film—is found Off- or Off-Off-Broadway or on the Fringe, and I urgently suggest that you try the same on your own next trip to London or New York.

A Visit to the New Paris

Five Recent Additions to the "City of Light" Have Made It the World's Unchallenged Leader

However magical it has always been, it has been made better. In 15 years, the great city of Paris has acquired five monumental new attractions. And suddenly, what was once a mere equal among the several top capitals of the world is today, in my opinion, the indisputable leader, without peer or contender. It stands alone.

If your own last visit to the "City of Light" was more than five years ago, then you haven't felt the combined impact of the five new wonders—the d'Orsay, the Picasso, the Beaubourg, La Villette, and the enhanced Louvre—as a single experience. That treat, a form of cultural gluttony, is at last fully available, and best pursued from mid-November through mid-April, when the city's trade shows abate a bit and hotel occupancies drop. Then you can tour the museums in comparative calm; pay as little as $60 a night for a double room in a charming small hotel; devour bistro meals that engage your senses, indeed lift you to the skies, for all of $25.

The **Picasso Museum** (late 1980s) should perhaps be your first choice. In the resplendent Salé mansion built in the 17th century in the historic Right Bank district of the Marais, the French government has mounted a permanent display of nearly 200 paintings from Picasso's own collection, his obvious favorites, together with ceramics and sculptures acquired in payment of the massive estate taxes levied upon the artist's death. And though you may think you have earlier experienced the titanic genius of this 20th-century master, you will be stunned—left weak but uplifted—by the works on view. Some are seen here for the very first time; all are grouped into the major periods or styles through which the artist passed, and all are brilliantly described in posted commentaries translated into English.

The **Beaubourg** (early 80s), or **Centre Georges Pompidou,** oldest of the four, is Paris's block-long collection of 20th-century art, reached on foot and with ease from the Picasso Museum. In a giant building as modern and joyful as its contents—with incongruous façade of water pipes, ducts, struts, and metal spars—visitors enter a tube of glass and ride up the outer wall to a top-floor permanent collection of surrealists, expressionists, post-impressionists, cubists, pop artists, and more, from Matisse and Mondrian to Andy Warhol and Salvador Dali. Outside are street buskers encouraged to entertain, while along one side—and often missed by tourists—is a water-filled playground for a team of impishly comic industrial robots, all dipping, dousing, and spraying water from garden hose–like appendages. What other city would have had the audacity to place such a fanciful construction into a traditional area?

La Villette, as it's commonly called (because of its location next to the Porte de Villette Métro station), is the brand-new science and industrial museum of Paris, resembling a world's fair of several structures. Although only a portion of the ambitious project is completed, what you will see today is a display of ultramodern technology ranging from rockets, robots, and lasers to humanlike computers. In the style of so many museums, visitors are encouraged to step through and/or handle the items on display, but

It provides a kind of cultural gluttony, best experienced from November through mid-April.

what distinguishes this exhibition is its vast size, surely larger (when completed) and more varied than any other on earth. It should be seen.

The **d'Orsay Museum** (late 1980s) is the other recent addition to the list of not-to-be-missed Parisian attractions, and the subject of reams of recent travel literature. In its showing of 19th-century masterworks of art, especially those of the French impressionists—Monet, Cézanne, Degas, Toulouse-Lautrec, Renoir—it provides a logical prelude to the more recent art of the National Museum of Art and the Picasso. And though I personally find it to be a confusing place with its 80 different galleries, its impact is staggering, as one explores the vast floors of a magnificent railroad station converted at great expense into an elegant museum of size and grandeur. It fills the niche between the largely ancient art of the Louvre, and the modern and contemporary art found elsewhere in Paris.

And then there's the enhanced and expanded **Louvre,** entered through the glass pyramid designed by I. M. Pei.

A brilliant pyramid. With its futuristic spaceship-like form and transparent modern walls, juxtaposed against the ancient ornate face of the grand palace, it reminds you that several hundreds of years have passed since construction of the latter. It makes "time visible." It does not detract from the Louvre and its courtyard, as an opaque building would have done, but highlights it, proclaims its age. With the vast public space underneath it, greatly increasing the exhibition areas of the Louvre, Paris has taken a further quantum leap in its visitor facilities.

As always, the glue that binds together your activities in Paris is food. If you carefully avoid the restaurants that cater to tourists, and patronize only those supported by residents, you will eat magnificently at moderate cost. Recently I strolled along the Seine at night until I was out of range of the bright lights, and there, *Voilà!*, was a restaurant filled to every seat with Parisians. They did not let me down. I began with a salad of mixed greens topped with razor-thin shavings (to keep the price down) of pâté de foie gras, the whole sprinkled with a subtle dressing. I had sole with oysters under a light pie crust with deep-green stringbeans (*haricots verts*) alongside. I had three desserts—brie, crème brûlée, a strawberry tart—with black coffee. And earlier, a half bottle of white Mâcon-Village. The tab? Just $25 for a meal that caused me to sing and leap my way home.

A pyramid that makes "time visible."

Friends who had dined that same evening at a better-known "name" restaurant—filled with Japanese, and other affluent foreigners—ate dismally at three times the cost. In Paris, if the restaurant is a household word, you're 10 years too late.

Food and fine art, culture and cuisine, sights of the most awesome beauty—all this adds up to Paris, and Paris today, in my stubborn view, is the top attraction on earth.

Guided Walks Through the Cities of Europe

You meet them at a carefully prescribed address ("the northwest corner of Kongens Nytorv"), or under a famous statue, or along a bridge. They await you in clean but scruffy clothes—a worn tweed jacket, a frayed and mended shirt—for none earns more than a marginal living.

But in their eyes, their manner, their speech, glows pride in their profession. And in the next two hours, they are exuberant, they literally bounce, as they share an overweening love for the city they inhabit by escorting you on a walking tour of a tiny portion of it, a historic quarter, a cluster of ancient homes.

All over Europe, unauthorized, unlicensed entrepreneurs have set themselves up as one-person tour companies to provide the visitor with a view of "Europe on foot."

They gain their clientele through leaflets scattered in budget hotels, or via index cards tacked to subway bulletin boards, or—if they're lucky—through a guidebook mention.

And would you believe it? Tourists in large numbers are responding, as the realization spreads that intimate walk-throughs provide the finest possible experience of Europe.

In Copenhagen

The pioneer in the art is a 60-ish former motorcoach guide named Helge Jacobsen, a Dane. A little more than 30 years ago he sent me a letter, which I printed in a book then called *Europe on $5 a Day.* "I am tired," he wrote, "of having to speak two, three, or even four languages on the same bus, and of rushing by everything of interest in a hurry. The best way to see any city is on foot." And thereafter followed a list of multiple walking tours offered weekly from April through mid-June and daily from mid-June through mid-September.

In a number of capitals, unlicensed, unauthorized entrepreneurs have turned themselves into one-person tour companies to conduct the visitor on walks through historic areas.

Mr. Jacobsen has been leading such tours ever since. Recently, I appeared for his Saturday-afternoon walk through the bohemian Christianshavn district of Copenhagen, and was regaled for two and a half hours (along with 10 other tourists, some touring with him for the third consecutive day) by a witty, intelligent, deeply felt commentary on a single but important urban quarter constructed in the 17th century. The tour—like the performance of an accomplished actor, against a backdrop of period courtyards, cul de sacs, and small churches into which we strolled—was the stellar highlight of my short Copenhagen visit, and cost all of 30 kroner ($5.75). For additional information on seven different daily walking tours, contact **The Guide-Ring, 91 Kongelundsvej, Copenhagen (phone 51-25-90).**

In Stockholm

The Swedish equivalent of Mr. Jacobsen's enterprise is a tiny firm called **Old Town Walks,** for which tourists are asked to gather daily in summer at 6:30pm in front of the Obelisque on Slottsbacken; no advance reservations are necessary. Price of the two-hour tour: 30 Swedish kronor ($4.50); theme is the daily life of Stockholm through the ages.

In London

The many historic districts of London, with their intimate courtyards and curving lanes too narrow for traffic, are custom-made for walking tours, and no fewer than a dozen tiny companies vie for the patronage of intellectually curious tourists. Every day of the week, March through October, at 11am and 2pm, and some evenings as well, they offer "Legal London," "Literary London," "Aristocratic London" (Mayfair and St. James's), "Historic Pubs," and other crowd-pleasers of two hours' duration, for a uniform £4.50 ($7.20) per tour. You meet each time at a designated subway exit. For other details, see the "Walkers' London" section of the chapter on "The Other London."

The most distinctive of the companies, but perhaps too drily intellectual for some tastes, is Citisights. Founded by professional archaeologists in 1981, it reflects their tastes with such predictable themes as "Celtic London," "Roman London," "Medieval London," and "Victorian London," to name but a few. For further information, contact **Citisights, 145 Goldsmiths Row, E2 (phone 739-2372).**

City Walks, Streets of London, and London Walks are all fierce competitors of Citisights, and a bit more popular in their approach. All lay a heavy emphasis on such sure-fire themes as "On the Trail of Jack the Ripper," "In Search of Sherlock Holmes," "Ghosts, Ghouls, and Haunted Taverns" (an evening walking tour), and "The World of Charles Dickens," and all charge a standard £4.50 ($7.20) per two-hour tour. But each company stresses its own periodic "exclusives" (which are soon imitated by the other firms).

Currently, City Walks is particularly proud of its two-hour "Beatles' London" (on Wednesday at 11am), which takes you past the place where John and Yoko first met, to the recording studios where renowned albums were made, and to the present-day site of Paul McCartney's office. For complete details, contact **City Walks, 9 Kensington High St., W8 (phone 937-4281).**

Streets of London features as its current "exclusives" "The London of Henry VIII," "Islington—A London Village," and "In and Out of Fleet Street—Home of Sweeney Todd." For more information, contact **Streets of London, 32 Grovelands Rd., N13 (phone 882-3414).**

At London Walks, the emphasis is on "The Historic City" and "The Famous Square Mile." For current details, contact **London Walks, 10 Greenbrook Ave., Hadley Wood, Herts EN4 (phone 441-8906).**

Typical of the smaller one-person walking-tour operators is John Muffty's Historical Tours, with guaranteed near-daily departures in every month but December. I particularly like his "Inside Some Hidden Interiors of Old London," which takes you to a 16th-century dining hall still in use, a 12th-century church, and to the 18th-century Old Curiosity Shop, among others. Contact Mr. Muffty at **Historical Tours, 3 Florence Rd., South Croydon, CR2 (phone 668-4019).** Or consider Peter Westbrook's Londoner Pub Walks, leaving from the Temple Underground station at 7:30pm every Friday of the year. For details, contact **Peter Westbrook, 3 Springfield Ave., N10 (883-2656).**

A variant on the standard walking tours of London are the one-hour backstage tours of famous London theaters offered by Barbara Kinghorn's Stage by Stage Ltd. for £6 ($11.20); these are given Tuesday through Saturday at 11am. A different theater is visited each day, and brought alive for you by one of a dedicated staff of actors

> "**I** am tired," he wrote, "of having to speak two or three languages on the same bus, and of rushing by everything of interest in a hurry. The best way to see any city is on foot."

and actresses. Bookings are made at the **Edwards & Edwards desk in the British Travel Centres at 12 Regent St. or 156 Shaftesbury Ave. (phone 379-5822) or directly from Stage by Stage (phone 328-7558).**

In Brussels

The one-man **Babbelbus** organization (his name is Philippe Baeyens) runs three-hour English-language walking tours of the central city daily except Monday from April through September at 10am, for 300 Belgian francs ($10), including a drink at the end, at a typical workingfolks tavern in the Marolles district. Phone 673-1835 for all the details.

In Rome

And finally, an order of Dutch nuns conducts walking tours of sights in the Eternal City—an entire morning devoted to one building, or to one of the Catacombs, or to a section of the Vatican Museum—for tourists seriously interested in history and culture. Tours leave on Tuesday, Thursday, and Saturday at 9:30am, except in August, from the Foyer Unitas in the lovely Pamphili Palace at via di S. Maria del Anima 30, and a small contribution to their work (the equivalent of a dollar or two) is asked at the end. Always phone 686-5951 for reservations.

Puerto Rico, Turnabout in the Caribbean

Because It Has Preserved Its Own Culture and Civilization, Our Own American Commonwealth Is Again King of the Tropics

The resurgence of tourism to Puerto Rico is one of the big travel stories of the year. Suddenly, from San Juan to Mayagüez, from Ponce to Dorado Beach, developers are rushing to complete new hotels and marinas on a coastline that now receives more visitors each year than any other island in the Caribbean.

Gone are the days of shuttered resorts, or of other lodgings visibly deteriorating before your eyes. A dozen large properties have been refurbished or are about to be; the most spectacular of all—that splendid, cliffside giant of a hotel, **El Conquistador**—has recently reopened, better than ever before. The old Normandie, near the Caribe Hilton, has reemerged as an elegant pink-walled Radisson. The sprawling Cerromar Beach, under new Hyatt management, sports a $4-million winding river of a swimming pool that's one of the great wonders of the resort world. In Old San Juan, period buildings of the 17th century have been restored and are as impressive as they once were.

No one better deserves such a turnaround than the Puerto Ricans. To come from a week among them, as I recently have, is to be refreshed and enlightened by a generous, warm-spirited people. As their economy has improved—and it continues to do so, with discernible dips in unemployment and poverty, the building of a major middle class, a near-halt in emigration elsewhere—so has their mood. Pride breeds security, and the old chip-on-the-shoulder days of *West Side Story* are like ancient history, replaced by almost unvarying courtesy, a dignified hospitality, and a sense of caring for the visitor.

Add to this a series of concrete improvements in tourist conditions. Apart from massive recent investments of private and government funds in hotels and attractions, four other factors, in my opinion, contribute to the upswing of tourism to Puerto Rico:

1. **Cost.** Although hotel prices here are marginally higher than on many other islands, everything else is dramatically cheaper. Food is reasonably priced, and meals in Puerto Rico are delicious, featuring many more fresh ingredients than are normally found in the Caribbean. The visitor delights in a broad range of just-caught seafood, accompanied by plantains and corn sticks (*sorullitos*), excellent local beer (try the India brand), and that most celestial of Puerto Rican specialties—a distinctively prepared, subtly flavored side dish of rice and beans.

2. **Culture preserved.** On this island of three million people, tourism is a relatively small activity, however large in numbers (it accounts for only 6% of the gross national product), and doesn't dominate the scene, as on so many smaller islands. Except in Old San Juan, the tourist is often invisible, and the Puerto Ricans are absorbed in their own concerns, their own history and language, their own boisterous politics. To me, this provides the best kind of setting for tourism, enabling those visitors to enjoy a foreign society and not a copy of their own.

3. **Variety.** A full 100 miles long and nearly 35 miles wide, Puerto Rico is a large island of cities and villages, mountains and rural valleys, rolling hills with cattle grazing, parks and beaches, theaters and schools. Evening cultural activities are abundant, and every sort of enterprise—from tuna canning to the production of pharmaceuticals, from Spanish-language Shakespeare to scuba-diving schools and thoroughbred racetracks—flourishes both day and night.

4. **Ease of access.** The decision by American Airlines to make San Juan its major "hub" to the Caribbean has brought dozens of daily flights to Puerto Rico from cities all over the U.S. Thousands of people headed for other islands are now brought first to San Juan, and an increasing number of them are staying over for a few days en route. No other tropical island enjoys such convenient nonstop access to and from so many major U.S. cities.

Here tourism doesn't dominate the scene, as on so many smaller islands.

Most visitors stay, of course, in the high-rise seafront resort hotels of San Juan; but other areas and categories seem far more desirable:

• **Off-beat Vieques and Culebra.** Off the east coast of Puerto Rico, reached by small plane or ferryboat, the cozy, country-like, laid-back, and barely developed isles of Vieques and

Culebra, with small hotels and guesthouses only, are becoming increasingly popular among unpretentious, intelligent "beachcomber" types. Here's the Caribbean as it was 30 years ago.

• **The low-cost beach hotels of the west coast.** A very special type of American, anxious to holiday among Puerto Rican vacationers, will head to the sprightly holiday areas at Boqueron Beach and Boqueron Bay, and to the *paradores* (country inns) on both the western and northwestern coasts. At Boqueron, rooms can be had for as little as $50 a night in high season, and though they're in modest structures they are clean and comfortable, and located smack in the heart of a bustling Spanish-style vacation industry, alongside an array of low-cost seafood restaurants, one better than the next. At the *balneario* (supervised public beach) of Boqueron, cottages housing up to six people can be rented for $40 a night total, even in the winter months (which are a low-season period for the Puerto Ricans themselves). Though Boqueron is nearly three hours by car from San Juan Airport, it's a prime choice for cost-conscious Americans willing to adapt to local conditions and amenities. They'll enjoy the dividend of closeness to the Puerto Rican people as the latter pursue their own vacations.

They are absorbed in their own concerns, their own history and language, their own boisterous politics.

• **The exquisite seaside haciendas.** Finally, tourists of the most highly refined tastes will opt for the elegant period seaside estates of Puerto Rico that have been converted into intimate high-quality hotels. The latest, completed in 1991, and now a jet-setter's favorite, is the 26-suite Horned Dorset Primavera Hotel near Rincón, on the west coast, just 15 minutes by car north of Mayagüez. Throughout a long, off-season period (April 15 through December 15), it charges a reasonable $245 a night for a two-person suite, for elaborate Spanish-style accommodations with canopied beds and luxury fixtures. My own room, with heavy mahogany antiques and an opulent bathroom, hung over the crashing waves of the Caribbean. I took cocktails in a well-stocked panelled library, supped gourmet dinners served by white-gloved waiters (a six-course banquet for $45), relaxed on a golden beach and on the powder-blue chaises longues at the quiet swimming pool area, almost as if I were the house guest of a titled Spanish family. Two former college professors—Kingsley Wratten and Harold Davies of Horned Dorset restaurant fame in upstate Leonardsville, New York—are the proprietors of the Horned Dorset Primavera, which serves as a model for what can be done with stately but ancient homes. For reservations, contact **Horned Dorset Primavera Hotel, Apartado 1132, Rincón, PR 00677 (phone 809/823-4030).**

What's ahead for Puerto Rico? The chief planned construction of future world-class hotels is taking place on the eastern and northeastern coasts of the island: an elegant Ritz Carlton near Humacao, two 400-room Princess Hotels near Rio Grande, a luxury Trafalgar House hotel near Ceiba, and the Western Hemisphere's largest marina (600 slips) almost next door.

Meanwhile, bustling hotel lobbies are a tribute to the spirit of the Puerto Rican people, who fought to erase an unfortunate image, and once again stand revealed as the gracious hosts they are.

A Trip to the Other Hawaii

If Our Vacation Budget Confines Us to the Tourist-Jammed Island of Oahu, How Can We Nevertheless Escape the Tawdry?

Wall-to-wall hotels. Awestruck, first-time visitors in matching muumuus or gaudy shirts. Fastfood restaurants with lines stretching far outside. Hokey Hawaiian performers leading organized songfests and drawn-out chants of "ah-loh-hah."

And if you present a tour voucher upon arrival at Honolulu airport, you get kissed on the cheek. No voucher, no kiss.

Hawaii's Tourist Ghetto

Let's face it: Some sections of modern-day Hawaii, especially overbuilt Waikiki, leave much to be desired. Some visitors to the 50th state are less than enchanted with the development of mass-volume tourism there, and seek an option—a pathway to the "other Hawaii," the "real Hawaii."

So do many longtime residents of Hawaii's heavily populated Oahu, who feel resentful of tourism, even enslaved by it. That, in part, is why Waikiki remains "ghettoized," in the words of a University of Hawaii anthropologist.

A thoughtful visitor runs from the tourist ghetto of Waikiki.

And as he further notes, that's just fine for many locals. It gives them the rest of the island to enjoy for themselves, a space in which they needn't be endlessly reminded of Hawaii's dependence on tourism.

The thoughtful visitor follows the same path, to areas of Oahu outside of Waikiki, and to the people who work in or inhabit those areas. But it isn't easy—it requires sensitivity and work.

The key word is "respect." That's the quality voiced to me by a dozen residents as lacking in tourists to Hawaii, and the essence of what would otherwise give them access to the "real Hawaii." People here have an overweening appreciation for courtesy—perhaps a by-product of the Japanese culture of the islands' largest ethnic grouping. They like questions to be prefaced with "Excuse me, could you please tell me?. . ." And if the resulting conversations should lead to an invitation to someone's home, where shoes are left outside the door, leave yours outside also. "Don't ask if you should take your shoes off. Just do it," said a long-suffering Hawaiian of my acquaintance.

People Places

Certainly the finest place to meet or mingle with the locals is the Ala Moana Shopping Center, largest outdoor shopping mall in the world, with close to 200 shops. Its Makai Market features dozens of food stalls offering international cuisine at low prices (less than $5 for large portions), and there you join locals in that ultimate conversational "bond" between tourists and residents: food.

After walking around the mall, go across the street to the pleasant Ala Moana Park, which has grass, picnic tables, and a lovely beach favored by locals. You can bring lunch from the Makai Market, or stop off at the Ala Moana Farmer's Market behind the nearby Ward Warehouse shopping complex; the latter features specialty foods of Hawaii: for example, a Hawaiian plate, from Haili's Hawaii, of lau-lau (dumplings made of ti leaves and stuffed with meat or fish), poki (raw fish), lomi salmon (smoked with tomatoes and onions), poi (sticky, pudding-like starch made from taro root), and haupia (coconut pudding), for a total of $3.60. And you won't see a single other tourist.

Traveling Elsewhere

For getting about and meeting friendly folk at the same time, the essential device is Honolulu's wonderfully efficient and inexpensive public transportation system, TheBUS (85¢ to any point in Oahu; call 808/531-1611 for the routes, and request a copy of the free brochure "Hawaii Visitors Guide to TheBUS"). According to many locals, use of TheBUS distinguishes locals from tourists. If you are friendly, you will soon find yourself in conversations about the food and weather, which often lead to weightier things. Cultivate the habit of listening to the residents; one local's explanation to me of what makes tourists so offensive is that they are "abrupt" and cut people off.

The Nonprofits

In preference to the commercial attractions and events assaulting you from every poster and glossy ad-filled brochure, patronize the attractions that aren't operated for money. Go to the **Campus Center of the University of Hawaii at Manoa (phone 808/956-7235)** and look at any of the numerous bulletin boards publicizing time and location of such cultural events as a Western Samoan music concert. Pick up a copy of the weekly *Ku Lame Bulletin* (at Bachman Annex no. 6), which lists several activities each day, including art exhibitions, theatrical productions, films, and lectures (a recent example: a breakfast meeting to discuss "The Pacific Attitude Toward Work"). Visit the University Bookstore for its "Hawaiiana section" of works on whatever aspect of Hawaii most interests you: from poetry and healing practices to mythology, ethnic difficulties, marine biology, whatever.

You can plan your activities, read your books, or perhaps participate in lively discussions at the **Coffeeline,** 1820 University Avenue (phone 808/947-1615) open daily except Sundays for both breakfast and lunch. A comfortable, open-air but roofed meeting place for the university community, the Coffeeline serves healthy, old-fashioned cooking at low prices (seafood gumbo, biscuits, lime pie, and coffee for $4; meals are prepared by food science/nutrition teacher Brigitte Campbell and the students she trains). And there are concerts here, usually, on Friday and Saturday evenings. You can also go to the sometimes boisterous university hangout, **Manoa Garden in Hemenway Hall,** open weekdays only: from 10:30am to 8pm when school is in session, from 11am to 6pm during vacations.

And then there's the **East-West Center,** established by Congress in 1960 to "bring together people from the United States, Asia, and the Pacific in studying and seeking solutions to problems of social, economic, and cultural change." By dropping in at Burns Hall on the East-West Center campus (adjacent to the university), you can pick up a copy of the event-listing *Centerweek.* From it, I was recently able to attend a free storytelling event by Hawaiian, Samoan, and Maori performers, "Na Mo'olelo O Ka Pakipiki—Legends of the Pacific" (followed by an engrossing, lively discussion). You can also scan the more detailed bulletin called "Today at the East-West Center" posted in Burns Hall, or phone 808/944-7283 for schedule information. Be sure to ask how early you should arrive to obtain a seat.

More Options

The thoughtful visitor can also obtain information on Hawaiian ethnic festivities by reading the local newspapers (*Star-Bulletin* and *Honolulu Advertiser*), or by calling the **Hawaii Visitors Bureau** (phone 808/923-1811). There you'll learn about such celebrations as the Japanese Bon Dance, which takes place at temples for the purpose of sending ancestral spirits to the "other world." Or you'll be given word of cultural activities in which you also can participate, such as Japanese tea ceremonies. If you'd prefer to arrange for this particular item on your own, contact the *Urasenke Foundation of Hawaii* (phone 808/923-3059), which offers tea ceremonies to the public on Wednesday and Friday from 10am to noon.

An excellent way to have a taste of Oahu's Asian communities is to **walk around Chinatown.** Wander down the main street, Mauna Kea, and look in the glass windows to see people making leis. Sample local foods—yellow bean cake and lotus root candy. Ask to be directed to a Chinese herbalist, Dr. S. Yee (on Mauna Kea Street), who charges $35 for acupuncture treatment and herbal prescriptions,

The quality voiced as lacking in tourists to Hawaii is "respect."

and by whom several of my Hawaiian friends swear. Stroll through the **open-air market** on King Street (most active on Saturday mornings), which displays produce, poultry, and exotic fish. Eat dim sum (assorted dumplings) for lunch, or at the famous Wo Fat, at the corner of Hotel and Mauna Kea Streets, for which dinner reservations are required. Take in the *Kuan Yin Temple* on Vineyard Street, whose impressive statues, altars, offerings, joss sticks, and incense reflect a mix of Confucian, Taoist, and Buddhist influences.

And if you must take a tour, at least opt for a walking tour of Chinatown. Both the "Chinese Chamber" (phone 808/533-3181) and the Hawaiian Heritage Center (phone 808/521-2749) offer full-scale explorations on foot of Chinatown and the Old Oahu Market District, dropping in at a Chinese noodle factory, cake shop, acupuncture clinic, herb shop, open-air fish market, and Asian food processor—a total of three hours and only $4. Both depart at 9:30am, on Tuesday in the case of the Chamber, on Fridays in the case of the center.

Around the Island

Now let's escape the city altogether and taste the pleasures of the "other Oahu." Following which, I'll talk about specific institutions that introduce you in general to the "other Hawaii."

The Road Less Traveled

Kamehameha Hwy. is your "yellow brick" path to the dream of Hawaii; it almost circumscribes the island, along the ocean on one side, with farmland and sloping volcanic hills on the other (where you'll see families hanging octopus to dry in the sun). In a rental car (as little as $23 for the day), you'll find numerous points from which to enjoy beaches unspoiled by tourists or development, cane fields, quaint towns, fruit stands, and lunch wagons. One visitor at a roadside pay phone was recently overheard calling home to complain about learning of this "paradise" so late in her stay.

For surfing and such, you use **Sandy Beach** on the far side of Hanauma Bay, or **Sunset Beach** on the north shore (but beware the dangerous waves). For simply enjoying the ocean and clear air, **Waimanalo Beach Park** and **Kailua Beach Park** are favorites of the residents whose town sits on their shores. **Haleiwa,** also on the north coast, is the quaint village site of still another charming beach.

Closer to Honolulu is the suburb of **Kailua,** with its soft, white sand beach of Lanikai flanked by aquamarine waters; from here you can take a 3½-hour excursion by inflatable boat (and for $45) to five uninhabited islands and a legendary sea cave—the kind of approach to unspoiled,

breathtaking nature that many visitors mistakenly assume can be had only on the more expensive outer islands of Hawaii.

In the course of your self-drive journey prior to reaching the Kamehameha Hwy. you can stop to visit **Manoa Falls,** an easy, one-mile hike through lush tropical rain forest entered by scarcely any tourists; if they did, they'd enjoy a major reward: a freshwater pool created by the gentle but high-up cascade.

And for other "roads less traveled," inquire of the **Sierra Club of Hawaii** (phone 808/538-6616) about their $1 hikes through still other unspoiled terrain of Oahu. These are generally scheduled for every Sunday (but occasionally on Saturday) and are often available on the other islands, too.

The Institutions That Assist You

Kawaiahao Church at 957 Punchbowl St. in Honolulu, which many call the Westminster Abbey of Hawaii, dates back to 1842 and figured prominently in the early Christian period as the church of the Ali'i (chiefs and chieftesses). Viewing the 21 graceful and lifelike portraits of the Ali'i here gives one a sense of the former Hawaiian kingdom and its rulers. Services, though open to everyone, are still conducted partly in the Hawaiian language, and there's no more awesome experience than the Sunday 10:30am program, suffused with the true aloha spirit, and frequently attended by parishioners dressed in the pageantry of Hawaii's past—not, mind you, to entertain the tourist, but in celebration of their heritage.

The **Bishop Museum,** at 1525 Bernice Street, phone 808/847-3511, displays relics of the art, transportation, war practices, and worship of ancient Hawaii. It's important, too, and charges an entrance fee of $7.95 for adults, $6.95 for children 6 to 17.

The Mission Houses Museum, also in downtown Honolulu at 553 S. King Street, phone 808/531-0481, where it displays home and workplace furnishings of 19th-century Protestant missionaries (admission is $5 for adults, $1 for children) is less interesting for its contents, in my view, than for its frequent (call for the schedule) guided walking tours of the historic downtown center of Honolulu. Tours depart from the museum on several days of the week, cost $7 for adults and $2 for children, require reservations (phone 808/531-0481), and are another introduction to the "other Hawaii."

The Honolulu Academy of Arts, 900 S. Beretania Street, phone 808/532-8701, is home to one of the world's finest collections of Asian arts, and is unusually pleasant to visit in its airy setting of courtyards with sculpture gardens. Open six days a week (closed Monday) for an admission charge of $5 to adults, it also offers classes, lectures, and films on the culture and art of Asia, the Pacific, and Hawaii, and serves lunch in its café for $5.95.

Temari Center for Asian and Pacific Arts, 1329-A Tenth Ave., provides semester-long courses to residents in Asian crafts, but also serves the tourist by scheduling single-evening lectures and demonstrations in such subjects as lei-making ($15 for three hours) or Japanese paper-making ($60 for a Friday-night lecture followed by Saturday and Sunday workshops). Phone 808/735-1860 for detailed information.

Discovering Authentic Culture

Tune your Walkman or your transistor radio to AM 1420—KCCN—the island's only Hawaiian-music radio station. Watch the newspapers for appearances by the Brothers Cazimero (best known of all the contemporary Hawaiian music groups), the Makaha Sons of Niihau, the Sons of Hawaii, or the Kahuano Lake Trio.

Waimea Falls Park, at 59-864 Kamehameha Hwy. in Haleiwa, on the north shore (phone 808/638-8511), offers exact performances of the original hula—considerably different from the contrived variety performed at Waikiki's Royal Hawaiian Shopping Center—daily at 11:30am and 1, 2:30, and 4pm. Additionally, a covey of shrines, burial caves, ancient game sites,

waterfalls, and arboretums make the park well worth visiting, even for its steep admission charge of $19.95 for adults.

"Luaus" are another means for entering into the life of Hawaii, but only if they are of the kind designed for local residents. Watch the newspapers or bulletin boards for announcements of one of the periodic community-sponsored luaus that rarely cost more than $10.

Nonstandard Resorts

Finally, with their otherworldly airs, their remoteness from industrial concerns, their mid-ocean location, it was inevitable that the islands of Hawaii would become capitals of the "New Age."

And that's exactly what is happening. Though Honolulu and its crowded Waikiki Beach have remained determinedly mainstream—with fast-food restaurants and souvenir stands at every turning—the remainder of the lush Pacific state is sprouting everywhere with "holistic spas," "Buddhist retreats," "channeling centers," and "meditation lodges." Even the recently built $300-a-night Hyatt Regency Waikoloa on the Big Island of Hawaii has announced that its central health facility will be devoted to "A New Age Restorative Approach" ("A.N.A.R.A.") consisting not simply of spa-like treatments, but of therapies with "depth and meaning . . . promoting a state of inner peace," according to a Hyatt official.

Use of "TheBUS" distinguishes locals from tourists.

Should you, who may have no sympathy at all for New Age concepts, nevertheless consider the use of such facilities for your next Hawaiian vacation? Yes, in my view, for the following reasons:

• The "spiritual," but nonreligious, resorts of Hawaii are all far from the overly developed areas, in remote settings of untouched, awesomely lovely nature. They assure you a noncommercial vacation.

• Their cuisine avoids the gluttony and over-indulgence of the tourist restaurants; you'll feast on bran muffins for breakfast, on tofu and sprouts for lunch.

• They tend to be cheaper than the standard resorts in all but a few instances. And finally,

• They put your own, standard views to the test, provoking thought, perhaps awakening your mind to new values, at least reducing stress and anxiety.

All this is found on three particular islands:

Maui Here's the most visible evidence of the burgeoning new philosophy in the form of count-less herbal and health-food stores, holis-tic medical centers, offices of "transformational counseling," and alternative bookstores, along the length of Central Avenue in the town of Wailuku, a short drive from the airport. The impressive commerce attracts large numbers of sympathizers from the mainland, who congregate particularly among the New Age books and crystals on sale at **Angels & Amethysts, 81 Central Ave., Wailuku,** where they gaze at a notice-filled bulletin board and peruse the free "Maui' Ana Magazine" monthly "Island Calen-dar of Events" listing massage classes, fire dance celebrations, acupuncture demonstrations, nutritional lectures, and other such esoterica across the island. Phone 244-8813 for Angels & Amethysts.

Hawaii Less evident to the eye, the New Age facilities of the Big Island are still vital and popu-lar. The leading New Age location is a laid-back retreat called Kalani Honua, consisting of 32 rooms grouped into four wooden lodges, rustic but elegant, on 20 acres of scenic lawns and for-ests about a mile from a black sand beach (and 30 miles down the coast from Hilo). Though outside groups schedule one-week workshops there during much of the year, individuals are always welcomed to occupy the small but charm-ing rooms, and to imbibe meals prepared with a careful attention to good nutrition—for example, homemade granola, sprouted-grain bread with

fresh berry topping, and fresh fruit, for break-fast. Hiking is particularly popular, to hidden lagoons, lava tubes, natural steambaths, and volcanic lakes. Room and board: a remarkable $50 per person per day, on average, exclusive of optional workshop costs. Contact **Kalani Honua, Intercultural Conference and Retreat Center, R.R. 2, Box 4500, Pahoa, HI 96778 (phone toll free 800/800-6886, ext. 669).**

On the same island, Wood Valley Retreat is a Tibetan Buddhist center (actual Buddhist temple and adjoining two-story residence) nestled in the woods near Pahala. Contemplation and calm prevail here, as contrasted with the sharing and sociability of other centers. Prices for retreats vary greatly, but often range about $40 a day for room and full board. Contact **Wood Valley Retreat, P.O. Box 250, Pahala, HI 96777 (phone 808/928-8539),** or send $5 to receive its mailings.

Oahu The pickings here are slimmer, but ac-cessible even to visitors staying at the standard hotels. By scanning the large bulletin board at the **Sirius Bookstore, 2320 Young St., Ho-nolulu, (phone 808/947-4910),** open until 7pm on weekdays, until 6pm on Saturday, you'll learn of a wide range of New Age seminars and meditations in the area away from Waikiki, and especially about the popular yoga classes taught for 23 consecutive years (and for $6 per hour) by the much respected Rick Bernstein at the Kilauea Recreational Center, two miles from Waikiki, at 9am on Tuesday and Thursday, and at other times (Tuesday and Thursday at 5:30pm, Saturday at 9am) in the airy structure behind the Japanese temple in Oahu's Nu'uanu Valley. Phone 808/732-7993 to speak with Rick.

Even if you stay on Oahu, you can visit the more exotic New Age facilities on Maui and the Big Island by flying there for a day visit; Aloha Airlines charges only $74 for any point-to-point trip within the islands, and offers discounts for AAA members and even cheaper packaged (air plus hotel) deals.

Tropical Trekking—A New Hawaiian Holiday

Through a Tangle of Jungle and Under-growth, Waterfalls and Rain Forests, Mountains and Coral Reefs

It seems an oxymoron, a contradiction in terms, a just plain absurdity. To the first-time visitor engulfed by the crowds at Waikiki, the skyscrapers of Honolulu, the traffic gridlock of Kalakaua Avenue, the notion that Hawaii can be visited for its wilderness aspects seems farfetched indeed.

Yet most of Hawaii remains a wilderness, a natural tangle of jungle and undergrowth, waterfalls and rain forests, mountains and coral reefs. Based on those riches—the perfect ingredients for adventure touring—a dozen, quite remarkable residents have begun operating tours that differ radically from the standard urban variety. And though their client base is still small, it is growing fast, and posing a strong challenge to the mass-market firms.

Here are a few of the "dissidents" in Hawaiian travel:

Hike Maui

The 52-year-old Ken Schmitt, owner of Hike Maui, brings greater-than-usual academic training (in anthropology, archeology, and geology) and vivid wilderness experience to Hawaii's second-most-popular island. When a hurricane destroyed the boat he had been using in the charter business, he went to live in the jungle/forest for an extended camping trip that lasted three years. No one knows the backcountry of Maui better.

> "Our trips," says an operator of Hawaiian adventure tours, "not only remove people from the framework of a standard vacation, but from the enclosures of a nine-to-five office job as well."

Schmitt leads hikes nearly every day of the year. They include a redwood forest trek, one to the waterfalls at Hana, others to coastal or mountain areas; but the hallmark trip—8 to 11 hours long—is into the other-worldly domain of Haleakala Crater, a panorama of changing colors, endemic plants and flowers, birds, and other wildlife, that Schmitt calls "a natural temple."

The accompanying commentary is both learned and inspiring. "What I aim to do," says Schmitt, "is to teach people how to be comfortable in nature, especially by using the knowledge of ancient peoples."

"This is particularly important to us today," he says. "What would we do if our homes were destroyed? I'm talking not simply of survival, but of how to enjoy living in the wilderness."

Most hikes start at $70 per person, and range from $100 to $110 for the 8- to 10-hour hikes to Haleakala (less for children). Schmitt will work with a minimum of two people, a maximum of six. When you phone his office and specify the date of your desired trek, he'll either advise you of the destination for that date or—if nothing is scheduled—permit you to pick the hike. Contact **Hike Maui, P.O. Box 330969, Kahului, Maui, HI 96733 (phone 808/879-5270)**.

Pacific Quest

Perhaps the leading adventure-tour company of Hawaii, so popular that reservations at least three and four months in advance are often required, Pacific Quest is the creation of Zane Bilgrave (a former "experiential educator" working out-of-doors with children under the auspices of the Hawaii Department of Education) and his wife, "M.J.," a former ranger at Volcanoes National Park. They now have a staff of several others who accompany scores of departures each year, each limited to between 10 and 16 people. Participants can be of any age and degree of experience, provided only that they regard themselves as active, adventurous sorts with a strong interest in the natural and cultural history of Hawaii.

Each day of the tours—there are 14-day, 8-day, and 1- to 5-day tours available—focuses on a unique aspect of Hawaii, almost always associated with its ecological environment. One day participants will be walking up a mountain and swimming under a waterfall; another day they may be ocean-swimming, hiking in the brush, and snorkeling. "And that," says Bilgrave, "leads to a heightened awareness of each day. It may even give people a different perspective on their lives when they return home. They try to get more out of each day. They begin to spend more time outdoors. Our trips not only remove them from the framework of a standard vacation, but from the enclosures of a nine-to-five office job as well."

Two basic tours are offered. The most popular, "Quest Hawaii" is a 13-day trip to the islands of Kauai, Maui, and the "Big Island" of Hawaii. Cost is $2,150 per person, which includes all lodging, ground transportation, inter-island flights, activities, instruction, and most meals. Nights spent camping alternate with stays in rustic inns. There is no backpacking.

One of their trips is operated partially at sea, and as always, the focus is on the natural history of Hawaii; all activities are "hands on," from helping to sail the ship to recording vocalizations of whales and dolphins. Your guides: a dynamic young couple, Mark and Beth Goodoni, she an experienced educator and marine biologist, he a licensed U.S. Coast Guard captain and naturalist.

One six-day, five-night trip led by them, "Earth, Fire, & Sea," begins on the west coast of the Big Island of Hawaii, goes trekking through the remote Waipio Valley (for flora identification and photography), then hikes across the crater floor of Kilauea (world's most active volcano), for a total of three days and two nights on land; and then boards a sturdy passenger ship for three days of whale-watching, exploring a coral reef, and sailing instruction. Total cost, virtually all inclusive: $995 per person.

A third trip of 10 days' duration, the company's only tour conducted solely on land, is called "Hawaiian Odyssey" and takes you hiking through each of Kauai, Maui, and the Big Island of Hawaii, with meals and overnights in B & B inns; $1,485 per person.

Contact **Eye of the Whale, P.O. Box 1269, Kapaau, HI 96755 (phone 808/889-0227 or toll free 800/659-3544).**

The Other New York

A World of Cultural Riches, Known to the Resident but Too Often Denied to the Tourist

I sometimes weep to think of the limited enjoyment and experience that most tourists derive from visiting New York.

To those of us who live here, the city—with its unparalleled cultural opportunities—is an endless source of new ideas, dynamic and stimulating. To the tourist confined to the standard attractions designed for the tourist, it is too often hackneyed and contrived, mindless and superficial.

So what to do? On your own next trip to New York, try alternating the usual sights with the following eight nonstandard activities:

1. **Go to a Speech:** With its massive, concentrated population of politically sensitive people from scores of ethnic and national backgrounds, New York plays host each night to dozens of free or inexpensive lectures, seminars, protest demonstrations, and

gatherings on every subject. Pick up a copy of the *Village Voice* (from any newsstand), turn to "Listings," and under the subhead called "Cheap Thrills" (meaning events that are either free or less than $2.50 in cost) you'll find announcements of verbal fireworks occurring nightly throughout Manhattan, on the part of speakers ranging from opposition leaders of Myanmar to spokespersons for Ralph Nader. Provocative as they are, the meetings gain additional interest from the intense, intellectual New Yorkers who attend, and both—the meeting and the audience—are fully accessible to the visiting tourist.

2. **Enter the New Age:** New York's Open Center is the nation's largest facility for inquiries—mostly in the form of nightly, one-time lectures, daylong weekend workshops, and group discussions—into the spiritual speculations and psychological experiments of those who champion "holistic health" or "New Age" thinking. Whether it be theories of meditation, reincarnation, or healing, or simple personal growth from advanced psychological approaches, you'll find it here nearly every day of the week, sometimes for free, never for more than a nominal charge. And you'll meet a special type of open-minded, modest, questing New Yorker of every age. For schedules, write or phone **New York Open Center, Inc., 83 Spring St., New York, NY 10012 (phone 212/ 219-3739).** And for numerous other such daytime or evening meetings sponsored by dozens of other New Age groups in New York, pick up the newspaper called *Free Spirit* at most health food or New Age bookstores, such as the one at 78 Fifth Ave., between 13th and 14th Streets.

3. **Folkdance in the Big City:** Every Sunday evening in Earl Hall on the campus of Columbia University (and for only $4), every Friday evening at the Ethnic Folk Art Center at 131 Varick St. (for about

the same), avid folkdancers from all five boroughs of the city engage in nonstop, joyous folk dancing of every variety. Newcomers and novices are accepted without question, and no better way exists to meet New Yorkers of every background, every age. Simply stand outside the line or circle until you've learned the step, and then break in.

4. **Attend Daytime Museum Lectures:** Every one of the city's major museums— the Metropolitan Museum of Art, the Museum of Modern Art, the Guggenheim Museum, the Museum of Natural History—offers daytime lectures for free or for a nominal charge, attracting New Yorkers of a highly developed artistic or scientific sense. The "Gallery Talks" of the Metropolitan Museum of Art ("Masters of the Early 20th Century" and "Buddhist Gilt Bronzes of China" were two recent themes) are especially popular, and take place daily except Monday, sometimes several times a day. Phone 212/879-5500 for specific talks or printed schedules.

5. **Head Off-Off-Broadway:** As the expensive Broadway theaters ($40 to $50 the average seat) turn increasingly to an escapist tourist or suburban audience, with flashy but vapid musicals and predictable plays, the serious, resident theater-goer heads Off-Broadway (about 30 shows nightly, in smaller theaters) or even Off-Off-Broadway (as many as 80 shows nightly, scattered about the city). The latter are found in tiny loft or basement stages seating fewer than 100 people, and there—behind the ugly façade of run-down buildings—beauty emerges, excitement prevails. To see experimental, avant-garde

> **T**he city is host each night to scores of inexpensive lectures, readings, seminars, gatherings on every subject . . . all fully accessible to the visiting tourist.

People and ideas— the key to a rewarding vacation—lend a new dimension to the experience of New York.

productions, revivals of classic works, new and serious efforts by young playwrights, consider taking in an Off-Off-Broadway show—and you may never again return to the larger houses. Full listings of Off-Off-Broadway plays are found in the Sunday theater/arts section of the *New York Times,* or in the weekly *Village Voice,* with partial listings in *New York* magazine.

6. **Attend an Acting Class:** The atmosphere of New York is considerably affected by the presence here of thousands and thousands of aspiring actors and actresses, and it's fascinating, in my view, to see them at work in the city's many acting schools, whose tuition they manage by waiting on tables in hundreds of restaurants. The famous **Herbert Berghof Studio** (one such school) will permit outsiders to visit a class (your choice of acting technique, scene study, or voice) for a fee of $5 per two-hour session; and it's the only one, in my experience, to do so. Phone 212/675-2370 for specifics.

7. **Take a Walking Tour:** In sharp contrast to the once-over-lightly approach of the escorted motorcoach tours, walking tours explore a particular area or activity in depth, and each is led by an individual literally in love with the city—the monetary rewards are slight. You'll tour with a small, intimate group. Each week, *New York* magazine lists at least 20 ad hoc walking tours in its "Cue Listening" section, but two year-round operators of multiple walking tours are **Adventure on a Shoestring** (phone 212/265-2663) and **Sidewalks of New York** (phone 212/517-0201), both charging about $10 a tour.

8. **Enroll for a One-Night Course:** A scattered 10 U.S. cities have one apiece of those trendy, new night schools that teach an entire course in one evening session of three hours; New York has four. On most nights of the week, tourists can join advice-hungry New Yorkers for instruction costing $29 to $39, in subjects ranging from career planning to computer usage to personal relationships to preparing sushi and sashimi. Some take the course as much to meet other class members as for the advice, but whatever your aim, you'll gain an insight into the urban life of still another slice of the population. Of the four schools, two—the **Learning Alliance,** at 494 Broadway, New York, NY 10012 (phone 212/226-7171), and the **92nd Street Y,** at 1395 Lexington Ave., New York, NY 10128 (phone 212/996-1100)—deal primarily with subjects of serious political and social concern. The other two—**Discovery Center,** at 245 W. 72nd St. New York, NY 10023 (phone toll free 800/777-0338), and the **Learning Annex,** at 2330 Broadway, New York, NY 10024 (phone 212/580-2828)—are considerably lighter in their themes.

Charlie Rose and Dustin Hoffman at 92nd Street Y. *Courtesy 92nd Street Y, photo by Robert A. Ripps.*

Write or phone for catalogs covering the period of your own visit.

Though none of these eight activities will ever replace or pose a threat to the standard commercial approaches to New York—the round-Manhattan sightseeing cruises, the skyscraper observation towers, the big Broadway musicals— don't they add a new dimension to your New York stay? Don't they begin to afford you a glimpse into how some New Yorkers make use of the enormous cultural resources of their city? If people and ideas are the key to rewarding, fulfilling travel, shouldn't some of the eight be added to your own itinerary?

The New World of Travel 1997

The life blood of the Arthur Frommer travel guides is the correspondence received from readers, commenting on the establishments recommended in the texts and recommending new establishments. Each such letter is carefully studied, and when a particular lead seems promising, it is followed up and personally checked.

It is hoped *The New World of Travel* will receive similar assistance from its readers. A yearly publication, issued near the start of each year, *The New World of Travel* will constantly grow. And since much of its contents relates to organizations that lack the means to market themselves properly, or come to the attention of a travel journalist, your help is invaluable in alerting me to the organizations—hospitality exchanges, alternative resorts, new travel clubs, and the like—that you have discovered.

If you become aware of a new travel organization, program, or development that deserves to be described in our next edition, *The New World of Travel 1997,* won't you please let me know about it? Send your letters to Arthur Frommer, *The New World of Travel,* 1841 Broadway, New York, NY 10023. All letters will be acknowledged, and all are warmly appreciated in advance, by the author.

The Future of Mexican Vacations

Pitfalls, Prospects— and Where to Go

The attitude of most American travelers toward Mexico has always been one of love and hate. We dislike the occasional stomach upsets (turista), the pestering vendors, the crowded airports and flights. Yet so great is our affection for the colorful culture and setting of Mexico that it overcomes all doubts. In 1995, more than seven million international visitors—most of them Americans—came to vacation in Mexico and made it the eighth-largest tourist destination on earth.

Recently, I attended the mammoth, annual travel trade show of the Mexican government in Acapulco, known as the Tianguis (from the Mayan for "marketplace"). And there it became perfectly clear that, for good or ill, Mexico would loom even larger in the vacation plans of us North Americans throughout the late 1990s. Never before in travel history has a government made a more determined effort to build tourism into its leading industry.

The plans are staggeringly ambitious: literally billions of pesos are being invested in new hotels and resort areas, and huge sums in overseas advertising. More and more charter flights are permitted, and U.S. tour operators allowed to drive their massive busloads of seniors right across the border and then—without changing vehicles—into the heart of the country. For the American travel industry, it's a whole new ballgame, and tourist figures continue to soar.

But can the quality of Mexican tourism survive the increase? In those coastal locations where gringos already overflow the sidewalks and turn once-quaint fishing villages into cheap bazaars, is it possible to import still more camera-toting couples without destroying the charm of Mexico?

There's no easy answer. Already, the single most heavily visited Mexican destination—the island of Cancún, off the Yucatán peninsula—is readily conceded by Mexican officials to be no longer Mexican in character but rather "Caribbean." Defending the rather high hotel rates of Cancún in relation to those in the rest of Mexico, they argue that Cancún's competition is other islands of the Caribbean and not the rest of Mexico. Therefore, they say, Cancún's price level is relatively low.

(Elsewhere in the Caribbean, one island after another is currently attributing its recent poor winter season to the lower-cost competition from new hotels in Cancún. One such deluxe property, the recently opened Hotel Club las Velas, the "Sails," offers a totally all-inclusive rate—room, meals, water sports, and all the daiquiris you can drink—for $130 per person per day, fully 30% less than at equivalent, but older, hotels in Jamaica.)

It is apparently the plan to create several more Cancúns, not only in new locations, but by adding to the resort capacity in older ones. Thus, a project called "Acapulco Diamante," at the extreme end of and beyond the great seaside bay that made Acapulco famous, will soon add thousands of rooms to the legendary strip of Mexico's first "Riviera." Already, a new Hard Rock Café, which does battle each night with a giant, new discothèque called Extravaganza, further lessens the feeling that you are in Mexico when you are in Acapulco.

An even larger resort development along the Bays of Huatulco, on the Pacific coast 200 miles south of Acapulco, is well under way, with several hotels (including a Sheraton and a Club Med) already open. Because the new development is nowhere near a traditional Mexican city, it, too, will be an isolated resort area, like Cancún, with nothing Mexican about it. Only the somewhat smaller resort communities now expanding

> **In those coastal locations where gringos already overflow the sidewalks and turn once-quaint fishing villages into cheap bazaars, is it possible to import still more camera-toting couples without destroying the charm of Mexico?**

at Los Cabos, at the southern tip of Baja California, seem both ecologically and culturally sensitive. Even the small cultural gains represented by the aesthetic Los Cabos are overcome by the immense, further development of sprawling Puerto Vallarta farther to the south, which continues to grow in a helter-skelter, unplanned, and—to my mind— unattractive, shabby, urban fashion.

One recent winter, at Christmas-time, I escaped the crowds of Puerto Vallarta (where I had been staying) by flying to Mexico City, of all places. And there, in a setting blessedly free of tourists, I wandered with delight to great museums, galleries, theaters, and shops, through ranks of mariachis and alongside Orozco and Rivera murals to pyramids and pre-Columbian excavations.

Imagine: To avoid the excesses of tourism, I had to flee to the nation's capital!

What other Mexican locations can a sensitive traveler choose for a satisfying vacation? More than ever before—and as simple-minded as the advice may seem—you must go to where the free-spending, disco-craving, shopping-mad tourists aren't:

• Go to **Oaxaca,** growing in tourist popularity but not yet inundated by it. Visit nearby Monte Alban, stroll through flower markets and crafts fairs, dwell again upon many vestiges and remains of the Spanish conquistadors.

• Go to the **State of Michoacan** and, in a rental car, follow the "hot springs route" from the state's eastern border to the northwest end of Lake Chapala. Top thermal resorts along the way, with pleasant rooms, meals, and heated mineral baths: San José Purua, in the village of Jungapeo; Agua Blanca, five miles from San José Purua; Atzimba, near the town of Zinapecuaro; Santa Rosa near Tuxpan. Staff at these hotels claim they can renew your energies, and even cure or reduce arteriosclerosis, neurasthenia, and outbreaks of the skin.

And yet the Mexicans hope to double their current, massive levels of tourism—50,000 new hotel rooms will be built.

• Go to **Zacatecas,** in the State of Zacatecas, a city of 500,000 residents whose vast central area is almost entirely colonial, with scarcely a single modern construction. Ten minutes from town is the renowned Convent of Guadalupe, with its marvels of handcrafted and painted art.

• Go to that circlet of well-preserved 17th-century Spanish colonial cities that surround the capital, about a three-hour drive away: **Patzcuaro, Querétero, Guanajuato.** Here you have culture treasures, charming hotels with interior courtyards, classic Mexican cuisine—and only a handful of North American tourists.

• Go, if you insist on a Pacific-coast beach resort, to the uncrowded southern half of the **State of Jalisco,** halfway between Acapulco and Mazatlán, and to such quiet resorts as the Hotel Coasta Careyes. From its solitary position on a private bay, it resembles the kind of place to which Mexico-bound jet-setters headed in the 1960s, and yet it charges a high-season average of only $90 for doubles, from $120 to $180 for suites. You get there by flying to Manzanillo, an hour's drive away.

• And finally, go to **Mexico City,** heart and soul of the nation. Go to its archaeological museum, among the greatest in the world. Go to the daily (late afternoon) flag-lowering ceremonies by a battalion of troops in the plaza of the National Palace. See the nearby Diego Rivera murals. Attend the Ballet Folklorico, or go to Garibaldi Square for the nightly impromptu concerts by mariachi bands looking for bookings. And stroll, in perfect serenity, past the enticing shop windows of the Zona Rosa. Unjustly maligned by exaggerating travel writers, Mexico City is as safe today as any large U.S. city for tourists taking reasonable precautions.

A vast country that's nearly a quarter the size of the United States, Mexico has scores of compelling attractions and locations that haven't yet caught the attention of mass-volume tour operators. By traveling on your own to the places they've overlooked, you still have a few remaining years to enjoy the Mexico that once was, the delightfully foreign country just south of the border. But rush—because more and more of it is growing less and less foreign each passing month.

Sweden: A Return to the World of Tomorrow

There's New Ferment in the Greatest Social Laboratory on Earth— and Special "Institutes" Can Reveal It All to You

To a teenager in the late 1940s (myself), magazine articles on Sweden supplied the same improbable combination of erotic images and high-tech fantasies that *Playboy* provides today. Imagine! Swedish men and women, it was seriously claimed, were living together before they got married. Wow! Day-care centers, like apparitions from Mars, were sprouting up for the children of working mothers. Neat! As wintry as its weather was said to be, Sweden seemed a dream of the rational future, and I, for one, longed to view it.

So did thousands of other foreign admirers, who flocked to Stockholm for special tours of contemporary life that the Swedes, with uncharacteristic immodesty, called "The World of Tomorrow." Then, as the rest of the world began cohabiting before marriage, and women flocked to offices and assembly lines, as progressive schools and cradle-to-grave security became a commonplace in dozens of nations, that special interest in Sweden began to wane, and all but disappeared by the early 1980s.

Well, it's time to return, but fast. Because those sly ol' Swedes are at it again, testing the limits of the possible, once more enacting the visions of social planners, revamping the rules of commerce and industry, and even family life. And since the rest of the world tends to emulate the Swedish model on a time lag of about 30 years, no thinking person can pass up this foretaste of what, arguably may be the world of the future.

As early as the ride on the airport bus into Stockholm, you begin to glimpse the Swedish penchant for innovation, if only in a trivial sense. It is a sunshiny summer day. Yet all the cars have their headlights on. "Why is this?" you ask the stately Swedish woman in the seat ahead. "Statistics show," she answers rather archly, "that even daytime accidents are sharply cut if pedestrians and motorists are made aware of traffic by oncoming headlights. Our parliament now requires them to be on throughout the day."

Once in town, engaged in conversation with the largely English-speaking Swedes, you quickly meet up with matters more monumental: much talk is of the awesomely ingenious proposal for "wage earners' funds" designed to overturn the very basis of industrial ownership in Sweden. Proposed a decade ago by Sweden's then governing Social Democrats, the funds would be entitled to 20% of the pretax profits of all corporations above a certain size. These monies would then be reinvested in exchange for new stock whose voting rights are held by labor unions and other public representatives of the employees in those firms. The aim is nothing less than to transfer control of all such corporations from shareholders to the employees in them, by 20 to 30 years down the road, in addition to ensuring the reinvestment of profits instead of their distribution to shareholders. While Sweden's opposition parties have pledged to dismantle the funds if they should ever go into effect, the razor-thin margins by which most Swedish governments gain and remain in power, and thus the probable Social Democratic reaccession in any event, makes the funds a lively topic for investigation and debate, both within Sweden and abroad.

A lighter topic for study (unless you're 12 or younger): spanking is now illegal in Sweden. Corporal punishment of the young in any form, even "humiliation" visited upon a child (like being made to stand in a corner), can now subject Swedish parents to a fine or term in jail. Though no one has yet been imprisoned, Sweden's child experts expect the altered home environment resulting from this legislation to produce no less than a better human race, at least in Sweden.

How do you, as a curious student of world trends, gain access to these experiments? How do you progress beyond the purely touristic realms into the actual test-tube settings of Swedish innovation?

You write to an "institute"—in this case, the Swedish Institute. Unknown to 99% of all American visitors, most European governments supplement the work of their tourist offices with "institutes" offering assistance far more profound to visitors pursuing special interests. Unlike the tourist offices, whose function is simply to attract more and more tourists, the institutes are broadly charged with promoting the culture and the image of the nation. And although many of the institutes are primarily concerned with language courses or library services—the Institut Français/Alliance Française, the Goethe Institute, the British Council, the Austrian Institute, do that—another batch (including, most prominently, the Swedish Institute and the Danish Institute) are heavily involved in arranging interviews and meetings with distinguished local figures or authorities for visitors from abroad.

You are, we'll presume, the vice president for labor relations of your company, or a teacher of political science, or vice chairman of your local political club, heavily involved in matters of social welfare. Or you're a medical administrator anxious to visit the Scandinavian hospitals, especially in a country whose life-expectancy rates are two years higher than ours. You advise the Swedish Institute that you'll be in Stockholm, say, from February 3 through February 12 (having first made all hotel and transportation arrangements yourself), and then: you describe your background, enumerate the topics you're desirous of pursuing, and ask whether a "program" might be prepared for your stay. Within a few weeks (faster in winter), and free of charge, you receive a carefully formulated schedule of appointments. At 11am on February 3 you're to meet for an hour or two with Professor Rasmussen of Uppsala University, an authority in the field you've cited. At 9am on the 4th, the appropriate English-speaking committee of the Center Party will wait to brief you at their party headquarters in downtown Stockholm. That afternoon, their opposite numbers at the Social Democratic Party will do the same. And so on and on. While none of this will be arranged for persons who simply describe themselves as members of the public (no matter how studious, sympathetic, or concerned they may be), it should not be hard to dredge up the titles or qualifications that will entitle you to receive these introductions to your "professional" counterparts in Sweden.

Next time you visit Europe, try an institute! No more fascinating travel activity exists. Contact: the **Swedish Institute (Svenska Institute), Sweden House (Sverigehuset), Kunstradgarden, Box 7434, S-103 91 Stockholm, Sweden or the Danish Institute (Det Danske Selskab), #2 Kultorvet DK-1175 Copenhagen K, Denmark (phone 135-448)**. And thus replace those rather mindless vacation weeks of sand and sea with intelligent travel, to destinations that may indeed presage the World of Tomorrow.

Viewing Their Cities vs. Our Cities

hen Americans travel on vacation to Europe, they tend to devote their time almost exclusively to museums and theatres, art galleries and cathedrals, spas and trendy boutiques.

I think they might profitably pay some attention to the organization of cities. The growing difference between the "patterns" of European cities, and those of the newly emergent, major cities of the United States (especially in the South), is so very pronounced as to touch off the most provocative ideas and comparative lessons. Nothing in travel can be more instructive.

Here's a short "travel guide" to the difference between European and American cities: what to look for, what to consider.

The average European city is a high-density metropolis, not a sprawling, spreading ink blot like Los Angeles, but a tightly compressed area like Boston or San Francisco.

Some major European cities have resisted the trend to decentralizing suburbs by surrounding their town limits with compulsory "greenbelts" in which further commercial development other than farming is prohibited. Others maintain programs encouraging the construction of high-density, multi-unit housing in the center of town.

By influencing the bulk of people to remain in or near the center, those policies have preserved that area as the focal point of all community activities. The downtown is a vibrant, colorful place in which people of all income classes mix and mingle, enjoying a sense of community.

The large numbers of people going downtown for their evening entertainment support a prolific theater and cultural activity—not the civic "art centers" or solitary, 2,000-seat auditoriums of our U.S. cities (with their bland and bloodless productions designed not to offend), but dozens of private theaters, cafés, cabarets, and art galleries, experimental and daring.

European cities are fanatical about preserving their historic and/or period buildings. In many cities, when one pulls down a turn-of-the-century (or older) structure to modernize it, one is required to rebuild its facade to the earlier design, down to the last milli-meter, sometimes using the same bricks as were there before.

In those several major cities whose historic inner centers were destroyed or badly damaged in World War II—London, Prague, Warsaw—people did not take advantage of that devastation to build a modern, new city, but rather they restored the historic inner centers to precisely their prewar appearance.

In such cities as Paris and Madrid, after some much-regretted deviations from the same path, people have now reached a near-universal consensus to locate modern, high-rise buildings away from the center, in districts of their own, preserving the city's inner core in its earlier, classic form.

In London, constraints have been placed on the construction of downtown office buildings; people believe that to erect more of these towers in place of older, smaller structures is to create oases of death in a living city, to reduce vitality and excitement rather than to improve matters.

Those are the policies. You may want to discuss them with the Europeans you meet in your hotel or pension, in the theatre bars or sidewalk cafés. Now, in the further course of your stay, relate those views to the wholly different paths taken by the major new cities of the American Sun Belt—Houston, Dallas, Atlanta, and Phoenix, among others. Here, the downtown in its traditional form has all but disappeared, to be replaced by office buildings, office buildings, office buildings. At night the streets surrounding these towers are scenes of desolation and death.

For the grand, rococo theatres that once were downtown, substitute the tiny cinemas in the suburban shopping malls. For a life of window-shopping and camaraderie, substitute long hours in an automobile, endlessly spent on highways cutting like an ugly scar through a once-pleasant scene of tree-lined streets and small or medium-sized buildings.

For high density, substitute the very opposite: sprawling tracts of one-family homes in areas a dozen miles and more from the city center. There live the middle class and rich who no longer see, meet, hear, or suffer the poor.

As for historic preservation, our most "dynamic" cities again follow a totally different course from that of Europe. In place of neo-Gothic churches, distinguished Victorian homes and clubs, modest but attractive department stores, they have erected still more of the office towers. On the former sites of magnificent train terminals, demolished without thought or contrition, they have thrown up box-like skyscrapers.

Now come the lessons and benefits of travel. Having made the comparison, ask yourself which form of city supports a higher quality of life? Which type—high-density European or low-density American—creates a greater sense of community, and reduces the alienation of modern life? Which maintains a higher level of culture, discourse and learning: London or Los Angeles, Munich or Phoenix?

Talk to the Europeans you meet. Ask them about their city as a city. How do they feel about having no automobile and making use instead of public transportation? Do they yearn for the suburbs? Would they prefer to replace their visits to the heavily attended theatres and movies of downtown with a smaller cinema in a shopping mall? You will receive a variety of answers—all of them instructive and a possible guide to your own life.

This year, as you rush from the Uffizi Galleries to the Pitti Palace, from the Louvre to the new Musée d'Orsay, pause to consider the contemporary life of Europe, and especially the organization of its cities. Nothing, as I have said, could be more instructive—a major dividend of your European trip.

The New World of Travel 1997

The life blood of the Arthur Frommer travel guides is the correspondence received from readers, commenting on the establishments recommended in the texts and recommending new establishments. Each such letter is carefully studied, and when a particular lead seems promising, it is followed up and personally checked.

It is hoped *The New World of Travel* will receive similar assistance from its readers. A yearly publication, issued near the start of each year, *The New World of Travel* will constantly grow. And since much of its contents relates to organizations that lack the means to market themselves properly, or come to the attention of a travel journalist, your help is invaluable in alerting me to the organizations—hospitality exchanges, alternative resorts, new travel clubs, and the like—that you have discovered.

If you become aware of a new travel organization, program, or development that deserves to be described in our next edition, *The New World of Travel 1997,* won't you please let me know about it? Send your letters to Arthur Frommer, *The New World of Travel,* 1841 Broadway, New York, NY 10023. All letters will be acknowledged, and all are warmly appreciated in advance, by the author.

XIII

Cost-Cutting Clubs and Organizations, Cost-Cutting Devices for Travel

Ten Varied Travel Organizations That Bring You Better, Cheaper Travel

Clubs and Exchanges, Schools and Retreats, Passes and Programs, Fitting into No Established Categories— An Assortment of Travel Firms That Can Change Your Travel Life

If Adam Smith returned to life (and I'm referring to the 18th-century economist, not the current-day journalist), he'd be rather pleased with the travel industry: it's largely a free-market dream. Except for the transportation element of it—increasingly dominated by a few large carriers—the activity consists of thousands upon thousands of relatively small and little-known entrepreneurs scrambling to improve upon their competitors' products.

Among those mini-units are a thousand particular firms whose approach to travel, in my view, is meaningful, innovative, and exciting, and it is that charmed number of organizations—1,200 or so, to be exact—that account for the bulk of our discussion.

A remaining 10 firms fail to fit, however, into any of our preceding categories. Hence the following chapter dealing with a few last miscellaneous and sometimes rather odd organizations that can nevertheless have a major beneficial impact on your next trip:

1. Networking the "A.T.s"

"Appropriate Technology" or "Alternative Technology" ("A.T.") is a massive worldwide movement of people who believe in a simpler, gentler, human-scale life, non-industrial, cooperative, participatory—the dramatic opposite of the factory-polluted, harshly competitive, and hierarchical world of autos and metallic wastes in which most of us live. Its advocates are found in every nation, on organic farms and in vegetarian restaurants, at "New Era" bookshops and solar-energy centers, in consumer co-ops and small utopian communities. And because they believe in pressing their views on others, they are the easiest people on earth to get to know. Regardless of your own beliefs, you add a new dimension and intellectual growth to your travels when you meet and interact with these mild-mannered but highly motivated, free-thinking people.

But how do you meet them? Though it wasn't intended for that purpose, the quarterly newspaper/newsletter called *TRANET,* for *Transnational Network for Appropriate Technologies,* is a highly useful "guidebook" to alternative technology people in every nation. Its primary goal is to apprise alternative technology advocates of developments in their specialties in other lands. But recent editions have contained extensive directories of addresses for the specific purpose of encouraging well-focused, carefully planned, international travel by persons exploring A.T. Thus, issue 48 listed 200 sources of "alternative travel," while issue 42 listed organizations engaged in "cross-cultural, people-to-people linkages" across national boundaries; by contacting them, one arranges to meet "people who are changing the world by changing their own lives . . . adopting alternative technologies." Issue 43 was called "Alternatives Down Under" and provided the addresses of scores of contacts in Australia and New Zealand for experiencing those approaches. Issue 51 has a similar directory to alternative movements and peoples in the otherwise highly conformist nation of Japan, and issue 53—did the same for Southeast Asia.

Such contacts are the supreme essence of meaningful travel, says *TRANET.* Journeys should produce not simply a "tolerance" of foreign people, but "a love of our differences. . . . We need to invite them to our homes, to visit them in theirs. We need to participate in their alternative celebrations, to eat their foods, to honor their ceremonies, to explore their wild places, to understand their human rights issues, to see how they confront their governments."

Though a year's subscription to *TRANET* is a hefty $30, back issues will be sent to you for $5 apiece. You'll want to start with the remarkable directory to Australia and New Zealand (no. 43), then perhaps go to the earlier one on "People-to-People Networking" worldwide (no. 42). Contact **TRANET, P.O. Box 567, Rangeley, ME 04970 (phone 207/ 864-2252)** or use e-mail: tranet@igc.apc.org.

2. Cattle-Herding Holidays

Consider, now, the latest initiative of the tireless Patricia Dickerman of New York City.

In 1948, alone in a battered coupe, she bumped along the rural dirt roads of America, persuading skeptical farmers to accept her guests and thus create a new holiday industry and a new source of income for themselves: farm vacations. She later did the same at working ranches. Her classic book of 1949, *Farm, Ranch, & Country Vacations* ($12 postpaid), updated approximately every three years, is the oldest continually published travel guide in America.

Now, fulfilling everyone's secret desire to lead the life of a cowboy, she arranges for actual participation by us city types in real-life cattle drives in Wyoming, Arizona, Colorado, New Mexico, and Montana, moving herds to pastures with better grass. Costs average $85 to $110 per person per day, including everything: chuckwagon meals, tents or sleeping bags under the stars, your own horse to ride. If nothing else, says Pat, "you'll have a new respect for a hamburger and the hard work that goes into producing it."

For her new book on cattle drives, *Cowboy Vacations,* send $10 to **Adventure Guides, 7550 East McDonald Drive, Scottsdale, AZ 85250 (phone 602/596-0226 or 800/ 252-7899)**.

3. A Reputable Student Exchange

The very finest form of travel, bar none, is a several-month stay in a foreign home, enjoyed in the teenage years of one's life. I weep for those students who miss out on these life-enhancing, maturing experiences simply because their schools haven't publicized the offerings (which happens more than you'd expect).

The solution: Acquire the information yourself and then deal directly with the sponsoring organization.

A 125-page publication from the Council on Standards for International Educational Travel describes the student programs offered by 55 reputable U.S. organizations and provides the facts for selecting the group from which to request further information. Listed are not simply the "giants"—Experiment in International Living, Youth for Understanding, American Field Service—but also the smaller, specialized ones as well, like the Educational Foundation for Foreign Study ($4,290 all inclusive, for 10 months in Europe with volunteer host families, while attending European public schools; note its full scholarship for students creatively talented in the arts); or the Iberoamerican Cultural Exchange Program ($775 for a six-week stay with a Mexican family, $2,500 for a full school year, excluding air fare). Scholarship aid is heavily stressed.

Request the *Advisory List of International Educational Travel and Exchange Programs 1991–1992* from **CSIET, 3 Loudoun St. Lessburg, VA 22075 (phone 703/ 771-2040)**, and enclose $8.50 for the cost of the booklet, postage, and handling.

4. King of the Discount Books

Though more than two million are sold each year, scarcely a copy appears in bookstores, and use of the so-called Entertainment Books is thus confined to those relatively few savvy Americans who purchase them from nonprofit clubs, service groups, and other civic organizations. Yet each book entitles the bearer to near-50% discounts at restaurants, sporting events, movies, live theaters, and other recreational facilities, even at scattered hotels in that person's home city—or in the 73 other major U.S. cities for which Entertainment Books are published.

Bulky as dictionaries, the books consist of perforated discount coupons offering "two-for-one" dining or admissions, or straight 50% reductions, at scores of establishments. Some 111 books are published each year, one for each of the 104 largest American and Canadian cities and regions, plus 7 international destinations.

Of course, the discount doesn't always work out to 50%. When two of you order a $15 and $11 entrée, respectively, at a listed restaurant, it is the cheaper entrée (the $11 one) that comes free; and drinks and dessert aren't included in the "two-for-one" offer. As for the hotel discounts, a major portion of them are valid for lightly booked weekend stays only. Yet though the dining discount works out to 30% on average, and some of the weekend hotel discounts are of dubious value, the savings overall are substantial indeed. Two million families wouldn't budge from their homes without their Entertainment Books.

Individual city books cost $27.95 to $48.95 apiece, depending on the city, and often pay for themselves in one or two days of travel or use. Almost all are sold in bulk to nonprofit organizations that then quietly resell them to members in fund-raising programs. But since Entertainment Publications, Inc. (a 30-year-old publicly owned company), has offices in most of the largest cities, they can usually be contacted directly by the public (and books purchased) by simply looking up the words "Entertainment Publications" or "Entertainment Passbooks" in your local phone directory. Or you can go directly to the headquarters of **Entertainment Publications, Inc., 2125 Butterfield Rd., Troy, MI 48084 (phone 313/637-8400)**, If you do contact them directly, consider buying the condensed one-volume nationwide Entertainment Book called *Travel America at Half Price* ($37.95).

5. Vacations from a Barter Firm

"Barter" is the exchange of product for product, and nowhere is the activity more intensely pursued than in the travel industry. Airlines trade seats for radio commercials, cruise ships trade cabins for stationery and supplies, hotels trade rooms for ads on the sides of buses. Since each of the "traders" has unused capacity or excess merchandise, they are exchanging items that might have gone unsold in any event—thus the trade costs them nothing (so goes the theory).

But who ends up sitting in the airplane seats, or sleeping in the hotel rooms and cruise-ship berths, that have been "bartered"? Since there's an obvious limit to the number of trips that radio station personnel and staffs of advertising agencies can themselves use (or else they'd be on perpetual vacation!), the excess "travel credits" are sold by dozens of so-called barter companies to large corporations or special groups, at prices heavily discounted from normal levels. Among those firms, a small but growing number (a handful, really) are currently selling their credits—sharply reduced air tickets, cruises, car rentals, tour packages, hotel stays—directly to individual members of the public, among others.

In the Southeast, the behemoth of the barterers is **Lino and Associates, 6950 Central Avenue, Suite 140, St. Petersburg, FL 33707 (phone 813/384-3700)**; and it is willing to deal with the public (I asked). Call, write, or visit, and you'll pick up a broad variety of trips and tickets at substantial discounts. In the East and West, the leading firms are, respectively, **Travel World Leisure Club, Inc., 225 W. 34th St., Suite 909, New York, NY 10122 (phone 212/239-4855 or toll free 800/444-TWLC)**, and **Communications Development Corp., 1454 Euclid St., Santa Monica, CA 90404 (phone 310/828-2122)**. Both sell deeply discounted tour packages, cruises, and air tickets, and have no objection to selling them in "ones and twos," to even a single person or couple contemplating a trip. For precisely what were these tours, cruises, and tickets originally exchanged? For a TV spot late at night, or a billboard in the country, or even a paint job in the airline's office!

6. "RV" Travel to Europe

Ever heard of "caravanning"? People with recreational vehicles—motor homes, camper vans—meet up at a departure point and travel as a group to attractive destinations. There they use their bed-equipped devices for overnight accommodations, but every day board a single sightseeing motorcoach for touring, exactly as they would on a standard, escorted tour.

Popular for many years within the United States, "caravanning" is now being offered to Americans for touring overseas. How? By flying recreational vehicle enthusiasts to a foreign site, and there providing them with rented, foreign recreational vehicles, again as part of a group.

Creative World Rallies and Travels, 606 N. Carrollton Ave, New Orleans, LA 70119, (phone 504/486-7259 or toll free 800/REC-VEES outside Louisiana), is by far the leader in the activity. Although it has been organizing domestic group trips for 18 years, its overseas caravans—on which travelers drive a motor home temporarily assigned to them—are of far more recent vintage. Yet the program has already grown to include three scheduled caravans to Australia and New Zealand, one ambitious trip to Eastern Europe (fly to Munich and pick up a German motorhome there for touring through Germany, Poland, and Czechoslovakia), and one of "Alpine Europe" (Austria, Switzerland, and Bavaria), always in spring, summer, and fall.

Durations of stay are lengthy—they average 32 days—and yet the cost is less than $3,900, including round-trip air from Atlanta (or, if requested, from other U.S. cities), a large number of restaurant meals en route, extensive sightseeing, use of the motor home, all campsite fees, and group leaders. "For what other people spend for two weeks staying in hotels," says Creative World's founder and president, 41-year-old Bill LaGrange, "we can provide five and six weeks abroad in a motor home." And is this not an exceptional travel method, staying close to the land and peoples of the countries you visit?

7. Visits to a "Homestead"

Next, a short trip to bask in the glow of the late Scott Nearing, who remained handsome, vigorous, and creative until his recent death at the age of 100. He, as you may recall, was the 1920s radical ousted from teaching positions because of his far-advanced views. Whereupon he and his wife, Helen, determined to end their dependency on society by moving first to Vermont and then to an abandoned farm in Maine, where they developed the practice of homesteading to a fine art: producing goods and services for their own consumption, self-sufficiently, without the intervention of a market or the use of cash.

A stream of books from their fertile pens— *Living the Good Life, Continuing the Good Life,* and *Simple Food for the Good Life,* among others—brought thousands of visitors each year to their Forest Farm and stone house built with their own hands, where Helen and Scott demonstrated the virtues of a fresh-food diet, gardening, composting, pond and dam building, and lectured on other, broader social themes. Despite Scott's death, 91-year-old Helen is still willing to receive visitors, provided they make advance contact with the nearby **Social Science Institute, Harborside, ME 04642 (phone 207/ 326-8211)**, to which royalties from the Nearings' books are assigned, and which also sells their books through the mails (request a catalog). According to Helen Nearing, it is possible to visit Forest Farm during the summer and fall. She devotes the other seasons to travel and writing. Accommodations and meals are available in the town of Blue Hill, approximately 20 miles away.

Care to change your life? The farm and books of Scott and Helen Nearing have done that for multitudes before you.

8. Foam-Rubber Bus Travel

From the innards of a large motorcoach, all the seats have been removed and then replaced by a foam-rubber platform. Why? So that 38 adventurous souls can stretch out to sleep, their heads on knapsacks or rolled-up coats, while the bus hurtles through the night. Daytime, the same passengers recline in varying positions, while some strum guitars or play the classics on a reedy flute. In vehicles so oddly outfitted, enabling an obvious lowering of travel costs (and an obvious camaraderie), the most casual (but perhaps the most insightful) of American tourists are today exploring geographic wonders of the U.S.A., Mexico, and Canada.

Some use the foam-rubber method to cross the country. Once every two weeks or so from May through mid-October, from each coast (New York and Boston in the East, San Francisco in the West), buses of the celebrated Green Tortoise line embark for an 11-day transcontinental adventure traversing 5,000 miles each way, yet costing only $299 to $329 per person. The buses drive mainly at night. In the day, passengers go river-rafting on the Colorado, explore major national parks (Bryce, Zion, Yellowstone, Badlands, Tetons, depending on itinerary), and go wandering about all over the continental states.

Other Green Tortoise trips go to Baja California and mainland Mexico in the winter, to Yosemite throughout the year, up and down the West Coast. Though singles predominate, Green Tortoise urges—and receives—patronage from families and senior citizens. On one four-week tour to Alaska, the average age aboard was 45.

On all trips, passengers contribute about $7 each per day to a food "kitty" used to purchase vittles for a twice-daily cooperative cookout. Breakfast is coffee, eggs, and rolls purchased at various truckers' stops, or else "gourmet vegetarian" if participants are bestirred to purchase and prepare the necessary ingredients.

One of the few survivors of a number of alternative bus companies established in the late 1960s—they included the Briar Rabbit and the American Gypsy—Green Tortoise is no Greyhound, but still a flourishing company that publishes an irresistible periodic tabloid, *Tortoise Trails,* about its most recent tour successes. For detailed information, contact **Green Tortoise, 494 Broadway, San Francisco, CA 94133 (phone 415/821-0803 or toll free 800/ 227-4766 outside California).**

9. British Motor Homes

Ever vacationed in a recreational vehicle? Then why not do so in Britain? The campsites and trailer parks there are as numerous as here, and large fleets of what the English call "motor caravans" are available for rental from numerous firms, at rates of $364 to $483 a week for the June-July-August use of a "camper/van" sleeping four adults, while larger and more luxurious motor homes in summer go for $427 to $533 a week (sleeping four) and for $490 to $623 a week (sleeping six). Rates are considerably less in all other months, and cover everything except

gasoline, food, and nominal charges for campsites. In a vehicle fully equipped with beds and sleeping bags, toilets, and all cooking and eating utensils, you'll wander the British Isles without fear of high hotel rates or fully booked hotels, and share the company of camping English people, all at marvelously low rates. Among the largest of the British firms (300 motor homes for rent) is **Apex Leisure Hire, London Road, Staines, Middlesex, U.K. TW18 FJJ (phone 07/8446-3233).**

10. Chautauqua

From late June to the end of August, the village of Chautauqua, New York, 100 miles from Buffalo, is filled to the eaves—and I use the word advisedly—with 10,000 visitors at a time, all in search of intellectual stimulation, spiritual balm, and cultural enrichment. If you're to be among them, or at least housed in acceptable accommodations, you've got to make your reservations early in winter.

Chautauqua, once described as an "intellectual Club Med," is a Victorian village frozen in time, virtually unchanged from its appearance in the 1890s. Then, and through the 1930s, it was a cultural capital of America, a national forum whose "institute" sponsored book clubs and traveling speakers (the "Chautauqua circuit") to bring new ideas and the latest developments to communities across the nation. Its own lecture platform welcomed the key celebrities of the time—Ulysses S. Grant and Theodore Roosevelt, Leo Tolstoy and Amelia Earhart; its meeting halls housed important world conferences.

Today, in summer, the multiple theaters, concert stages, lecture halls, conference and classrooms, and giant 6,000-seat amphitheater of Chautauqua provide a dizzying daily array of morning, afternoon, and evening speeches and seminars, concerts, recitals, and performances of every sort—English-language opera, theater, orchestras, political and inspirational talks, educational courses, arts and crafts workshops, and

Great Books seminars—supplemented by all the standard summer recreations. Speakers in 1995 ranged from Supreme Court Justice Sandra Day O'Connor to author Kurt Vounegut to children's advocate Marion Wright Edelman.

"Gate tickets" to all daily events and courses at Chautauqua cost a reasonable $10 for the day, $28 for both day and evening sessions for adults (but only $150 per week), free for children 12 and under. To this you add widely varying accommodations and meal costs (all quite reasonable) in Chautauqua's dozens of hotels, apartments, inns, and bed-and-breakfast homes, which expand each summer to accommodate thousands each night. But to get the best rooms at the best prices—sometimes to get any room at all—you should reserve before spring, or by mid-spring at the latest.

For literature or for a free accommodations directory, write or phone **Chautauqua, P.O. Box 1095, Chautauqua, NY 14722 (phone 716/357-6200 or 800/836-ARTS)**. For bookings, or immediate information, call the **Accommodations Referral Service (phone 716/357-6204 or toll free 800/ 333-0884)**.

Reductions in Price for the Traveling Theater-Goer

Discount Ticket Stands Have Proliferated Throughout the Country—And Around the World

Travelers to New York City usually pay $40 to $50 and more for the average theater seat. Residents of New York City frequently pay $20 to $25 for the very same seat.

Travelers to London, Paris, and a dozen other major theater cities almost always pay the same full price. Knowledgeable residents there often pay half.

Surely the largest single gap in travel information relates to the half-price facility for theater-going that's made available in every major theater city of the world. Though guidebooks often refer to the famous half-price "TKTS" (tickets) booth in New York's Times Square, they almost always overlook the very same facility in a dozen other towns, thus depriving their readers of an important opportunity to save.

All the booths below sell same-day tickets (when available) for half the normal price, plus a small service charge (usually 75¢ to $2). Some also sell full-price tickets for future dates, but that's not the main reason for patronizing them.

London: The half-price booth on Leicester Square, clearly marked and easily found, sells tickets to all 40 or so West End theaters, and for some concerts too, and is open daily except Sunday from noon to 2pm for matinees and 2:30 to 6:30pm for evening shows.

Paris: Just behind the Madeleine Church on the Right Bank (place de la Madeleine, 15; Métro stop is Madeleine), the Kiosque Théâtre sells seats at half price on the day of performance, and is open Monday through Saturday from noon to 8pm and on Sunday from noon to 4pm. A supplementary Kiosk is operated in the Gare Montparnasse. Tickets are often available for concert recitals and variety cabaret, in addition to the standard plays and musicals.

> The smart traveler buys tickets as residents do—on the day of performance, for half price.

Sydney, Australia: You pick up last-minute half-price tickets for theaters, and for musical and dance events as well, at Martin Place, City Center, on Castlereagh Street; open weekdays from noon to 5:30pm and on Saturday from noon to 5pm.

Toronto: "Five Star Tickets," at two locations—the main lobby of the Royal Ontario Museum, and on Yonge Street near Dundas Street, outside the Eaton Centre—sells half-price tickets to the great majority of the city's plays and musicals, including those of small nonprofit companies. It's open Monday through Saturday from noon to 6pm and on Sunday from 11am to 2pm.

New York: There are two "TKTS" booths attracting heavy patronage: on a traffic island in Times Square (at 47th Street, open daily from 10am for matinee seats, from 3pm for evening performances), and in the World Trade Center (building 2) in the financial district, open Tuesday through Friday from 11am to 5:30pm and on Saturday from 11am to 3:30pm). The latter location is far less busy than the booth on Times Square, and rarely requires standing in line. New York also operates a Music and Dance booth selling day-of-performance half-price tickets to concerts, recitals, and ballet, on 42nd Street between Fifth and Sixth Avenues, just along-side Bryant Park; open Tuesday through Saturday from noon to 2pm and 3 to 7pm and on Sunday (selling Monday seats as well) from noon to 6pm.

San Francisco: Its "STBS" (pronounced "Stubs") booth on Union Square (at 251 Stockton, between Post and Geary Streets) is an "interdisciplinary" outlet selling half-price tickets for theater, music, and dance, open Tuesday through Saturday only (it sells Sunday and Monday tickets on Saturday) from 11am to 6pm, Tuesday through Thursday, 11am to 7pm on Friday and Saturday. On the weekend when I researched this chapter, it had half-price tickets available to 17 shows—pity the uninformed tourist who paid full price!

Minneapolis/St. Paul: In this highly active center of the performing arts, half-price tickets are broadly available, Tuesday through Saturday from noon to 6pm, at the "Tickets to Go" outlets in the IDS Center of downtown Minneapolis, and in the Town Square of St. Paul; Sunday tickets can be purchased on Saturday. These are almost always for theater performances only, but occasionally as well for the St. Paul chamber orchestra and mime troupe.

Washington, D.C.: "TICKETplace" is the spot, at the Listener Auditorium on the campus of George Washington University, 730 21st Street NW (corner of H Street, two blocks east of the Foggy Bottom metro stop), noon to 4pm from Tuesday through Friday, 11am to 5pm on Saturday (when you can purchase tickets for Sunday or Monday). You can also phone 202/842-5387 to learn what half-price tickets are available that evening—a service most other cities don't offer.

Boston: "BOSTIX," in Faneuil Hall Market Place, at the corner of Congress and State

Streets, is occasionally stocked with same-day half-price tickets for sports events, in addition to the more usual reduced-price seats for theater, music, and dance. Open Tuesday through Sunday from 11am to 5pm.

Chicago: "HOT TIX" discounts to nearly 50 theaters, from locations at 24 South St. in the heart of the Loop, the Park Square Atrium in Oak Park, and 1616 Sherman Ave. in Evanston. Figure hours of 10am to 3pm generally, but until 6pm at the Loop location. Tuesday through Saturday; Sunday tickets can be purchased on Saturday.

Denver: The "Ticket Bus"—a bright-red British double-decker—is parked at 16th and Curtis Streets, downtown, from noon to 6pm on weekdays and 11am to 3pm on Saturday (when you can also buy half-price Sunday tickets).

San Diego: Try the "Times Arts Tix Booth" in the lobby of the Spreckels Theatre at 121 Broadway, at the corner of First Avenue; open Tuesday through Saturday from 10am to 6pm. On Saturday you can purchase not only Saturday tickets but those for Sunday and Monday as well.

Pittsburgh: "TIX," at U.S.X. Plaza, at the corner of Grant and Sixth Avenues, open Monday through Saturday from 11am to 6pm, is a final half-price outlet for tickets to theater, music, and dance. Buy Sunday tickets on Saturday.

You might want to keep this chapter in mind for a future trip, because—to my knowledge—news of such reductions is rarely conveyed to tourists, and certainly isn't available from another single source. But at the very least, it may cause you to make inquiries about half-price tickets whenever you travel to a theater town. Like airplane seats and cruise-ship cabins, theater seats are perishable commodities—and wherever that's the case, discounters are at hand.

Like airplane seats and cruise-ship cabins, theater tickets are perishable commodities—and wherever that's the case, discounters are at hand.

XIV

Traveling in the Mature Years

Our Greatest Retirement Bargain—Extended-Stay Vacations

A Month in Spain for $999, Including Air Fare

If I could bestow an academy award for travel, it would be to the operators of extended-stay vacations to Spain in the winter months. Next to the values offered by these one-month (and longer) sojourns, all other tour programs seem tawdry rip-offs, high-priced scams.

I am standing, in my fantasy, on the great curving stage of the Dorothy Chandler Pavilion in Los Angeles. I rip open the envelope and shout to the world: "The winners are" (pause): "Sun Holidays of Boca Raton and Grand Circle Tours—for their 'Extended Stays'!"

And as they drag me to a psycho ward (overlooking the blue Pacific), I struggle to explain the concept:

Almost by definition, an extended-stay vacation takes place overseas in the off-season setting of a popular summer resort.

The hotels are desperate. Built to accommodate the great warm-weather crowds, they now stand empty and losing in the chillier months. Along comes a U.S. tour operator with the following pitch: "If you will rent us your rooms for $6 a night, we'll fill them off-season with retirees staying for at least 30 days. You'll still lose money, but you'll lose less. And your staff will be happy to stay active and receiving tips."

Almost by definition, an extended-stay vacation takes place overseas in the off-season setting of a popular summer resort.

To the airlines, a similar appeal: "Our one-month clients don't need the popular dates. Give us seats for $300, and we'll fill your flights on Tuesday nights."

To the public: "Why go in the winter to a mildewed motel and the plastic meals of fast-food chains? We'll fly you for less to glamorous foreign resorts. Sure, it's no longer hot in those places. But it's sunny and mild, and filled with exotica."

Thousands of mature U.S. travelers (and their numbers are growing) now say "Yes" to these attractive offers. They receive one of the great travel bargains, which seem particularly well packaged by the following:

Sun Holidays, to Spain's Mediterranean Coast ($999)

The undoubted price champion of the extended-stay companies, Sun charges a flat $999 from November 1 to March 31, for a full winter month on the Costa del Sol of Spain, including air fare. It flies you there and back from New York, Boston, or Miami ($110 more from Boston or Miami) on Iberia Airlines, meets you at the airport of Málaga, and transfers you by bus to the modern, high-rise Timor Sol Apartments on the beach of bustling Torremolinos (Europe's most heavily visited resort city in summer) with its dozens of hotels and varied tourist facilities. And there you stay for four weeks in a studio apartment with fully equipped kitchen, either making your own meals or taking them at restaurants nearby, enjoying maid service, an entertainment program, and the mild winter climate of Spain's southernmost shores (where it's too chilly at that time for ocean swimming, but otherwise entirely pleasant—and emptied of its often-oppressive summer crowds). For $196 more per person, you get a one-bedroom apartment for the month; for $105 per person per week, you get additional weeks. And thus, for as little as $1,319 per person, including air fare, you can stay for a full eight weeks on the Mediterranean coast of Spain!

Vacationing in this fashion, America's middle-aged and mature adults can now vacation in dignity at a modern, beachside resort and eat off linen and fine china at quality restaurants staffed with attentive Spanish waiters, instead of spending the fall and winter at a shabby, rusting motel of Miami Beach or Phoenix, and taking their meals at noisy fast-food restaurants.

The Sol Timor, "lead hotel" on Sun Holidays' extended stays. *Courtesy Sun Holiday.*

But why is winter so cheap on the Costa del Sol? Reason: it's no longer "swimming weather" there in the fall and winter. Indeed, it occasionally gets chilly at that time, even overcast, and traditional vacationers from Western Europe stay away. But the average autumn and winter afternoon highs are in the mid-60s, the sun usually shines, a sweater is required only at night, and the area has become heavily patronized by fall/winter "snowbirds" from the U.S.A.

When I first heard of these fall/winter "extended stay" vacations several years ago (and of the competing programs offered by other senior citizen specialists), I was skeptical as to whether the $999 figure was simply a "come-on," rarely available. I was then advised, and independently confirmed, that Sun Holidays now makes use of the entire 400-room capacity of the Timor Sol Hotel in which passengers paying the $999 are placed, and of the entire 350-room capacity of the nearby, upgraded Sol Aloha Puerto Hotel, at which persons paying $1,235 for a month (including air) are placed. Persons booking as late as November of this year are virtually assured of getting the $999 price, except perhaps for the Christmas period.

So many thousands of American retirees are now flown to the Costa del Sol each fall and winter, that their numbers now permit the operation of evening, English-language group activities, English-language movies, and daily tours with English-language commentaries to famous nearby cities of Andalucia (Seville, Granada, Cordoba, others). Indeed, this fall and winter, some operators will be providing three free-of-charge tours to their one-month clients, going to nearby small villages and towns in the mountains. The Spanish government tourist authorities and the villages themselves help subsidize those free excursions, as a gesture of welcome to the vacationing Americans.

Although there's no formal minimum age for the program, it's obvious that mature retirees are usually the only persons who can devote a month and more to a fall/winter vacation. Even if you're not in that category, you might want to bring these opportunities to the attention of friends or relatives of mature age, who will bless you for doing so—they're among the few travel programs that genuinely deserve to be called "miracles."

Sun Holidays has been operating these tours in close concert with Iberia Airlines for 15 years. Though a half-dozen other companies attempt the same thing—including such well-known senior-citizen specialists as Grand Circle Travel and Saga Holidays, no one else comes remotely close in price or value. An Oscar is clearly deserved. For a colorful free catalog describing several such lengthy stays in various resort areas of Spain, and a similar miracle of pricing for one-month winter vacations in Venezuela, near Sorrento, Italy, and on the Algarve coast of Portugal, contact **Sun Holidays, 7280 Palmetto Park Road, Boca Raton, FL 33433 (phone 800/243-2057).**

> **W**hy endure a shabby Miami motel and fast-food chains when Spain awaits?

Grand Circle Tours (also to Spain)

"Extended Stay Vacations" are also offered by other senior-citizen specialists, including the large **"Grand Circle Tours"** of Boston **(phone 800/859-0852)**, but not for as little as is charged by Sun Holidays. Write for their catalog covering the November-through-March period and you'll be able to spend such a holiday on the Mediterranean coast of Spain at a string of hotels differing from those used by Sun Holidays, at higher per-month charges. But less than a year ago, Grand Circle dramatically announced that it would henceforth operate such one-month-long vacations in the months of April and May as well, and that has created broader-than-ever options for mature travelers.

The details are in a four-color, 32-page catalog called "Spain & Portugal—February–May," available free from Grand Circle at the number listed above. Transportation to Spain is this time on Royal Air Maroc via Casablanca (and you stay in Casablanca for a night on the return trip). The hotel is the beachfront Hotel Bajondillo in a kitchen-equipped, utensils-equipped studio or (at a further additional charge) one-bedroom apartment. The one-month price is obtained by booking Grand Circle's $995 two-week tour of Torremolinos, and then adding extra weeks at $95 apiece, for a grand total of $1,195 (see pages 6 to 10 of the catalog). Departures are on Tuesdays and Thursdays through late May, and stays therefore extend into June! Though we're a bit concerned about this tough, competitive challenge to Sun Holidays, the pioneer, it's good to see another heavyweight of travel (Grand Circle moves more than 40,000 persons a year) creating budget-priced vacations for seasoned, mature travelers. Sun Holidays remains, of course, cheaper in the winter months, when its prices and hotels should be carefully compared with those of Grand Circle.

The Battle for the Older American Traveler

Five Major Travel Firms Are Following a Unique Approach in Their Sale of Vacations to Seniors

In the world of travel, what do older Americans really want?

That inquiry is the topic of the year among airlines and tour operators. As if, without warning, a new planet had swung into their sight, they've discovered that a startling percentage of all travel expenditures are made by people 55 and older. Not yuppies, not preppies, not even baby boomers, but rather senior citizens are today the "name of the game" in travel.

Young folks, it appears, go to the movies; older ones go on vacation.

"Our senior citizens," says one tour operator, "are feeling better about themselves, and that's why they're traveling more. They're healthier, living longer, more affluent. They have a new conviction that life is to be enjoyed for quite a while more, and this fairly recent attitude makes them the fastest-growing segment of the travel market."

Given that fact, it is surprising, as an initial note, to find so few companies serving the needs of the older American traveler. Apart from local motorcoach operators and purely ad hoc programs by regional firms, only five really major U.S. companies deal exclusively with the marketing and operation of far-ranging tours for seniors, and three of these are headquartered in one city: Boston. They are: Saga Holidays, Grand Circle Travel, Inc., and Elderhostel.

Having journeyed to Boston to view the first three, and phoned the fourth in California, I've been alternately impressed, startled, dismayed, and educated by several uniform ways in which they do business. Traveling seniors may want to consider the following observations on the major "tour operators for older Americans":

They Mainly Sell "Direct"

Not one of the "big five" deals with travel agents or sets aside a single percentage point of income for the latter. Each one heatedly insists that the processing of seniors' tours is a specialty requiring direct contact between them (the tour operators) and their clients (the actual senior travelers), usually via toll-free "800" numbers. Because the five firms adhere fiercely to their position, their brochures and catalogs are unavailable in travel agents' racks and can be obtained only by mail. Nor do they advertise in the general media. If you are not already on their mailing lists, you must specifically request their brochures by writing to the addresses listed below. Once you do, you'll soon receive a heavy packet of attractive four-color literature and application forms.

Not yuppies, not preppies, not even baby boomers, but rather senior citizens are today the "name of the game" in travel.

They Cater to "Older" Americans

Although people can theoretically use the services of the senior-citizen tour operators when they reach the tender ages of 50, 55, or 60 (50 for Gadabout and RFD, 55 for Grand Circle, 60 for Saga and Elderhostel), in practice they don't. The average age of Grand Circle's clients is 67, that of the others only slightly less. The apparent reason is that Americans no longer feel removed from younger age categories until they reach their early or mid-sixties. Advances in health care and longevity, better diets, and attention to exercise keep most of us youthful and vigorous into our late fifties, and reluctant to cease socializing—or vacationing—with younger people. (I recall growing apoplectic with rage when, on my 50th birthday, the mail brought an invitation to join AARP.) Who any longer even retires at the age of 65?

Their Clients Insist on the Exclusion of Younger Passengers

But when those mid-sixties are in fact reached, the newly elder turn with a vengeance to services of the specialists. After an initial reluctance to confine their travel companions to a single age group, today's 65-year-olds discover that they are of a different "mind set" from their younger co-citizens. Brought up during the Depression, sent to fight or work in World War II, denied the easy travel opportunities enjoyed by our blasé younger set, they better appreciate the joys of international travel, react with gratitude and awe to wonders of the world, enjoy the companionship of people who feel the same way.

They Possess a Historical Perspective Denied to the Younger Generation

Clearly, they share a wealth of experience and a common outlook; come from an education in the broad liberal arts as contrasted with the crudely materialistic, vocational outlook of so many of today's youth. And when they travel with younger people, they are often upset by the young folks, failure to share the same values or to be familiar with the events that so shaped their own lives. What mature American can enjoy a trip through Europe or the South Pacific with people who are only dimly aware of Franklin Roosevelt or Winston Churchill, of Douglas MacArthur or Field Marshal Rommel, of the Normandy Invasion or the Holocaust? Accordingly, they respond with eagerness to tour programs limited to persons of their own age.

Their Clients Receive Distinctly Different, Custom-Tailored Travel Arrangements

In addition to confining their groups to an older age range, the major tour companies earn their allegiance by providing arrangements that are significantly different from those designed for a general clientele. "We avoid the modern hotels, with their small public spaces, their in-room videos and bars," explains a specialist. "We look for traditional buildings with large lobbies for congregating and sitting—our clients prefer camaraderie to in-room movies! We also insist on a location within distance of everything important."

"We pace our tours to avoid overly long hours on a bus," explains another. "But we keep our passengers active, always on the move. Older travelers have had enough of sitting around at home; they want constant experiences and encounters."

Though the tours are of a longer duration than the normal variety, they are rarely for more than three weeks at a time. "People in retirement like to take two and three trips in a year," says the president of one firm. "They tour a particular destination for two or three weeks, then want to try something else."

In planning tours for the older American, the great majority of departures are scheduled for off-season periods—not in July or August to Europe, for instance, but in the "shoulder" and "off-peak" months when retired people are the best possible prospects for travel. "We get better rates for them that way," says a tour official. "And they're better appreciated at that time by the suppliers. They get more and better attention."

But Their Prices Are Higher Than the Norm

So much for the good news. The bad news is that the tours planned for senior citizens only are generally higher priced than similar trips sold to all ages. This is not to say that the former do not use better hotels, provide closer and more personal attention, supply more tour ingredients. They may or may not. But except for Elderhostel—whose prices are truly remarkable—not one of the senior-citizen specialists has opted to service the needs of intensely cost-conscious Americans; their tour products are generally $100 to $300 higher than the motorcoach programs or "stay-put" holidays available from several of the low-cost tour operators serving a general public, sometimes for suspiciously similar features. This, to me, is a serious mistake on their part, limiting their programs to an upper-middle-class clientele and bypassing the budget-limited majority of the older generation. When a tour company—perhaps a wholly new one—begins offering modestly priced tours for exclusive use by older citizens, it will, in my view, be flooded with bookings (as Elderhostel is).

> Tour companies earn their allegiance by providing arrangements that differ significantly from those designed for a general clientele.

The Programs Themselves

What do the specialists offer, and how do they differ one from the other? Here's a quick rundown:

Saga Holidays, 222 Berkeley Street, Boston, MA 02116 (phone 617/262-2262 or toll free 800/343-0273 outside Massachusetts), is perhaps the largest of the lot, resulting from the activity of its British parent company, which each year sends over 250,000 senior citizens on vacation. To tap into that major movement (and the bargaining power it represents), the U.S. organization routes many of its transatlantic tours through London, there to combine its older American travelers into one group with older British and Australian passengers. Such blending of English-speaking nationalities adds "zip" to any tour, they claim, and I agree. On board the buses, frolicsome passengers quip that Saga means "Send-a-Granny-Away" or "Sex-and-Games-for-the-Aged" (the latter very much tongue-in-cheek).

After traveling with Saga, passengers are invited to join the Saga Holidays Club and receive a quarterly magazine supplemented by newsletters. The latter's most appealing feature is a page of travel "personals"—older people seeking other older people to join them on a trip. But primarily, the literature establishes a feeling of kinship with other members, who all must be 60 years of age.

Saga's major stock-in-trade is escorted motorcoach tours: heavily (and throughout the year) within the United States, heavily in Europe, but also in Mexico, in Australia and the Far East, and in South America. Although it also offers cruises and extended stays, it is the escorted motorcoach, competitively priced, that most of its clients demand. Recently, an ingenious "Road Scholar" plan of serious lectures delivered en route has added more than the usual content to several popular motorcoach itineraries.

Grand Circle Travel, Inc., 347 Congress St., Boston, MA 02210 (phone 617/350-7500 or toll free 800/248-3737), is the oldest of the U.S. firms dealing only with senior citizens, but recently rejuvenated through its acquisition by an enterprising travel magnate, Alan E. Lewis, who has injected considerable new resources and vigor (quarterly magazine, *Pen Pal,* and travel-partner service) into it. In business for 37 years, it enjoys a large and loyal following, who respond especially to offers of extended-stay vacations in off-season months, and to low-cost foreign areas with mild climates. The greater number of Grand Circle's passengers are those spending, say, 2 to 20 weeks on the Mediterranean coast of Spain, in a seaside kitchenette apartment supplied with utensils, china, and cutlery. Others go for several weeks to Portugal and Madeira, the Canary Islands, the Balearics. Wherever, the tour company argues (and quite successfully) that older Americans can enjoy a "full season" at these exotic locations for not much more than they'd spend to Florida or other domestic havens. While neither Spain nor Portugal offers swimming weather in winter, their low prices enable seniors (even those living mainly on Social Security) to vacation in dignity, enjoying good-quality meals and modern apartments in place of the fast-food outlets and shabby motels to which they're often relegated here at home. Grand Circle's extended stays are supplemented by nearly a dozen other programs—Alaskan cruises, Canadian holidays, inexpensive homestays, tours to Europe and the Orient—booked by thousands, but not yet as popular as those "stay-put" vacations for several weeks in a balmy, foreign clime.

Elderhostel, 75 Federal St., Boston, MA 02110 (phone 617/426-7788), is, in a nutshell, the much discussed, increasingly popular, nonprofit group that works with 1,900 U.S. and foreign educational institutions to provide seniors 60 and over with residential study courses at unbeatable costs: $320 per week for room, board, and tuition (but not including air fare) in the U.S. and Canada; an average of $2,500 for three weeks abroad, this time including air fare. Accommodations and meals are in student residence halls or underused youth hostels.

Those are the "nutshell" facts, which can't do justice to the gripping appeal of Elderhostel's course descriptions. Who can withstand "The

Mystery and Miracle of Medieval Cathedrals" (taught at a school overlooking the Pacific)? Or "Everything You Always Wanted to Know About Music But Were Too Afraid to Ask" (at a university in Alabama)? Or "Gods, Kings, and Temples" (at a classroom in Cairo)? They make you yearn to be 60!

With more than 300,000 traveling students anticipated for 1996, Elderhostel is the once-and-future travel giant, fervently acclaimed by its elderly devotees. "Thank you, Elderhostel!" wrote one senior in a recent publication. "We've built beaver dams in Colorado, explored temples in Nepal, ridden outrigger canoes in Fiji, sat on the lawn sipping coffee at Cambridge University, eaten with our fingers at private homes in Bombay, where they venerate older people!"

Gadabout Tours, 700 East Tahquitz Canyon, Palm Springs, CA 92262 (phone 800/952-5068 or 619/325-5556), 29 years in business, specializes in escorted tours of the United States, and utilizes an innovative method (on many, but not all, tours) of avoiding the fatigue and stress of packing and unpacking as participants go from place to place. Rather, it places its groups into one hotel "base" per region, and then operates circular trips every day from there, returning each night to the same hotel, where participants stay for the entire duration of their tour. They unpack only once. It's an approach that has found much favor with its mature customers. Though a few summer trips are scheduled to Europe, a few winter ones to Central and South America, Australia and Asia, most departures are to the standard national parks, country music hot spots (Branson, for instance), and the

historic towns of New England. A decided plus: rather moderate prices averaging only slightly more than $100 a day for domestic tours.

RFD Travel Corporation, 5201 Johnson Drive, Mission, KS 66205 (phone 800/ 365-5359), is similarly priced, a larger organization (indeed, one of the giants in the senior citizen field) in business for 23 years, and a particular favorite of midwestern travelers in their senior years. Its programs span the world, utilizing every form of transportation; concentrate on rural villages, country inns, farm visits and the like in Europe; and, while limiting its groups to persons 50 and over, has recently added several "grandparents and grandchildren" tours to domestic locations, like an "American Heritage" tour to colonial Williamsburg, Washington, D.C., Philadelphia, and the Blue Ridge Mountains. Specify the area of the world in which you're interested when requesting catalogs.

The Prices They Charge

Those are the five specialists. Why aren't they (with the exception of Elderhostel) cheaper? With such huge resources and immense followings, the senior-citizen tour operators are capable of achieving major price breakthroughs for their elderly clientele. The disquieting thing is that they don't.

A leisurely trip to Rome.
Courtesy Trafalgar Tours.

In the area of extended stays, a well-known nonspecialist, **Sun Holidays, 7280 Palmetto Park Road, Boca Raton, FL 33433 (phone toll free 800/243-2057)** takes people of all ages to modern apartment-hotels on Spain's Costa del Sol, in winter, for a charge per month (the first month) of $999 per person, including round-trip air fare from New York on Iberia Airlines. Two of the major senior-citizen specialists (I am of course excluding Elderhostel) charge $100 to $400 more on most of their winter departures for virtually the same one-month stay (although the costlier tour includes a night, with meals, in London at both the start and end of the trip, and a slightly larger apartment). The senior-citizen companies also include insurance worth about $30.

In the field of escorted motorcoach tours, the well-known **Trafalgar Tours,** selling to young and old alike, charges $1,688 for a 15-day tour of Britain, air fare included, and $1,888 for a classic 16-day tour of Europe, air fare included. One of the major senior-citizen specialists (I am again excluding Elderhostel) charges $1,899 for a 16-day tour of Britain, air fare included, and charges $2,159 for a quite similar 17-day tour of Europe, air fare included. Another so-called specialist charges over $2,000 for nearly everything. While hotels on the highest priced of these tours are marginally better than Trafalgar's, they do not support (in my opinion) a differential of that magnitude; and most other features of the tours are similar.

Should companies be surcharging the senior citizen by $100 to $400 per person for the right to travel only with other senior citizens? Shouldn't older Americans, of all people, enjoy the lowest of travel costs? Especially when they are dealing directly with the tour operator, saving that company a travel agent's commission?

In private conversations, travel industry people will speculate as to whether the senior-citizen companies are relieved of normal competitive pricing pressures by the semi-captive nature of their clientele—who have no independent travel counselor to steer them to a cheaper course. Whether or not this is so—whether, as the companies claim, their tours are worthier because of their attention to needs of the elderly—those prices quite obviously need some analysis, and perhaps revision.

Traveling Alone in the Mature Years—Plight or Opportunity?

The Problem Is Not

Confined to Women;

the Question Should

Be Rephrased to Ask:

"Can a Single

Woman, or Single

Man, Travel Enjoyably

Alone? And Can

This Be Done at a

Mature Age?"

Out-of-breath and weary, I end my eager speech—that overlong lecture on travel that I deliver, somewhere, each month—and throw open discussion to the floor. Within four minutes, never more, it comes, that inevitable, inescapable, and utterly harrowing question: "Can a single woman travel safely, and enjoyably, alone?"

Amazing how persistent the inquiry, how it reveals a major, near-universal concern among a large portion of all potential travelers.

The questioner is usually a widow in her late middle age, her forehead furrowed with worry. She explains that she and her husband had

Loners on Wheels. *Courtesy Loners on Wheels.*

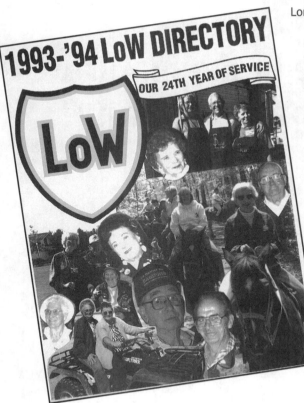

The Glib Response

Though my answer, generally, is "Yes," I wish I could state it with greater conviction than I do. But the issue is complex, surrounded by ifs, perhapses, and maybes.

In this respect I differ from a great many more impulsive travel lecturers who teach one-evening courses at urban night schools, under the title "Traveling Solo: The Joys of Going It Alone." These people claim that we should always travel unaccompanied, even if we don't have to. Why? Because such is the road to romance and adventure, to chance encounters with foreign citizens, invitations to foreign homes. And the practice, as they tell it, is deliciously selfish: you do only what you desire, without compromise. You do not alter your itinerary or schedule to suit the tastes of another human being.

For the first time in your life, you are *free*.

The message of these trendy singles (almost all in their mid-twenties) is of course based on the assumption that a compatible travel companion doesn't exist; that, almost as if by some law of nature, two people traveling together must necessarily have widely divergent views, inclinations, and tastes. Having themselves never experienced true friendship, love, or compatibility, they proclaim the resounding advantage of traveling alone.

I can't go quite that far. For surely, only the most naïve pollyanna can believe that the pleasure of traveling with a cherished companion—the joy of sharing reactions to renowned sights and experiences—can now be duplicated or replaced in the absence of that person. At best they can be experienced differently, with adequate enjoyment, but not usually with the profound satisfaction of

enjoyed memorable trips abroad, that travel for her is a cherished activity, but that now she is anxious, even frightened, about undertaking further journeys on her own.

As she talks, a nervous movement occurs in the auditorium among men of a similar age. Though they—the men—never initiate the question, they now lean forward in rapt attention, concentrating on every word. And suddenly it is obvious: the problem is not confined to women; the question should be rephrased to ask: "Can a single woman, or a single man, travel enjoyably alone? And can this be done at a mature age?

Before discussing the ways to travel alone, it's important to note that you don't have to.

discovering them in the company of a like-minded friend.

The Alternatives to Solitude

Therefore, before I discuss the ways to enjoy a solitary holiday trip, to "make a go" of traveling alone, it's important to note that you don't have to. By simply mailing $39.95 for a three-year membership in the Saga Holidays Club operated by **Saga Holidays Ltd., 222 Berkeley Street, Boston, MA 02116 (phone 617/262-2262 or 800/343-0273)**, or applying for a similar membership (without charge) in the Grand Circle Travel Club, operated by **Grand Circle Travel, Inc., 347 Congress St., Boston, MA 12210 (phone 617/350-7500 or toll free 800/248-3737)**—both of them companies dealing exclusively in travel for mature persons—you can obtain the names of potential companions for your next trip. Both clubs distribute quarterly magazines with "Pen Pal" or "Penfriend" features listing dozens of applications by mature singles for travel partners. These, in effect, are "travel personals," but proper to a fault, and fascinating to read as they detail the varied goals of the mature, experienced travelers submitting them.

(Members of the Saga Holidays club also receive considerable discounts off flights, cruises and tours, including $50 off any Saga tour.)

For more extensive listings (over 400 "travel personals"), send $25 for a one-year subscription to **Partners-in-Travel, P.O. Box 491145, Los Angeles, CA 90049 (phone 310/476-4869)**, and you'll receive (a) the bulky directory of 400 singles wanting to share their love of travel, as well as a later, mid-year update of it; (b) a list of tour operators that package vacations solely for singles; and (c) a brochure addressing specific concerns about solo travel. All material is personally written by the irrepressible Miriam Tobolowsky, who attracts a zestful following and ads peppered with jaunty exhortations: "Let's go—life is for living!" One recent listing assures that the applicant is "caring and considerate, but won't hover. Want ardent traveler who travels light, dependable driver, honest and open communication, brisk walker." Though Partners-in-Travel does not limit its services to mature persons, a full 70% of its subscribers appear to be over 50, most in their early sixties.

And for a near-guarantee that you will find a suitable travel "match-up," but at rates of $36 for six months (you can also request simply a copy of their most recent, 26- to 36-page newsletter for only $5), contact **Travel Companion Exchange, P.O. Box 833, Amityville, NY 11701 (phone 516/454-0880)**, founded by the well-known travel figure Jens Jurgen. His is the most elaborate of all travel match-up services, supplying you with literally thousands of available listings, all carefully grouped by computer into helpful categories ("smokers," "planned destinations," "wishes to travel with same gender," and the like) to enable a wise choice. Highly recommended.

Traveling Only with Singles

As a substitute for seeking a travel companion, one can travel with groups consisting only of singles. Although the prestigious **Singleworld Cruises & Tours, Inc., P.O. Box 1999, Rye, NY 10580 (phone 914/967-3334)**, does not limit participation to mature persons only, its programs are heavily booked by the mature, and its tours are only for single people. Join them and your problems of "singlehood" vanish.

As a substitute for seeking a travel companion, one can travel with groups consisting only of singles.

Loners on Wheels, Inc., P.O. Box 1355, Poplar Bluff, MO 63901 (phone 314/785-2420), is still another travel organization confined to singles. An RV club, it forms caravans of singles only, and takes them to rallies and campouts all over the country and occasionally to Mexico too. Annual dues: $36, plus an initiation fee of $5 (the first year only).

Activities Where It Doesn't Matter

Your other option is to travel abroad with groups pursuing an intense social, political, scientific, or educational purpose. In that context, the fact that some are singles, some couples, becomes of minor significance: people are engaged in a communal activity, living helter-skelter in group lodgings, so intent on their work that they mix and mingle easily.

The study tours operated by the famous **Elderhostel, 75 Federal St., Boston, MA 02110 (phone 617/426-7788)**, are that kind of program. Elderhostel sends people over the age of 60 to attend one- to three-week classroom courses of instruction in the U.S. and around the world, using university residence halls—sometimes even dormitories, segregated by sex—for lodgings. It makes no guarantee of single or double rooms, charges one standard fee without single supplement, and thereby attracts a heavy number of singles to its continually fascinating curriculum (singles make up a full 30% of Elderhostel's volume, and two-thirds of those singles are women). But because Elderhostel passengers are focused so intently on ideas outside of themselves, the fact that they are alone or accompanied dwindles in importance, fades from consciousness; and people glory in the camaraderie and joint activities of the entire group.

The trips sponsored by **Earthwatch, P.O. Box 403N, Watertown, MA 02272 (phone 617/926-8200)**, are also that sort of program. It sends its volunteers on scientific research projects (tagging fish, measuring acid rain, interviewing rural residents), making use of a catch-as-catch-can array of housing accommodations (local schools and community centers, tents, and private homes) in which people are lodged as conditions permit. Its charges ("contributions") are uniform per person, with no single supplement, and the composition of its "teams" is heavily slanted to singles. "We were an unlikely group," wrote one recent Earthwatch participant, ". . . a history teacher from Ohio, a Long Island college student, a retired real estate investor from Arizona. . . ." A full 20% of all Earthwatch volunteers, I am told, are 56 to 65 years old; nearly 10% are over 65.

Similar in character, largely erasing the distinction between couples and singles, and attracting a heavy percentage of singles, are the "adventure tours" (camping safaris, treks in Nepal and the Andes, outdoor nature expeditions) sponsored by an increasing number of tour operators. Though they require a certain minimum vigor (but less than you might think), they cater to people of all ages, attract a heavy turnout of mature singles, and house them in tents or improvised accommodations. Scan the catalogs of **Overseas Adventure Travel, 625 Mount Auburn Street, Cambridge, MA 02136 (phone 617/876-0533 or toll free 800/221-0814)**—which carried an 82-year-old woman on a recent camping safari to Tanzania—or **Mountain Travel/Sobek Expeditions, Inc., P.O. Box 1089, Angels Camp, CA 95222 (phone 209/736-4524 or toll free 800/777-7939)**, for additional examples of purposive trips in which all participants became undifferentiated members of a cohesive group, without regard to marital status. The same applies to volunteer "workcamp" tours engaging in socially conscious projects around the world: contact **VFP International Workcamps, Tiffany Road, Belmont, VT 05730 (phone 802/259-2759)**, and specify the trips open to all ages; or to politically oriented trips, some heavily feminist in nature, organized by groups such as **Global Exchange, 2017 Mission Street, #303, San Francisco, CA 94110 (phone 415/255-7296 or 800/255-7296.**

While all such trips appeal to only a segment of the mature audience, they provide the perfect antidote to the "single travel blues."

It is primarily—let me suggest—on the standard, traditional trips, with their single supplements and couples-only atmosphere, that the problems of traveling alone are most sharply felt.

Enjoying the Standard Trips

So how, then, do you travel alone for normal sight-seeing or recreational purposes? How, as a mature single person, do you best vacation in new lands, or travel to visit important cultural exhibits or simply to refresh the mind and body?

The problem centers on that edifice known as a hotel—that ultimately boring and impersonal institution, with its inescapable "single surcharges." The obvious solution is to avoid the use of standard hotels and replace them with a people-friendly form of lodgings. Staying with families while abroad serves the triple purpose of avoiding loneliness, gaining new friendships and insights, and lowering costs: you not only escape from that burdensome single supplement, but start from a radically lower base of costs. Indeed, some mature singles even lower their lodgings expense to zero by joining the public-spirited, worldwide membership of **Servas, 11 John St., Suite 407, New York, NY 10038 (phone 212/267-0252)**, which believes that free and frequent people-to-people contacts, through home visits, serve the cause of world peace. On the eve of a trip, they obtain from Servas the names and addresses of families in every major city who have expressed their willingness to receive other Servas members into their homes (for short stays) free of charge, because they believe in the profound moral aspect of such hospitality. (Yearly fee for Servas membership: $55.)

Other mature singles opt for a more commercial form of homestay, but inexpensive and without the single supplement, by utilizing the services of homestay organizations in every major country. For a comprehensive list of several dozen national homestay organizations (and of other interesting travel activities), send $5.95 (plus $1 for postage and handling) to **Pilot Books, 103 Cooper St., Babylon, NY 11702,** for a copy of the 72-page *Vacations with a Difference*. This little book lists homestays in Canada, France, Australia, Tahiti, and Scandinavia; homestays with Unitarians, humanists, Mennonites, and Quakers; homestays with farmers and wine growers; homestays for as little as $85 a week, including all meals. What you yourself may have done as a teenager—a month and more abroad with a foreign family—is now available in your mature years, and for reasons obvious and profound, no other travel experience quite compares to it.

The most relaxed and adventurous of mature singles stay in youth hostels both here and abroad, now that the international youth-hostel organization has removed all maximum-age restrictions on the right to use their facilities. Particularly in the fall and winter months, when young people are in school, the predominant clientele of many youth hostels is today middle-aged and elderly! But even when one shares these multibedded rooms or dorms with young people, one pays an inexpensive charge, without a supplement. And one stays in a lively setting of international conversations and encounters. For information, contact **Hostelling International/American Youth Hostels, 733 15th Street NW, Suite 840, Washington, D.C. 20005 (phone 202/783-6161)**.

One rather affluent and mature U.S. lawyer of my acquaintance, who has traveled extensively by herself in the South Pacific, actually favors hostels, though she could afford much better. "They offer a wonderful way to meet people, including local people traveling in their own country," she points out. "The kitchen is a great social center, with perhaps 12 people each attempting to cook dinner for one—a hilarious scene. By the time the various dinners are ready, you're all old friends."

Revising Your Attitudes

If, despite this advice, you're determined to keep going on the standard trips and to use standard hotels, you may need a new mental outlook for coping with the problems of solitary travel—a confident and positive outlook. Though at the outset I was careful to stress my own view that traveling in twos is usually superior to traveling alone, there are nonetheless some attractive aspects to the latter experience.

You might regard that first experience as a zesty challenge, a chance to shape yourself for the better. Whatever your usual personality, you must of necessity attempt to be more outgoing and convivial.

Introduce yourself to the people around you. Ask other tourists for advice on restaurants and sights. Suggest the sharing of a meal at some celebrated establishment. Just as the same human necessities breed invention, so traveling by oneself often leads to increased openness, receptivity to new people and ideas, greater self-assurance and pride.

Among some single travelers—certainly not all, but some—the experience soon takes on a mood of surprised exhilaration. They find they're more sensitive to the people and culture of the destination. The absence of a familiar companion removes them from the familiar cocoon of their own language and culture, and teaches them a new language, a new culture. (And,

incidentally, traveling alone is the fastest—some say the best—way to learn another language.)

These new solitary travelers become less self-conscious. After that first nerve-wracking dinner alone in a large hotel restaurant—when every eye seems focused, accusingly, on them—they suddenly realize that in reality no one is terribly concerned with or interested in the fact that they are dining alone. It is a liberating bit of knowledge. On all subsequent evenings they bring a book or magazine to the dinner table, and revel in the luxury of thus relaxing at a high-quality meal.

Though it may not be all that it once was, traveling while alone is soon recognized to be immeasurably more satisfying than the alternative: moping at home alone. And with every succeeding trip, the experience gains in pleasure, ease, and depth; it keeps us alive. As that canny voyager (Miriam Tobolowsky) who operates Partners-in-Travel puts it: "Travel isn't something you do in old age; it is something you do *instead of* old age."

Travel is thus far too important to be dispensed with when a companion is unavailable; it is part of a civilized life, our birthright. The most vital of our fellow humans travel, whether alone or not—and so should you!

Some Travel Options—
Good, Bad, and Indifferent—
For the Mature American

As the Travel Industry Scrambles to Win Over the Senior Citizen, a Mixed Bag of Programs Emerges

Maybe it's my widening girth, my whitening hair, my increasing nostalgia for "slow music." But the travels of senior citizens interest me more and more, and provoke these comments on recent developments.

That 10% Lure: Call me a grouch, but I'm not impressed with the discounts for mature travelers offered by most hotel chains and airlines. In the majority of cases these consist of 10% reductions off room rate or air fare. Since that's the exact amount that hotels and airlines pay out to travel agents, and since most senior-citizen travel programs require (in effect) that passengers avoid the use of travel agents, the hotels and airlines are frequently saving 10% on their senior-citizen programs— and then simply passing on that 10% saving to the senior citizen.

In other words, they're not spending a red cent to obtain their senior business. Which seems a bit chintzy.

Best Hotel Bets

Does anyone do better by America's elderly? A few do. And they deserve acclaim as a means of nudging the others to do more. Here's a sampling:

Sheraton Hotels: Though they caution that the discount can be withheld during periods of peak business, and is not applicable to minimum-rate rooms, virtually all Sheratons give a 25% discount to persons 60 and older. Phone toll free 800/325-3535.

Ramada Inns: Many (about three-quarters) give the same 25% off to persons 60 and up. Phone toll free 800/2-RAMADA.

Marriott Hotels: At more than 190 Marriotts in the United States, AARP members receive 10% off normal rates, up to 50% off with a 21-day non-refundable advance purchase, and 20% off on food and non-alcoholic beverages. AARP members also receive 10% off at Marriott's Fairfield Inns and Courtyards by Marriott (two subsidiary chains), and 15% off at Marriott's Residence Inns. Phone Marriott itself at 800/228-9290, Courtyard by Marriott at 800/346-4000, Residence Inn at 800/331-3131, and Fairfield Inns at 800/322-4000.

> **C**all me a grouch, but I'm not impressed with the discounts for mature travelers offered by most hotel chains and airlines.

La Quinta Inns: Offer 10% off to people age 55 and older. Phone toll free 800/531-5900.

Holiday Inns: Give up to 50% off room rates, 10% off meals, to those over 50 joining their Mature Outlook club for $9.95 a year. Phone toll free 800/336-6330 for membership and to learn the identities of participating inns.

Days Inns: From 15% to 50% (usually 15%) off at 850 participating inns, hotels, suite-hotels, and "Day Stops," to members (50 years and older) of their September Days Club; also offers 10% off meals, and discounts on Alamo Car rentals; send $12 to September Days Club, P.O. Box 4001, Harlan, IA 51593 (phone toll free 800/344-3636).

Howard Johnson's: Take 10% off for seniors 60 years and older, and 20% to 30% off for AARP members, at more than 85% of the nation's H.J. hotels. Phone toll free 800/634-3464.

Airline Offerings

As for the airlines, some of them also confine their senior-citizen air-fare discounts to 10% and simply pass on the 10% they've saved by subtly influencing senior citizens to book direct. In fairness, they also provide self-promoting newsletters for senior travelers, and diverse other discounts and features (for hotels, car rentals, and the like). Some, in handsome style, give 15% off to travelers 65 and older, while other airlines sell valuable coupon booklets or yearly $1,600 or $1,900 passes for extensive travel.

Such programs have been overtaken by events. The introduction of radically reduced "MaxSaver" fares, and the continuation of "SuperSaver" fares—as little as $99 to fairly distant points—lessens the worth of these programs considerably. Unless one travels with absurd frequency, it is often cheaper simply to pay individual advance-purchase rates than to commit to the use of a yearly pass.

Clearly, unless the airlines now devise new programs keyed to the levels of, and kept below, their own "Saver" fares, they must—in my view—brace for outcries of protest from the seniors who purchased their fixed-price coupons or year-long passes.

Rehearsals for Retirement

Happier news—of a bright, new use of holiday travel to scout potential sites for retirement. Though the idea is obvious, it's easier said than done.

When middle-aged people go off to test the retirement attractions of Florida or Arizona, of Costa Rica or Cuernavaca, they often return as uncertain as when they left. Simply to look at a retirement area is not to ensure that you obtain reliable, relevant information about its suitability for retirement. For the latter, you need to meet with real estate people and lawyers, with municipal officials and other retirees.

So reasoned Jane Parker, a retired schoolteacher of Modesto, California. And thereupon she formed a tour company called Lifestyle Explorations that performs all the advance preparations for a meaningful research trip. Arriving at the destination, her groups engage in scheduled interviews, appointments, seminars, and briefings on the pros and cons of that area's retirement possibilities. The information is supplied by on-the-spot specialists, who undergo a withering cross-examination by tour participants; the latter stay at the area's best hotels and enjoy gala dinners while doing so.

Lifestyle Explorations' most popular trip is to Costa Rica. Four are scheduled each year, in February, April, August, and November, and at least two of these consist of two groups at one time. Price for the 12-day journey is $1,965 per person from Miami, with a single supplement of $690. The same is charged for thrice-yearly trips to Honduras, exciting considerable attention nowadays.

Twice a year, Lifestyle Explorations takes groups to the Algarve coast of Portugal for $3,660 per person including air fare, and twice again to Uruguay/Argentina for $2,990 per person, including air.

Note carefully that in the hot month of August, Lifestyle Explorations operates several "economy" versions of its scouting tours to different retirement destinations, at prices radically reduced from the prices we've cited, sometimes for as little as $1,090 to Costa Rica or Honduras for as many as 12 and 14 days. These may bring its trips to within your own budget.

For additional information, or to book, contact **Lifestyle Explorations, 101 Federal Street, Suite 1900, Boston, MA 02110 (phone 508/371-4814.)**

Having a high regard for Mexico as a retirement location is a well-established firm called **South of the Border Tour and Travel, Inc., 40 Fourth Street, Petaluma, CA 94952 (phone 707/765-4573, fax 707/778-1080)**. They operate monthly departures of an eight-day tour to Guadalajara, Lake Chapala and Ajijic, in Mexico, for precisely the purpose of judging that nation's retirement potential. In the words of their brochure, you meet, at several cocktail parties and dinners scheduled throughout the week, with "professionals, government officials and retirees who will share accurate and up-to-date 'insider' information on all that is needed to make informed retirement decisions about Mexico." On one occasion, you meet only with "a select group of long-time Lake Chapala retirees." On another, you go into private homes of retirees to gain "insights into [their] lifestyles." At a farewell dinner in Ajijic, you are again joined by "special guests and lakeside retirees." Though the week is also filled with standard, daily sightseeing by escorted motorcoach, the emphasis is on gaining real estate information, legal and medical advice, and on seeing homes.

The cost is a relatively modest $1,649 for the eight days, which *includes* round-trip air transportation from a number of cities (New York, among them), all lodgings, sightseeing, transportation and guides, all meetings and seminars, visits to private homes, and a number of high-quality meals described in South of the Border's brochure. The same organization (Loujean La Malfa is its president) also promotes a quarterly newsletter, "Retire in Mexico Updates," for persons who are especially serious about retiring in low-cost Mexico (apparently, close to a million Americans already live there), and for which a charter subscription is $39 a year. Request the free brochure first.

A "Club Med" for Seniors

At $28 to $38 per person per day (based on double occupancy), including two large meals daily, private facilities, and morning-till-night activities—all limited to people over the age of 60, from November until April 30—that, in a nutshell, is the pricing policy of "Florida's Club Meds" for senior citizens: four large hotels in highly desirable cities on the west coast of the Sunshine State.

These are not, of course, real "Club Meds"—that's only my term for them. The owning company is Senior Vacation Hotels of Florida, in business for 32 years—longer than any Club Med in the Western Hemisphere.

But the offerings—and atmosphere (adapted for an older generation)—are almost those of a Club Med: you receive not only your room but also two grand repasts daily, parties, live entertainment and free movies, bus excursions, theme nights, beach trips, and more—for one fixed, and remarkably low, price.

What's the catch? Well, first, there's the required minimum age, and I should point out that most guests appear to be over the age of 65 (but they're an unusually lively lot of over-65ers). More important, you must normally stay for a minimum of one month, usually starting at the beginning of the month. Provided you do, you pay only $875 per person per month (based on double occupancy) in November, December and April, $995 to $1,095 per month in January (depending on location), $1,025 to $1,195 in February and March. Single room supplement: $325 per month.

The hotels in question are the large Sunset Bay and Courtyard in St. Petersburg, the Regency Tower in Lakeland, and the Riverpark in Bradenton. For a lively four-color brochure on these veritable "Club Meds for Senior Citizens," and for application forms, contact **Senior Vacation Hotels of Florida, 7401 Central Ave., St. Petersburg, FL 33710 (phone 813/345-8123 or toll free 800/223-8123.**

Savings for the Older Skiier

And would you believe there are discount-granting clubs for mature skiiers into their eighties? One, the Over the Hill Gang (its motto: "Once you're over the hill, you pick up speed") has 3,200 members in all 50 states, accepts members starting at age 50, and promises major discounts. Members not affiliated with local groups can obtain lifetime memberships for $245; most group members pay $88 for three years, $37 for one year, and join periodic ski tours of the group (they also go on sporting-type summer trips). Contact: **Over the Hill Gang, 3310 Cedar Heights Drive, Colorado Springs, CO 80904 (phone 719/685-4656).** For skiiers older still, the 70 Plus Ski Club was founded by the remarkable Lloyd Lambert, who still skis at the age of 93. For a lifetime membership fee of $5, skiiers over the age of 70 receive his excellent newsletter, which lists 221 ski resorts that permit septuagenarians (and older) to ski for free. Write directly to Lloyd, who personally registers new members, at **70 Plus Ski Club, Ballston Lake, New York 12019 (phone 518/399-5458).**

A Guide to Mature Travel I

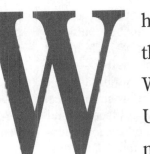

As a Mature Adult, Do I Travel Differently from When I Was Younger? You Bet I Do! With Age Comes Travel Wisdom . . .

When I was barely 22, at the time of the Korean War, the long arm of Uncle Sam plucked me from law school, dressed me in khaki, and flung me to Europe. That was more than 40 years ago, and I've been traveling ever since. First in the army, and then as the author or publisher of more than 70 travel guides, I've journeyed to foreign continents like other people commute to the suburbs— daily, weekly, unremittingly, traversing millions of miles to nearly 100 nations.

Have I learned anything from all this? As a mature adult, do I travel differently from when I was younger? You bet I do! With age comes travel wisdom, and wisdom consists of life-improving rules and reflections, healthy lessons for future conduct. In my case, I now vacation better than I ever did before, by following 12 basic courses of mature travel:

1. *I combat jet lag by going to sleep immediately upon arrival.* Time was when I would "hit the streets" after an overnight ocean crossing and go dashing into museums and shops, enjoying that false sense of vigor that the excitement of a foreign land often brings. No longer. As the years have passed, jet lag becomes harder, not easier, to overcome, and the mature traveller who fails to nap on arrival becomes so overly tired as to be unable to sleep—and thus condemned to a "white night" and disoriented fatigue thereafter—when evening falls. Having tried every "jet lag" diet and routine ever suggested, I now simply pass up that immediate round of sightseeing and instead go immediately to sleep for a few hours upon arriving at my overseas hotel (and this, regardless of whether I've been able to sleep on the plane). In mid-afternoon, upon arising, I devote the few remaining hours of daylight to casual, relaxed activity, and then fall asleep again for a fresh, full night of rest. While, to some, I may be "wasting" my first full day in London or Bangkok or Seoul, I have instead, to my mind, achieved the transition to a new time zone; I have regained a clear head and make more effective use of the days ahead; I do not wander like a zombie in my first week abroad, as do so many younger travel zealots who go charging off their overnight flight to the counters

> In my mid 60s, I follow 12 new approaches to vacations and tours that improve upon my travels of earlier years.

> The mature traveler who fails to nap on arrival becomes so overly tired as to be unable to sleep—and thus condemned to a "white night" and disoriented fatigue thereafter—when evening falls.

at Harrod's or the halls of the Louvre. Frommer's time-tested, mature remedy for jet fatigue? Go to sleep!

2. *I prepare for my trips with histories and art appreciations, more than with guidebooks.* In my early years of travel I thought nothing of flinging myself to the most remote, exotic foreign destinations without spending so much as a single evening in a library studying the history and culture of the places I was about to visit. Result: I arrived in Zurich, or Cairo, or New Delhi, literally as an untutored ignoramus, confused and bewildered, unable to discern the age or history of the structures about me, puzzled by the comments of people or the lectures of tour guides, failing to derive 90% of the enjoyment—and intellectual growth—that could have been mine had I come mentally equipped. No more. I now prepare for my trips. I approach them with mature deliberation, without youthful impetuousness. If I am going to the Far East, I read about the concepts and institutions of Buddhism. If I am off to the cities of Germany or France, I refresh my memory about the history and evolution of the Gothic Cathedral. If I am visiting Scandinavia, I read appropriate articles about the provocative new social experiments of the Danes, the Swedes, the Finns. Although I consult the practical guidebooks for hotels and shops, I spend far more time reading about the political developments, contemporary achievements, cultural treasures, historical trends, in the cities or countries I am about to see. I arrive with an advance framework for understanding. And through this mature preparation my trips become infinitely more meaningful than those headlong travel flings into the unknown that proved so painfully confusing, and ultimately lacking in satisfaction, when I was 22.

3. *I pack less and enjoy more.* Youthful vanity once dictated that I bring an outfit for every conceivable and far-fetched social occasion. Yuppie morals required that I avoid repeating an item of apparel on successive days. I traveled like a beast of burden, with multiple suitcases, collapsing in sweat at every hotel, laboriously packing and unpacking suitcases of unwashed laundry, carting about trendy sports jackets, or dress shoes, or silk neckties never once worn in the course of a trip. No more. Just as I now accept that I will never be president of the United States, so does my increasing age cause me to reject unjustified travel expectations: I've come to peace with the probability that I will not be invited to a garden party on my two-week holiday to Spain; that I will not attend the sold-out opera in Sydney or Vienna; that I will not be asked to meet the Queen. I no longer pack with those possibilities in mind. And as for the repeated use of the same pieces of clothing, I rejoice in the mature wisdom of doing exactly that! I take a quarter of what I used to, pack only one replacement set of underwear, socks, and sport shirts, wash them out in my hotel room at night, travel with a single, medium-size suitcase half full, and thus go about the world with more "youthful" freedom and lighthearted independence than certain popinjays of the new generation, who groan under the weight of their self-imposed fashion needs!

4. *I equip myself with the names and addresses of competent, English-speaking physicians.* No longer the eternal optimist about health and illness, I travel ready for that unsettling event—becoming ill in a foreign land—that sooner or later always occurs as you travel through the mature years. And sometimes it occurs on safari in far-off Kenya, or in an isolated village in the south of France, or in the remote suburbs of Rio. A doctor arrives, his command of English shaky, his competence questionable; he prescribes for you, and yet you become sicker and sicker as the trip proceeds, until a new doctor is summoned; he visibly recoils as he reads the prescription of the earlier savant, cancels it forthwith, and brings you back to health. This, believe it or not, has happened to me on two occasions in my recent travels, once because the first physician's command of English was insufficient to catch the nuances of the symptoms I described; once because the doctor in question was simply a dolt.

I now phone up my own doctor on the eve of a trip and obtain his recommendations of a colleague or two in the places I am about to visit. If he has none to suggest, I contact the life-saving **International Association for Medical Assistance to Travellers (IAMAT), 417 Center Street, Lewiston, NY 14092 (phone 716/754-4883)**, and obtain their list of capable, well-trained, English-fluent doctors in every major tourist destination. And ever since I've achieved the mental calm that comes from such a list, I have never once become sick again in the course of my travels!

5. *I bargain over the prices of travel purchases.* In my twenties, thirties, and forties I regarded the act of bargaining as beneath youthful dignity, something for hysterical fishwives or tobacco auctioneers, but certainly not for proud young achievers like me. What errant nonsense! As I've grown wiser to the ways of the world—seen the rampant rebating and discounting in the travel industry, the notorious last-minute "sales" and cut-rate disposal of rooms, seats, and cabins, the ability of tour operators to negotiate the rates in half for purchasers of travel "packages"—I now shed that juvenile modesty and bargain at the drop of a hat, openly, unabashedly, proudly. I walk to a hotel counter and announce that I am looking for a room, "but only if it costs less than $60." And somehow, mysteriously, such a room is found for me.

With the years, I've learned that attitudes toward bargaining are all in the mind; that bargaining is neither degrading, demeaning, nor humiliating; that it can be done courteously and without loss of face. By acting like a smart senior determined not to waste money, I now

> **I** shed that juvenile modesty and bargain at the drop of a hat, openly, unabashedly, proudly.

> **N**o mature stomach can possibly tolerate an endless routine of those overly rich, overly sauced restaurant meals abroad.

take advantage of the single most significant phenomenon in travel: the utterly perishable nature of all hotel rooms, charter-airplane seats, and cruise-ship cabins. Since these items are a complete loss to their owners if unsold for a particular date or departure, such people react favorably to requests for discounts if that is the course required to sell off remaining rooms, seats, or berths. "Ask and it shall be given," says ancient wisdom. As a mature traveler, rid of youthful modesty, I now ask—and it is given more often than you'd ever expect!

> **I take advantage of the single most significant phenomenon in travel: the utterly perishable nature of rooms and airplane or cruise tickets.**

6. *I take one meal a day "picnic style."* Entering into my mid-forties, traveling all the while, it slowly dawned on me that no mature stomach could possibly tolerate an endless routine of those overly rich, overly sauced restaurant meals abroad. As metabolism slowed and waistline increased, I resolved—and have ever since succeeded—to make one meal a day out of simple, cold ingredients purchased in a foreign grocery or delicatessen and consumed from a park bench, a river's bank, or in the privacy of my hotel room. In this manner I not only eat sensibly, healthily, and cheaply—but better! Why? Because the ingredients of a picnic meal overseas are a gourmet's delight, almost always superior to the same food items enjoyed at home. It is a fact, as unfortunate as it may be, that the quality of the bread, for instance, found in nearly every foreign country, is superior to the bread we bake in the United States. The same for pâtés, cheeses, fresh olives, tomatoes, local red wine— all the other ingredients that make up those memorable picnic-style meals consumed while traveling in foreign climes. I now invariably have a simple, cold lunch from items I've purchased at a grocery counter abroad, and then wait patiently until evening to dig into those garlicky escargots or escalopes, those subtly flavored fish fillets swimming in sauce au vin blanc, or juicy tournedos doused with sauce béarnaise. Mature travel has taught me that meals like that can be had with safety perhaps once a day, but never twice!

Rules 7 through 12 of "mature travel"? Turn the page.

A Guide to Mature Travel II

My Mature Travel Tastes Are for the Places As Yet Uninundated by Commercial Tourism

Though it may seem like a dream come true, a life devoted to constant, unending, almost-weekly foreign travel isn't nearly as romantic as you might think, dear readers: it is fiercely fatiguing (listen to me complain!), full of both tedium and mishaps, disorienting. And it gets harder, not easier, as you move into the mature years—as I am now doing, at the age of 65. In the first part of this discussion, I wrote that a lifetime of near-continuous travel had at last caused me to adopt 12 totally new approaches to my trips, wholly different from the rash fashion in which I used to fling myself abroad. Specifically, I now (1) combat jet lag by going to sleep immediately on arrival, (2) prepare myself culturally for the cities I'm about to visit, (3) pack less and enjoy more, (4) equip myself in advance with the names of competent, English-speaking physicians at the destination, (5) bargain over the prices of travel purchases, and (6) take one meal a day "picnic style."

What else do I do? Read on!

Rules 7 Through 12 of Painfully Acquired Vacation Wisdom

7. *I bring along a small but select assortment of travel products.* And I emphasize the reference to "small"; the average trip requires only a handful of tiny gadgets or medicines, but smart older tourists are clear about what they should be: eyeshades to ensure your continued morning sleep when sunlight invades the room and easily pierces middle-aged eyelids; earplugs to blot out the occasional snores of your travel companion; a small immersion heater for that late-night coffee indulgence; Tums or Maalox for indigestion. And, of course, adapters and converters for enabling your electric appliances (travel irons, hair dryers, and the like) to work on foreign currents and in foreign sockets. Don't take another thing! The traveler who arrives in London or Paris—birthplaces of the pharmacy—with suitcases of Band-Aids, Kleenex, and iodine, is simply woefully uninformed about the highly developed state of most foreign capitals; even Katmandhu has a late-night drugstore!

But there is one final product that mature travellers will almost always procure in advance of arrival abroad: comfortable walking shoes, even ultra-comfortable walking shoes, however unsightly the latter may be. Cushioned, crepe-soled shoes, even some of the new cushioned running shoes, are travel footwear rarely found on youthful feet—but they're the losers for all of that! When one has marched for miles on the uneven

> **A** lifetime of near-continuous travel has at last caused me to adopt a new approach to my trips, wholly different from the rash fashion in which I used to fling myself abroad.

cobblestones of a medieval city, or sloshed along the muddy paths of Bangkok, or shuffled through the yellow clay of Aswan or Abu Simbel, one begins to envy those senior citizens who have rejected style and conformity in favor of bouncy, springy, comfy, molded walking shoes.

8. *I acquire, in advance of departure, the names and addresses of people to look up at the destination.* Ultimately, the experienced traveler concludes that people are the highlight of any vacation trip—people in the form of foreign residents with whom one converses by chance on a train or in a café, and who sometimes invite you to their homes. We all know that these are the single most memorable events of travel, yet in our early trips abroad we approach such contacts helter-skelter, without a plan. After many years of random approaches to people, I now devote time to ensuring that such encounters will in fact take place. I pester friends, associates, or relatives for the names of their own acquaintances in the cities I am about to visit. If I have more time, I apply for the names of people who have indicated to several nonprofit organizations that they are willing to provide hospitality in their own home cities to visitors from overseas. Among such groups are **Servas, 11 John Street, New York, NY 10038 (phone 212/267-0252), or INNter Lodging Co-Op, P.O. Box 7044, Tacoma, WA 98407 or Visiting Friends, Inc., P.O. Box 231, Lake Jackson, TX 77566.** With maturity, with the personal humility that comes with years, I now want to know what other inhabitants of this planet are thinking, and I value the chance to meet them as a supreme travel goal, fully as important as the many minor museums and lifeless monuments to which the younger tourists are madly dashing.

9. *I make use of government tourist offices and "institutes."* In the early years of travel we tend to be "do-it-yourselfers," arriving in cities without advance information of any sort, stumbling from festival to festival without knowing their dates, bereft of addresses, learning only from hard knocks and chance discoveries. It only gradually occurs to us, as the years unfold, that every major city, every island, every country seeking to attract tourists, maintains offices in the United States for the purpose of aiding would-be visitors to their land. And only then do we write to these entities for lists of hotels and private homes, events and services, the advance information that proves such a balm to mature travel. The most experienced of travelers actually pay visits to these government tourist offices, in New York and Miami, in Chicago and Los Angeles.

Such was the "wisdom" I finally acquired after, say, 20-or-so years of aimless travel. I'm even more ashamed to disclose that it was only in the past two years that I became aware of a parallel organization—the government "institutes"—that most nations maintain, some with offices in the United States, others only in their home capitals (for which addresses will be provided by the tourist offices). Unlike the tourist offices, these have the broad goal of promoting their nation's culture and image by assisting the formation of study tours, or by scheduling appointments and interviews with experts for travelers pursuing special interests in their countries. By simply writing to the Swedish Institute, or the Danish Institute, the British Council, the Institut Français, or any number of others, Americans can obtain the most extraordinary free assistance toward meeting and conversing with the single most accomplished individuals in those nations, enjoying a "program" of timed interviews with professors, government officials, technicians, and artists. By taking the time to do just that in my latter-day trips, I've experienced the most profound forms of mature travel. You can do the same.

10. *I stay calm and roll with the travel "punches."* If maturity teaches anything, it is that the world is a turbulent place filled with people who often err—especially in travel. Uncertainties and omissions, delays and goofs, are an inherent element in travel, and part of what makes the activity so dynamic and appealing. How dull the world would be if all the countries

in it hummed and purred and worked like Switzerland! Recognizing this, I no longer rant and rail when the airport clerk announces a two-hour delay; I whip out a paperback book and savor an interlude of leisure. I no longer gnash teeth and feel the ground swaying underfoot when the hotelier admits an overbooking; having experienced the futility of protesting against such a situation on so many occasions, I ascribe it all to "karma"

> **U**ltimately, the experienced traveler concludes that people are the highlight of any vacation trip and takes time to ensure that encounters with people will take place.

and, Zen-like, begin calmly exploring the alternatives. In short, I now accept the inevitable vagaries of vacations, and travel to undeveloped and inefficient lands precisely because they are so unlike the mechanical society we know at home. If the point of life is simply to enjoy an uneventful, slumbering routine, then why travel? Maturity, instead, is the acceptance of the improbable and unexpected, the spice of life; and mature travelers stay relaxed and unperturbed in the face of unscheduled problems.

11. *I buy various forms of cheap travel insurance before departing on a foreign trip.* I never did so when I first traveled, but oh, how I learned, I learned! Travel, let me tell you, is a complex activity in which many things can and sometimes do go wrong. Luggage is lost or misplaced. Strikes or weather delay your return flight. Cables arrive advising of the illness of a relative at home, requiring that you prematurely cut short your trip, forfeiting hotel deposits or the benefit of your return air ticket. The door of a Paris subway closes on your arm, severely bruising it.

The financial consequences of each of these potential mishaps can be offset by various forms of inexpensive travel insurance, yet only a tiny fraction of all American travelers ever buy such policies before departing on a trip. Youthful optimism is one explanation. Youthful inexperience or confusion about the whereabouts of such policies is another. The mature traveler, by contrast, takes time to survey the field, and soon discovers that both Citicorp and BankAmerica traveler's checks are currently making available quite respectable policies (covering baggage, trip interruption, and trip accident losses) for as little as $8.50 total per person; you simply apply for the policies in the same transaction at the bank in which you purchase your traveler's checks. With rates so low, and policies so accessible, no mature traveler should ever forgo the peace of mind, and real protection, afforded by reputable travel insurance; and that, too, is a lesson derived from three decades of travel all over the world.

We've seen the world as none of our forebears could, and we can continue to do so— even better— into our mature years.

12. *I avoid the heavily touristed and opt for the undiscovered.* Finally, having had my fill of all the massively popular destinations—the Londons and the Acapulcos, the Romes and the Honolulus—my mature travel tastes are for the places as yet uninundated by commercial tourism: the Bonaires and Nova Scotias, the Maltas and the peninsulas of Jutland. Give me a beach where I alone lie sheltered by a waving palm, reading a paperback classic undisturbed by chattering charterloads of people. Take me to the village cafés whose patrons look up startled but genuinely pleased to see an outsider in their midst. Show me the shopkeeper for whom a tourist is still an event! There remain such places on earth, and the mature traveler searches them out. We've learned, with age and experience, how tawdry and dull are the contrived nightspots, souvenir shops, and mindless tours of the mass-volume cities and resorts. We crave good music, not discos; good talk, not loudspeaker commentaries; good companionship, not crowds. And we find these in the quieter spots not yet on the tourist map.

Think back on it: your fondest travel memories are of the islands and towns where you arrived before the others did, where prices and amenities were gently human in scale, where residents smiled as you approached. In the last analysis, mature travel consists of continuing to act as a travel pioneer, always seeking out the new, keeping juices and spirits flowing, pursuing the dream of discovery and challenge, retaining the very best form of "youth," that of an ever-questing open mind.

Travel: it is today an essential requisite for a civilized life. We who are now in our mature years have been the first generation in history to enjoy travel in its fullest. With jet airplanes at our disposal, crossing from continent to continent in a few short hours, we've seen the world as none of our forebears could, and we can continue to do so—even better—into our mature years.

XV

The Time, the Resources, and the Attitudes for Proper Travel

The Scandal of American Vacation Time

While Other Developed Nations Provide Their Citizens with Five Weeks and More of Paid Leave, We Squeeze Out a Meager Two—Or Two and a Half

Thoughtless, at the very least. Barbaric, at worst. Inhuman, certainly. Short-sighted and ill-advised. Miserly. Unhealthy.

Depending on the depths of your passion, those are the words you may want to use to describe employer attitudes toward vacation time in the United States.

We Americans put up with the shortest, most miserably limited vacations of any advanced, prosperous nation. The result is a stunted quality of life and (if that doesn't bother you) a stunted commercial travel industry.

To gauge how bad things are, place yourself, hypothetically, into one of four national contexts:

- Imagine, first, that you are "Wilhelm Preizendorff," a young Austrian, and that you have just gone to work as an office clerk for a Viennese stationers. From the moment you enter the mailroom door, you are entitled by law to five weeks per year of paid vacation.

- Or you are "Nigel Lawson," floor manager of a small Sydney, Australia, department store. Each year, by practice of your firm, common in Australia, you receive six weeks of paid vacation. Sometimes you store up three months of vacation and take the family on an around-the-world trip.

- Or you are "Chantal Lasserre," buyer for a Paris dress shop. You are this time entitled, by minimum guarantee of French law, to five weeks' paid vacation per year. You take a month off every summer, which you then supplement with a week in winter or spring.

- And now you are "Mary Jones" or "John Smith," an American. This year you have no vacation at all: you have recently changed jobs and lost the time accrued under your former employer. Next year: one week with pay. The year after that: two. After five years of consecutive employment with the same firm, you will have three weeks per year of paid vacation—but never more than that. All your working life: three weeks per year.

Is this an exaggerated comparison? I wish it were. In numerous studies of vacation time, only a single one shows the American public enjoying as many as two and a half weeks, on the average, of vacation time. Most other reports fix the average figure at two weeks—or even less.

Two weeks. Even two and a half weeks. Those compare with the five weeks enjoyed in numerous other advanced industrialized nations, and with the remarkable six-week policy of Australia. Even in nations having nowhere near our own material prosperity or per capita income—such as Britain—the average working person enjoys nearly four weeks per year of paid vacation. (My British statistics are from a survey by the respected *Economist* magazine of London.)

And it gets worse. Not only is the American average a paltry two or two and a half weeks, but even that brief interlude is enjoyed under the most fragile of circumstances. Leave your job and you lose your vacation time. Painfully, patiently, you must start all over, accruing new vacation privileges from a new employer. The past counts for nothing.

No law protects the vacation. Though the United States subscribes to the Universal Declaration of Human Rights—which prescribes "the right to rest and leisure, including . . . periodic holidays with pay" as a fundamental privilege of life—not a single federal or state law, to my knowledge, guarantees a single day of paid vacation to anyone.

We Americans put up with the shortest, most miserably limited vacations of any advanced, prosperous nation.

Either we Americans are the workaholics of the world, or we are exploited in this regard, or in our drive for improved wages we have simply neglected to secure the time in which to enjoy the fruits of our pay.

However the neglect came about, it contributes to a serious decline in the quality of our lives. A barrier to our cultural growth. Inadequate time for study or reflection, human relationships, the eternal verities. Burn-out. Even, perhaps, worsened health.

Shouldn't we all consider whether the time for leisure is fully as important as other aspects of material prosperity? Would it not be worth a trade-off to enjoy greater respite from constant labors? A life more dignified and fulfilling? When the political pendulum of the United States begins to shift from its present rightward course, as must inevitably happen; when labor again becomes aggressive in its collective bargaining; when ordinary people once more demand improvements to their lot—shouldn't the goal of increased vacation time be high on the national agenda?

And if these quality-of-life arguments don't suffice, shouldn't we at least consider the impact of increased vacation time on our commercial travel interests?

The U.S. travel industry is also a victim of limited vacation time: it is puny in comparison with its European counterparts. Because of their enhanced vacation periods, tiny Benelux countries send as many people to winter vacation destinations in Spain and North Africa as the entire United States sends in that period to certain major islands of the Caribbean. With nearly four weeks of paid vacation available to their clientele, at least a dozen British tour operators each handle several hundreds of thousands of vacation arrangements each year, while here in the United States, with four times the population, the same companies are perhaps six in number.

Either we are the workaholics of the world, or we are exploited in this regard, or have simply neglected to secure the time in which to enjoy the fruits of our pay.

Every day of vacation time added to the American average would create a need for hundreds of new hotels and resorts, tens of thousands of new jobs in leisure areas, additional airplanes, trains, and buses. The multiplier effects are dazzling.

And each such result comes about at lesser cost to employers than higher wages or other traditional fringe benefits. In service industries, and especially in those smaller economic units where vacation time is particularly meager, people take on extra tasks—work harder and in broader functions, take up the slack—when their colleagues go on vacation. The common experience of all of us confirms that increased vacation time costs less to employers than other employment benefits.

Who ideally should agitate for increased vacation time? I suggest the more than 250,000 Americans who work as travel agents. No other social change could better secure their futures, add to their opportunities, expand their industry, while at the same time performing an act for the common good. One could even argue that only travel agents and other travel professionals possess the kind of direct, compelling self-interest in the matter, and the political numbers, capable of changing American vacation policies.

But is it likely that travel agents will head such a drive? Not under their present leadership. Notoriously short-sighted, almost automatically conservative, officials of the American Society of Travel Agents—a profession that is 70% female—recently battled congressional efforts to secure maternity leaves for working women (it would raise their payroll costs). Imagine their reactions to proposals for additional vacation time.

Someday this may change. Someday both the men and women of America's travel agencies will realize that though they work in small storefront locations, they need not possess the souls of shopkeepers. Someday the sophistication of their travel lives will lead to a corresponding sophistication in their social outlooks, and they will champion the fight for civilized standards in vacation policies.

The way to do it? A modest, one-sentence addition to the Federal Wages and Hours Act: "All persons engaged in interstate commerce shall receive a minimum of three weeks each year of paid vacation." By bringing along those persons enjoying less than three weeks, such legislation would surely add at least half a week to the national average, setting off an explosive increase in this nation's vacation facilities and travel-related industries. What more business-like way to improve the lives of all of us!

And then we ought to work for four or five weeks of yearly vacation time. Why should Americans enjoy less than the Scandinavians, Austrians, Germans, or French?

Ethical Travel: Does Tourism Cause More Harm Than Good?

Rethinking the "Rights" and "Wrongs" of Our Vacation Trips

At the bar of a tropical nightclub, on an island whose language is Dutch, two tipsy young tourists are exchanging loud comments on the "childish behavior" of the natives. "They haven't any concept of time." "They're so disorganized." "They move in slow motion." Nearby, overhearing each word, his English near perfect, a bartender stands seething with anger.

• In the marketplace of a Hindu village, a traveling couple bargain over the cost of a trinket. Though the price is that of an ice cream at home, they're determined to pick up "a steal." Resignedly, the shopkeeper reduces her quote to a marginal level, hardly enough to bring her a single rupee of real income.

• On the streets of a Mexican city, two confident visitors in costly tennis clothes go strolling in high spirits to a favorite bar. Unseeing, uncaring, they pass clusters of ragged children, who in turn stare at the elegant pair with envy and resentment.

• In the air-conditioned restaurant of a Nigerian hotel, owned by a multinational chain, guests dine on tournedos flown in from Argentina and wash down the steak with a fine French wine. Of the monies charged for their meals, only the tiniest part remains in Nigeria.

• Onto the tarmac of the Bangkok airport steps a group of German tourists, all of them male. They have come for prostitution. Included in their "package," at no extra charge, is a young Thai farm girl for the entire week.

Does tourism involve ethics? Should tourists be trained to act responsibly? Are travel practices—and institutions—in need of reform? Each of these questions was recently studied by a group of American church people at a conference in San Anselmo, California. Their gathering came several years after the organization of similar groups abroad.

Some years ago, a conference of Asian church leaders in Penang, Malaysia, issued a broad condemnation of tourism as it was then practiced in their countries. They decried the boorish antics of tourists to Asia, the harmful role models offered to impressionable Asian children by foreign tourists, their patronizing attitudes and harsh demands, the pollution of authentic settings and communities by modern hotels, the disrespect for Asian cultures by numerous tourist groups, the heavy use of prostitution as an Asiatic tourist lure, the monetary inflation and social trauma caused by a sudden touristic influx.

The capacity for harm is deeply ingrained in the very practice of tourism, which often brings more injury than good to poor nations.

But their criticism went deeper. In a dizzying outflow of bulletins, pamphlets, newsletters, and even a quarterly magazine (*Contours*, standing for "concern for tourism") occurring in the years since, the Ecumenical Coalition on Third World Tourism (ECTWT, the continuing organization) has appeared to argue that the capacity for harm is deeply ingrained in the very practice of tourism; that it brings more harm than good to poor nations; that it is, in effect, a new form of economic colonialism; that all of us should step back and rethink the methods by which tourism is conducted; and that the problem is worldwide in scope, erupting wherever the Rich visit lands of the Poor.

Think for a moment about the geographical directions of tourism. On an international level, most vacation travel consists of people from the "First World" (United States, Europe, Japan) traveling to visit islands, beaches, and picturesque towns of the "Third World" (Mexico, the Caribbean, Africa, Southeast Asia, India). Most of it occurs for the purpose of returning for a short time to a simpler way of life—to lost innocence, in settings old-fashioned and open-air.

But though we opt for the "tropical paradise," we demand that it come with all the comforts of home. So we drop glass-and-steel hotels next to peasant villages or fishermen's huts, creating luxuriant, forbidden facilities that no resident would dare enter, let alone use. We instantly separate *us* from *them*.

Within these bright new edifices, we staff all the servile posts—waiters, busboys, chambermaids—with native labor, but bring in executives from our own developed world to run the show (when, in the tropics, did you last see a native-born general manager?).

We then parade our wealth before people who can never enjoy our incomes. Though we ourselves may be only modestly well-off, we pay prices of a staggering size in local terms. Our very presence creates the most appalling contrasts.

In the course of our stays, we make no use at all of the lodgings that residents use, or of their transportation or dining spots. We create our own.

We arrive without the slightest advance knowledge of their ways of life, customs, or culture. We challenge them to quickly brief us on the spot ("orientation sightseeing tours"). We demand that they pose quaintly for our Kodaks and Minoltas, dance for our amusement ("Thursday night: native entertainment"), show us their funny clothes. We care not a fig for their politics, but expect them to admire our own. Unlike the great travelers of the past—Marco Polo, Rubens, Byron—we show no real regard for their achievements and discoveries, art and literature, but expect them, in essence, to have adopted our culture, at least a bit: to speak the same language we do ("luckily, they all speak . . ."), to stock our newspapers and our books in their newsstands and shops.

In short, we pay them massive disrespect. We assault their human dignity; we necessarily imply that they are inferior to us. Some—especially the young in Emerging World nations—begin to believe just that.

We injure them.

But if this is the situation, what is the solution? Having read my way through a stack of the literature on ethical tourism, I intend no slight of the various Ecumenical Coalitions when I state what they would readily admit: that their work to date has defined the problem but rendered less satisfactory solutions.

Still, some solutions have emerged. They begin with a frontal, public-relations attack on

> **Though we opt for the "tropical paradise," we demand that it come with all the comforts of home. So we drop glass-and-steel hotels next to peasant villages or fishermen's huts.**

A Code of Ethics for Tourists

1. Travel in a spirit of humility and with a genuine desire to learn more about the people of your host country. Be sensitively aware of the feelings of other people, thus preventing what might be offensive behavior on your part. This applies very much to photography.

2. Cultivate the habit of listening and observing, rather than merely hearing and seeing.

3. Realize that often the people in the country you visit have time concepts and thought patterns different from your own. This does not make them inferior, only different.

4. Instead of looking for that "beach paradise," discover the enrichment of seeing a different way of life, through other eyes.

5. Acquaint yourself with local customs. What is courteous in one country may be quite the reverse in another—people will be happy to help you.

6. Instead of the Western practice of "knowing all the answers," cultivate the habit of asking questions.

7. Remember that you are only one of thousands of tourists visiting this country and do not expect special privileges.

8. If you really want your experience to be a "home away from home," it is foolish to waste money on traveling.

9. When you are shopping, remember that that "bargain" you obtained was possible only because of the low wages paid to the maker.

10. Do not make promises to people in your host country unless you can carry them through.

11. Spend time reflecting on your daily experience in an attempt to deepen your understanding. It has been said that "what enriches you may rob and violate others."

—Issued by the Ecumenical Coalition on Third World Tourism

the most blatant exploiters of Emerging World people for touristic purposes: in particular, the operators of sex tours using women coerced by poverty (or physical force) into a criminal world of prostitution; the decriminalization of that activity, eliminating the exploiters, is a goal of some of the ecumenical organizations.

The solutions include political opposition to the worst excesses of tourist development: the sprawling airports and monumental hotels plopped into the midst of small villages and rural beauty.

The solutions involve encouraging the greater use of simpler, indigenous lodgings and facilities for visiting tourists; supporting and even subsidizing the operation of small guesthouses and guest-accepting private homes, pensions, and farms; promoting the sale of purely local crafts to tourists and the consumption of local food products; arranging visits by tourists to meetings of local service organizations and, indeed, to people's homes.

The solution means marketing—giving badly needed publicity to—those underfinanced travel organizations that practice "integrated tourism," placing visitors into the facilities used by local people themselves.

Finally, and perhaps most important, the solution involves educating travelers to comport themselves properly in the Emerging World. A recent victory of the Ecumenical Coalition was to persuade Lufthansa to show a film of advance cultural preparation and ethical conduct on its holiday flights to certain Emerging World nations. Another has been the widespread dissemination and increasing acceptance of a code of ethics for tourists: "Travel in a spirit of humility. . . . Be sensitively aware of [their] feelings. . . . Cultivate the habit of listening and observing. . . . Realize [they] have time concepts and thought patterns different from your own. This does not make them inferior, only different. . . . Do not expect special privileges. . . . Do not make promises [you cannot] carry through. . . ."

Once the exclusive domain of Asian and European groups, the drive for ethical travel practices is now on the march in the United States. Its "general" is Virginia T. Hadsell, her recently formed organization is the **Center for Responsible Tourism, 2 Kensington Rd., San Anselmo, CA 94960 (phone 415/843-5506)**, and the organization now holds periodic conferences in different U.S. cities. Send her a large self-addressed stamped envelope, and she'll send you literature, including the interesting Code of Ethics for tourists.

Or you may make a direct contact with the **Ecumenical Coalition on Third World Tourism, P.O. Box 9–25, Bangkhen, Bangkok 10900, Thailand,** requesting a copy of the fascinating *Contours*. They'll mail it to you free, but you're invited to send a small contribution—say, $3 or so—to defray the costs.

A Plea for "Social Tourism"

Isn't It Time We Brought the Benefits of Travel to All Our Citizens?

In all the years you've read the Sunday travel sections, have you once observed a reference to "social tourism"?

Probably not. It is a concept known to every prosperous nation other than our own, to every rich continent other than North America, to every major language other than English.

"Social tourism" is tourism for the poor.

Here in America, we don't push it. Apart from various "fresh-air funds" sending underprivileged children to summer camp, not a single major program brings away-from-home vacations to low-income groups. While you and I enjoy all the widely recognized benefits of travel— the awesome beauties of an outside world, the broadening impact of foreign cultures, the mind-tingling sense of human possibilities—

the same rewards are simply unavailable to persons of adult age who happen to be poor and living in the United States.

But should this be? If the ability to enjoy rest and leisure is a fundamental human right—and it certainly is—shouldn't we concern ourselves with travel opportunities for the poor? With "social tourism"?

Apart from various "fresh-air funds" sending underprivileged children to summer camp, not a single major program brings away-from-home vacations to low-income groups.

In Europe as far back as 1956, leading travel figures met to discuss the contradiction between low income and the right to travel. From those talks emerged, years later, the Bureau Internationale du Tourisme Sociale, headed by a former chairman of the European Travel Commission.

That director presides over some 90-odd organizations of "social tourism" in Europe and North Africa, in South America and the Pacific Rim—but not, astonishingly, in the United States. Though their work may seem utterly basic, even a bit simple, it is of remarkable importance.

The Vacation Itself

They agitate, first, for the fundamental right to a yearly paid vacation by people of all income strata. Sounds self-evident, right? Yet in an America that mandates (in effect) the 40-hour week and the 8-hour day, no law protects the right to a paid vacation, and numerous low-income persons fail to receive one. What maid, for instance, enjoys the security of an assured, paid period of rest?

Access to the Vacation

They seek to persuade governments, owners of the railways, to provide poor persons with a free or drastically reduced round-trip rail ticket, once a year, to a vacation destination. By eliminating

or lowering that transportation cost—as France, Portugal, and Switzerland have done—they bring proper vacations into the financial reach of a great many of the poor.

A Fulfilling Vacation

They attempt to eliminate the substandard, cinder-block motel and fast-food restaurant as the sole affordable facility for vacationing poor. They promote the construction and operation of dignified, low-cost "vacation villages" in seaside and mountain areas, by political parties of both the left and right, by labor unions and philanthropic societies, all receiving low-interest loans, grants, or tax rebates for the purpose, from local or national governments.

(I have visited several such "social resorts" in Europe. They permit the poor to experience nature and the finer aspects of culture, solitude, rebirth; they encourage the self-esteem of their guests; leave them replenished in energy and spirit for an assault on their own poverty. In short, they provide the poor with the same vacations that you and I enjoy—and isn't that an unarguable goal?)

Filling Unused Accommodations

They enroll farmers with large and partially underutilized homes, or educational institutions with vacated residence halls, to list those facilities for holiday use by the poor, at low rates, and then disseminate such availabilities to a low-income population, helping both the user and the provider.

A Host of Other Measures

They work for the creation of "land banks" or additions to national parks, preventing the wholesale private purchase of scenic areas, which would block their use by persons of lesser means. They develop camping facilities—the cheapest form of meaningful travel—and caravaning; issue reduced-price travel vouchers and credit facilities for travel by the poor; advocate staggered vacation schedules as the most efficient means of reducing the cost of vacations for low-income persons; and perform a multitude of other needed functions.

But now you undoubtedly have questions.

First, isn't "social tourism" a form of subsidized tourism? Of course it is—but so is "commercial tourism." When the nonpoor travel, who pays for the highways on which they drive their cars? Who funds the aviation authorities that secure the safety of their flights? Who maintains the port facilities, docks, and marinas at which they park their boats and yachts? Because the taxpayer is already so heavily supporting travel by middle-income and high-income Americans, common justice demands that at least some resources be spent on travel for the poor.

Second, don't we provide any semblance of "social tourism" in this country? Not really. Some unions maintain holiday facilities for their members—but those are not the "poor." Several hundred companies belong to the National Industrial Recreation Association, operating travel programs for their employees— but neither are those the "poor." While state and national parks are "social" in their character, their long-stay facilities (lodging, restaurants) are notoriously unsuited to the needs of the truly poor.

The "poor" of which I speak are those 50 million Americans living either below the federal poverty line or perilously close to it. At their levels of income, almost absurdly low, the road to travel and tourism is effectively blocked.

How, then, do the "poor" vacation in the United States? The overwhelming number never leave their homes. Those who do, in my experience, squeeze out a stay of three or so days near theme parks or casino cities, whose attractions and activities are of the basest sort—dumb and contrived, consumerist. Just as low-income groups have failed to receive adequate low-income housing from private industry, so the American poor have been abandoned almost entirely by the commercial travel industry. They simply have no access to vacations of worth and meaning. Yet such interludes are surely the birthright of every American, the essential requisites for a civilized life.

If the ability to enjoy rest and leisure is a fundamental human right—and it certainly is—shouldn't we concern ourselves with travel opportunities for the poor?

Don't we need an Institute for Social Tourism in this country? A private body to devise, coordinate, and encourage efforts in this field? And shouldn't persons in the travel industry be the leaders of that movement?

Franklin Roosevelt said that "from those to whom much is given, much is expected." Those who earn handsome incomes from the commercial industry of travel should be the first to labor at extending the benefits of travel to those less favored.

I plan to write more on "social tourism." And I'd be grateful to have your comments and suggestions. Send them to the address listed in our introduction, and they will find their way into a subsequent edition of this book.

XVI

Some Unresolved Problems of Travel

Infringements on Our Right to Travel

What Provisions of the Constitution Enable Our Government to Designate the Lands to Which Freeborn Americans Can Travel in Peacetime?

Several years ago, armed agents of the United States Treasury Department entered the offices of the single most distinguished travel firm in America, seized certain of its records, and confiscated its major bank account.

The office was that of Lindblad Travel, its head the late, revered Lars-Eric Lindblad, one of the few living persons at that time to have been named to the Travel Hall of Fame by the American Society of Travel Agents.

His "crime"? He planned to operate tours to Vietnam and Cambodia. For attempting to enable Americans to reach their own conclusions about conditions in those troubled lands, his business was gravely threatened and he himself burdened with the need to litigate against the mighty

United States of America. Several hundreds of thousands of dollars of legal fees later, he went bankrupt, and was forced to work throughout his remaining years as a featured guide and lecturer on "adventure cruises." He died in 1994. By then, the Treasury Department had lifted its ban on traveling to Vietnam, just as casually as it had earlier imposed it.

By what right did all this occur? What provision of the Constitution enables our government to designate the lands to which freeborn Americans can travel in peacetime? (Such bans presently exist against travel to Cuba and several other lands).

Government, after all, is our servant, not our master. And one of the ways in which we, the masters, select our government is by traveling internationally to test the wisdom of the foreign policy practiced by a particular administration. We journey to view conditions in other countries, meet their citizens, ask questions and listen, communicate.

Travel is thus a form of education, perhaps the very best form of education. Absent the most compelling wartime conditions, government has no more right to interfere with that educational process than it has to prevent us from listening to a lecture, attending a course, or reading a book.

Astonishingly, these views about the importance of travel do not seem to be shared by the majority of Americans. Witness the complete lack of any public reaction at the time to the steps taken against Lindblad, or even any tangible concern on the part of travel professionals.

Although the travel trade press reported the seizure, not one word of real protest was heard from *Travel Weekly, Travel Agent, Travel Trade, A.S.T.A. Travel News, Tour and Travel News,* or *Travel Management Daily.* A single, brief editorial in *Travel Weekly* confined itself to restating the facts, and then asked the Treasury Department "to explain" what it had done.

How about the American Society of Travel Agents, which bestowed its highest award on Lindblad for opening numerous areas of the world to tourism? Any word from them? Not one.

Any reaction from the United States Tour Operators Association, of which Lindblad was a member? Not a peep.

Yet why shouldn't Lindblad have operated such tours? And why weren't we Americans able at that time to visit Vietnam/Cambodia, or any other of the nations proscribed by our government? In Southeast Asia particularly, site of one of the greatest foreign policy blunders in our history, shouldn't we have been particularly sensitive about reaching conclusions on our own? Here, of all places, weren't we entitled to validate what we were told by government with our own on-the-spot observations?

Is any other consideration more important than our right to know? Were we, for instance, still at war with Vietnam? That would have surprised a great many people, and yet it was the Trading with the Enemy Act upon which the Treasury Department based its asserted power to prevent organizations like Lindblad's from operating tours to Vietnam, Cuba, and elsewhere. In 1975, long after hostilities had ceased, regulations were issued under that act by an interdepartmental committee of the Executive (not by Congress), finding that an emergency still existed which warranted a ban on all commerce (including tourism) between the U.S. and Vietnam. Findings as debatable and outmoded as those should not have been used to nullify the precious right to international travel.

The hypocrisy inherent in our government's ban was no less staggering. For years we had officially protested the refusal by the former Soviet government to permit the late Andrei Sakharov to travel to international conferences. For decades, American presidents had stood at the Berlin Wall and roundly condemned the refusal of East Germany to permit its citizens, among other things, to visit the West. It was wrong, apparently, to prevent them from visiting us, but all right to prevent us from visiting them!

How can we now overcome these repeated denials of our right to travel? It will require, I fear, long-term efforts by all of us to make our public and our public officials, including our judges, sensitive to the values of international travel. Currently, our courts offer little promise in that regard, and the decisions of the Supreme Court in this area are not among its most distinguished. Although the Justices have repeatedly held that foreign travel is a presumptive right of every American, they have also said, confusingly, that the right is protected only by the Due Process clause of the *Fifth* Amendment, and not by the stronger terms of the *First* Amendment. In other words—and this is the necessary conclusion from their reasoning—that right can be abridged if officials follow the proper steps.

Such distinctions, in my view, mirror the unconsidered and quite subliminal beliefs of judges (and of the public) that travel is a bit of fluff, a mere recreational activity, unrelated to any higher purpose. It is the same viewpoint, widely held, that considers the Sunday travel section to be the toy department of the average newspaper.

Enlightened Americans know better. With the increasing sophistication about the world brought about by large-scale international travel, a growing number have come to realize that travel is experiential education of the finest sort; that it impacts the mind in a way that no other activity—even that of widespread reading—is quite capable of doing; that the ability to travel internationally has now become an essential part of an enlightened life; that it cannot be choked off without destroying precious constitutional freedoms of discourse and information-gathering. It is, in short, as wrong for our government to prevent or hinder Americans from traveling to Cuba and elsewhere as it was for the former Soviet-bloc governments to prevent their citizens from traveling to meet with us.

We must press these views upon public officials, upon legislators, upon the courts. We must express, and give, support to the new Lars-Eric Lindblads that will inevitably emerge. We must demand the right to travel. It is too precious a birthright to be abandoned in the face of attacks upon it by right-wing ideologues who prate about freedom for business interests, but seem curiously uninterested in political freedoms for the ordinary citizen.

Slave Labor on the Love Boats?

Too Often It Is the Shockingly Low Level of Wages Paid to Ordinary Seamen That Permits the Cruise Lines to Offer Their Remarkable Bargains

Except perhaps for the dance instructor, and the social director with his white dinner jacket and gleaming smile, when did you last see an American employed on a cruise ship?

You haven't. Apart from the social and entertainment staff, almost everyone else is foreign, and nearly 80% of them are from Southeast Asia (Indonesia and the Philippines, Thailand and Sri Lanka) and Poland.

The reason is wages and working conditions: as little as 75¢ an hour for work weeks of 80 and 90 hours, with perhaps a single day off per month, and a closet-sized berth in which to sleep. Those shockingly low wages paid to the ordinary seamen who staff each vessel enable the cruise ships to offer what is generally considered to be the finest value in travel today: elegant cruises of tropical waters, including several meals a day, comfortable cabins, and countless amenities, for as little as $150 a day per passenger.

But are these bargains ethical? Is it morally proper for Americans, who constitute 97% of the passengers on these ships, to enjoy their vacations at the expense of other human beings? Is it acceptable to dance the night away while others labor in the bowels of the vessel for a dog's wages?

If a manufacturer were to import Indonesians to staff a clothing factory in North Carolina at 75¢ an hour, would we not all be aghast? And refuse to buy the products made in that manner? In what way does this differ from the activity of a cruise ship picking up and delivering American passengers to an American port?

By signing on as cosponsors of legislation dealing with shipboard wages and working conditions, 30 members of Congress have expressed their own disgust over practices in the cruise-ship industry. In what should be an era of heightened sensitivity to moral concerns, we all should examine their arguments and proposed solutions.

The legislation is primarily aimed at those Americans and American companies who discovered, a decade or two ago, that it was possible to avoid the labor laws of this country by simply registering their ships under foreign flags. Many of the so-called love boats are owned by prominent Americans, but technically incorporated in Panama, Liberia, or Honduras—countries scarcely known for their interest in human rights.

By making their vessels into "runaway ships," even though they continued dealing almost exclusively with American passengers, owners were able to rid themselves of their American crews with their pesky insistence on minimum wages, decent working conditions, the right to organize, and so on. The American component of the world's merchant marine was decimated. When the practice was challenged in lawsuits, courts were quick to hold that Congress had

never intended American labor laws to apply to ships flying a foreign flag.

"H.R. 3283," introduced in the House of Representatives by Congressman William Clay of Missouri and 29 others, would change all that. If a ship were regularly engaged in transporting passengers to or from a port in the United States (including Puerto Rico), its crew would receive the protections of the National Labor Relations Act (right to organize unions, right to protest working conditions without being fired) and the Fair Labor Standards Act (right to receive the minimum wage of $4.25 an hour). Although the latter statute exempts seafarers from the limitations of a 40-hour week, it otherwise would clothe the crews of cruise ships with numerous well-known benefits and protections.

At a committee hearing on the bill, witnesses presented heart-searing testimony to Congress and exhibits on the conditions endured by most crew members aboard cruiseships. One of them, the Rev. James Lindgren of the New England Seamen's Mission, represented an organization of nearly 200 Christian port chaplains who go on board ships when they dock in the United States to speak with ordinary seafarers, and who are often the only outsiders to whom a seafarer can safely talk without fear of reprisals. He told of seafarers who "generally work seven days a week and often have no time off for up to a full year of employment," all under "onerous conditions . . . in cramped quarters and . . . in some cases on marginal diets." In short, he concluded, "conditions and rates of pay long outlawed in the United States for U.S. workers are prevailing on ships which, except for the flag they fly, are, *de facto,* American ships."

And lest he be misunderstood, Rev. Lindgren pointed out that such conditions prevailed "especially [on] cruise ships," and that "the majority of the seafarers on these cruise ships are neither officers nor employees who receive tips in the course of employment."

In interviews conducted by me with observers in the field, descriptions were especially poignant about the recruitors of cruise-ship labor on the streets of Manila and Bangkok. I was repeatedly told about workers lured by promises of major earnings, who later learned that their round-trip air fare to the Caribbean, and other expenses, would be deducted from their pay, leaving a much diminished and paltry sum for a year's arduous labor.

The opposing view was most strikingly presented at the hearing by the "International Committee of Passenger Lines," which represents the 17 companies accounting for 85% of the international cruise trade. Surprisingly, their testimony was limited to a short but punchy four pages that called the legislation "misguided" and a contravention of "international law. . . . and treaties," but contained no detailed refutation whatever of the accusations of exploitation and abuse that had been leveled against the industry. Rather, the shipowners responded with a threat: "If the bill were ever to become law, foreign-flag passenger vessel operators would be impelled to transfer their operations out of the United States. . . . Attempts by Congress to export American labor and wage concepts to foreign-flag ships are bound to be no more successful than efforts to export concepts of American democracy to certain foreign countries of the world."

Is the threat credible? Will these shipowners simply pack up and leave our ports if principles of humanity are enforced? Where else would they go to operate their three-night and four-night cruises between Florida and the Bahamas? What Caribbean island could today accommodate the cruise passengers pouring each day into Miami, Ft. Lauderdale, and Tampa? How difficult would it be to extend the legislation to prevent subterfuges of it?

On the average cruise ship carrying 1,000 passengers, the crew amounts to approximatley 500 in number. An increase in price for the cruise of $15 per passenger per day would generate up to $105,000 a week for that vessel, more than enough to guarantee the U.S. minimum wage to every seafarer aboard. Indeed, $10 a day could do it. I for one cannot believe that the American public, once apprised of the situation, would not be willing to ensure civilized conditions aboard the vessels they sail by paying that much more for a luxury cruise. And is there no space in shipowners' profits to cover a bit of that extra $10 or $15?

In the short time that Mr. Ted Arison has been operating Carnival Cruises, he has become one of the richest men on earth (*Forbes* magazine lists his fortune as $2.9 billion).

In the holiday weeks, as we read Christmas literature, is the image of Ebenezer Scrooge to be confined simply to our imagination, to literature? Or does the evil of Ebenezer Scrooge still prevail in our time?

Excessively Lavish Travel As an Improper Priority

Around the World by Concorde—On $4,000 a Day

Apparently emboldened by recent political developments, a number of American tour operators have announced that they will soon be offering additional, three-week, around-the-world tours by Concorde jet, costing upward of $40,000 per person. The rush to provide such adventures to the wealthiest of tourists is seen not simply as a confirmation of recent right-wing themes, but as a particular victory for the conservative talk-show host, columnist and author, William F. Buckley, Jr., who pioneered in conducting a similar tour six years ago. At that time, he led a Concorde flight around the world at a cost of $39,000 per person, and inspired a group of 90-or-so other affluent Americans to book aboard. They paid almost $80,000 a couple, or nearly $4,000 a day when other incidentals were included.

Though Buckley's role is now history, it casts a helpful light on the current round-the-world extravaganzas, undoubtedly including similar elements.

The fare for his group included air transportation by chartered British Airways Concorde jet (the famed supersonic plane stayed with the group throughout the trip), elegant hotels, three meals a day, and, at some point in the air journey, the right to sit next to Buckley. (The affable commentator apparently rotated his seating aboard the luxury jet.) Participants were also invited to attend on-the-spot tapings of Buckley's PBS television program "Firing Line," as he interviewed heads of state and other political figures en route.

For weeks the travel trade press was agog over this record-breaking tour, which was surely among the most expensive ever offered. *Travel Weekly*, the industry's most important publication, actually featured the trip on its front page, drawing special attention to the good fortune of those travel agents who had been able to find clients wealthy enough to book the flight. One had made a single call to a prospective customer who phoned back to report that she had persuaded three friends to go along with her, thus earning a commission of $16,000 for the agent in that one contact. "Isn't it fun?" gushed the agent.

No travel publication, to my knowledge, ever discussed the ethical character of the tour, either then or since, or even betrayed the slightest awareness that questions of morality might be at stake. Advertising has appeared in the trade press for imitations of Buckley's tour throughout 1995.

The itinerary of the Buckley flight was a curious one. Though the Concorde was a joint project of Britain and France, the plane stopped only in London and not in Paris. I've always felt this was due to the fact that the French that year were celebrating the 200th anniversary of their Revolution against similar aristocratic excess.

The plane, however, was carefully scheduled to include a prominent African country among its stops. No explanation was ever provided by the trip's sponsors—either by Buckley or by Lorraine Travel of Miami, his collaborator in the venture—of why their $4,000-a-day couples were deliberately alighting among a population 80% of which lived in the most abject squalor. And thus spreading hatred for Americans wherever their sightseeing limousines went.

The Concorde was financed by the taxpayers of Britain and France. After spending billions on its development, the British and French governments wrote off those start-up costs and in effect made a free gift of the aircraft to British Airways (subsequently privatized by Prime Minister Margaret Thatcher) and Air France, which proceeded to use it—witness the Buckley trip—as a plaything for the rich. Neither British Airways nor Air France would respond, through their public relations offices, to my request for a comment on the morality of using this plane for such a blatant display of sheer wealth.

Am I alone in feeling revulsion over the trip of these merry millionaires? In a world of widespread hunger and homelessness, and when our nation has such unmet social needs, is it wrong to believe that travel expenditures of this size are excessive? That people so fortunate could find a better use for their wealth?

One thing is certain: people of the Emerging World are beginning to feel exactly that way. Some time ago, a charter load of high-living German tourists, arriving in an impoverished state of India, were met at the airport by pickets demanding that they go away. Signs advised the tourists, among other things, that the high-rise hotel they were about to use—replete with lobby waterfalls and the like—was diverting scarce water resources from nearby villages.

I do not know whether pickets marred the tour of Mr. Buckley's group, or will do so with respect to their 1996 counterparts. But I myself would have dearly loved to greet their return to

JFK Airport in New York with a stack of paper diplomas. To every passenger: the Marie Antoinette Award for supreme indifference and selfish indulgence.

And to Mr. Buckley: a special citation for reviving the image of the "Ugly American" in the world of travel.

The New World of Travel 1997

The life blood of the Arthur Frommer travel guides is the correspondence received from readers, commenting on the establishments recommended in the texts and recommending new establishments. Each such letter is carefully studied, and when a particular lead seems promising, it is followed up and personally checked.

It is hoped *The New World of Travel* will receive similar assistance from its readers. A yearly publication, issued near the start of each year, *The New World of Travel* will constantly grow. And since much of its contents relates to organizations that lack the means to market themselves properly, or come to the attention of a travel journalist, your help is invaluable in alerting me to the organizations—hospitality exchanges, alternative resorts, new travel clubs, and the like—that you have discovered.

If you become aware of a new travel organization, program, or development that deserves to be described in our next edition, *The New World of Travel 1997,* won't you please let me know about it? Send your letters to Arthur Frommer, *The New World of Travel,* 1841 Broadway, New York, NY 10023. All letters will be acknowledged, and all are warmly appreciated in advance, by the author.

The Unchecked Decline
of Our Railroads

You stare at the wheel, you tap the dashboard, you fume and you boil. Your Florida vacation, which started so promisingly, has sputtered to a halt on Interstate 95. From Boca Raton in the north to Miami in the south, the highway is a sluggish mass of barely moving cars.

All over America, traffic gridlock in key resort areas is wreaking havoc on holiday plans. At different times of the day, you hardly move anymore on the Long Island Expressway, on Highway 101 outside San Jose, California, on scores of other key arteries.

The solution? It isn't more highways. Experts estimate that an absurd 44 parallel lanes would be needed to handle the north–south traffic on Florida's east coast projected for 10 years from now. And it isn't more airplanes. Already, numerous large airports are simply incapable of accommodating more landings and takeoffs.

The answer from every standpoint—that of ecology, energy, efficiency, and expense—is the train, and especially new modes of high-speed rail that can propel large numbers of passengers at 185 miles an hour, or slightly smaller groups at an astonishing 300 miles an hour.

The technology exists, and has existed for more than a decade. In Japan and Western Europe, scores of "bullet trains" *(shinkansen)* and TGVs (ultra-speed railway cars) are currently in daily operation along major routes, at 185-m.p.h. velocities. Within the next six years, all of Western Europe will be covered with similar service. In northern Germany, on a 20-mile test track, railroad cars using "maglev" (magnetic levitation) capabilities are currently flashing along on elevated monorails at 300-m.p.h. speeds, completing the experiments that will soon lead to their commercial introduction.

And what have we in the offing, here in the United States? A single, 17-mile "maglev" project from Orlando Airport to the tourist action, that possibly, may commence construction in three or four years. Although numerous states have established "high-speed rail commissions" to explore the new technology, every other contemplated project remains in the wishing stage, a full 20 years behind Europe and Japan. Consider the following and weep:

- **California/Nevada:** "Reports" are still forthcoming, and commissions still "studying," a high-speed line between Anaheim and Las Vegas, and from San Diego to Los Angeles to San Francisco. Not a penny has yet been appropriated, and even if work were already underway (which is not the case), the year 2004 would be the earliest starting date for service.

- **Oregon/Washington:** "Studies"—and nothing more—are underway for a proposed line from Portland to Seattle.

- **Georgia:** Though numerous groups have called for a line from Atlanta to Macon to Savannah, not even a study has yet been authorized, and no commissioners yet appointed by Georgia's governor.

- **Pennsylvania:** Though studies have been made of a Philadelphia–Harrisburg–Pittsburgh line, still another several-year-long inquiry has recently been authorized.

- **Massachusetts/New York/Washington, D.C.:** On the important route from Boston to New York to Washington, D.C., where air service has reached limits of congestion, Amtrak is petitioning Congress for funds to develop high-speed tracks and trains, but has only a dubious chance of passage in the near future.

- **Ohio:** For the Cleveland–Columbus–Cincinnati route high-speed proposals have been submitted by private interests, but nothing has been done about them.

- **Colorado:** Legislation was introduced, but is languishing, for a high-speed line from Pueblo to Colorado Springs to Denver to Boulder.

- **Texas:** A recently appointed state commission is "getting ready" to consider proposals for a line from Dallas/Fort Worth to Houston to San Antonio and Austin.

- **Great Lakes:** A study is "underway" for service from Minneapolis/St. Paul to Madison, Wisconsin, to Chicago—and perhaps from there to Detroit. Completion date for the study? Your guess is as good as anyone's.

Why the delay? Why the inaction? It is tradition and ideology—damaging ideology—that keeps us from moving.

Tradition: Unlike other nations, we have no real tradition in the United States of using public funds to build new railways. In the last century, vast amounts of public lands were given free to railway companies which were always private, but that practice ended in 1872. Thereafter, bankruptcy ultimately brought about the creation of Amtrak, which Congress keeps barely alive with funds for operating purposes. Airports and highways are built with public funds, but so strange is our attitude toward trains that even the proposals by different states to create high-speed rail lines are designed to take effect without such funds. Rather, all sorts of alternative, complex, risky, and time-consuming financial guarantees and tax-free bond issues are suggested, requiring many years and much uncertainty to work out.

Ideology: For two decades now, ideologues have told us that no matter how pressing the public need is, tax increases are never justified for anything. As contrasted with Justice Holmes's famous statement that "taxes are the price we pay for civilization," their simple riposte is that all taxes are bad. Period. And thus we Americans will continue to stew in our cars, and vegetate at airports, reducing the quality of our lives, and incurring billions of dollars of lost time, rather than tax ourselves a moderate sum to improve the quality of our lives.

We also, by our failure to expend public funds on high-speed railroads, are surrendering another major new industry to foreign hands. The company building that short maglev line in Orlando is a consortium of German and Japanese firms. The company proposing to operate a high-speed line from Miami to Orlando to Tampa is a partnership of Sweden and Switzerland.

These overseas operators have reached those capabilities because their governments have far-sighted industrial policies, and spend money for the research and development that no private firm could afford. In Germany, public funds spent on maglev research has now exceeded $1 billion. By contrast, recent proposals for U.S. maglev research are for a pitiful and ineffective $10 million. The cost of a single Stealth bomber would enable the U.S. to reach German levels of maglev research.

Which will it be? Continued U.S. backwardness in developing high-speed trains? And all the attendant horrors of clogged highways and airports? Or a willingness to tax ourselves a moderate sum to improve our travel lives?

Index

Photo Credits

Adventure Center, page 139
Archeological Institute of America, page 65
Center for Global Education, page 23
Dartmouth Alumni College, photo by Sherwood Burnett, page 40
The Expanding Light at Ananda, page 1
Pauline Frommer, page 266
Green Tortoise, photo by Stephen D. Lawrence, page 305
Marriott, Inc., page 316
Ocean Connection, page 222, 345
Overseas Adventure Travel, page 356
Structure House, page 190
Vermont Bicycle Touring, page 147
World Explorer Cruises, page 173
The Wedgewood Inn, page 84